Gerhard Friderich Müller was born in Westphalia and studied in Leipzig. In 1725 he moved to Russia to teach as one of the first members of the Russian Academy of Sciences. Müller's fifty-eight years with the institution were spent at or near the centre of intellectual and political activity in his adopted land. His writing interpreted Western culture to Russians and helped to create the West's image of its vast neighbour.

Müller was a founder of modern Russian historiography. He explored and catalogued the resources – particularly historical – of Siberia during a remarkable decade-long expedition sponsored by the Russian Academy. He edited Russia's first popular journals, advised monarchs, helped to reform the school system, and acted as liaison between the Academy and its western European counterparts.

Black's discussion of Müller's professional life as a historian and his descriptions of Müller's scholarly contacts, including battles with fellow academician Lomonosov, provide valuable insights into Russian social and political history. Müller is mentioned in almost every study of eighteenth-century Russian intellectual life, but this book is the first full-length biography. His long association with the Academy of Sciences also provides the setting for a definitive account of the birth and growth of one of Russia's most important institutions.

J.L. Black is a professor of history and director of the Institute of Soviet and East European Studies at Carleton University. His books include *Citizens for the Fatherland* and *Nicholas Karamzin and Russian Society in the Nineteenth Century*.

G.-F. Müller and the Imperial Russian Academy

J.L. BLACK

McGill-Queen's University Press
Kingston and Montreal

© McGill-Queen's University Press 1986
ISBN 0-7735-0553-9

Legal deposit second quarter 1986
Bibliothèque nationale du Québec

Printed in Canada

This book has been published with the help of a
grant from the Canadian Federation for the
Humanities using funds provided by the Social
Sciences and Humanities Research Council of
Canada.

Canadian Cataloguing in Publication Data

Black, J.L. (Joseph Lawrence), 1937–
    G.F. Müller and the Imperial Russian Academy
    Bibliography: p.
    Includes index.
    ISBN 0-7735-0553-9
    1. Miller, Gerard Fridrikh, 1705–1783.
    2. Historians – Soviet Union – Biography.
    3. Akademiia nauk SSR. 4. Historiography –
    Soviet Union. I. Title.
    D15.M83B58 1986   907'.202   C85-090799-3

To Janice, Joe, Jen, and Laura

In his manner of thinking, there was something great, just, and noble. In relation to the merits of Russia ... he was a warm patriot ... In the literary field he was as Field Marshal Münnich was to the military.

A.L. von Schlözer on Müller, 1761

Contents

Preface

The year 1983 marked the two hundredth anniversary of the death of G.-F. Müller (1705–83), a German scholar who contributed to the enlightenment of Russia for nearly sixty years. Although he was one of the founding fathers of Russian journalism, geography, archival work, and ethnographical and historical studies, Müller has been regarded by nationalistic Russian and Soviet writers with a somewhat jaundiced eye. There are, however, striking ambiguities in their opinions of him. He is labelled incompetent as a historian by some and an enemy of Russian enlightenment and nationhood by others; but his tireless efforts at collecting documents and his studies of Siberia and its people are still awarded considerable praise.

No major studies of Müller have been published in English. Although a substantive dissertation on him was completed by S.H. Cross for Harvard University in 1916, it has not been printed. The few English-language books on the history of Russian historiography (A.G. Mazour, G. Vernadsky) allot only limited space to Müller. Specialized books on Russian culture and enlightenment (S.R. Tompkins, A. Vucinich, H. Rogger, to name but a few) all note Müller's importance but add little in the way of detail. Works on the history and geography of Siberia and on the exploration of its coastlines (L. Bagrow, G. Barratt) allude to Müller's significance in that field of study as well, but fail to pursue the issue very far. This omission is understandable, for Müller's own interests were so broad that he may well have appeared on the periphery of many disciplines while mastering none. The one exception is Raymond H. Fisher, who was attentive to Müller in his recent books on Dezhnev and Bering.

The authors mentioned above, however, all had broader themes in mind, so that the small space that they afforded Müller was appropriate to their studies.

As a glance through the bibliography of this work will show, German scholars have taken the initiative in re-evaluating Müller's contribution to Russia's enlightenment in the eighteenth century. In so doing they have illustrated his important contributions to contemporary Russian journalism, to the Academy of Sciences in St Petersburg, and to the evolution of Russian geographical studies. Eduard Winter, Uf Lehmann, Peter Hoffman, and Annelies Lauch all have printed large portions of Müller's correspondence in connection with their work on contemporary scholars such as Leonhard Euler, Johann Gottsched, P.S. Pallas, and H.L.Ch. Bacmeister. In 1976 Hoffman wrote an article in which he placed Müller at the forefront of geographers of Siberia in particular, and in the mainstream of eighteenth-century geography generally. J. Tetzner (in 1956) and H. Grasshof (in 1970) delineated Müller's importance as liaison between editors of periodicals in Russia and Germany; Winter (in 1959 and 1964) and Lothar Maier (in 1979) have written about his eminence in Academy affairs. Maier's latest piece, published in English in 1981, is the first to look carefully at Müller's role as an adviser to the Russian government. Yet German scholars have yet to deal at length with Müller's part in the evolution of Russian historical studies.

The purpose of this book is to study Müller's career at the Imperial Russian Academy of Sciences in general, and to outline his contribution to the development of Russian historical studies in particular. Because it is dedicated solely to Müller's activities and treats other individuals only insofar as they were associated with Müller, the book may leave readers with the incorrect feeling that the main function of the Academy Conference was to serve as an arena for highly charged battles between its members. It may also seem that the famous polymath M.V. Lomonosov (1711–65), whose career was inextricably entwined with Müller's after 1743, expended almost all his energy trying to make life miserable for his German colleague.

Such inferences would be unfortunate, because the Academy accomplished a great deal in the scientific disciplines. Individuals such as the Bernoulli brothers, F.U.T. Aepinus, Joseph N. de l'Isle, and especially Leonhard Euler (whose association with the Academy coincided almost exactly with Müller's) had international reputations as scholars of the first rank. More than 150 well-known European scholars were made honorary members of the Russian institution in the eighteenth century, 90 of them before 1765. The famous Christian Wolff at Halle was active in Academy service during the first two decades of its existence, 1725–47. Voltaire (1746), Diderot (1773), and Benjamin Franklin (1789) added lustre – if not much else – to its later list of members. A number of the Academy's own members were invited to be associated with similar institutions elsewhere.

At home the Academy performed invaluable service in the field of cartography, the translation of foreign books, the publication of journals, and, above all, the scientific exploration of the Russian Empire. Lomonosov's varied pursuits and incomparable accomplishments for Russian science and literature are illustrative enough to need no defence here.

Books could be written about Müller as geographer and cartographer, as ethnographer, explorer, or journalist, and this study will contain much on those subjects. The emphasis here, however, will be on Müller the historian, because that was his chosen profession and the one in which his contribution remains controversial to this day, and on the Academy of Sciences, because that was his place of work.

Nearly all the dates found in this book are old style, that is, according to the Julian calendar, which was adopted for Russia by Peter the Great in 1699. In the eighteenth century, this calendar was eleven days behind the Gregorian calendar, which was used by most western European countries. Dates found in correspondence sent to Russia from Europe are cited as they appeared in the original letter; in their initial form as well are all titles of eighteenth-century books and articles. For the most part, I have used the system of transliteration from the Cyrillic alphabet applied at the Library of Congress.

A number of individuals and institutions have contributed to this study in a variety of ways. Carleton University and the Social Sciences and Humanities Research Council of Canada have provided some funds for travel, research, typing, and other related needs for a period of some five years. The interlibrary loans staff at Carleton University, the Chicago Research Libraries, and the Russian Research Center at the University of Illinois, Urbana-Champaigne, also have been very helpful. I have been able to use the Eighteenth-Century Russia microfiche collection at McGill University in Montreal for several years; the Soviet embassy in Ottawa has been instrumental in obtaining useful material for me from archival collections in the Soviet Union. Special thanks are due to James Cracraft of Harvard and the University of Chicago, who read the first draft in 1982 and made a number of valuable suggestions; Judy Benner of Ottawa read another draft and provided me with commentary of editorial value; Donna Harper, of the Institute of Soviet and East European Studies, Carleton University, typed bits and pieces of the manuscript over a period of several years. All this assistance is much appreciated.

PART ONE

Present at the Creation

CHAPTER ONE

Leipzig and the Founding of the Russian Academy 1705–31

I consider you the most qualified person for this position and I hope very much to have you with me. I can
tell you that it is just as comfortable in St. Petersburg as
it is in Germany ... The Library is superb.

J.P. Kohl to Müller, April 1725

Gerhard Friderich Müller was born on 18 October 1705, in Herford,
Westphalia. If parental inclinations can ever be said to influence a
child's selection of profession, it is not surprising that Gerhard
Friderich and his older brother, Heinrich Justus, were to spend most
of their lives studying and teaching. Their father, Thomas, was rector
of the Herford gymnasium, and their maternal grandfather, Gerhard
Bodinus, was a professor of theology and superintendent of schools
in Rinteln.[1]

There were certain drawbacks, however, to being the son of a
schoolmaster. Müller's friend, first biographer, and distant relative,
A.F. Büsching (1724–93), relates a local tale in which it was said that
when Tsar Peter I, "the Great," of Russia travelled through Herford in
1716, Thomas Müller locked his youngest son's shoes in a closet so
that the boy would not desert his studies in order to observe the
Russian emperor pass by. Apocryphal as the story may be, it lingered
on in Herford as the reason why Gerhard Friderich decided one day
to go to Russia to seek his fortune.[2] Whether such strictness was due
to his role as teacher or parent, or more likely both, Thomas Müller's
methods were successful in that his youngest son proved to be an apt
student. Büsching, whose own career saw him serve as a rector of a
gymnasium in Berlin, as a professor of theology, and briefly as a
pastor in St Petersburg, said that Gerhard Friderich's progress
through the lower-school ranks was unusually rapid.[3]

Having completed his first studies in the gymnasium over which his
father presided for nearly forty years, Gerhard Friderich left Herford
in 1722 to continue his education in Rinteln. A year later he journeyed

to Leipzig to attend university. At Leipzig, Müller studied with Johann Christoph Gottsched, a twenty-three-year-old instructor in poetry, and with J.-B. Mencke, official historiographer of Saxony and one of the university's senior scholars. Recognizing the young man's potential, Mencke helped provide some financial security by arranging employment for him in the university library, then under the charge of the church historian Johann Peter Kohl. Müller also assisted Mencke in his private library, which was described by J.D. Schumacher as an excellent, "full history library."[4] This was a fortunate beginning indeed for a student who was one day to be the dean of historical studies in imperial Russia.

The intellectual atmosphere in which Müller found himself was a heady one. Johann-Burkhard Mencke (1674–1732) had been a professor of history at Leipzig since 1699. Appointed historiographer in 1708, privy councillor for Saxony in 1709, and a member of the royal societies in Berlin and London, he was one of the most highly regarded men-of-letters in Germany. His reputation was due in part to his activity as a historian, but he was best known in Leipzig as editor and publisher of *Acta eruditorum Lipsiensium* (Acts of the Learned Leipzig) and as president of the city's Society of German Poetry, the purpose of which was to propagate and purify German literature. The *Acta eruditorum* was a family enterprise inaugurated by Mencke's father, Otto, in 1682 and carried on after 1752 by his own son, Friderich Otto. In 1712 J.-B. Mencke began to print a German rendition of the Latin-language *Acta eruditorum*, thereby increasing its audience and at the same time drawing from a far wider region for his articles. Among his other family publications was the journal *Neue Zeitungen von gelehrten Sachen* (1715–84), comprising reviews, references to the contents of foreign periodicals, letters from scholars, and notices of publications and other "learned" events. He wrote as well a biographical dictionary, several regional histories, bibliographies, and biographies. Thus, the young student and employee in Mencke's library learned to gather and sort information from a consummate publicist and antiquarian.

Johann-Christoph Gottsched (1700–66) was a newcomer to Leipzig, arriving there only in 1723. He too became a protégé of Mencke, who turned the Society of German Poetry over to him in 1726. Gottsched proceeded to make the society into a model for similar groups in most of the leading German universities, and Leipzig itself into a centre for German literature during the 1730s. Gottsched's disciples urged scholars to write in High German and to cleanse the language of French phrases and elements of Latin and provincial dialects.

Although he was only seven years older than Müller, J.-P. Kohl (1698–1778) already was an established historian in 1723. He contributed regularly to *Acta eruditorum* and in 1723 published a tract entitled *Ecclesia graeca Lutheranizans* in Lübeck. This was an expanded version of a paper that had been presented to Peter the Great in 1717 as a contribution to a current debate over the merits of a union between the Russian and western churches. Kohl's study traced similarities between current Greek and Russian practice and also noted doctrines that Orthodoxy and Lutheranism had in common – and where they contradicted each other. He concluded that the Graeco-Russian and Lutheran faiths might well unite. Kohl later was the first scholar seriously to investigae church Slavonic literature and use philological techniques to show the importance of Slavic translations for the study of old Greek words. So he too was a scholarly devotee of historical sources.

Also at Leipzig was Johann Jakob Maskov (1689–1761), a historian whom the distinguished polymath G.W. Leibniz (1646– 1716) tried to recruit for work on an ambitious project to gather and publish all the important sources of German history (*Scriptores rerum Germanicum*). Because Maskov travelled extensively and Leibniz died before the proposal obtained support from imperial authorities, their potential collaboration never reached fruition. Instead, Leibniz produced a collection of sources for the history of the House of Brunswick-Lüneburg (*Scriptores rerum brunsvicensium*, 1707–11), which became a model for large regional histories based on original documentary sources that were to be copied at length and exactly as they appeared in the original. Leibniz also gathered documents for a history of the Guelphs, which he hoped to expand into a vast study of medieval Germany. He advocated the use of the native language (as opposed to Latin) and insisted that all old sources, even legends, cannot help but bear an element of truth in them.

If there was a Leibniz school in historical studies, Maskov was a charter member. His *Geschichte der Teutschen bis zu Anfang der fränkischen Monarchie* (10 volumes, Leipzig, 1726), which had several editions and was translated into most European languages (but not Russian), was prepared in the manner advocated by Leibniz. Maskov used critical methods for determining the authenticity of his sources, cited them exactly as they were in the original, and, even though he respected them as relics of bygone ages, refuted many of the conventional legends. His emphasis on cultural and religious affairs along with political matters was innovative for that era.

There was another side to Maskov's historicism, however, because he wrote for students as well as for scholars. In 1722 he published a survey textbook on the history of the "German" state (*Abriss einer vollständigen Historie des teutschen Reichs*, Leipzig), which was reissued many times. This book was intended primarily for his own students at Leipzig, where he had been a teacher of law since 1719. It was written in current, even idiomatic German and reflected a sense of German – as opposed to more parochial – national feeling. Generally, Maskov and his colleagues assumed that the job of a historian was to accumulate material. They stressed primary documentation above all other sources for history and differed from their seventeenth-century predecessors only in that they favoured current languages over Latin. Although there is nothing specific to suggest that Müller undertook any studies directly with Maskov, later remarks demonstrate that he was well aware of Maskov's work.

The ideas of *Aufklärung*, that is, the German enlightenment, reigned supreme at the University of Leipzig in the 1720s. Gottsched acknowledged the famous philosopher Christian Wolff (1679–1754) as the master whom he hoped to emulate. Aside from Mencke's and Maskov's publications, the most widely read historical and political treatises at Leipzig were those by Samuel Pufendorf (1632–94). Müller probably read Pufendorf's *Einleitung zu der Vernehmsten Reiche und Staaten* (1682), which had chapters on both Poland and Muscovy. Although the latter chapter was not very complimentary to the Muscovites, Peter the Great called for its translation into Russian in 1718 and 1724. G.S. Treuer's *Einleitung zur Moscowitischen Historie bis auf den Stolbowischen Frieden* (Leipzig, 1720) would also have been readily available if Müller had been interested in reading it. In the 1750s, he rather harshly reviewed a book on Russian genealogy published by Treuer in 1731.

Pufendorf's *De Statu Imperii Germanii* (1667) emphasized *raison d'état* and exhorted individual German states to sacrifice their special interests in order to strengthen all of Germany. His historical work, which included histories of Sweden, Charles Augustus x, and Frederick William the Great Elector, had no clear narrative and no criticism of sources. He saw history as a record of the activities of prominent people, a tool with which to demonstrate the laws of politics. But his work carried rational rather than ideological interpretations, thereby making it an integral part of the new history, and applied archival and other documentary evidence to his conclusions. Pufendorf and Wolff, a pupil of Leibniz, were both rationalists who eschewed religious intolerance and believed that rulers had a duty to govern in the best interests of their subjects. Both men aspired to a well-ordered society, however, and assumed that subjects in their turn were obligated to obey the laws established by rulers. Generally, their assumptions mirrored the *Aufklärung*'s search for some inner harmony in knowledge and for a rational order in politics.

The University of Leipzig, in fact, had a rationalist tradition of its own. It was there that a professor of natural law, Christian Thomasius (1655–1728), had defended the Pietists, attacked superstition, and been influential in having trials for sorcery stopped in Germany. Thomasius lectured in German, rather than in the customary Latin, published journals that were both scholarly and humorous – and so worried the authorities that he was forced to leave the university for Berlin in 1690. Four years later, he helped plan a university for Halle where he became a colleague of P.J. Spener, the founder of Pietism, August Francke, a Pietist responsible for the organization of charitable schools, and Wolff. The fact that Thomasius was invited back to Leipzig in 1709 suggests that, even though he did not return, the spirit of rational inquiry that he promulgated was well established there by the time of Müller's arrival.

The attitude that Thomasius and the Pietists exemplified was both devoutly religious and socially utilitarian, with a predilection for charity, education, and simplicity. Sentiments expressed in a testament prepared by Thomas Müller for his son in 1725 indicate that Gerhard Friderich was comfortable with such ideas before he settled in Leipzig:

Let honesty be in your heart, let not deceit be on your tongue, and worship God with true piety. Make sure that others approve of your way of life and manners – that you please the good and displease evil men ... My adored son, with these monsters [idleness, pleasures, maliciousness] you must do battle with mind and heart strong and brave. You must be humble of spirit and countenance and you must labour to help someone, if you can, and hurt no-one ... Hear much, say little, keep confidence and learn to spare the weaker, yield to the stronger, and endure your equal. Remember to be sober, wakeful and truthful, ready to love the good and tolerate the evil. Above all, revere God who sees and learns everything, whom in the end no-one can deceive.[5]

While Müller was being introduced to the theories and practices of *Aufklärung* at Leipzig, J.D. Schumacher was one of several aides of Peter I who were trying feverishly to complete arrangements for a long-planned Russian Academy of Sciences. Peter's interest in education already had resulted in sporadic attempts to open military, mathematical, and medical schools at the secondary level, mainly to supply technicians and bureaucrats for his army, navy, and civil administration. In 1716 Peter was urged by Leibniz, with whom he had been corresponding for some years, to establish a three-tiered educational system that would include an academy dedicated to the pursuit of scientific knowledge.[6] Nevertheless, by the 1720s Russia still had neither a university nor a major research institution.

Not until 1721, when the so-called Great Northern War between Russia and Sweden finally ended, was Peter able to release the large sums of both money and energy needed to work out a systematic program of schooling for his subjects. He hurriedly created agencies through which Russia would be kept strong: the *Ecclesiastical Regulation* of 1721 and the Table of Ranks of 1722 were expected to help channel Russia's spiritual and human resources to the full advantage of the state. In both projects Peter decided that one's level of education should play a leading role in determining the heights an individual might reach in the civil, military, or ecclesiastical hierarchy.[7] He was also anxious that the newly named Russian Empire should have its own scientific community so that Russia might never again be caught short of trained personnel or modern technology. Also, the emperor hoped to change the European image of Russia as one of a backward, barbaric state to that of a respected equal. An academy of sciences and a university would contribute enormously to such an image. Peter was well aware, however, that in order to provide Russia with a pool of native-born experts, he must first look to Europe for their instructors.

To that end, agents were sent abroad to meet with Christian Wolff (Leibniz having died in 1716) and others for the purpose of obtaining advice and professional talent. Laurentius Blumentrost, Peter's personal physician, travelled to Germany in 1719 hoping to persuade Wolff to return to Russia with him. He delivered a letter from Peter in which the emperor stated that he was planning an academy with accompanying university and gymnasium. Wolff did not go to Russia. He advised Blumentrost that his ruler would be better served by the establishment of an active university and lower schools to act as a feeder system to a future scientific institution. But Blumentrost and his ruler were determined to have an academy right away.

Two years later, Blumentrost sent his assistant, Schumacher, who was the imperial librarian and supervisor of the St Petersburg *Kunstkamera* (museum), to Paris, London, Berlin, and other European centres. Schumacher was ordered to converse with scholars and purchase books for the proposed academy.[8] Like Blumentrost, he too tried to persuade Wolff to come to Russia, but in vain. He also talked with abbé Bignon, director of the Académie des sciences in Paris – and took with him several Tibetan manuscripts in order to impress the French academicians with the success and seriousness of Russian-sponsored exploratory expeditions to central Asia. These also were shown to Mencke, who reproduced some of them in his *Acta eruditorum*.[9] In a report to Peter in 1721, Schumacher said that he had already hired two French scholars for Russian service, the astronomer Joseph N. de l'Isle and the zoologist and surgeon Johann-Georg Duvernois. He said also that he had purchased the necessary scientific equipment. But the structure and aims of the new institution were not formulated until January 1724. At that time, Blumentrost and Schumacher presented Peter with a general plan, which he made into law on the 22nd of that month.[10]

Fully aware that Wolff's precautionary recommendations were reasonable, Blumentrost and Schumacher noted first that the purpose of the Academy was to 'advance the fame of the empire' and 'to serve the needs of the country.' Then they proceeded to counter Wolff's warnings:

The establishment of a simple Academy of Sciences ... will not quickl, ʰear fruit among the people. Even less will be accomplished by the foundation of a university, because so far [we have] no regular schools, gymnasia and seminaries, in which young people can be taught fundamentals ... Therefore what is most needed here is that there should be established an association to consist of the most scholarly people who are willing to: (1) promote and perfect the sciences; (2) publicly instruct young people in those sciences; (3) take for private instruction a few individuals who can teach young people the rudiments of all the sciences. In this way one institution may with only minor difficulties accomplish with great benefit what is performed by three separate institutions in other empires.

Blumentrost was named the Academy's first president and was for many years the only important person at the Academy who was Russian-born. This situation was to cause serious dissension during and after the 1740s. Schumacher became secretary-general. In April, Blumentrost announced the founding of the Academy in Mencke's *Neue Zeitungen von gelehrten Sachen*. In September he presented the emperor with a list of fourteen scholars who had agreed to come to St Petersburg to take positions.[11] This list included people recommended by Wolff, Schumacher, and V.N. Tatishchev, a member of the Russian trade commission in Sweden.[12]

Wolff recommended learned men of the sciences and mathematics. For the "Humanities" class of the Academy, Blumentrost turned to Mencke, who submitted nine or ten names. Of these only Kohl suited Blumentrost's specifications. Since Russia still did not have a school system from which to draw persons qualified for university work,

Mencke was asked to suggest a student to come with Kohl, study in the university, and teach at the gymnasium. This was the capacity in which Müller was invited to Russia. In fact, Peter the Great had stipulated that with each new foreign professor the Academy should try to recruit two Slavic-speaking students who would be able to learn Russian more readily than German- or French-speaking candidates. But such students were hard to find. Kohl, who was hired as a professor of rhetoric and church history, and as director of the gymnasium,[13] left Leipzig on 7 February 1725. Müller was to follow.

Müller did not leave Leipzig with Kohl because he felt some concern over what his fate might be in Russia. He wrote much later that his father and others strongly advised him against going to Russia because it was Orthodox and barbaric (see Appendix A). They warned him that he might never be allowed to return, "so great was their prejudice then against Russia!"[14] But Kohl wrote to Müller from St Petersburg assuring him that living conditions there were "as comfortable as Germany," that the library was excellent, and that he would be able to mingle with serious scholars. Kohl added, "[You are] more qualified for this position [student of humanities] than others, and I hope strongly to have you with me." Shortly thereafter, Kohl wrote again, saying that Schumacher was very well educated and that he (Müller) could be kept "up-to-date by the Librarian [Schumacher]. Crede Mihi!"[15] In fact, the Russian government was compelled to make its offers exceptionally attractive, or very few scholars could have been persuaded to emigrate. Schumacher himself wrote of this to Blumentrost in April 1724, "Here are several answers to our letters. From them you can see that everything is going well, but at the same time it all depends upon money and you know, kind sir, that we are not known so much for our generosity and remuneration."[16]

In August 1725, a Berlin banker was authorized to advance Müller the equivalent of 100 rubles to cover expenses for his voyage to St Petersburg.[17] Still apprehensive, he left Leipzig in October and travelled overland to Lübeck, whence he embarked by ship for Russia. He arrived in St Petersburg on 5 November. Müller fully expected to return to Leipzig after his year's contract had expired. In the interim he hoped to set aside enough money so that he might undertake a magister's degree.[18] If he had been allowed a glimpse forty years into the future, the twenty-year-old student would have been astounded to see himself as Fedor Ivanovich Miller, senior member of the Imperial Russian Academy of Sciences, about to leave St Petersburg forever to take up a new career – in Moscow!

Four professors and two student-teachers settled in St Petersburg during the winter of 1725: Jakob Hermann (mathematics), Christian Martini (logic, metaphysics, and physics), G.B. Bülfinger (physics), and Kohl as professors; and Ch.F. Gross (moral philosophy) and F.Ch. Mayer (mathematics) as student-teachers. The latter two were appointed professors in January 1726. Müller was preceded also by the Bernoulli brothers, Daniel and Nicolaus, both mathematicians from a famous Swiss family of scholars, M. Bürger (chemistry), C. Goldbach (mathematics), Duvernois, and de l'Isle. De l'Isle's half-brother, Louis de l'Isle de la Croyère (astronomy), G.Z. Bayer (Greek and Roman antiquity), J.S. Beckenstein (jurisprudence), and J. Weitbrecht (physiology) arrived in November and December 1725. Weitbrecht, Gross, and Mayer joined Müller as teachers in the gymnasium. By the end of 1725 sixteen European scholars were resident in the Russian capital: thirteen Germans, two Swiss, and one French. Half were experts in mathematics or related subjects and took up posts in the first and second classes.

The original project called for a fairly large bureaucracy: an elected president; a curator; a director, with two associates; a financial "commissar"; a secretary to keep protocols and to carry out correspondence with foreign scholars; a librarian, who was to have a budget for books and scientific equipment; and a rather vaguely defined "High Protector," chosen from the academicians to chair public assemblies. From the beginning, however, the only real officials of the Academy were Blumentrost, who was appointed – not elected – president by Catherine 1 in December 1725, and Schumacher, who had the prerogatives and duties, if not the titles, of the remaining positions. In fact, most of the other positions were not filled. Directors were not named until the 1730s, and they were Schumacher's choices as long as he was at the Academy. The budget was set at a moderate 24,912 rubles, to be drawn from "revenues from customs dues and export-import license fees" collected in various Baltic cities.[19]

The three classes of the Academy were divided according to subject and also represented an order of seniority. The four persons assigned to the first class were responsible for the "Mathematical Sciences": one to study arithmetic, algebra, geometry, and theoretical matters, another for astronomy, geography, and navigation, and the final two for mechanics. Four others were included in the second class, one each for physics, anatomy, chemistry, and botany. The three members of the lowest class in the hierarchical scheme were charged – at least according to the plan of 1724 – with such disciplines as rhetoric, ancient and modern history, natural and public law, politics, and moral philosophy.

Perhaps the most ambiguous part of the original plan was its explanation for the establishment of Russia's first university. Because the Academy was intended as an institution for research and invention, it was declared that a university – "an association of learned individuals who teach young people by means of the high sciences, Theology, jurisprudence, medicine, and philosophy" – and a gymnasium would be part of the overall Academy structure in St Petersburg. After outlining carefully how such organizations are fully separated in Europe, the plan went on to say that in Russia they would be combined because there were no native schools from which to draw qualified teachers and students. Thus a newly appointed academician might see service also as a university professor, or even as a gymnasium instructor. In fact, Peter was quite open about the need to attract both faculty and students from Europe. No Russians attended the opening academic session in November, which marked the first discussion on Russian soil of the ideas of Newton and Descartes. The foreign atmosphere of the Academy was such that minutes of its meetings were dated according to the Gregorian calendar until 1728.[20]

Peter I had died in January 1725; thus in August the first professors were presented to his widow, Catherine I. She listened to speeches by Hermann in French and Bülfinger in German. These speeches and the rather grandiose ceremonies that surrounded them were also reported at length in Mencke's *Neue Zeitungen von gelehrten Sachen*.[21] Informal meetings of the still embryonic assembly, or Conference, began in September, and the initial public assembly took place in November. Duke Karl-Friedrich of Holstein (husband to Anna, Peter's daughter by his first wife), prince of Hessen-Homburg, and a representation sent by the king of Sweden were among the foreigners in attendance. Russia's most senior officials, Grand-Admiral F.M. Apraksin and Prince Alexander Menshikov, brought greetings from Catherine, who did not attend. The church hierarchy was present in the person of an archbishop (*arkhiepiskop*) and several bishops. After speeches and introductions, the academicians were fêted by the duke of Holstein. One can imagine that the celebration was somewhat strained, for the temporary setting of the Conference was unheated – which was the explanation for Catherine's absence.[22]

In spite of her absence, proponents of the Academy were optimistic about its future because Catherine was enthusiastic about the project. Indeed, only a few days after Peter's death, Blumentrost had notified Wolff, Mencke, Hermann, and Russia's ambassadors in Paris (Prince B. Kurakin) and Berlin (A.G. Golovkin) that the empress was anxious to complete all existing arrangements for the Academy.[23] Blumentrost's presidency was confirmed by Senate *ukaz* in early December,[24] and Catherine seemed to have given the scholars *carte blanche* to act on behalf of their disciplines. Blumentrost was respected and popular among the academicians. He attended all the academic sessions and was seen by members to have the best interests of the learned community at heart. According to Müller, Blumentrost was versed in "the philosophy of Leibniz, mathematics and medical science, physics, natural history ... Above all he was courteous and friendly."[25] All in all, the institution had a very propitious beginning.

Unfortunately for the academicians, however, the organization provided by Peter in 1724 did not include a careful delineation of their duties and privileges. It recommended that members examine and report on inventions, keep abreast of all "good authors" in their fields, and prepare extracts of their own works for use in Russia. They were also required to meet weekly to discuss experiments and scientific developments, to provide the government with information requested of them, and to have all their work translated into Russian. Each member was obliged to prepare a course of lectures to disseminate his expertise among "young people" and to teach in the university.[26] But these instructions were not made law, and they were subject to various interpretations. The Academy had no charter in which administrative lines of authority and specific obligations of members were outlined clearly. Nor was it obvious to anyone yet whether the research emphasis of the new institution should be theoretical or practical, or both.

A.K. Nartov, an intimate of Peter I, had drawn up a proposal in December 1724 for a separate academy of arts, in which architecture, mechanics, design, sculpture, and engraving would be taught.[27] But the new academicians were more interested in theoretical studies, and Nartov's plan was discarded after Peter's death. Instead, Nartov was put in charge of an auxiliary service department, the function of which, as far as most Academy members were concerned, was to maintain their sophisticated equipment.[28]

It took a year or two for the absence of a formal charter to cause difficulties. The professors believed themselves to be guaranteed freedom from both the real and imagined restrictions for which Russia was already famous. In his recent book on the founding of the Academy, Iu.Kh. Kopelevich draws at length from a letter Bülfinger sent to Bayer in November 1725. Bülfinger fairly gushed over the funds he foresaw coming to scientific projects and over the Academy's "full immunity from Russian jurisprudence." He praised the library and laboratory facilities, exclaimed that he and his colleagues had "everything necessary for the growth of science," and concluded by saying that he was convinced that in no other academy or university were there "such privileges and guarantees." Goldbach wrote to Bayer that the quality of life in St Petersburg was better than in Prussia and that conditions of employment were excellent. Bayer's own words of praise for St Petersburg, the Academy, Blumentrost, and Schumacher were printed by Mencke in Leipzig in 1726. Gross also sent similar letters to former associates in Frankfurt. The fact that during their first few months in St Petersburg the new academicians were treated to free provisions, wine, and housing, and to lavish banquets in the homes of the city's wealthiest citizens, could not help but prompt glowing reports of their good fortune.[29]

There are a few later examples of such unbridled enthusiasm. When Catherine died in 1727, the court moved to Moscow; and Peter II showed very little interest in academic affairs. The Russian treasury still had not recovered from the Petrine wars, and the taxes from Baltic cities were an unreliable source of income. Funds for the Academy were already running short. In August of that year, Blumentrost prepared a long report outlining its material requirements: instruments, laboratory equipment, printing materials, living quarters, translators, and medical and chemical supplies.[30] But none of these pressing needs was redressed that year. Early in 1728 there were signs of bickering among the scholars. The first of many complaints was lodged with Schumacher from professors who had been attracted to Russia by visions of substantial material gain, but by 1728 were not even being paid regularly. Seeds of further dissension were sown when Schumacher began to give positions of some responsibility to students and teachers, whose annual salary ranged from 200 to 266 rubles, rather than to academicians who were promised sums between 400 and 1,800 rubles.[31] "The students will fulfil their duties because they hope for a promotion" was his frank admission to Blumentrost.[32] There were more compelling reasons why Schumacher assigned editorial, library, secretarial, and other chores to the junior associates of the Academy, among them the simple fact that regular members felt that such assignments were beneath their dignity.

In 1727 the title adjunct was introduced and awarded to Müller, Weitbrecht, and new arrivals Leonhard Euler, G.W. Krafft, and J.G. Gmelin. These particular adjuncts and gymnasium teachers were not far removed from many of the academicians in qualifications or even in age. Krafft, at age twenty-six the eldest of the five, Gmelin – the youngest, at eighteen! – and Weitbrecht all held magister degrees from Tübingen, where they had either studied under or were well known to Bülfinger and Duvernois. Gmelin continued to study medicine with Duvernois in Russia. Euler had earned his magister at

Basel, where he had been a student of Johann Bernoulli, one of the greatest mathematicians of the time and father of the two Bernoullis who were at the Russian Academy. It was Daniel Bernoulli who persuaded Euler to come to Russia. Of the first group of regular members to arrive in 1725–6, only Hermann was in his forties (which earned him the title *professor primarius*); most of the others were in their late twenties or early thirties. The younger Bernoulli was the same age as Müller and only two years older than his friend Euler. Even Blumentrost was then only thirty-three years old. By 1730 four of the original professors had returned home, three had died (Bürger, Mayer, Nicolaus Bernoulli), and seven new professors had arrived. Kohl was among the departing professors. He returned to Hamburg in 1727 suffering, it was said, from "melancholy." A.L. Schlözer insisted some years later that Kohl actually suffered from a case of unrequited love for the princess Elizabeth Petrovna, whom he described as one of the great beauties of her time.[33] At any rate, because of their experience, ambition, and apparent stability, Müller and his four fellow adjuncts were logical appointments to administrative positions.

By August 1728, it was apparent that Schumacher also was looking to the adjuncts for allies against the increasingly obstreperous academicians. At that time he complained to Blumentrost that Búlfinger and others were going over his head to the six-member Supreme Privy Council (*Verkhovny tainy sovet*), the senior administrative unit in Russia, which had been created only two years earlier, on matters of salary.[34] Five months later the regular members petitioned Peter II to allow them to elect their own directors annually (or even semi-annually), to participate in making the budget, to have a "patron" named to the Academy from among the "highest of Your Ministers," and to establish a clear set of rules and ranks for both members and administrators. They asked, in fact, that academicians be made the equal of college councillors,[35] which would have placed them on the sixth, and hereditary, grade of the Table of Ranks. This first broadside in what was to be a long struggle between Academy members and Schumacher was ignored by the emperor. The young tsar, his confidant, Prince Ivan Dolgorukii, and other representatives of the old Russian nobility in Moscow were emotionally attached to their city and were not in the least inclined to grant favours to foreigners who resided in St Petersburg.

The academicians quickly forgot the high opinion they had had of Schumacher in 1725–6.[36] Some were unaware of his academic qualifications (a magister and Laurea Poetica from Strassburg) and his valuable administrative experience. Schumacher had come to Russia in 1714 and served as foreign secretary to Robert Erskine (Areskin),

Peter I's physician before Blumentrost. He became Blumentrost's aide on Erskine's death in 1718 and proved to be Peter's most efficient envoy to Europe's seats of learning in 1721.[37] Schumacher's contacts at court were also impressive. When he married the daughter of Peter's favourite cook in 1723, the emperor and many very highly placed persons attended.[38] In fact, it has been successfully argued that Blumentrost and Schumacher together had more direct influence on Peter's planning for the Academy than had either Leibniz or Wolff.[39]

Schumacher received his contract directly from Peter I. In February 1724, he had been relieved of his duties as librarian in Blumentrost's medical office in order to manage the everyday affairs of the Academy at an annual salary of 800 rubles. A month earlier, Schumacher had been appointed Academy librarian, and his duties were clearly outlined: to purchase, catalogue, and oversee all books; to conduct the official correspondence of the Academy; to supervise the copyists and translators; to establish a drawing class to provide technicians for work on charts, atlases, and folios; and to prepare the budget for equipment and members' salaries. As well, he had been in charge of the *Kunstkamera* since 1722. In fact, there were few activities within the Academy in which Schumacher was not directly involved.[40] When Blumentrost moved to Moscow with Peter II's court in January 1728, Schumacher's hand was strengthened even more. A Blumentrost order of 12 January left the management of the Academy entirely to him and required him to send only the "most important business" to Moscow.[41] To assist Schumacher, and perhaps to appease the academicians, the president instituted a temporary system in which three professors were to act as Schumacher's assistants for a year, each taking a four-month term. However, this gesture failed. Hermann, the first assistant recommended by Blumentrost, refused to work as an "aide" to someone he considered beneath him in rank. Müller wrote that the professors avoided participation so as to prevent "jealousies" – the result of which was that Schumacher was still left "to govern arbitrarily." To compensate for the lack of co-operation from the professors, Schumacher created the Chancellery, a bureaucratic unit that was to govern the Academy without receiving formal authority to do so until 1747.[42]

Müller had little to do in 1726 and 1727. He was one of the instructors at the gymnasium, which had slightly over 100 students in its first year.[43] He attended lectures which were read somewhat irregularly at the university. But he had only seven fellow students at the latter institution, and enrolment at the gymnasium declined quickly and drastically.[44] Aside from Müller and J. Blyda, a student who also came to St Petersburg with Kohl, the university students were all Austrian subjects, from Vienna, who spoke Slavic tongues. Although most students at the gymnasium spoke Russian, they were sons of foreign families who resided in the St Petersburg region. Müller was personally responsible for educating two gymnasium students, Vasilii Adodurov, a young nobleman from Novgorod, and Panajota Condoidi, a Greek from Corfu, and nephew of a member of Russia's Holy Synod. As neither student spoke German and Müller could not yet converse in Russian, they communicated at first by means of written Latin. Both young men were to have long and successful careers in Russian service (Condoidi became a physician and privy councillor; Adodurov, adept at languages, remained at the Academy as a translator from Russian to German and became an adjunct member in 1733, the first Russian to be so named).[45] In the mean time, however, Müller had ample time to avail himself of the resources of the Academy library, where he served as Schumacher's assistant. Peter the Great's large library of some 1,600 books had been transferred to the Academy in 1725. About a tenth of these were works on history and geography, subjects that Müller taught. The young scholar had prepared himself enough by May 1726 to venture a lecture to the Academy Conference on the history of literature.[46]

Early in 1728 Müller's opportunities to work on his own became less frequent. This was a particularly busy and unsettling year for the academicians. In the spring, unmarried members were moved from their quarters in the home of exiled former vice-chancellor and senator P.P. Shafirov to a new residence on Vasilevskii Island. The *Kunstkamera*, which was integrated with the Academy officially only in 1728, and the library were also relocated there, in a new building. Both were opened to the public. A formal opening of the new location took place in November. A new, large printing press arrived from Holland early in the year and broadened considerably the potential of the small printing house that had been operating under the Academy's auspices since October 1727. This was one of only two printing presses in St Petersburg. The other was attached to the Senate and was used to print government announcements. The Holy Synod was authorized to act as a censorship board for anything printed at the Academy. By this time the Academy establishment numbered eighty-four persons, of whom seventeen were academicians.

On 6 January 1728, Blumentrost transferred Müller from the gymnasium to the Academy archives to organize German-language dispatches on current affairs ("kuranty") and raised his salary by 100 rubles.[47] It was at this time that his experience in Mencke's library began to serve him well. In March, Müller – who still barely read Russian – was asked to edit the newly established *St. Petersburg Gazette* (*Sankt-Peterburgskie vedomosti*).[48] The *Gazette* carried translations from European newspapers, reported important military and political events, and printed official notices. It also covered happenings at the Academy, the appearance of new books, and even noted theatrical productions and other gala events of capital-city life. The paper appeared twice weekly. Between five and ten times per year it was accompanied by a supplement that explained in greater detail incidents noted in the *Gazette*. A German-language version of the *Gazette*, the *St. Petersburgische Zeitung*, edited by Gross and Beckenstein, was printed simultaneously.

Müller's energies were taxed further in 1728 by the addition to his editorial duties of a monthly supplement called at first the *Monthly Historical, Genealogical, and Geographical Notes to the Gazette* (*Mesiachnye istoricheskie, genealogicheskie i geograficheskie primechaniia v Vedomostiakh*), but later referred to simply as the *Notes* to the *Gazette*.[49] It was purposely written in a style designed to make its content readily comprehensible to literate Russians from all walks of life and, according to comments later made by Müller, was very popular. It included translations from the English *Spectator* and other journals and short articles on such topics as health, agriculture, anatomy, and basic mathematics. Some poetry and literary notices appeared as well. This was the first Russian-language organ for the promulgation of general information.

Müller's friend Krafft was a constant contributor to the *Notes*, as was Müller himself, and there grew around it a coterie of translators who later were to be important participants in the Russian component of the Academy and in Russia's schools (M. Shvanvits, M.I. Alekseev, and I.I. Iakhontov; and, in the 1730s, Adodurov, J.-K. Taubert, and S.S. Volchkov). Although a German version of the *Notes* was also published after 1729, Müller later stated in his memoir that he was especially anxious that the magazine be addressed mainly to a Russian audience and said that it served as a clear precedent to a much more popular journal, *Monthly Compositions*, which he was to edit at mid-century.[50]

This early publishing activity at the Academy was especially important for Russia's small literate community because an edict issued by Peter II in 1727 allowed only two of the many printing presses established by his father to remain in business – one in Moscow for church-sponsored titles and another in St Petersburg for government laws and notices, and for "historical books which are translated into the Russian language." The same edict, however, called for the establishment of a printing house at the Academy. This press was expected to print only school books, but in fact it accounted for almost all the secular books published in Russia during the next thirty years. In its first few years it printed only laws, public notices, calendars, and newspapers. Thus, Müller quickly became a central figure in the project to propagate knowledge among Russians. The Academy's role as the sponsor of secular culture in St Petersburg was accentuated in 1728 when a special office for selling books (*knizhnaia palata*) was founded and put in its charge, and the *Notes* to the *Gazette* was exempted from Synodal censorship.[51]

It was also Müller's job to keep European centres of learning aware of research done in St Petersburg. He therefore kept in touch with Mencke, who continued to co-operate by including general information about the Russian Academy in his *Neue Zeitungen von gelehrten Sachen* and printing summaries of completed research in *Acta eruditorum*.[52] But editorial work was not the only responsibility handed to the young German. When Goldbach, who was acting as secretary to the Conference, went to Moscow with Blumentrost, Müller was charged with recording the minutes of the academic sessions, organizing Chancellery reports, and handling foreign correspondence for Schumacher. He served also as proof-reader at the printing house, prepared protocols for the gymnasium, and continued to help care for the library.[53]

The plan approved by Peter I in January 1724 had placed special emphasis on the Academy as a disseminator of scientific information to his subjects. To achieve that ambition, the Academy began, also in 1728, to issue Russia's first scholarly publication, *Commentarii Academiae Scientiarum Imperialis Petropolitanae*. Printed in Latin, the international language of scholarship, it covered three categories: mathematics, physics, and history. An abbreviated Russian translation of the first volume also appeared in 1728. That practice, however, was continued only on a very irregular basis,[54] so that the main audience of *Commentarii* consisted of scholars in Russia and in Europe.

Müller edited the first two volumes of the *Commentarii* and assisted with the third, which appeared in 1732. The first volume included mathematical pieces by Bülfinger, Daniel Bernoulli, Duvernois, and Mayer, as well as essays by Bayer on the origins of the Scythians, on Herodotus and the Scythians, and on the Caucasus region. The publication was issued sporadically – fourteen volumes between 1728 and 1751 – and was dominated by articles on mathematics and astronomy. But there were enough items on the history and geography of the Russian empire to attract the attention of its young editor to those subjects. Müller, as the Academy's main, if unofficial, editor, probably read and digested more finished research material than any other member.

While at the archives, Müller was contracted in 1729 to prepare a genealogical chart for Count Peter Sapieha, a favourite of Catherine I and friend of the powerful Prince Menshikov. Müller's work was an adaptation from a previously printed chart and so did not involve protracted study on his part. He wrote later that it represented his first efforts in genealogy and stimulated his interest in Russian history.[55] In late 1729, Blumentrost put Müller in charge of a project to translate into Russian a German-Latin lexicon written by E. Weismann. Müller acknowledged that his contribution to this project was slight in this instance as well, for at the time he still "had almost no knowledge of the Russian language."[56] In any case, his academic horizons and administrative responsibilities were expanding quickly. In January 1730, Schumacher went to Moscow, leaving Müller to oversee the library and the Academy journals and entrusting him with all but the most "important matters" having to do with the Academy.[57] Thus Müller seemed to have settled in quite comfortably, and there is no evidence to suggest that he was still planning to further his own education at a European university. He was soon to discover, however, that there were drawbacks to this kind of success.

Writing in the 1760s, M.V. Lomonosov referred to Müller's role as liaison between Schumacher and the Academy membership in very disparaging terms. He accused Müller of serving as a spy for Schumacher (whom he called *Flagellum professorum*): "To strengthen the power he had appropriated for himself, Schumacher won over the student Müller ... [and,] without formal legislation, placed him in the Chancellery ... He recognized that this Müller, a youthful student and a man of unlikely future in the sciences, would eagerly adapt his own trade on the hope of a speedier acquisition of honour. In him, Schumacher was not disillusioned."[58] Müller was Lomonosov's bitterest enemy when this diatribe was written, so it cannot be considered an unbiased report. But it was not far from the truth. While the academicians fought the unofficial but none the less stifling authority wielded by Schumacher, Müller kept the secretary-general informed about complaints sent to the empress and to individual members of the Senate and gathered details of arguments between Bülfinger and Daniel Bernoulli. In fact, some fifty years later, Müller admitted to having had hopes of becoming Schumacher's "son-in-law and successor in office."[59]

Lomonosov went so far as to accuse Müller of causing the rancour between Bülfinger and Bernoulli, "by transmitting insulting speeches of one to the other." In this case, however, Lomonosov's charges were quite unfair. Angry exchanges between Bülfinger and Bernoulli had taken place already in 1727 and had reached a stage of snarling hostility by 1729. Bernoulli propagated various Cartesian principles against Bülfinger's defence of Newtonian hypotheses, and their respective viewpoints were featured regularly in the first two volumes of the *Commentarii*. Since the Conference protocols made no mention of the controversy, it was left to Müller, whom Blumentrost appointed to an investigatory committee with Mayer and de l'Isle, to provide Schumacher with the only detailed account of it.[60] Schumacher's use of the reports to demonstrate to Blumentrost that the professors were petty and grasping, and could not be trusted to run their own affairs, can hardly be blamed on Müller. By ignoring the protests of the academicians, Blumentrost allowed Schumacher to build up his Chancellery to such an extent that it completely subordinated the activities of the Academy to its authority.[61]

In the summer of 1730 Müller was able to escape the indignation of those Academy members who suspected him of being Schumacher's informer. Their animosity toward him had been made clear in March, when he, Euler, Gmelin, Krafft, and Weitbrecht had all requested promotions to the rank of professor. Blumentrost asked the academicians for their opinion, and only Müller was not recommended by the Conference. According to Schumacher, Blumentrost decided to include Müller in the promotions anyway because he believed that the Conference judgments were prejudiced.[62] Müller's contract, which came into effect 1 January 1731, granted him a four-year term as professor of history at the Academy assembly. His salary was set at 400 rubles for the first two years and 600 rubles for the final half of his tenure. An extra 60 rubles were allowed annually for quarters, firewood, and candles.[63] The other four young men were awarded similar terms.

Although his appointment as a historian was later derided by Müller's opponents, his credentials were not unreasonable by contemporary standards. His academic promise had been noted by both Mencke and Kohl, established scholars and historians themselves. While writing a history of the Academy in the 1770s, Müller remembered his lack of formal training as a historian. But he added, "I relied upon my literary knowledge and upon my acquaintance with the books and manuscripts held in the Academy library, which I began to read with the aid of an interpreter. Bayer, who explained ancient Russian history and geography from Greek and northern writers, supported me in this undertaking."[64] It should be remembered also that Bayer was then the only historian at the Academy, that Müller was well versed in the historicism of Pufendorf, which he had studied at Leipzig, and that he had worked in Mencke's historical library.[65] At any rate, there are no recorded complaints about his skills as a historian at the time of his appointment, which may indicate only that his scientific-minded colleagues-to-be had little interest in the discipline of history.

His father's death in late 1729 and consequent "family matters" were the reasons Müller offered when he begged leave to return home in May 1730. Fortunately for him, the request was a particularly timely one for the Academy, which was in the midst of a very awkward period. The leading lights of St Petersburg had removed to Moscow again in the fall of 1729 for Peter II's wedding. But Peter's illness and sudden death in January 1730, and the subsequent succession crisis, meant that the interests of the academic community were of little concern to the Russian government. Salaries, which were to be paid on a quarterly basis, arrived intermittently or not at all, and several members had to rely on money-lenders for survival. The Chancellery saved some money by releasing three draughtsmen from Nartov's division, all foreigners. The promotion of the four adjuncts to relatively low-salaried professorial positions also saved the expense of more costly help from Europe.

The succession of Anna, duchess of Courland, second daughter of Peter the Great's half-brother Ivan v, brought with it chaos at court. With support from the gentry and the palace guards, the new empress was able to restore the prerogatives of autocracy, which were threatened by members of the Russian *dvorianstvo*, or old nobility, in 1730. She abolished the Supreme Privy Council, imprisoned or exiled most of its members, and established a new cabinet presided over by her favourite, Ernst Biron. The role that Biron, who was made a count in 1730, and other Baltic Germans played – or were perceived to have played – in Anna's success and during her harsh regime harmed the Academy. Anna had no interest whatsoever in the institution, and pent-up hostility among Russians against foreigners was to be directed against the Academy when she died in 1740.

With such goings on in Moscow, the future of the Academy seemed considerably less rosy in the early 1730s than it had a few years earlier. Hermann and Bülfinger returned to their homelands in 1730, and both Blumentrost and Schumacher (who on personal grounds was quite relieved to see them go) worried that they might malign the Academy in Europe. Schumacher already had been forced to defend the Academy from very unfavourable remarks made by Christian

Martini, professor of physics, logic, and metaphysics, who had been discharged for alleged incompetence in May 1729. Two years later, Martini published a book *Nachricht aus Russland* (Frankfurt and Leipzig) that was very uncomplimentary toward Russia generally, and the Academy particularly. To forestall any complaints from Hermann and Bülfinger, however, Blumentrost appointed them honorary members of the Academy and put them on pension. In return for 200 rubles per year, they each signed testimonials that spoke very highly of service in Russia. But this was an uncertain quarantee of the Academy's reputation. Blumentrost and Schumacher therefore were glad of the opportunity to use Müller as a public-relations representative of the Academy in Europe.[66]

Schumacher granted Müller a Russian-language passport for Kronstadt and Holland on 16 July 1730, with a note to the effect that he was a salaried employee of the Russian Academy with permission to be absent. It was undersigned by officials from the Admiralty and by the police. Eight days later Müller obtained a second passport signed by Field-Marshal Count Burkhard C. Münnich, who was in charge of military affairs. It was written in German, apparently so that Münnich's reputation might protect the young traveller from being impressed into the army of the Prussian king, to whom Müller was still officially subject.

The Academy president had issued a clear set of instructions to him in June.[67] He was to travel to England, Holland, and Germany to arange for the purchase of new books from specifically named dealers in Amsterdam (where he was also to buy engravings), Leipzig, Hamburg, and Danzig. And he was to establish long-term business connections between the dealers and the Academy in St Petersburg. In England Müller was expected to find unspecified booksellers and arrange similar commissions. He was also instructed "to become acquainted with scholars everywhere" who might consider becoming honorary members of the Russian Academy. Eleven people were mentioned by name, including Mencke and Sir Hans Sloane. Sloane, president of the Royal Society in London, was named a foreign member of the Russian institution in 1733. Persons who might consider entering Russian service directly were also to be approached, "especially scholars of jurisprudence, experienced physicians, and men familiar with the Eastern languages." Above all, Müller was ordered "in all circumstances to observe the interests of the Academy, and report everything that happens in his travels to ... the president of the Academy of Sciences." In his own account of these orders, Müller said that the final instruction meant that he was expected to refute any unfavourable tales of the Russian Academy that he might overhear in Europe's leading circles.[68] Müller later related one or two incidents in which he was able to counter bad impressions of Russia. One occurred in Leipzig, where Johann Buxbaum, who had left the Academy in 1729, had taken to wearing a sheepskin coat and cap, saying that all professors wore them in St Petersburg. Müller credited himself with dispelling this myth simply by his appearance in normal Western dress.[69]

Müller accomplished all that was expected of him and probably considerably more. He left St Petersburg on 2 August with his "best friends, Gmelin, Euler, Weitbrecht, and Krafft," who accompanied him as far as Kronstadt, and reached London at the end of the month. He presented Sloane with books and Russian engravings, was shown through the Royal Society museum and library, and was invited to attend a meeting of its assembly set for 22 October. In the mean time, Müller conversed with other British scholars, journeyed to Oxford, commissioned a book-dealer (Nicholas Prevost) to send books to Russia, and ordered a Newtonian telescope. On being introduced to the Royal Society in October, he presented books and copies of the *Commentarii* to the assembly and, a few days later, was invited to allow his name to stand for membership, which he did with pleasure.[70] Müller left for Rotterdam during the last week of November, having spent two-and-a-half hectic but very successful months in England. He was elected a fellow of the Royal Society on 10 December 1730.

Müller's agenda in Holland followed the pattern that he established in England. He talked to scientists, booksellers, and writers in Rotterdam, The Hague, and Amsterdam. At the end of December he spent a week in Leyden, enjoying long conversations with the famous chemist, botanist, and instructor in medicine Hermann Boerhaave and with the historian Jean Rousset de Missy, who was later to write histories of both Peter the Great and Catherine the Great. Boerhaave was made an honorary member of the Russian Academy, and in the 1730s he recommended several important European scholars to Russian service. Müller must have been especially persuasive in the case of Boerhaave. He had written Blumentrost in early April 1731 that the Dutchman "was very prejudiced" against the Academy because of stories spread by Martini and Buxbaum.[71]

After Leyden, Müller spend some time in Utrecht, leaving there on 13 January 1731 for Herford.[72] Occupied with family matters for three months, he was not able to travel to Rinteln until April. From there he made his way to Leipzig, where he was saddened to find Mencke in very weakened circumstances, physically and mentally. In Leipzig, as elsewhere, he arranged commissions with book-dealers, conversed with more learned men, and disproved – at least to his own satisfaction – Buxbaum's exaggerations about Russian customs. He also invited several people to St Petersburg: the naturalist Johann Ammann, who joined the Academy as professor in 1733; G.F.W. Juncker, who had studied with Müller at Leipzig in 1724 and was appointed adjunct to the Academy in 1731; George Jakob Kehr, who arrived in St Petersburg in 1732 to serve as a professor of Eastern languages and translator for the College of Foreign Affairs; J.Ch. Hebenstreit, who finally took up a post in Russia as professor of botany in 1749; and J.F. Schreiber, a physician who did not go to Russia but was made an honorary member of the Academy.[73] Müller also renewed his acquaintance with Gottsched and was invited to join the Society of German Poetry. His Leipzig experience proved esecially gratifying for Müller, whose pride of accomplishment bursts through even in a much later account when he asks readers to imagine his joy at being accepted as a worthy companion and fellow scholar by persons to whom he had been a mere student only five years earlier. Among other things, he was given a tour through Maskov's private library by the great man himself. At that point in his career, however, Müller had no intention of making historical studies his main avocation, and so his brief association with Maskov did more for his ego than it did for his education as a historian.

After Leipzig, Müller went to Dresden and Berlin, where he spent time at the Academy once presided over by Leibniz. He left Berlin on 13 June for Hamburg and remained there for a while with Kohl, who had recovered enough from his illness to publish an important book on sources for Slavic history and literature, *Introductio in historiam et rem literarium slavorum* (Altona, 1729).[74] This work was in part a result of political and religious arguments that had dominated Russian "learned" circles before Kohl arrived in St Petersburg. The most prominent person in Russia's small group of learned men was Feofan Prokopovich (1681–1736), who befriended Kohl in 1725. Prokopovich had been educated at the Kievan Academy, was converted to the Uniate Church, spent several years studying Catholicism in Rome, and was then reconverted to Orthodoxy during the first decade of the century. Much in the manner of Bishop Jacques Benigne Bossuet (1627–1704), bishop of Meaux and apologist, by means of biblical references, for Louis xiv's claims of a divine right to rule, Prokopovich defended Peter i's absolutism against those Russian churchmen who clamoured for the restoration of the Patriarchate. Prokopovich wrote the *Ecclesiastical Regulation*, which gave the state full authority over the church, and by 1724 had been raised by Peter to the archbishopric of Novgorod.

Prokopovich encouraged Kohl to pore over old books and manuscripts in order to clarify the history of Orthodoxy and its relation to
other Christian churches. The *Introductio* included descriptions of
work undertaken by Patriarch Nikon, whose attempts at ecclesiastical
reforms in the seventeenth century resulted in a great schism (*raskol*)
in the Russian Orthodox church. Also contained in the *Introductio*
were a Latin translation of the documents about Nikon's excommuni-
cation, information on the schismatics, a translation of their *Book of
Faith*, and many other sources for church history. Kohl also lauded
the Academy and the milieu for scholarship in Russia and even spoke
well of Schumacher. It seems that Müller discussed these sources with
Kohl at length, though his interest in history as a career was still
slight. From Hamburg, Müller set out for St Petersburg. He reached
his destination on 2 August, exactly one year from the day he had
departed.

While on tour, Müller had received a number of letters from
Schumacher. They included orders for equipment, names of book-
dealers and scholars to contact, and some general news about the
situation at the Academy. In one letter, dated 2 January 1731,
Schumacher lauded Müller's earlier work as editor of the *St.
Petersburg Gazette* and complained about his successor, A.B. Kramer.
Schumacher urged Müller to have done with his trip so that he could
resume editorship of the paper and take on as well the role of tutor to
Princess Elizabeth (Anna Leopoldovna) of Mecklenburg, thirteen-
year-old niece of the empress.[75]

After such encouragement from Schumacher, and flushed with a
sense of considerable achievement in Europe, Müller was shocked to
discover after his return that somehow he had incurred his patron's
hostility – or so he alleged later in his memoir. His writing cupboard
had been searched, and all the letters he had received from Schumacher during 1728 and 1729 had been removed. Moreover, the
position of tutor to the young princess had already gone to Johann
Conrad Henninger, Schumacher's brother-in-law.[76] In discussing
these matters with Kramer and the comptroller, Jakob Hoffmann,
Müller learned that the search and theft had been ordered by
Schumacher. Müller also found it very difficult to collect compensation for expenses that he had contracted while travelling in the
employ of the Academy. He requested 1,000 rubles reimbursement,
but Schumacher granted him only 200, saying that Müller had not
been an official Academy agent sent abroad. Unfortunately, Blumentrost's instructions carried no financial promises. Arguing that he
would never have gone to England or Holland had he not expected

some monetary assistance, Müller continued to pester the Chancellery. He received a further 200 rubles in 1732, but this still left him far short of what he said were his expenses. The case was not resolved until 1736, when the Academy's then president, Baron J.A. Korff, appointed a special committee to look into the case. Even so, Müller was granted no further compensation.[77]

Twelve years later, while writing to G.N. Teplov on another matter, Müller disclosed that Schumacher's "hatred for me began in 1732, when the Senate ordered the professors to examine the academic organization created by Schumacher. I then thought it my duty to ask to join the other professors, my friends, in this task, and since there were many things in the structure which needed rejection, I did not hesitate to express my opinion ... This brought down Schumacher's wrath on me."[78] This seems a more reasonable explanation for the falling-out between the two men than the charge that Müller made in his memoir to the effect that Schumacher was pushing Henninger forward at his expense. Müller asserted that Baron A.I. Ostermann, who was responsible for the education of the princess, preferred him, but we have no evidence to corroborate such an allegation. In fact, Müller's assertion sounds a little like sour grapes, for Ostermann would have been a formidable patron. He had arrived in Russia in 1704, also from Westphalia, was a member of the Supreme Privy Council 1726–30, and was in charge of foreign affairs under Anna, whose ascent to the throne he helped to engineer. Nepotism was a common practice, and Müller would have been quite willing to benefit from a similar arrangement himself. Further, the princess would have had a long wait if Ostermann had insisted on having Müller, and so Henninger was a logical choice. Schumacher's parsimonious reaction to Müller's financial requests need not have been for personal reasons. When it came to monetary settlements, the Academy's secretary was renowned for treating everyone equally by giving them as little as possible. His own budget was quite limited. The confiscation of Schumacher's letters to Müller may also be explained quite simply. The succession crisis of 1730 made it expedient for all senior officials to protect themselves by destroying potentially sensitive correspondence from the previous reign.

However, Schumacher must have been furious when Müller, whom he had nutured so carefully as a protégé in th 1720s, went over to the professors in 1732. It is also possible that Müller's success in Europe, and his new status as professor, prompted Schumacher to curb potential competition from a rising young man. Schumacher had hoped to wield full control over the young adjuncts and in the early 1730s wrote to Blumentrost about them as if they were still boys. "One must wave a finger under their noses constantly, or they will play pranks," he said in a letter of 1731. In another note, he wrote that if "one yielded to the young rascals then they will become impudent."[79] Some of Müller's later remarks imply that his young colleagues – he does not admit to misdemeanours himself – were a rowdy lot. Whatever the cause, Müller's new self-assurance was not likely to win him many friends at the Chancellery, and so his career took a sudden turn for the worse. The only consoling event was the appointment of his older brother, Heinrich Justus, who had returned to Russia with him, as a teacher of Latin at the gymnasium in St Petersburg.[80]

CHAPTER TWO

Fledgling Historian at the Academy 1731–3

I had no choice but to seek out some other learned thoroughfare; that was in Russian history.

Müller memoir, circa 1732

Having lost one avenue to a long and successful career, Müller had to find some other "learned thoroughfare," as he called it. He had resumed editorial functions with the *St. Petersburg Gazette* in September 1731. Kramer stayed on as his assistant. Six months later he was asked also to edit the German version of the paper, and the *Notes* were again put in his charge – all of which suggests that Schumacher could not yet have turned against him completely.[1] But Müller did not wish to embark on a career as an editor, nor did the prospect of being a university lecturer appeal to him. Instead he made up his mind to make his way as a scholar of "Russian history, which I intended not only to study industriously myself but to make known in compositions from the best sources. A bold undertaking, since I had so far done nothing in this subject and was still not entirely skilled in the Russian language." Müller pointed out later, however, that his father's "large" library, his association with Mencke, and his own continuous labour in libraries from the Leipzig days had instilled in him a "disposition" toward history.

In St Petersburg he collaborated with Bayer, who, Müller said, planned to put him to work on primary sources until "I succeeded in learning the Russian language, of which he had no doubt, because I was young and active. Now that is what happened: I began with a proposal for the improvement of Russian history through the printing in separate issues of a collection of various items relative to facts and events [in the history of] the Russian Empire. When I subsequently ... read a specimen of this in the usual meeting of the Academy, it was received with approval by everyone, even by Schumacher. It was immediately printed in German and Russian and put into circulation. In the same year, the first issue of the [*Sammlung russischer Geschichte*] was published. In the next year, 1733, I printed the second and third issues."[2]

Whether or not the proposal was Müller's own, as he maintains, or a project initiated by Bayer, which is more likely, it is true that it sparked immediate interest. Mencke published a detailed announcement of it in the *Neue Zeitungen von gelehrten Sachen* and included an outline of the geographical and historical components of the undertaking. Paul-Emile Mauclerque, who corresponded regularly with Bayer, announced it in the *Bibliothèque germanique*, a journal published in Amsterdam.[3] The work to be done was exhaustive. Müller called for the publication of existing sources, among them the *Kniga stepennaia* and the *Primary Chronicle*; genealogical tables; geographical accounts; descriptions of ancient coins and medals; natural history reports; church histories and the lives of saints; histories of schools, of regions, and of the non-Slavic peoples in the Russian empire; and specifically named works by Bayer and Duvernois. The proposal was therefore fully in accordance with the historical research undertaken at Leipzig, where Bayer had also studied briefly, and indeed throughout most of Germany.

The project attracted attention within Russia too. V.N. Tatishchev, who had begun reading Russian history sources while in Sweden during the mid-1720s and who had spent some time during 1726 and 1727 poring over Russian chronicles with Bayer, wrote Schumacher for further information about Müller's plan.[4] Tatishchev previously had printed a series on mammoth bones found in Siberia in a supplement to the *St. Petersburg Gazette*[5] and had carried on a mild debate with Gmelin on the matter. He too had outlined a number of topics for study in Russian history, including a study of seventeenth-century Russian currency and a genealogical table of the Russian great and lesser princes.[6]

Tatishchev's had been the most articulate of about a dozen proposals set before the Supreme Privy Council during the disorders of 1730. He was well versed in the ideas of *Aufklärung* generally and of Christian Wolff, whose world-view included faith in constituted authority. Wolff's interpretation of natural law placed the conception of obligation and duty above individual rights, and Tatishchev used this assumption to provide a rationalistic appeal for autocracy. Using "proofs" drawn from Russian history and geography, he concluded that autocratic government was more useful and less dangerous than all others.[7] Thus he attached a great deal of importance to the study of the national past. Although they did not meet again after 1727, Tatishchev and Müller were to enjoy a long, though often futile co-operation in their mutual efforts to prepare for a definitive history of Russia. In 1732 the task seemed imposing. Bayer and the novice Müller, both Germans who were weak in the Russian language, were the only two people recognized in any official way as historians of Russia. This irony was probably lost on them at the time, but would return to haunt Müller years later.

This is not to say that there were no Russians anxious that a national history be prepared or that there were no records of Russia's antiquity available. Baron C.H. von Manstein was probably quite sincere when he reported that in the 1740s Russians seemed to have little interest in their national heritage.[8] But he could not have been aware of the many medieval chronicles that were still preserved in monasteries and that were known and consulted by scholars in the seventeenth century. In his own time, an increasing number of interested scholars and patriots were turning to the old records and showing concern for their preservation and vertification. By mid-century the themes of such annals, the earliest extant form of which – the so-called *Primary Chronicle* (or Tale of Bygone Years), attributed to the monk Nestor of the Crypt Monastery in Kiev and dated between 1111 and 1113 – was soon to be subject to acrimonious debate.

The Nestor version of the *Primary Chronicle* asserted clearly the celebrated – or notorious – tale that in 862 Slavic tribes invited the Varangian Russes "from beyond the seas" to provide them with a centralized form of government ("Our land is great and rich, but there is no order in it. Come and rule and reign over us!"). From these Russes, "the region of Novgorod became known as the land of Rus'."[9] It was asserted also in the *Primary Chronicle* that Christianity was introduced to the Slavs in Kiev by the apostle St Andrew himself, and that he predicted God's favour for the "great city" that would arise on the hills where Kiev was later constructed. The chronicle explained the "origin of the land of Rus', the first rulers of Kiev, and the way in which the land of Rus' had its beginning,"[10] by weaving together Byzantine and Arabic writings, old legends, folk-tales, and biblical references. Later annals carried more specific political themes and often reflected the dictates of rulers who wished to justify their power both to contemporaries and to posterity. From the early sixteenth century, annals also gave form to the notion that Moscow was the new seat of Christian orthodoxy, having replaced the heretical and fallen Rome and Constantinople to become God's permanent city on earth – the Third Rome.

One such work was compiled for Ivan IV sometime in the 1560s by Metropolitan Makarii and his successor, Afanasii. Called the *Kniga stepennaia tsarskago rodosloviia* (*Book of Degrees of the Tsar's Genealogy*), its tone was set in an introductory paragraph where the authors proposed to trace "God's confirmed holders of sceptres" from St Vladimir to Ivan IV. The legend about St Andrew was repeated. Although the book started its series of hagio-biographies with Vladimir (980 – 1015), Ivan was awarded an unbroken lineage to Riurik, the semi-legendary figure whom the earlier chronicles credited with founding the "Russian" state in the ninth century. In his turn, Riurik was related to a certain "Prus," mythical brother of Augustus Caesar.[11] In this way, Ivan could boast a royal ancestry second to none. All later Kievan and Muscovite princes were granted saint-like characteristics and were extended absolute powers, derived directly from God, by the authors of the *Kniga stepennaia*.

In the seventeenth century the government in Moscow delegated the recording of a national history to a special administrative body. A registry department (*Zapisnoi prikaz*) was instituted by Tsar Alexei in 1657 to gather documents for the preparation of a history of Muscovy after the reign of Ivan IV. Apparently the proposed work was intended as a continuation of the *Kniga stepennaia*. Nothing, however, seems to have been written, and the undertaking was abandoned after two years;[12] but the Romanovs achieved their historical pedigree in 1669 anyway, when Fedor Griboedov wrote the *History of the Tsars and Great Princes of the Russian Lands*. The book was used at court, where Griboedov was an official, but was not circulated to the public. In it the rulers were listed so as to portray Muscovy as the rightful heir to Kievan political lands and its "autocratic" great princes. The Romanovs were traced back to Ivan IV's family, to "Prussus," the alleged founder of Prussia and brother of "Augustus, Caesar of Rome" – and to Riurik.[13] Griboedov's reliance on the *Kniga stepennaia* was apparent throughout.

A similar message was carried in a chronicle compiled by Feodosius Safonovich, the father superior of the Mikhailovsky Monastery in Kiev. His was a highly selective account of Kievan history alone, but it was at the same time a representation of the fact that humanistic European scholarship had made inroads in Kiev, if not yet in Moscow. Safonovich used old chronicles and remarked on the intrinsic value of knowing the national past. A similar view was expressed in a foreword to an unpublished "Historical Book" written at the command of Feodor Alekseevich (tsar 1676–82). Its anonymous author allotted to historical writing the task of teaching readers by searching for the truth in the past. History is a source of lessons for the present, he said, and insisted that it must be used to improve mankind by praising good and criticizing evil; but fables must be disproved and discarded. The manuscript contained extracts from classical historians (Thucydides and Tacitus), from emperors and kings (Alexander the Great, Julius Caesar, Justinian), and others to demonstrate their interest in and use of historical knowledge.[14] This work was not typical of the age in Russia, however. Compilers of historical information within Muscovy continued to rely on the traditional legends and, more specifically, on material gathered by Polish chroniclers, who tended toward the theological and teleological in their interpretations.

A good example of this tendency appeared with the publication of the *Sinopsis* in 1674. The *Sinopsis* contained biblical legends, extracts from mainly Polish sources, and both religious and fabulous explanations for events in the history of old Rus'. The book was unique, however, in that it was the first printed book on Kievan history and had twenty-five reprintings before 1762. It remained the most widely read book on medieval eastern Slavic history until the nineteenth century. Introductory chapters of the *Sinopsis* claimed that the ancient Slovenes, or Slavs, "exceeded all others in strength, manliness and bravery" and so derived their name from *slava* ("glory"); that the Russians ("*Russkie*") descended from the Slovenes and earned their name from their "dispersion" ("*rosseianie*") over vast territories; that the prince of Rosh ("*Rosska*") referred to by the Old Testament's prophet Ezekiel might have been one of their early leaders; and that the Muscovites descended from Mosoch (Meshech), the Slovene-Russian grandson of Noah, who also appeared in the book of Ezekiel. Eighteenth-century additions gave Moscow a central place in the *Sinopsis* as the "God-preserved city,"[15] but the bulk of the text still dealt with the history of Kiev to the invasion of the Tatars in the thirteenth century, and with Dmitrii Donskoi in the fourteenth century.

Two reprints of the *Sinopsis* were ordered personally by Peter I, who appreciated the educative and even propagandistic potential of history more than any of his predecessors. The founding of Russia's first public library, civil typography, and newspaper, and the simplification of the Russian alphabet, are signs of the importance that Peter assigned to the printed word. He was also concerned with having his version of his reign preserved for posterity. One striking example of this was the "History of the Swedish Wars," which was compiled in detail between 1718 and 1722 under the supervision of Peter himself. The tract documented events of the long conflict with Sweden as well as later contests with Persia, explained Russian diplomacy, and described the evolution and administration of the Russian army. Yet it remained in manuscript until Prince M.M. Shcherbatov published one rendition of it in two volumes, 1770–2. Vice-Chancellor P.P. Shafirov's *Discourse Concerning the Just Causes of the War between Sweden and Russia, 1700–1722* (*Razsuzhdenie kakie*

*zakonnye prichiny ego tsarskoe Velichestvo Petr Pervyi ... k nachatiiu voiny
...*) St Petersburg, 1717, 1719, 1722) was an equally important example
of Peter's attempts to justify Russia's diplomatic and military causes to
his contemporaries. It also had English and German printings. The
Book of Mars (*Kniga Marsova* [St Petersburg, 1713]), a collection of
engravings and short accounts of military events over the first decade
of the eighteenth century, and a Russian translation of Pufendorf's
Introductio ad historiam Europaeum (1718) indicate the diversity of
Peter's interest in history.[16]

According to contemporaries, the national history was a continuing
passion for Peter even though he had little time to spend on it. His
friend A.K. Nartov reported that "the ruler loved to read chronicles
and ... often asked Feofan Prokopovich, 'when will we have a full
Russian history?'" Jakob Stählin, academician 1735–85, professed to
have heard from Schumacher that Peter judged all works on Russian
history written abroad to be "good for nothing. What can foreigners
say of our history? We have written nothing on the subject ourselves
... I know very well that the materials are scattered up and down the
empire, and buried in the dust of monasteries. It is long since I formed
the project of snatching them from the destruction that threatens
them, and of doing all in my power to facilitate the composition of a
good history of Russia by some able pen."[17]

The emperor included ancient and modern history among the
professorial chairs in the humanities section of his proposed Academy
and ordered that the first up-to-date history of Russia be written. In
spite of Peter's encouragement and enthusiasm, however, Baron
Heinrich van Huyssen, Fedor Polikarpov, B.I. Kurakin, Feofan
Prokopovich, G. Skorniakov-Pisarev, A.I. Mankiev, and Tatishchev
all tried but failed to make an encompassing history of Russia
available for public, or private, use during his reign.

The well-educated van Huyssen (1666–1739) first was hired by one
of Peter's agents in 1699 to improve Russia's image abroad, but when
he went to St Petersburg in 1705 he was asked to serve as tutor to the
tsarevich, Aleksei. He also took on special diplomatic missions for
Peter. Van Huyssen was responsible for the publication and distribution in France of a short pamphlet about the history of Peter's reign,
but never completed a larger version of Russian history that he was
commanded to prepare. Polikarpov (early 1670s–1731) taught at the
Slavic-Greek-Latin Academy in Moscow during the 1690s, became an
editor and later director of the Moscow typography, and from 1726 to
1731 was in charge of the Holy Synod printing press. In December
1708, he was commissioned by A.I. Musin-Pushkin, head of Peter's
monastery department (*Monastyrskii prikaz*), to write a history of

Russia's rulers from the first decade of the sixteenth century (Vasilii III, 1505-33). In spite of Musin-Pushkin's prodding, even harassment, however, the work was not ready until 1715 and then was deemed unsuitable for publication by Peter.[18]

B.I. Kurakin (1676-1727), author of several diaries and accounts of current events, was Russia's foremost diplomat in Europe after 1709. He got as far as outlining a full account of Russian history from ancient times, but completed only a description of Peter's reign for the years 1682-94. Finished two years after Peter's death, it was not printed for another century and a half.[19] But Kurakin's proposal had an important new characteristic. Only one-third of his outline was dedicated to the period before Peter began his reign. This and other historical projects of the era clearly were intended as pragmatic, rather than theological, rationalizations of the present. They represented one of several dimensions of Peter's aim to secularize his state.

Prokopovich's accomplishments as a historian are somewhat more difficult to determine, in the main because the authorship of many works usually attributed to him has recently been called into question by James Cracraft. There is little doubt, however, that the Kiev-born and -educated archbishop of Novgorod was either author, co-author, editor, or supervisor of many publications, one of which was a *History of Emperor Peter the Great from His Birth to the Battle of Poltava* (*Istoriia Imperatora Petra Velikago ot rozhdeniia ego do Poltavskoi batalii*), first printed in 1773.[20] Moreover, Prokopovich and fellow members of Peter's Holy Synod steadfastly expounded the merits of "learning" generally and of history particularly. Prokopovich saw history as an ideal means for national moral regeneration, and as a wellspring for religious and political education.

Prokopovich's concern for history was actuated in large part by practical considerations. The *Ecclesiastical Regulation*, which he either wrote or supervised, called for the establishment of seminaries in which Russia's youth could be educated and heresies combated. "Many say that education is responsible for heresy," stated the *Ecclesiastical Regulation*, "[but] learning is beneficial and basic for every good, as of the Fatherland, so also of the church." Prokopovich believed that "obstinacy and ignorance" were the main causes of heresy and of disloyalty. In short, he hoped to counter the influence of both Catholicism and recalcitrants within Orthodoxy by means of "good and sound" learning. Since his opponents cited regularly from classical writers and justified their position by referring to history, he decided to fight them with their own weapon. The *Ecclesiastical Regulation* insisted even that grammar be taught by having students read books of history and geography.[21] After Peter's death, Prokopovich patronized Tatishchev and Antioch Kantemir and with them formed Russia's self-styled Learned Guard, a small group of thinkers who saw themselves as defenders of learning in Russia and in that way helped futher to spread the seeds of humanism in Russia. Unfortunately, however, there were no literary forums in which their ideas could be broadly disseminated. School systems only barely functioned, and researchers at the Academy were not yet interested in sponsoring a popular Russian history.

Another member of Peter's ambassadorial corps, F.S. Saltykov, also submitted a strong recommendation that a history of Russia be prepared. Like Prokopovich and Peter himself, Saltykov was motivated by practical concerns. According to his "Propositions," which he wrote in London between 1712 and 1714, a history of the Petrine state system should be compiled and translated into European languages so that Russia's cause might be better known.[22] This suggestion may well have provided the initiative for Shafirov's *Discourse*, but the historical dimension of the project went the way of other plans for writing history during Peter's administration. Apparently undaunted, neither Prokopovich nor his emperor ever gave up the idea of Russian history.

In 1722, Peter enjoined Skorniakov-Pisarev, a close associate of the ruler, director of the Naval Academy, and eventually port-master of Okhotsk, to prepare a new Russian chronicle, and this he was able to accomplish by collating and drawing extracts from known chronicles, rank books, and chronographs – that is, surveys of universal history made up from biblical stories and scattered historical information. Once again, however, the results of one of Peter's history projects remained hidden from the public eye. Skorniakov-Pisarev's *Detailed Chronicle from the Beginning of Russia to the Battle of Poltava* (*Podrobnaia letopis' ot nachala Rossii do Poltavskoi batalii*) was not printed until 1798–99.[23]

Although the emperor's wish that a "true history of ancient Russia" be compiled was not satisfied, his desire that the "raw materials for a Russian history [which are] hidden in cloisters and monasteries throughout the realm" be assembled was partly served. In December 1720 he charged all governors, vice-governors, and *voevody* (governors) to make copies of old charters "and other original curious letters, also historical books – printed and in manuscript" located in monasteries and send them to the Senate. Fourteen months later Peter ordered that all chronicles, chronographs, and genealogical tables be collected and deposited in the library of the Moscow Holy Synod.[24] This project had only barely begun to show results by the time Müller took an interest in old documents, but at least the first step toward the gathering – and preservation – of Russia's written heritage had been taken.

Sometime toward the end of Peter's reign a proposal for a general history and description of the Russian empire was drawn up, but apparently not acted on. The historical spectrum of the work was to stretch from ancient times to the present, and it was to conclude with a full statistical accounting of the contemporary realm. Its scope was very wide in comparison with earlier projects, for it was to include information on ancient settlements and migrations, wars and religion; the morals and customs of all peoples that make up the empire; a description of its natural resources; an outline of the important cultural and religious events and institutions of Russia's past; early and recent forms of government, and some account of the practices of early princes and tsars; and full descriptions of the provinces. Although neither the author nor the recipient of this document has been identified, it remains as a reflection of the thirst for information that permeated Peter's bureaucratic circles. If it was not drawn up by Tatishchev, it certainly mirrored his ambitions and foreshadowed his actual research – just as it did those of Müller.[25]

The one general history of Russia to be completed during Peter's reign was written by A.I. Mankiev, secretary to Prince A.Y. Khilkov, Russia's envoy to Sweden. Entitled *Kernel of Russian History*, the manuscript was written while Mankiev sat out the Russo-Swedish war in a Swedish prison. Although he repeated the legend that the Russians were descended from Mosoch, Mankiev said that they came "from men, not Gods," thereby taking a major step away from the religious explanation offered by the *Sinopsis*. He retained the notion that the Slavs had earned their name by early "glories," and he connected Riurik to "Prussus" and Augustus Caesar. The book was openly patriotic and praised Peter for deeds which, he said, surpassed those even of Nebuchadnezzar, Alexander the Great, and Ulysses.[26]

Wherever possible, Mankiev used Russian sources in lieu of the Polish ones on which the author of the *Sinopsis* had relied. For a prisoner in a foreign country, he had access to a remarkable number of such materials. The gymnasium in Västeras, where he was free to roam, held several chronicles (including Safonovich's), the *Kniga stepennaia*, and quite a few useful books deposited there by a prominent Swedish historian who had lived briefly in Russia. Mankiev used classical writings, Swedish books, and some Polish works, the most important of which was M. Stryikowski's *Kronika Polska* (late sixteenth century). The *Kronika* had already been used by the author of the *Sinopsis* to corroborate the doctrinal legends about

Mosoch and *slava*. It also contained extracts from a huge number of Polish, Russian, Lithuanian, Ukrainian, western European, and Greek works, along with autobiographical materials from the author himself. Tatishchev was regularly to use the *Kronika* as a source.[27] Another innovative feature of Mankiev's *Kernel* was the fact that it contained accounts of events down to his own time, that is, to 1712. By lauding Peter's cultural and other reforms, the book marked the first expression of Russian national self-consciousness in terms of the history of human achievement.[28] It is worth noting that Mankiev's book was not written on Peter's command. Thus its contemporaneity and patriotism were independent reflections of the age in which the manuscript was prepared.

Mankiev saw history as the best source of moral and practical guidelines for his contemporaries. Tatishchev also stressed the didactic role of history in his multi-volume *History of the Russian Empire from Earliest Times* (*Istoriia rossiiskaia*). Although he showed an interest in the subject from the first decade of the eighteenth century, Tatishchev began to write the history seriously only in 1729 and was not able to submit a draft of his work to the Academy until January 1740; a more complete version was ready in 1746. For the next thirty years, the long manuscript provided ammunition for debate between proponents of different interpretations of Russia's antiquity. It contained extensive extracts from and reproductions of entire chronicles, including some that were lost forever in a fire of 1750. Tatishchev's thoroughness in bringing together information from both foreign and Russian sources – he boasted of having used more than a thousand books – made his material especially valuable to researchers.

Tatishchev was the first Russian to test the traditional legends about the ancient Slavs against a wide variety of documentary sources. He rejected the story that St Andrew had introduced Christianity to the Slavs, ridiculed those who traced Riurik back to Augustus Caesar, and found the theories about Russian descent from Mosoch or Rosh wanting. But he accepted as reasonable the idea that the name Slav derived from "glory." Tatishchev went to great lengths to underscore the benefits of historical study. In a foreword he said that he wanted to honour and glorify his homeland, and later he noted that "no man, no condition of life, no profession, no science, no government, much less a single individual, can be perfect, wise and useful without a knowledge of history." His belief that both good and villainous deeds of the past must be portrayed in order to provide current readers with reason to practise virtue and avoid evil and his urge to correct "European historians who accuse us of having no ancient history"[29] were premises later assumed by Müller. Yet the lessons of history offered by Mankiev and Tatishchev remained lost to Russia's reading public until the final third of the century, when Müller was finally given permission to prepare their manuscripts for publication.

This scattered historical activity in seventeenth- and early-eighteenth-century Russia had only barely taken into account the progress made in historical studies in Europe. Generally, history in Russia meant chronicling the affairs of rulers and attempting to use real and imagined events from the past to inculcate moral and political lessons in a quite minute readership. Russian writers seemed virtually untouched by the advances made in critical, geographical, and humanistic historical writing in Europe as early as the sixteenth century. Müller, however, had the advantage of studying at an institution, Leipzig, where history was a well-developed science. Although he did not expect then that eventually his profession would be as a historian, he could not help but be influenced by the humanistic atmosphere and the respect given to professional inquiry at his university. He was favoured further in St Petersburg by his association with the only two professional historians in Russia, Kohl, until he left Russia in 1727, and G.-S. Bayer, the most influential person in Müller's development as a historian.

Gottlieb-Siegfried Bayer (1694–1738) once wrote that "history is the mirror of the world" and that "the main purpose in studying ancient history ... is to demonstrate good deeds for readers to imitate."[30] This did not mean, however, that his work was typical of the didactic historical pieces then being produced in Russia. Before going to St Petersburg, Bayer had studied the historical sciences at Königsberg, Berlin, and Leipzig – where he earned a magister in 1718. He was an expert as well in Semitic and Oriental languages and was an established scholar with publications in Mencke's *Acta eruditorum* and other learned journals before he took up residence in Russia. Blumentrost had been especially anxious to fill the chair of history at the Academy with an established historian and several times in 1725 asked Wolff to recommend someone who was capable of taking on the "rank of Historiographer." Bayer was finally persuaded to go to St Petersburg by Goldbach, a friend from his Königsberg days, and an offer of a chair of classical and Eastern languages at a salary of 600 rubles.[31] By that time, Blumentrost must have changed his mind about the position of historiographer, for it was to be twenty more years before the first such appointment was made. Although he never learned Russian or other Slavic languages, for which he was roundly criticized later by opponents of his theories on ancient Russia, Bayer's gleanings from non-Slavic sources were very important to Müller, Tatishchev, and others who were then concerned with Russian history. Bayer translated from Chinese, instructed young scholars willingly, contributed prolifically to the *Commentarii*, and conscientiously studied materials pertaining to ancient Russia. He also prepared an introduction to a short textbook of ancient history that Ostermann had ordered written for the young Peter II. After Kohl left Russia in 1727, Bayer agreed to direct the gymnasium, a post he held until 1737 when he withdrew from the Academy in order to return to Königsberg. Unfortunately, he died in St Petersburg the next year before he had a chance to leave Russia. Bayer's overall contribution to Russia's enlightenment was not great, but he was an important force in the lives of certain individuals. He was friendly with Prokopovich, Kantemir, and Tatishchev and was regularly at odds with Schumacher on behalf of his fellow academicians.[32] Above all, however, he made a serious researcher out of Müller.

More than thirty of Bayer's articles can be found in early issues of the *Commentarii*. Three (on the Scythians) were translated into Russian, and a historical study of Azov was reprinted in the second volume of the *Sammlung*, which Bayer edited in 1736. Of the items in the *Commentarii*, the most valuable for Müller and later historians of Russia were "De Varagis" (1729), "De russorum prima expeditione constantinopolitana" (1731), and "Origines russicae" (1736). These accounts were based on Greek, Scandinavian, and Arab sources, the most important of which were the *Annales Bertiniani* and *De administrando imperio*. The latter was compiled around 950 by the Byzantine emperor Constantine VII Porphyrogenitus. By collating such sources with the so-called *Primary Chronicle*, parts of which he was able to read in a German translation, Bayer concluded that the Varangian Rus' (Russes), whom the chronicles said were invited from "beyond the sea" by Novgorodian Slavs to rule over them in 862, were Scandinavian. Much later, this very controversial assumption came to be called the "Normanist" theory on the foundation of the Russian state, because Bayer used the term "Norman" to refer to the peoples of the Scandinavian peninsula.[33]

Tatishchev incorporated "De Varagis" and two other essays by Bayer into his own manuscript intact,[34] but he did not accept Bayer's interpretation without some qualification. He traced the Varangians to Finland and associated them ethnically with "Finnish" Sarmatians. Although he did not give the Varangians a Slavic lineage, he said that the Slavs were as old a people as any other and challenged foreign writers who insisted that they had no history before the ninth century. Moreover, Tatishchev proclaimed that large areas around

Novgorod had been governed for at least five generations before Riurik by the family of a Slavic chief, Gostomysl': "Gostomysl had 4 sons and 3 daughters. His sons died ... and to his middle daughter, who was married to the Finnish king, was born a son, Riurik."[35] So Riurik was granted a legitimate claim to leadership in the Slavic lands, a circumstance that Tatishchev said was proved in a Novgorodian chronicle that was lost soon after he used it. Since Tatishchev was anxious to find evidence in history to support his own advocacy of strong, centralized monarchy, this story suited his scheme well. In any case, Müller was acquainted with Tatishchev in the 1720s, but was not yet familiar with his historical theses.

There were others in St Petersburg besides Bayer who contributed to Müller's progress as a historian of Russia. Johann-Werner Paus, director of translators at the Academy and expert on Old Church Slavonic, acted as a translator himself for both Bayer and Müller. It was he who introduced them to the *Kniga stepennaia* and to a redaction of the *Primary Chronicle* that had been copied in Königsberg for Peter the Great in 1716. This version was also called the Radziwill chronicle. According to E. Winter, both documents were translated into German and Latin by Paus (but were not published) and were used in that form by Müller. In fact, Müller later blamed Paus for the errors that appeared in his own *Sammlung* piece on the chronicles (1732). In his turn, Paus complained that it was he who "was the discoverer of sources, the creator and interpretor of history," while Müller was a "plagiarizer, popularizer and braggart."[36] Thus, Müller's first foray into the field of history provoked a bitter reaction from Paus, whose ten months of concentrated labour on the translation were not acknowledged in print. In this case the accusations were private, and so they had little effect on Müller. Later crises over Müller's historical essays were to prove much more dramatic.

Müller rushed into his chosen career with enthusiasm and not a little recklessness. In September 1732 he printed extracts from the *Primary Chronicle* (Königsberg) in the first issue of the *Sammlung*.[37] His introduction to it and other old manuscripts was the first published discussion of eastern Slavic chronicles, but was marred then by the fact that Müller wrongly attributed the *Primary Chronicle* to a non-existent monk named Theodosius. Müller's first reference to the Varangians as Normans, who came "especially from the Norwegian kingdom," appeared in this introduction.[38] But he also printed extracts from old Norse sources that demonstrated the close connection between Scandinavian, Prussian Slav, and Rus' tribal leaders in the tenth and eleventh centuries. These publications revealed clearly Bayer's influence on Müller.

A few months later Müller addressed the Conference on the subject of the Kalmyks. Most of his information was taken from a diary written by a Russian military commander sent among them in 1722. This talk was printed in the first volume of the *Sammlung*, where Müller said that he planned to write a book on the history, religion, literature, and territory of the Kalmyks. He also reviewed a massive book by Nicolaas C. Witsen, mayor of Amsterdam and a friend of Peter I, *Noord en Oost Tartarye* (1692).[39] Müller already had published part of this work in the *Notes* in 1728 and singled out the information on Kamchatka as especially worthy of notice. Müller then prepared an account of the life of Alexander Nevskii, which he drew in the main from the *Kniga stepennaia* and several foreign sources, and edited more sections of the *Primary Chronicle* for inclusion in each of the remaining five issues of the first volume.[40] Thus he took seriously his own proposal of 1732, which formed part of the introduction to the *Sammlung*. He had promised to print materials that would lead "towards a full Russian history, and to a geographical description of the Russian Empire," even if the task took "twenty years or more" to accomplish.[41] Müller could not have recognized it at the time, but the routine for his career in Russia had already been established, that is, a perpetual, nearly frenetic busyness. Aside from the time-consuming self-imposed task of making himself into a historian, Müller still had other editorial and teaching chores. He tutored and shared his quarters with two sons of a Livonian nobleman named Rennenkampf, to whom he was expected to teach those sciences "which are suited to cavaliers," and gave two-hour daily lessons to Ch.G.P. Iaguzhinskii, stepson of Count von Prinzenstern, vice-president of the office of state.[42].

While Müller was thus occupied, the Academy itself was continually under political pressure. Warned by highly placed friends in 1731 that the Academy needed a "protector" against "intrigue," Schumacher asked the academicians to assist him in organizing a lobby at court.[43] The members considered his suggestion that they appeal directly to Count E.J. Biron.[44] But equivocation on the part of the Conference and Blumentrost's loss of authority because of the change at court forced Schumacher to act on his own. Blumentrost returned to the capital from Moscow again in January 1732 and a few months later was unceremoniously relieved of the presidency. The immediate cause of his dismissal was the death of Catherine Ivanovna, Empress Anna's sister and the mother of the girl whom Müller once hoped to tutor. Anna's wrath fell on Blumentrost in part because he was the royal physician, but the fact that his replacement was a nobleman from Courland – Count H.K. Keyserling – was an indication of the real reason for Blumentrost's vulnerability.[45]

In his one appearance at the Conference in 1732, Blumentrost told members that they were going to have to labour under a new set of regulations. He left them, however, with no idea as to the nature of the changes being contemplated.[46] In August 1732, the Senate requested a detailed report on the Academy's financial situation. At the same time it issued instructions for the establishment of observatories and for the preparation of a general map of the Russian empire. The importance that the Senate assigned to the map-making capacity of the Academy was indicated by an accompanying order that gave its agents the right to collect maps and charts from anywhere in the realm. The Senate also insisted that members fulfil their responsibilities by publishing regularly in Academy journals and that all expenditures be justified. Later memoranda requested information about Academy membership and its obligations, names of students, lists of books in the library, and all items held in the *Kunstkamera*. Members were allowed to respond individually; most criticized Schumacher, who had been trying to reorganize both the typography and the gymnasium.[47]

This marked the first time that the academicians were asked to express their views over the heads of Academy officials. Bayer took the lead by holding meetings in his home. The result was that ten members, including Müller, signed a statement which, while saying nothing about their own duties, reminded the Senate that they had not been paid for their previous year's service.[48] Euler and Krafft submitted a more detailed reply of their own, suggesting, first, an overhaul of the Academy administration, the better to fulfil Peter's wishes; second, that salaries be made more equitable; and third, that a professor be named vice-president, with a secretary and copyist. Finally, they suggested that more adjuncts (there were four at the time) and translators be appointed.[49] They did not criticize Schumacher. Blumentrost also sent a report to the Senate, complaining that not enough funds had been made available to the Academy to cover its service sector sufficiently; the journals, *Commentarii* and the supplement to the *Gazette*, could be printed only irregularly; the typography needed expensive repairs; and several promised buildings, including residences for staff, had not been constructed.[50]

It was clear to everyone concerned that most of the enthusiasm that permeated the institution during the first years had worn off. A visitor to St Petersburg from France noted in 1733 that the Academy was "in such great disorder that its principal members have requested permission to leave";[51] among those were Bayer and Bernoulli. In February 1733, however, salaries for the previous year were finally paid, and in June Keyserling was appointed president.[52] According to Müller, this change went a long way toward appeasing the Academy community.[53] Keyserling's term of office proved to be of short duration. But in that time he managed to place the administrative side of the Academy on a firm footing, to organize the budget, and to complete preparations for the second Kamchatka expedition under the command of Vitus Bering. When Keyserling departed from St Petersburg to take up a diplomatic post in Poland, he left instructions on the management of the Academy during his absence:[54] professors were again required to meet twice weekly in the Conference to read lectures; a secretary to the Conference was appointed (Charles Meder); a five-member directory (Goldbach, Beckenstein, de l'Isle, Duvernois, and Bayer) was put in charge of the Conference, each to take a monthly turn as chairman; resolutions of the Conference were to be decided by a majority vote of all members, except adjuncts; and Academy finances were to be managed by a committee comprised of Goldbach, Beckenstein, Bayer, and Schumacher. This was clearly a breakthrough for the academicians. They now had control over their own affairs. Or so it seemed at the time.

PART TWO

Charting Siberia

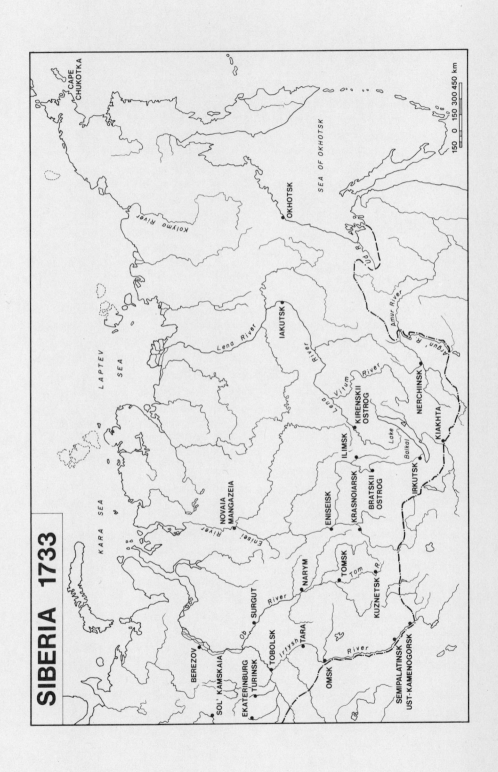

SIBERIA 1733

CAPE CHUKOTKA

OKHOTSK

SEA OF OKHOTSK

Kolyma River

LAPTEV SEA

Lena River

IAKUTSK

Lena River

Vitium River

KIRENSKII OSTROG

Amur River

Argun' R.

Ud R.

NERCHINSK

KIAKHTA

KARA SEA

NOVAIA MANGAZEIA

Enisei River

ILIMSK

ENISEISK

KRASNOIARSK

BRATSKII OSTROG

Lake Baikal

IRKUTSK

BEREZOV

Ob River

SURGUT

NARYM

TOMSK

Tom

KUZNETSK

Tom R.

SOL' KAMSKAIA

EKATERINBURG

TURINSK

TOBOLSK

Irtysh

TARA

OMSK

River

SEMIPALATINSK

UST-KAMENOGORSK

150 0 150 300 450 km

CHAPTER THREE

A Land and Its Past
1733–43

God grant that my Siberian business will soon come to
an end ... I do not wish to complain ... but there is
hardly a town or part of Siberia in which I have not
been.

Müller to Leonhard Euler, June 1740

Establishing an Academy of Sciences was only one of Peter's schemes
to build a reputation for Russia as a country concerned with modern
science. Leibniz informed him in 1716 that "the extensive lands of the
Russian Empire ... offer excellent opportunities ... for new discoveries by which the sciences are advanced." He further suggested that
Peter might "render a great service" by ordering the exploration of the
northern seas and the geographical relation between Asia and
America. Leibniz also observed that the huge empire would undoubtedly "yield many plants, animals, minerals, and other natural objects
that have not yet been discovered."[1]

These suggestions were timely, if not decisive, in Peter's decision to
explore and open up the vast potential of his domain. The search for
minerals in Siberia had intensified already in the middle of the
seventeenth century, and administrative and military centres (*raz-
riady*) were organized in Siberia by Peter's predecessors. Geographical and ethnographical data were being collected in the 1670s, and
several maps, the most important of them by Semen Remezov, were
completed by the turn of the century.

Leibniz, who raised the subject regularly after 1697, when he first
mentioned it to François Lefort, Peter's adviser, was merely the most
persistent of those who advocated that the Russian government
expend more energy on discovery. One of Peter's own subjects,
Saltykov, made similar recommendations in his "Propositions"; and
John Perry, an English engineer who served in Russia from 1698 to
1712, reported in 1716 that Peter several times expressed an interest in
discovering whether Japan could be reached via the Arctic but that

the long war with Sweden made such ventures impossible.[2] Only after Russia's success in the war seemed assured – and after regular reports of disorder, lawlessness, and finally rebellion on the part of the Cossacks and native peoples between 1710 and 1714 – was Peter persuaded to appoint the Great Kamchatka Command in 1716. Its purpose was to survey northeastern Siberia from the Kolyma to the Amur, but, because of quarrels between various authorities at Iakutsk, the expedition came to nothing.

The next year Peter discussed the geography of Siberia with Guillaume de l'Isle, Joseph Nicolas's older brother and member of the Académie des sciences in Paris. In 1706 Guillaume de l'Isle had printed a map that implied there might be a chain of mountains connecting Siberia and "quelque autre Continent."

Peter was therefore both aware of and interested in the question of the degree to which North America was accessible by land – or by sea – from regions claimed for the Russian monarchy. His first concern, however, was to evaluate the material potential of his holdings in Siberia. To accomplish this, he contracted Daniel G. Messerschmidt in 1718 to explore western and central Siberia, with orders to catalogue its natural history, plants, and human resources. Many of the items that Messerschmidt brought back with him in 1727 – rocks, plants, and animal specimens – were housed in the *Kunstkamera*. More important, however, was the confirmation by Messerschmidt, and others, of major deposits of copper in the Urals, iron around Tobol'sk, and silver at Nerchinsk. The acquisition of such minerals soon surpassed the fur trade in significance. Messerschmidt was accompanied in 1721–2 by P.J.T. Strahlenberg, a Swedish officer who lived in Tobol'sk as a prisoner of war from 1711 to 1721. He had charted parts of Siberia during his internment and later wrote the first detailed description of that region. *Das nord und östliche Theil von Europa und Asia* was printed in Stockholm in 1730 by Strahlenberg himself and was available to Russian explorers before Müller left for Siberia in 1733.[3]

Other exploratory groups were organized by Peter's government and sent to the Caucasus in 1718. One such expedition resulted in the production of detailed maps of the Caspian Sea coastline by S.I. Soimonov and others. A year later, geodesists Feodor Luzhin and Ivan Evreinov travelled to Kamchatka and prepared maps and reports on the region and on the Kurile Islands. They had secret instructions to discover whether Asia and America were joined, but this they were prevented from doing because of a sea accident.[4] Also in 1719, Tatishchev presented Peter with a proposal for a full land survey of Russia, with accompanying maps of the various administrative regions of the empire. Peter agreed to sponsor the undertaking and suggested that it be expanded to a broad geographical description of his possessions. But the project foundered when Tatishchev was sent to Siberia in March 1720 to administer the state factory systems in the Urals.[5] Nevertheless, Peter was as tenacious in his geographical ambitions as he was in his attempts to prepare for a Russian history: by virtue of a statute issued in February 1720, geodesists were ordered to describe "all boundaries, rivers, cities, towns, churches, villages, forests, and so on," in the Russian empire. A supplementary order of May 1721 called for even more detailed accounts of the realm.[6]

Questions of science, discovery, and economics were not the only stimuli for Peter's desire to gather such information. Wars with Turkey, successful ones in 1695–6 and unsuccessful ones in 1710–11, and conflicts with Persia in 1722–3 made it necessary for Peter to secure his frontiers on the Caspian Sea, in the Caucasus, and on the Dnieper River. Geographical information was therefore essential to military planning. The emperor recognized the need for allies and for diplomacy on a large scale, which was the most compelling reason for his extended tour of Europe in 1697. Central Asia was also important to Peter, in part because of the potential of the region's natural resources, but also as a stepping-stone for trade with India as well, and for reasons of military security and territorial aggrandizement. Diplomatic missions to Mongolia, to China, and to Japan were all part of an ambitious scheme to modernize, secure, and strengthen his newly established "empire."

Before accomplishing such goals, however, Peter had to provide the huge territory with an efficient administration and develop both internal and external trade – for which he needed further geographical data. In 1708, all Russia was divided into eight provinces (*Guberniia*), of which Siberia and Perm were two. A governor for Siberia was appointed at Tobol'sk with more autonomous authority than governors of other provinces. When this arrangement proved not to come up to Peter's expectations (the governor was hanged for corruption in the 1720s), Siberia was divided into regimental districts, with each military group responsible for a town and its surrounding region. Peter thus undermined the long-standing supremacy of the Siberian Prikaz (Office), which had administered Siberia from Moscow since 1630. Since he tended to send non-nobles as administrators, whereas nobles traditionally had gone to the region to act as *voevody* and line their pockets, there developed a certain amount of personal animosity and competition for authority in Siberia.

Ironically, the first comprehensive corpus of geographical, historical, economic, and statistical information on the Russian empire, *The Flourishing Condition of the All-Russian State* (*Tsvetushchee sostoianie vserossiiskago gosudarstva*, 1727), was not completed until shortly after Peter's death. Its compiler was Ivan Kirilovich Kirilov (1695–1737), chief secretary of the Senate. Kirilov had an active career in Peter's bureaucracy, mainly with the Senate in various capacities, but also with the commission of commerce. *The Flourishing Condition of the All-Russian State* was printed in two parts and contained detailed information on twelve regions of the empire. It remains to this day one of the most important sources for the study of Russia's national economy at the time of its preparation. A few years later Kirilov sponsored the publication of the first atlas of the empire (*Atlas rossiiskoi imperii*, 1734), and during the final three years of his life he directed the Orenburg scientific expedition and the construction of a line of fortresses on the central Asian frontier. His efforts represent the best of the many Petrine initiatives to create an administration based on a systematic gathering of knowledge.[7]

In December 1724, Peter commissioned Vitus J. Bering to lead the first Kamchatka expedition to the easternmost point of the Russian empire. Bering set out from St Petersburg by land in January 1725, with his lieutenants, Alexei Chirikov and Martin Spangenberg, and a hugh team of geodesists, navigators, seamen, shipbuilders, and soliders. Bering had a number of specific tasks to perform: to find out whether there was a northeastern route by land between Asia and America, to prepare detailed maps of the empire, to enumerate its resources, and, above all, to reconnoitre the coast of America.[8] During five years of extreme hardship he reached Okhotsk, built a ship, transported goods to the west side of Kamchatka, provoked a bloody rebellion on the part of the Kamchadals (1730–1), constructed another ship, and sailed north beyond what is now called Cape Chukotka. Bering returned to St Petersburg in March 1730.

Although Müller was responsible for printing an official notice about Bering's exploits in the *St. Petersburg Gazette*,[9] he was not much interested at that time in Siberia or Kamchatka. After his return from Europe in 1731 and his clash with Schumacher, however, Müller's newly found interest in the history and geography of the Russian empire drew him immediately to proposals Bering had made for another trek to Kamchatka.

Exactly a month after his return, Bering presented the Admiralty College with two sets of proposals for a second, more grandiose exploratory trip. There is some question about his motivation, and a number of writers insist that the Senate was dissatisfied with the results of his first expedition. Be that as it may, Bering was promoted to the rank of captain-commander and awarded a large sum of money, presumably because of his recent services to Russia.[10] Bering was sent to Moscow in December to discuss his propositions with the Senate, which received them favourably. It took more than two years of administrative activity, however, before Bering's proposals were given final form in orders issued under Empress Anna's name. These called for a vastly complex and expensive project of exploration, reorganization, and mapping of eastern Siberia and Kamchatka; the charting of the arctic coast of Siberia; and visits to the coasts of America and Japan for the purpose of setting up trade relations. In June the Senate formally approved a plan to involve the Academy of Sciences directly in the expedition and appointed a group of professors to undertake scientific research in Siberia and Kamchatka.[11]

It had not been easy to persuade the government to sponsor Bering for the second time. Aside from a general malaise caused by the succession crisis in 1730 and the advent of a new monarch – and new favourites – there was no longer the interest in discovery for its own sake that had been a feature of Peter I's court. Moreover, Joseph Nicholas de l'Isle persuaded the Admiralty College that Bering's charts were inaccurate. In fact, Müller later said with justification that de l'Isle's own map, which the expedition was obliged to use, "hindered the discoveries beyond Kamchatka more than it helped them."[12]

Bering was fortunate, however, to have the support of three prominent figures at court, I.K. Kirilov, N.F. Golovin, and Baron Ostermann. The most important of these to the expedition was Kirilov, who, Müller wrote, was the "primary driving force" in the planning of the second Kamchatka expedition. In his turn Kirilov persuaded Ostermann, the guiding light of Anna's small cabinet of ministers, to support Bering by emphasizing the potential such an enterprise represented for trade, missionary work, and profit from natural resources. Count N.F. Golovin, vice-admiral and a senior member of the Admiralty College, also spoke in favour of Bering because of the advantages his explorations of the arctic coastline might have for Russia's navy. All three of these men had been prominent during Peter's reign and so may well have retained some of the broad visions that were characteristic of the early 1720s.[13]

While official negotiations (and wild rumours) about what was known variously as the great northern, or second Kamchatka expedition were taking place, Müller developed his scholarly interest in eastern subjects. His attention was directed toward Siberia, anyway, both because Bayer and Paus were eastern specialists, and because Müller himself had read the book by Witsen on Tatary, as well as a study by J.G. Gerber on towns in the Caucasus and Bayer's work on the town of Azov. Müller fully intended to expand his study of the Kalmyks and actually printed essays on the Samoeds in both the *Notes* and the *Sammlung*.[14] He became directly involved with the expedition when Kirilov asked him to translate communiqués on the subject for Biron, and in February 1733 Schumacher instructed him to give daily lessons in geography to six students who were already named to take part in the enterprise. But in the long run, Müller said, it was "Bering – to whom I was very well known, who stimulated in me a desire to join the voyage even when there seemed to be no chance of my going." Müller also had acted as Bering's interpreter during the captain-commander's discussion with de l'Isle.[15]

The original Academy appointments to the expedition were Gmelin and Louis de l'Isle de la Croyère. Providentially for Müller, Gmelin fell ill and was excused from participation. Müller "offered [his] services to describe the civil history of Siberia and its antiquities, with the manner and customs of the people, and also the occurrences of the voyage, which was likewise approved by the Senate." Kirilov and Ostermann both supported his application, which Müller said was put forward by Bering himself.[16] Official sanction was given to Müller on 23 March 1733; he now had his opportunity to escape "the chaotic circumstances of the Academy ... and far from hatred and enmity [he] could enjoy quiet and peace with independence." Then Gmelin's health improved – allegedly after drinking two full bottles of the "best Rhine wine" – and he was reinstated to the expedition with no prejudice to Müller's participation.[17]

On 5 July 1733, Müller, Gmelin, and de la Croyère were given their general instructions from the Chancellery. De la Croyère was told to make astronomical observations, and Gmelin was expected to report on "everything that concerns natural history."[18] Müller's task was "to describe the history of those peoples" whose paths he crossed while in the company of Bering. He was also to observe and comment on their religions, village life, customs, commerce, military and political institutions, languages, and costumes, the regions in which they dwelt, "and especially to examine in detail the habits, customs, and so on of those peoples who live on the north side of the Amur River, because it is rumoured that a Russian people lived there in ancient times." As we shall see, the Academy's professed interest in the ethnographic characteristics of people who lived along the Amur was not strictly a matter of scientific curiosity. This was a task set by the government for political and strategic ends. Müller was also to keep "an accurate journal in the Latin language."[19] As Gmelin put it in a memoir that he published nearly twenty years later, their job was "generally to learn everything that has scientific interest."[20] A tall order indeed!

About 600 persons were assigned to the second Kamchatka expedition.[21] They were divided into three attachments. An Admiralty section was to go overland, build ships at Okhotsk, and sail to the coasts of Japan and America. Bering's group was to proceed to Tobol'sk and from there explore the arctic coastline. The Academy contingent was to follow Bering to Tobol'sk, then travel with him to Okhotsk and to Kamchatka. Two landscape artists, a physician, an interpreter, an instrument-maker, four surveyors, five students to assist the professors, and fourteen guards (including one drummer) accompanied the academicians. Joining them also, against the wishes of both Müller and Gmelin, was a French subject named Francesco Locatelli. At that time, Locatelli called himself Rocquefort (or Roccaforte) and professed to be a French nobleman fleeing from Paris in order to escape a marriage contract. He was sponsored by de l'Isle and de la Croyère, with the cautious assent of Kirilov. Thus, the younger professors were compelled to accept his presence.[22]

Nine wagonloads of instruments, including four large telescopes, a library of more than 200 books (to which they constantly added titles), writing paper, paints, drafting materials, and other items considered necessary for scientific endeavours, were dragged along by some forty pack-horses. Several kegs of Gmelin's favourite Rhine wine went along with them – presumably for medical reasons! The academicians carried official documents authorizing them to examine any archive collection and to requisition interpreters and guides at local expense. They received an enormous increase in salary (Table 1) and permission to purchase items at Academy expense.[23] Further, Müller and his two colleagues were granted the privilege of private quarters, the right to demand assistance from Bering for their exploratory side-trips, and freedom from his authority. All in all, this amounted to quite a coup for the newly appointed professors. Müller was then twenty-eight years old, and Gmelin was only twenty-four.[24] They had little idea, however, of what they were getting into, how rough and potentially dangerous Siberia could be. Nor did they have any notion of how their presence and privileges were to complicate Bering's administrative chores.

The expedition departed from St Petersburg in stages. Captain Spangenberg, Bering's second in command, had departed with the heaviest equipment in February 1733 on his way to Okhotsk. Bering following in April, going first to Novgorod, then to Tver', Kazan',

TABLE 1

Accounts for Academy Professors on Kamchatka Expedition 1734

SALARIES

Rank and Name	Rubles	Copecks
Professor Müller	1,260	
Professor Gmelin	1,260	
Professor de l'Isle de la Croyère	1,260	
Arist [Johann] Berkan	500	
Drawing Master [J.-W.] Lursenius	400	
Geodesist Andrei Krasil'nikov	220	46¼
Geodesist Nikofor Chekin	220	46¼
Geodesist Moisei Ushakov	220	46¼
Geodesist Alexandr Ivanov	220	46¼
Student and translator Il'ia Iakhontov	120	
Student Stepan Krasheninnikov	100	
Student Fedor Popov	100	
Student Vasilii Tret'iakov	100	
Student Luka Ivanov	100	
Student Aleksei Gorlanov	100	
Instrument apprentice Stepan Avsianikov	72	
Total　16 men	6,253	85

VICTUALS*

Rank	Puds†
Three professors, each 40 puds, thus	120
Twelve men under them, each 24 puds, thus	288
Two artists, each 30 puds, thus	60
Four men under them, each 24 puds, thus	96
Two Geodesists, each 30 puds, thus	60
Four men under them, each 24 puds, thus	96
Six students, each 30 puds, thus	180
Three men under them, each 24 puds, thus	72
Instrumental apprentice	24
One corporal, twelve soldiers, one drummer, according to *Ukaz*	–
Total, besides soldiers	996

Bering, 15 February 1734

*Meal, barley, oil, and salt.
†One pud = 36.11 pounds.
Source: Materialy, 2 (1886): 446–7.

Ekaterinburg, and Tobol'sk. The Academy contingent, which was to take the same route, did not leave until 8 August. Müller and his colleagues had a private audience with the empress and other members of the royal family already in the spring and were sent off then with great fanfare. Ominously, however, the group could not at first find adequate transportation out of the capital city, and its departure had been delayed.

Because of the size of their entourage and the bulk of their supplies, the academics achieved "often not more than 12 or 15 versts per day" (eight to ten miles). They did not reach Tver' until the second week of September.[25] Unforeseen incidents delayed them as well – the breakdown of Müller's wagon, and a "small crisis" when the student Ivanov for some reason shot a woman who lived in the house where he was quartered.[26] In a detailed report to St Petersburg from Tver', the Academy was informed that Gmelin already had found "new or unnamed grasses and trees" and also had listed all known plants and their locations along the way. In Novgorod Gmelin and Müller visited monasteries while de la Croyère set up his astronomical equipment and recorded observations. Müller also studied epitaphs and other sources of genealogical information about Russia's nobility. A routine was thus set which they tried to follow throughout their long trip to Siberia. The reports also included careful accounts of their expenditures, a practice that was eventually to prove valuable in later quarrels with the Chancellery over reimbursements and salaries.[27]

Terrible weather during their two weeks at Tver' prevented Gmelin and de la Croyère from compiling botanical and astronomical reports. Müller was more fortunate; he discovered a few documents pertaining to the lives of former great princes. It was also at Tver' that they first realized that their special orders from St Petersburg might carry less and less authority as they moved eastward in the Russian empire. The artist Johann Berkan was arrested in Tver' when priests from the church he was sketching became suspicious of his motives and had the local constabulary take him in. By the time Müller obtained his release night had fallen. Berkan could not complete the sketches because they had to depart the next morning on a large, well-supplied barque left them by Bering. They proceeded in relative comfort along the Volga to Kazan', and arrived there on 18 October.

The voyage from Tver' proved very fruitful. At the juncture with the Mologa, Gmelin discovered more new rocks and collected samples to send back to the *Kunstkamera*. He and de la Croyère twice daily noted barometric and meteorological conditions, and they made corrections on their maps of the Volga. Müller listed and described the tributaries, islands, rapids, towns, and villages of the great river. At Uglich, he found genealogical information on princes of that town and of Rostov. At Iaroslavl', however, he was prevented from pursuing such investigations by church authorities who simply ignored his orders from the Senate.[28] At Nizhnii Novgorod, Müller found a much more co-operative cleric who showed him documents on nineteen members of Russian great princely families. Further downriver, at Cheboksary, he and Gmelin tried for three days in the company of an interpreter and two soldiers to get information from Chuvash villagers, but with little success.[29]

Both their successes and failures proved exciting to Müller and Gmelin. Forty years later, Müller was still able to convey the exhilaration he felt while travelling along the Volga and when he first sighted the towns of Uglich, Iaroslavl', Kostroma, Nizhnii Novgorod, and Makar'ev, the "Cheremis and Chuvash in their environment," and the great monasteries.[30] Within three days of their arrival in Kazan', the rivers froze over, so that they had time to examine that "remarkable city." Although the commandant of Kazan', K.I. Musin-Pushkin, assisted them only reluctantly, Müller was able to report on its Tatar features, the remnants of ancient Tatar townsites, churches, and a seminary that he visited, conversations with individuals who had travelled from Kazan' to Astrakhan and Persia, as well as the effects of Russian schooling on speakers of Tatar, Chuvash, and other indigenous languages. Assisted by a Major La Mothe, he also watched Tatars and Votiaks taking oaths on the Koran as they were inducted into the Imperial Russian army.[31]

Gmelin spent much of his time observing the rites of the Tatar religion, while Müller compiled a simple vocabulary of the non-Russian languages of the Kazan' region. Among the peoples he referred to specifically were the Tatars, Chuvash, Mordvins, Cheremis (now Mari), and the Votiaks (now Udmurts). He took key words, most of which reflected their way of life, and gave them Latin equivalents. He used and added to this list for the next ten years. Meanwhile, his artists depicted costumes, dwellings, religious sites, and villages.[32] He was also shown and had drawings made of ancient Tatar coins. While his staff worked, Müller prepared detailed descriptions of the leather industry in Kazan', which he said was the most advanced in the empire, and admired a "fabric factory" that employed over a thousand people. By the end of 1733, Müller had organized his research on the peoples of Kazan' into a paper for publication. He sent this to St Petersburg, but it was not until 1756 that it was printed.[33]

To a certain extent, the staggering multiformity of Müller's interests was forced on him, and on his companions, by the Academy Chancellery. In October 1733 the Academy insisted that Latin and Russian-language copies of all "astronomical and magnetic observations, the history and inscriptions from the Cathedral, churches, and monasteries of Novgorod, descriptions of the mountains near Bronnits and its different plants, either in drawings or actually impressed in paper; and two charts, one of Novgorod, the other of the mountains," be sent back to St Petersburg. In their turn, the professors pestered the Academy for medicines (which the Senate ordered Bering to release from his own supply), Academy publications, scientific books, and money to pay local coachmen and scribes.[34]

To facilitate communications between the expedition and the capital, Bering had been instructed to establish a monthly postal service from points east of Moscow. He was to arrange this system in consultation with local officials, but the dearth of men, horses, and roads, and the vast uninhabited distances that the couriers had to cover, turned this scheme into another of the Senate's unrealized projects.[35] Increasingly, communications among Senate, Admiralty, and Academy and their respective charges in Siberia were characterized by long and frustrating delays. The situation was made worse for Bering in that he had not been granted authority over the academicians or even over regional officials.

De la Croyère, who had continued to take astronomical and "magnetic" observations at Kazan', left there on 8 December 1733. The expedition saw the last of Locatelli at Kazan' as well. He applied to go to the Persian border, where a Russo-Persian war had been dragging on for several years, to serve with the prince of Hessen-Homburg. But complications over his travel permit led to his arrest by La Mothe. Locatelli's life was complicated further by a European war over the Polish succession, which had broken out in September 1733, with the French and Russian governments on opposite sides. The Russian authorities suspected Locatelli of being a spy for France. The governor sent him under guard to Moscow in order that his status be cleared up. Locatelli later recounted his experiences in a book, *Lettres moscovites* (Königsberg and Paris, 1736), which Müller said was filled with "lies and slanders" and which had both an English and a German translation.

Müller and Gmelin set out from Kazan' three days after de la Croyère. They made their way by sledge along the Kama to Sarapull and Osa and then overland to Kungur and Ekaterinburg, where they caught up with de la Croyère on 29 December. At Ekaterinburg they were received by Lieutenant-General George von Hennin, who was more amenable to their wishes than had been his counterpart at Kazan'. Hennin had resided in the region since 1722, when he had been sent to Kungur to replace V.N. Tatishchev as director of mining and manufacturing for the Urals and Siberia. Like Tatishchev, Hennin was an avid collector of historical and current information on Siberia. With his extensive knowledge of both the geological and geographical nature of the region, he proved to be especially useful to Müller and Gmelin.[36]

It was Müller's opinion that de la Croyère regularly pushed on ahead of his colleagues because he wished to avoid having witnesses to his incompetence. Whether or not that was the reason, de la Croyère left for Tobol'sk on 9 January 1734, leaving Müller and Gmelin to visit several local mining sites. A letter from Bering, however, urging them to make haste to Tobol'sk, prompted Müller to leave a week later. Gmelin had not completed his observations and so followed shortly thereafter. Having stopped to visit iron mines at Sysertskii and Kamenskii (the oldest iron mine in Siberia), Gmelin then travelled northeast to observe the spectacular annual fair at Irbit. Irbit's agricultural fair had been a regular event since 1631 and brought together merchants from all over the empire. Hennin accompanied Gmelin as far as Irbit, and so the young academician had been treated by locals with deference. After leaving Irbit for Tiumen', however, Gmelin found that his prestige diminished rapidly when Siberia's officialdom was not close by. Tatars at Tiumen' refused to give his group a change of horses and said that their ancient rights precluded them from adherence to such orders. He had to hire some instead.[37] Thus the Academy expedition came to be scattered into separate groups, which added to its expense. De la Croyère, Müller, and Gmelin drifted into Tobol'sk between 15 and 30 January 1734.

Situated as it was just east of the Urals, at the confluence of the Tavda, Tobol, Ob, and Irtysh rivers, Tobol'sk was at the centre of trade routes between European Russia and Siberia. It had been the administrative and Orthodox church headquarters for Siberia for a long time. A sign of its importance was its number of stone churches, government buildings, and officials' homes. In fact, it was the only Siberian City to have a stone wall, on a hill inside the city. With fourteen churches and over 3,000 dwellings in the 1730's, it was a bustling and imposing community. Merchants from western Europe met there with merchants from central Asia and China. Native caravans, especially of Kalmyk and Buryat merchants, were prominent there as well.

Müller and his colleagues had the good fortune to find in Tobol'sk Alexei L'vovich Pleshcheev, a senior official anxious to assist them in any way that he could. Governor of all Siberia from 1731 to 1741 and himself the author of a historical-geographical manuscript on Siberia, Pleshcheev was well qualified to direct their activity. In Müller's own words: "Pleshcheev ... was a distinguished man who made it a rule to supply us with all possible means to undertake our scholarly pursuits. With great promptness he ordered the provincial chancellery to provide me with information on anything about the regional towns and surrounding areas which I requested. But I recognized that I still did not know what it was I should be asking. For that, I needed practical information which is learned only by experience. Here I began to search through Siberian archives and to have copies made of all those documents which could help explain the history and geography of the area."[38] According to Müller, the Tobol'sk archives did not "go back before the time of the [Russian] conquest" of Siberia. He did find an old Siberian illustrated chronicle, about the authenticity of which he was certain. He sent this back to St Petersburg "as especially precious" and later included it in the first part of his Siberian history.[39]

Many other items were catalogued and copied by Müller's assistants. His four and a half months' experience in Tobol'sk proved to be of inestimable value, for it afforded him the time and necessary co-operation from the authorities to work out a method for his later searches. Müller was concerned primarily with documents. His general approach was first to rearrange the old rolls (stolbtsy) and books chronologically, noting their contents and designating those to be copied. This work usually followed questions he submitted to regional chancelleries, placing the onus on them to locate documents for him and to provide both translators and clerks to make extracts.

Brandishing the authority granted him by the Senate, Müller and his staff prepared descriptions of towns, islands, mining sites, trade patterns, settlements, religions, and other features of the regions they visited. He and Gmelin sought out artifacts and relics; they purchased drawings, idols, weapons, items from grave sites, samples of clothing, and coins from the native people. In 1734 Müller began to prepare maps of Siberia, and within a year he was able to send charts of the Irtysh and Ob regions to the Academy.[40]

There was much more than just work available to the academicians in Tobol'sk, for it was here that they saw frontier life at its wildest. At least one Gmelin account is worthy of reproduction in full:

I saw nothing in particular at Tobol'sk until the 17th of February: but on that day, the first of carnival [week before Lent fasting], everything seemed to come alive. The wealthiest gentlemen visited with each other and enjoyed various amusements. All the people went mad: night and day they paraded, shouted, revelled and fought. It was difficult to go out into the streets because there were so many men, women, animals and sleds. While passing in front of an inn one evening, I saw a particularly unusual sight – a large number of men had made a pile of snow in front of the house beside a small river; they sat on the snow, drank, sang, and ate delicacies. Whenever they needed more to drink, one of them simply went to the cabaret, bought more provisions and they continued in their pleasures. They did not seem to mind the cold in the least, and they invited passersby to join them. Women enjoyed promenades and sometimes there were up to eight on the same sled; it was remarked upon how often they too rather reeked of wine. Every night there were further scuffles, fights and noise. One junior naval officer threw a woman onto the street and beat her so severely over all her body with a rope's end that she died a few days later.

At the Tobol'sk Cathedral they listened while all the former tsars, patriarchs, and even Ermak, who was fêted as the "conqueror of Sibir," were praised as holy people. Müller also observed a Tatar wedding, a funeral, and other local ceremonies and noted that all the many special days (birthdays, namedays, etc.) called for banquets and great celebrations. "A lover of eating and drinking can thus find no better place in the world than here," wrote Gmelin; at the same time, however, he complained that the abundance of food and cattle ("I have never seen a place where there are so many cows wandering about") made the people of Tobol'sk "very lazy."[41]

In spite of all the festivities and good living, the first Tobol'sk stay was especially productive academically. Before he left the region Müller had posted a list of ancient Tatar and Armenian inscriptions, translated into Russian; a history of the origins of Kungur; notes on the history of Kazan' and Siberia; vocabularies of Tatar and Vogul; and a translation of a prayer book into Vogul. Gmelin sent observations on natural history, which included depictions of caves at Kungur, notes on the water of the Sylva River, drawings and descriptions of Kalmyk cows and sables, and an account of the Irbit market.[42]

In May 1734, the group left Tobol'sk armed with a new general order from Pleshcheev to all vice-governors and *voevody* confirming the Senate's instructions and journeyed south on the Irtysh to Para, Omsk, Zhelezinskaia, Iamyshevskaia, Semipalatinsk, and Ust'-Kamenogorsk. Müller described these areas as the "most pleasant in Siberia. Granted, we later came to regions which were not secondary to these, near the Chinese border. Here, however ... we came to a paradise of flowers comprising of completely unknown herbs, into a zoo where we found the rarest animals of Asia gathered before us, into an antiquarian shop of old heathen graves ... in short, into regions which had not been travelled for the purpose of scientific knowledge. Thus, many opportunities and discoveries spurred us on to unusual diligence."

De la Croyère left them again at Omsk and accompanied one of Bering's captains to Iakutsk, arriving there in the summer of 1735. Bering had gone to Iakutsk in the spring of 1734, after a year in

Tobol'sk supervising the construction of a vessel (the *Tobol*) large enough to carry the first task force north on the Irtysh to the Arctic Ocean. There were many delays, not the least being that caused by the leisurely manner in which our heroes had made their way to Tobol'sk. They had with them the surveyors and instruments Bering needed to make final plans for his voyage.

A few days after the *Tobol* sailed, Bering had gone to Iakutsk. There he found that no provision had been made for him, and his supplies did not arrive until the following spring (1735). Nevertheless, Bering was able to build two more ships. He sent these also to the Arctic, this time along the Lena River. One ship was to turn west and chart the coast to the Enisei; the other was to turn east and chart the coast as far as possible. Bering remained in Iakutsk in order to construct more ships, dwellings, iron foundries, and an entire complex from which to supply and organize the various parts of his expedition. But administrative road-blocks caused long delays. They were the consequence, in part, of a falling-out between Bering and Major-General Pisarev, harbour-master and de facto governor of Okhotsk. Bering had forwarded supplies and builders to Okhotsk, and the final stages of the expedition were to be launched from there. The bureaucratic obstructionism and increasing rancour between Bering and the local officials eventually eroded Müller's and Gmelin's enthusiasm for Kamchatka.

Pisarev once had been director of the Naval Academy in Moscow and chief procurator of the Senate, but had been exiled by Peter II in 1728 for insulting Prince Menshikov. In 1731, he was ordered to Okhotsk to build a port, but he spent most of his time at Iakutsk. He and Spangenburg were so hostile to each other at one point that their men were armed and prepared to make battle. Spangenberg and Bering sent charges against Pisarev regularly to St Petersburg, and Pisarev returned the favour for them.

In the mean time – blissfully ignorant of Bering's problems – Müller and Gmelin set out northeast for Tomsk, Eniseisk, and Krasnoiarsk in the late spring of 1734. As Müller later wrote, the joy of discovery was still upon them, and "everything that we saw was new to us." They had still not faced the discomfort, privations, and even physical perils that were to confront them later. But their first inkling of danger had come already in June at Tara, when they were joined by twenty Cossacks sent by the governor to protect them against marauding Kirgiz-Kaisaks. Pleshcheev also had insisted that two cannon be added to each of their vessels; but it would not be for another two years that Müller and Gmelin recognized the necessity of such precautions.

Their enjoyment of the natural surroundings was curtailed considerably sooner, however. They found Tomsk unpleasant because an epidemic of some sort had killed "all but ten cows [of more than 100] and left only two or three horses," the summer before their arrival. In contrast to the surfeit of cattle on which he had remarked at Tobol'sk, in Tomsk Gmelin grumbled that there were more mice than he had ever seen before in one place, and that even the local cats could not keep them under control. Moreover, he guessed that at least one person in each household suffered from syphilis because of the "loose living" that predominated.[43]

The academicians reached Kolyvan' on the Ob during early August 1734. There they watched the operation of silver and copper mines that had been founded by Akinfei Demidov only five years earlier. Müller noted that the worth of these mines was still not generally known and suggested that the "patriotic governor" sent them there for that very reason. Gmelin wrote later that the mining complex at Kolyvan' already was superior in scale and richness to anything he had seen in Europe. Although Müller failed to mention it in his account, Gmelin also noted that the majority of the people living in the factory villages and fortresses were Old Believers who "would neither drink nor eat from the dishes which had been used by Orthodox Russians, would not enter a Russian church, and fully abstained from vodka."[44]

Throughout the spring and summer of 1734, Müller and Gmelin suffered their first real experience with mosquitoes, which Gmelin insisted were so vicious in Ilimsk that they tormented cattle to death. Members of the expedition were forced to sleep under hot screening and to wear veils on their faces and gloves on their hands at all times. At Eniseisk they encountered a cold spell in December that was so drastic that "birds fell out of the sky as though dead and froze if not immediately taken into a warm room." According to Müller their food and drink "froze before we could bring it to our mouths." But they continued doggedly to compile information. A caravan of some 200 camels driven by Russians, Tatars, and Bukharans arrived in Tomsk while they were there, and so Müller was able to gather considerable data on trade. At Krasnoiarsk Müller again was informed about trade routes by means of long discussions with Kalmyk and Buryat merchants who took part in the caravan system of that region.

In his turn, Gmelin discovered a "musk deer," which seems to have been unknown to European naturalists at the time, and sent sketches and a skeleton back to the Academy. It was from this area that they reported large copper deposits. Very old deserted mines and an abundance of copper tools and weapons in old graves persuaded them that it would be profitable for the Russian government to sponsor mining operations there. Müller later took credit for having recommended a profitable copper mining venture that was opened on the Lugasa in the late 1730s.

March 1735 found Müller and Gmelin en route to Irkutsk. There they had some difficulty in persuading the vice-governor, Colonel Andrei Grigorievich Pleshcheev, to allow them access to the archives, or even to arrange supplies for their retinue. Pleshcheev demanded immediate payment for any service rendered and countered their complaints by saying that it was they who worked for him – he was under no obligation to the Academy. Finally, after many frustrations, on 24 April the academicians took the initiative by simply sending soldiers to the market-place to requisition all the horses they could find – and left for Kiakhta, the way station for Russian trade with China, a few hours later. On this tour, which was also to take them to Selenginsk and to Nerchinsk, they had their first taste of extended desert travel and found the heat almost unbearable.[45]

At Kiakhta Müller discussed matters of trade with Brigadier Ivan D. Bucholtz, who had been responsible for border security and commerce in the city since 1728 and who founded Omsk in 1716. Müller also observed both private trading and the organization of a government caravan. At Nerchinsk he completed a long report on the Tungus language and customs (which appeared in the *Commentarii* in 1747). He and Gmelin also spent some time in consultation with two of Bering's land surveyors who had been in Nerchinsk for nearly a year trying to obtain guides and supplies for a mapping trek to the Ud River. Their purpose was to find a practical route from Nerchinsk to the Pacific, and it was in part because of their subsequent lack of success that Müller concluded that Russia's commercial interests would best be served by taking control of the Amur from the Manchus.[46]

In his memoir Gmelin showed contempt for the local habits and complained of "shameful vices," rampant disease, drunkenness, and laziness among the people who lived along the border. He also wrote that the Russian local *voevoda* was corrupt and incompetent. Returning to Irkutsk in September, they arrived at Lake Baikal to find it so cold that they had to spend a full day in bed. Because of violent storms and wind their trip across the lake took four days. They lost much of their equipment and very nearly their lives. Müller later wrote that local inhabitants regarded the lake as a holy sea, to which sacrifices of coins had to be made, and that Gmelin committed some sort of sacrilege against the custom. He implied that the locals saw this as the cause of their difficulties. Perhaps cautioned by this experience, and finding Pleshcheev somewhat more amenable, they stayed on at Irkutsk until January 1736. The apparently strait-laced Gmelin expressed his displeasure with the inhabitants of that city as well, saying that they "loved idleness, wine and women to excess." He was especially shocked at the drunkenness that prevailed at the Christmas season which, he complained, "seemed to be a celebration of the devil rather than of God."[47]

Be that as it may, 1735 was another fruitful year for the Academy contingent in general, and for Müller in particular. Among the many articles he sent back to St Petersburg were ancient and more recent Chinese coins; a description of the old town site that had been called Sibir and in Müller's time featured a saltpetre works; some historical documents from Tobol'sk; chronological notes on an old calendar that dated everything from the Creation; two stones, one with the head of a bear, the other a ram; copies of documents from the Tara archives that referred to Russian history; genealogical notes about the Romanov family; calculations of the distances from Tobol'sk to Tara, Tara to Tomsk, and Tomsk to Verkh-Irtyshevskii; vocabularies of the Kalmyk and Bukharan (Uzbek) languages; measurements of the Iamyshevskaia salt lake; and notes on grave sites and towns along the Irtysh. As well, some fifty other items were crated and shipped that year. All were listed in a report that Müller compiled for the Senate in 1746. Gmelin's bulletins were as detailed, if not so varied.

From Irkutsk our travellers moved north on the Angara to Ilimsk and from there they portaged to the Lena, which they followed to Iakutsk after the ice broke up in May 1736. Their passage was not without extreme difficulty. Gmelin wrote that local members of their escort (*sluzhivye*, irregular soldiers) spent most of their time intoxicated and that on the Lena oarsmen for their twelve boats constantly deserted. To solve this dilemma, the expedition was forced to impress peasants, but these were usually exchanged for political exiles and common criminals by area authorities. A vigilant watch had to be maintained by the regular soldiers, and harsh punishment was exacted against deserters from the expedition. The loss of men still continued at such a rate, however, that gallows were raised in all big towns along the river – though Gmelin said that he never saw them used. In his opinion, there was no other way to deal with the Sibiriak other than with the "utmost severity: [because] neither honesty, nor kindness, nor benevolence" would persuade them to work properly.[48]

Still, there were some accomplishments of note on this leg of their long trip. Gmelin explored the large mica quarries on the Vitim River, and at Ilimsk Müller adopted a new system for searching out archival material. Instead of randomly examining registry lists and checking those items that he wished to see, he now divided documents chronologically, concentrated on material from specific eras, such as the "Time of Troubles," and left other well-defined categories to his assistants.

After Ilimsk the Academy group split up again in August. De la Croyère left for Iakutsk first, followed by Müller ten days later and then by Gmelin, who wished to explore the Vitim further. By mid-September, however, they were all gathered together at Iakutsk where they spent the winter of 1736–7 with Bering and the remainder of the Kamchatka expedition (which had now grown to about 800 persons).[49] This was their first protracted association with the harassed Bering, and the proximity was not to their liking. The professors complained about their quarters ("not good enough even for students"), went over Bering's head to local officials, and generally made a nuisance of themselves. They did acquire better lodgings for themselves and their men, but even these were not up to their exaggerated expectations. Nevertheless, one can sympathize with them. In describing the interiors of most dwellings in Iakutsk, Gmelin remarked on the constantly foul air. The stoves on which everyone slept often had outlets directly into the rooms, "so as to lose no heat; others had vents to the outside so as to avoid [some of] the sulphurous odours which the stoves emitted ... [but] these vapours caused headaches, trembling, nervousness, nausea, vomiting, drowsiness, and finally would take away one's breath and even life – but they have not the slightest effect on most of the Russians, perhaps because they are accustomed to them from their infancy."[50]

Out of resentment at the indifference shown them by the local *voevody* and Bering, Müller and Gmelin wrote to St Petersburg that Bering and Spangenberg (who was then in Okhotsk but had left behind a reputation for bullying and cruelty) had "had little success in whatever they undertook. Everything went on so slowly that one could not foresee when the trip to Kamchatka would begin."[51] Pleading a lack of necessary academic supplies – and safe transportation – Müller and Gmelin avoided making the trip to Kamchatka when the opportunity finally arrived. In their stead they sent the student Krasheninnikov. The propriety of their decision may be open to question, but there is no doubt that it had far-reaching consequences: Krasheninnikov was able to turn his experiences into a successful career; Müller and Gmelin survived the expedition; and the most exhaustive study of Siberia during the eighteenth century was allowed to continue.

Fierce cold, high winds, and generally harsh living conditions also had dissipated the academicians' passion for further northern travel. Gmelin reported that the Lena was frozen to the depth of a yard and a half by September, that his windows, constructed of ice, let in too little light to work by, and that he had to wear furs from head to toe when outside. Moreover, they had been contracted to the expedition for five years and so felt that if they moved further northeast they could not possibly return to the capital within the allotted time. As Müller said in a letter to Euler, written in May 1737, "God grant that we soon either make the trip to Kamchatka or return [to St Petersburg], and not be stuck here forever."[52] Perhaps to justify in part their failure to complete the mission to Kamchatka, Müller and Gmelin sent reports back to St Petersburg in which their respective illnesses were featured prominently alongside tales of Bering's incompetence and overbearing attitude.

As usual, however, the two young professors kept busy at the task of compiling information about Siberia. They were assisted in Iakutsk by a former associate of Strahlenburg, Heinrich Busch. A Dutchman who had served Sweden until he was captured and sent to Siberia in 1706, Busch had settled in Iakutsk. Between 1714 and 1716 he toured Okhotsk and Kamchatka, and so he was able to give Müller a first-hand – if dated – description of the area.

A fire at Iakutsk in November destroyed half of Müller's money supply and most of Gmelin's notes, books, and equipment.[53] In June 1737, they therefore were compelled to retrace their steps up the Lena in order to record again Gmelin's observations. They arrived at Kirenskii ostrog in September. Gmelin spent the winter there while Müller went on to Irkutsk in November. Gmelin joined him in March. While in Kirenskii, Gmelin noticed that most of the exiles on the Lena were merchants who had been banished from Russia because of debt. This procedure was very helpful to Siberian development, he said, because most of the exiles fell back on their entrepreneurial skills in order to survive in Siberia. Many were flourishing in commerce. Gmelin also remarked with some awe on the scale of an iron-mining enterprise near Irkutsk run by four local merchants who had purchased a monopoly from Moscow.[54]

Müller's health was instrumental in his decision to go to Irkutsk, for he knew that a physician was wintering with a caravan in that city. In spite of increasing ill-health, Müller had found the time in Iakutsk to prepare a series of notes on Kamchatka, detailing the surrounding geography plus the customs, commerce, and settlements of the Kamchadals, Koriaks, and Kurils. These reports, compiled from interviews and from materials located in the Iakutsk archives, were passed on to Krasheninnikov in June. The selection of Krasheninnikov for the trip to Kamchatka from among his peers had been unanimous. The student already had completed several minor expeditions on his own, and both Gmelin and Müller respected his abilities. In turn, he reported to them regularly during his three months in Okhotsk before he left for Kamchatka.[55]

While Müller was in Irkutsk and Gmelin in Kirenskii ostrog, they each sent requests to St Petersburg for further assistance and authority. The fact that their petitions were quite similar suggests that they were planned well in advance. According to the minutes of the Academy Chancellery, the professors asked above all that the Senate "grant them by general decree the power to demand of local administrations that they execute, under penalty of heavy fine, all the requests of the said professors, because the delays and other aggravations caused by the same administrations and other local officials are quite intolerable." One can well imagine that the presence of the young, haughty, and demanding academicians was intolerable to most local government officers. Müller and Gmelin appealed also for another professor of history, two geodesists, two copyists (one for German and one for Latin), a "Russian clerk with complete knowledge of bureaucratic style," and money to pay small salaries to meteorological observers "so they would perform their tasks with greater application."

Müller's condition had worsened that winter, and so in his application of 16 December 1737 he also requested that, "unless his health improved," he be relieved of all further duties in Siberia. According to Büsching, Müller's symptons were "depressed spirit, bloatedness, fears and pressure on the chest, and extraordinary coldness of the feet, especially the soles ... and a hefty heart beat." The cure does not sound very reassuring either: "nerve-strengthening medicines with all sorts of rubber ... ammonia spirits with wine residue and 17 bloodlettings, each of about five to six ounces.[56]

Neither his illness nor the doctors' treatment seems to have slowed Müller down to any great extent. He continued to work on his various historical and ethnographical projects, but used the pending request to St Petersburg in order to avoid any commitment to Bering. Müller did present Bering with a report based on information that he gathered from explorers, sailors, and the Iakutsk archives on the "frozen sea" supposedly separating Asia from America. He even found reports of annual seventeenth-century voyages from the Lena to the Kolyma. One account reported that a small boat with S.I. Dezhnev as captain had sailed from the Kolyma around the Chukotka Peninsula to the mouth of the Anadyr in 1648, thereby preceding

Bering through the Bering Straits by nearly a century.[57] The north-eastern tip of Asia is now named Cape Dezhnev.

Müller later wrote, with some sarcasm, that even though he had posted this information to St Petersburg Bering still felt it necessary to prove geographical phenomena that he, Müller, had already demonstrated. His digust is understandable, if unwarranted. Müller and the other academicians were convinced that the primary purpose of Bering's explorations was to discover whether Asia and America were joined by land. They had no idea that the Admiralty and the Senate also wanted exploration of and trade reports on the American coast.

The two young professors wintered at Eniseisk in 1738–9 and investigated the languages, customs, and history of the Buryats and Tunguses. But they suffered some anxiety because of rumours of unrest among the native peoples – especially the Buryats. On the way to Eniseisk, at Bratskii ostrog in August 1738, they had seen fifty Buryat and Tungus prisoners whose chiefs were charged with sedition and heard tales of potential revolt in Udinsk and Ilimsk.[58] Although there was not an actual uprising, they were relieved to have left those areas behind them. On 31 March 1739, they received a senatorial decree allowing Müller to return to the capital if he continued his researches on his way home. The Academy ordered G.W. Steller, who had been assigned to the expedition already in July 1736 and who was with them for several weeks at Eniseisk in 1739, to act as Gmelin's assistant.[59] When Steller also went to Kamchatka, Gmelin was sent another aide, named Martini. J.E. Fischer was commissioned to replace Müller, and Jacob Lindenau, who was to become an eminent ethnographer, joined them as a translator.[60] Gmelin's plea to return to St Petersburg was denied, and Müller was ordered to turn over all his documentation and folios to Fischer. Though they were more than pleased to have Steller, neither Müller nor Gmelin was satisfied with the results of their respective petitions. On 8 May, however, they were both instructed instead to prepare a "complete description of the Siberian provinces ... their geography and natural history ... in order that the Russian state reap some benefits from the Kamchatka Expedition." Three copyists (one each for Russian, German, and Latin) and two geodesists were sent to assist them. The Russian-language copyist and the extra sums for "meteorological observers" were to be paid from Siberian administration coffers.[61]

The reasons for the Academy and Senate decisions are not known, but the fact that Schumacher was involved may help explain their perverseness. He suspected that the two men, Müller especially, were malingering. A 1738 memorandum to the Senate signed by

Schumacher and Korff acknowledged their agents' poor health, but implied that it was Steller and Krashenninikov who were doing the real work for the Academy in Siberia, and for much less pay than the professors. Later, in 1740, Schumacher filed a note to the effect that if Müller were to stay in Siberia, then his expenses should be covered by local government agencies, not by the Academy.[62] But a more compelling reason for the Senate to demand some return for its huge investment was the fact that it was beginning to despair of the Bering expedition altogether. Reports from Siberian officials who disliked Bering had placed the entire project in jeopardy again, as Martin Spangenberg learned to his distress in 1740. Spangenberg's successful voyage to Japan in 1738 had so depleted the Okhotsk detachment of supplies that Bering's long-awaited departure for Kamchatka had to be postponed. Nor was the expedition allowed to rejoice in Spangenberg's noteworthy accomplishments, which included the charting of the Kurile Islands. While on his way to St Petersburg to report his findings to the Senate, Spangenberg was intercepted in July 1740 at Kirenskii ostrog, accused of deception, and ordered to repeat his voyage to Japan.[63] Thus Bering's departure for Kamchatka was delayed again.

In fact, the intrigue and jealousies at the court and Academy had caught up with the Kamchatka expedition. The office of Academy president was in a state of constant flux, and this complicated matters further. In November 1734, Baron J.-A. Korff replaced Keyserling and promptly ordered that the Conference minutes be recorded in German (rather than in Latin). Korff was born in Courland and served at Anna's court before she became empress of Russia. Since 1730, he had been a courtier in St Petersburg. His appointment to the Academy officially was not as its president, for it was not clear that Keyserling would not return. For that reason Korff was assigned the rather imposing title of Supreme Commander.[64] He tightened up procedures in the Conference and insisted that the minutes be recorded in a systematic fashion and that the archives be put in order. He also requested that all manuscripts prepared by Academy members be carefully scrutinized, that is, censored, in the Conference before they went to the printer's for publication. In March 1735, he ordered the establishment of a Russian Assembly within the Academy for the purpose of modernizing the Russian language and orchestrating accurate and rapid translation of scientific books into Russian.

Korff also instituted a geography department, in 1739, and spent large sums of money on books for the Academy library. Unfortunately, however, a number of these books, purchased by Schumacher with Academy funds, went directly to Korff's private library. This may have been an attempt by Schumacher to curry favour with his chief, but it was also a sympton of the irresponsible budgeting at the Academy. All in all, however, Korff's contribution to the modernization of the Academy was substantial. Yet he was away often – nearly the entire year of 1736 – and so relied on Schumacher to put his policies in practice. Thus, the clash of wills between Schumacher and the academicians continued unabated. These tensions were compounded by the fact that the empress seemed determined to transform the Academy into an institute for the study of industrial design, fine arts, and instrument-making. Studies on weights and measures, the process of coin-making, and machine-tooling were set in motion in the early 1730s. A chair of mechanics was established in 1735 under the directorship of J.-G. Leutman, professor of optics and mechanics since 1726. When Leutman died in 1736 his administrative and teaching duties were assigned to A.K. Nartov, whom Anna had appointed as instrument master the previous year. By the end of Anna's reign, in 1740, slightly over half of the Academy's complement of 400 teaching – and learning – personnel were associated with 'artistic subjects', that is, industrial and fine arts.[65] Its official establishment had risen to 158, whereas the number of academicians had dropped to fourteen, and two of these were honorary members.

Relations between Schumacher, the scientific academicians, and the design sections of the Academy were further strained when Korff was somewhat abruptly appointed envoy to Denmark in 1740. His replacement was Karl von Brevern, who was related by marriage to Keyserling. Brevern, the third successive president of the Academy to come from the Baltic region, spent much of his time at court, where he had been a secretary of the cabinet since 1734.[66] But there was no security at court during the years 1740–1. His term was cut short by Anna's death in October 1740 and the succession of the infant Ivan VI, who ruled under the regency of his mother, Anna Leopoldovna, princess of Brunswick. She had won the regency by supporting a coup by Field Marshal B. von Münnich against Biron, whom Empress Anna had designated as regent. Biron was exiled to Siberia, and most of his protégés were dismissed from their posts by Münnich, who became "first minister." The bizarre story of court intrigue continued to unfold when Ostermann forced Münnich out of office in March 1741. Eight months later, in November, both Germans and a number of their supporters followed Biron to Sibera as a result of a second coup, this time in the name of Elizabeth, daughter of Peter the Great. Throughout this chaotic time, Academy affairs were left to Schumacher, who had been appointed a director in 1738.[67] By 1742, however, even his position had become precarious when a wave of anti-German sentiment permeated Elizabeth's court.

This situation aggravated Bering's difficulties. Always at odds with Siberian officials, who neither wished nor could afford to deplete their meagre resources to assist the expedition, and left to manage a vast enterprise with too little authority, Bering lost control of his finances. Costs soared. His first estimates to Anna's chancellery had called for a sum that ranged between 10,000 and 12,000 rubles (apart from salaries, provisions, and shipbuilding materials). By 1737 actual costs had gone beyond 300,000 rubles, and Bering had accomplished nothing to show for it.[68] Some members of the Senate suggested that the entire project be recalled; S.I. Soimonov, by then chief procurator of the Senate, proposed that Spangenberg replace Bering; and the Admiralty pressured Bering to start out for Kamchatka. In 1737 Bering was deprived of his supplementary salary, with the warning that it would not be renewed until the expedition got under way once again.

Bering was finally ready to leave Okhotsk in the summer of 1740, but a number of unforeseen incidents – the change in orders delivered by Spangenberg at the last moment, an accident that cost them valuable supplies, and a revolt by harshly overworked native peoples – resulted in his not reaching Kamchatka until September. By then it was too late in the year to undertake the voyage to America. Only in June 1741 were Bering's two ships, the *St. Paul* and *St. Peter*, able to set sail from Petropavlovsk. After suffering through six months of storm, cold, and raging disease that killed half his crew, the sixty-year-old Bering died. The famous Danish explorer was buried on a desolate island that later bore his name. The second Kamchatka expedition was officially terminated in 1743 but actually limped on until 1749 under two of Bering's captains. Little more was accomplished in the way of exploration or discovery after 1742.[69]

In the mean time, Müller and Gmelin were still studying Siberia. They travelled north to Novaia Mangaseia in June 1739 and were so fascinated by the fact that there was little difference between night and day there that they spent an entire night watching the sun. They returned to Eniseisk in time to participate in the great trade fair held annually there in August.[70] In September the academicians made their way south to Krasnoiarsk and set up headquarters for a series of tours by horseback around the region between that city and Abakanskoe. They bribed Tatars to plunder tombs of their ancestors for artifacts and not a little wealth in the form of gold and silver ornaments and jewellery. Back in Krasnoiarsk they observed on two separate occasions the punishment of women who had killed their husbands.

The murderesses were buried alive up to their necks and allowed slowly to die of thirst – if sunstroke or insect bites did not kill them first. One of the women had already languished for twelve years in prison.[71]

In February 1740, Müller departed for Tomsk – leaving Gmelin in Krasnoiarsk. To his surprise he found that the archives in Tomsk contained not one historical act. Indeed, the entire collection consisted of current documentation. Although Müller was informed that the earlier materials had been destroyed by fire, he discovered to his horror that the local *voevoda* had thrown all the old documents in the Tom' River shortly before his arrival.[72] From Tomsk Müller sailed up the Ob to Narym and Surgut, where he met Fischer in June. He had already written to the Academy a year earlier to express his concern over the decision to have Fischer take possession of his manuscripts. In that letter he had stressed the difficulties of his task at the best of times, stating categorically that he could not complete his research without constant access to the material he had already collected. Müller also pointed out that Fischer was a novice in historical and ethnographical studies and so could not possibly make good use of his documentation. Although there is no evidence to suggest that Müller had a reply from the Academy by the time he confronted Fischer, he kept much of the folio material for himself anyway and sent the rest back to St Petersburg.[73]

Fischer's lack of preparation worried Müller, and Gmelin's charge that he was an unwilling worker further exacerbated his anxiety.[74] As a result, Müller rushed to complete a detailed series of instructions for Fischer to use while gathering information on the history and peoples of Siberia. The instructions included a large number of briefly stated points, over 1,200 in all, categorized under six headings: authoritative journals, geographical descriptions, present circumstances of towns and their regions, examining archives and accounts of Siberian history, accounts of antiquity, and describing the morals and customs of peoples. The prospectus also included instructions on preparing maps and drawings, what items to collect for the *Kunstkamera*, and how to add words to the dictionary that Müller had started in 1733. Müller had been composing this guide since 1734, and so Fischer's coming was not responsible for its inception. Indeed, in 1740, Müller had found a similar but shorter questionnaire that Tatishchev had left in Krasnoiarsk and that helped him to consolidate his own.[75]

After Surgut, Müller proceeded northward on the Ob. In Berezov he found several important historical documents and heard enough "oral testimony," he said, to prepare a description of peoples who lived in the Arctic Ocean area. During the autumn of 1740 he went again to Tobol'sk. From there he wrote to the Academy that his recent tour had been especially beneficial, for he had gathered further information on the "customs and way of life of the Ostiaks [now Khanty], Voguls [now Mansi]," and the Samoeds. In long letters to Gmelin he also demonstrated his interest in natural history, describing shrubs, medicinal herbs, and birds at some length. One plant, which he called beard grass (*Borodskaia trava*), was a favourite with the Tatars because when mixed with honey "it comforts old and weak people and is also used as an aphrodisiac." Müller acquired a hunting falcon from a Tatar and described it in great detail to Gmelin. He seemed fascinated by this bird, telling Gmelin of its training, diet, and hunting practices. Müller even found archival records that told how such falcons were brought to Moscow in large numbers during the reign of Alexei Mikhailovich (1645–76).[76] But he complained that the Tobol'sk archives had fallen into "such disorder that many volumina, or so-called stolbtsy," that had been there in 1734 could no longer be found. Müller grumbled further about "coolness and slowness" on the part of local officials. A letter to Euler of June 1740 suggests that he had had his fill of Siberia: "God grant that my Siberian business will soon come to an end ... I do not wish to complain ... but there is hardly a town or part of Siberia in which I have not been"[77]

In March 1741, Müller went to Tiumen' and then to Irbit, and in July he reached Ekaterinburg. He studied thoroughly the surrounding areas during the summer and fall, going as far south as Cheliabinsk. He was reunited with Gmelin on the river Iset' in September, and together they returned to Tobol'sk. From Gmelin, Müller discovered how fortunate they both had been insofar as physical dangers were concerned. A few weeks earlier, Gmelin had passed through two deserted villages and learned that every man, woman, and child had either been killed, tortured, or taken away as prisoners by a band of renegade cossacks.[78] Apparently such large-scale acts of violence were becoming increasingly common. Bands made up of cossacks, Russian exiles and criminals of all kinds, and Tatars were provoking a situation of near civil war. In general the brigands were after horses and trade goods. The frontier troops seemed unable to stop them.

Müller and Gmelin stayed in Tobol'sk until January 1743, when they set out for Turinsk. There Müller prepared a long report for the Academy outlining the extent of his historical findings to date. He boasted to have found enough material to "bring into clarity the history of Siberia."[79] Müller pointed out, however, that he could find no Russian documents in this region on Siberian history prior to 1593, nor was there any information about Ermak's conquest of Sibir in 1581–2.

Müller was stricken with a violent fever while in Turinsk and thus was unable to complete further research until that summer. At that time he sailed north on the Tura River to Verhotur'e. There he met and married the widow of a German surgeon.[80] Having gathered almost everything he needed, Müller spent much of his time during 1742 writing and recuperating from recurring sickness. He probably completed the first four chapters of his history of Siberia before he got back to St Petersburg in 1743.[81] Perhaps aware that they might never again have the opportunity to travel east in the Russian empire, Müller and his bride returned to St Petersburg in a relaxed manner. They spent several weeks in Sol' Kamskaia, where they and Gmelin were impressed by the family of G.A. Demidov, son of the state chancellor: "We were especially enthusiastic about the habits of Demidov, son of the Councillor of State [wrote Gmelin]. His wife is no less civil than he; their children are raised in a way that is rare in this country; by their manners, their politeness, their knowledge and their ability, they are far ahead of what is normal for children of their age. This Demidov is versed in natural history ... He had a very beautiful garden and a truly regal orangery in view of the rigorous climate."[82]

Steller and Fischer also admired this garden in 1746. Steller spent more than a month with the Demidovs while recovering from an illness and making arrangements to return to the capital. Fischer arrived in Sol' Kamskaia with his family on his way back to St Petersburg. He had not gone even so far as Okhotsk in his travels, having stopped for some time in Tomsk while his wife bore their fourth child. He lost still more time while under investigation by the authorities – as a result of a false accusation – in the winter of 1743.[83] But Fischer's lack of accomplishment was not important to Müller in 1743. Leaving Gmelin in Sol' Kamskaia, the Müllers passed through Vologda and Beloozero and reached the Russian capital on 14 February 1743.[84] Gmelin followed three days later. According to Müller's own calculations, he had travelled 31,362 versts (about 24,000 miles) during his decade in Siberia.

Between 1735 and 1738 Müller submitted to the Chancellery fully prepared descriptions of the Kuznetsk (1735), Eniseisk, Mangazeia, Krasnoiarsk, Selenginsk (1736), and Nerchinsk (1737) regions. He also sent information about the industries in the mountains of Siberia and Perm, the silver mines in Irkutsk, and the fortresses along the Irtysh River (1735). In 1740 he forwarded a catalogue of natural history specimens and was ordered by imperial decree to prepare a full study of the Amur River area for the vice-governor of Irkutsk,

Lorents Lange, who was preparing to negotiate with the Chinese over trade rights and access to the Amur.[85] Müller's "Nachrichten von dem Amur-Flusse" was completed in early January 1741 and sent off to St Petersburg. In it he praised the Amur as one of the most important waterways in Asia. He saw it as the means to eliminate many of the difficulties faced by Russians wishing to travel to Japan or America. He referred to the Treaty of Nerchinsk (1689), which gave the Chinese full control of the river, as illegal and deserving of repeal. Later he said that, in making this report, he was fulfilling his "full patriotic duty."[86] Müller also wrote a short history of Irkutsk province and sent it to St Petersburg in 1736, and a memorandum on Russian northern sea voyages, written by Müller sometime after 1736, was published in the *Notes* to the *Gazette* in 1742.[87] Such reports (the Nerchinsk report was 115 pages) were made possible only through the use of questionnaires sent ahead to the officials of the region he wished to study. The results suggest that he received considerably more co-operation from Siberian officialdom than he was willing to acknowledge.

All in all, Müller's accomplishments in Siberia were remarkable. His collection of documents, abstracts from old records, and artifacts, many acquired through the services of grave robbers, have proved invaluable to later scholars of Siberia. His folios contained enough raw material to enable him to continue writing and publishing books and articles on Siberia for the ensuing thirty-five years.

Müller's ethnographical work was vast, but his efforts to catalogue, copy, and rearrange the historical documents in Siberia were even more prodigious. The Siberian archives contained a great number of official documents sent from Moscow in the late sixteenth and through the seventeenth centuries to provincial authorities, military commanders, and Church representatives. In many cases the originals had disappeared in European Russia. In Tobol'sk, Eniseisk, Iakutsk, and Verkhotur'e, the holdings were contained in large wooden buildings; in Tomsk they were stored in a damp stone room. Most were in a state of acute disorder. Müller and his assistants were the first to attempt to rearrange them into some kind of chronological order. These copies saved many records for posterity when the originals were lost to the ravages of fire and rot. That many documents disappeared in Tobol'sk and Tomsk during the six years that separated Müller's first and return visits to each place testifies to their high mortality rate.

Müller later insisted that local officials were reluctant to help if their assistance was to cost them money. He became more and more demanding, stridently proclaiming his rights in the name of the

Senate. Even though he sent requests and questionnaires along ahead of him, much time was wasted while Müller waited for local copyists. He had brought competent assistants from St Petersburg – his translator, Iakhontov (who died at Eniseisk in 1739), and the students Tret'iakov, Krasheninnikov, and Gorlanov. The last two, however, and the artist Berkan left him to go to Kamchatka. Berkan was replaced by Johann Decker, who, Müller said, "was good as a copyist but had no talent for drawing animals."[88] Generally, though, he had to rely on personnel provided by local authorities, and he complained regularly about the quality of their work.

In spite of such difficulties, Müller arrived at the Academy feeling, quite rightly, that he had accomplished something of great importance for that institution. His completed and catalogued collections included forty-two books of documents on the history and geography of Siberia, four books of chronicles, and books of descriptions of Siberia (ten prepared by Müller himself and three compiled by his students and overseen by him) and a large quantity of maps, drawings, and city plans. Further, he delivered fourteen thick files of reports, documents, letters, orders, and other communications between his group and St Petersburg between 1733 and 1743. Müller promised soon to hand over the journals of his and Gmelin's trips, a history of Siberia, a geographical description, and a detailed account of the commerce, administration, society, and customs of contemporary Siberia.[89] Invaluable as their scientific data proved to be for future researchers, Müller and Gmelin were both realistic enough at the time to point out that by far the most important immediate application of their information should be in the area of trade and commerce.[90]

It was unfortunate that both Kirilov and Bayer were dead by the time that Müller settled back into academic life in St Petersburg, because his new, self-taught skills would have delighted them both. The scientific information about Siberia that Müller gathered and organized in a systematic manner was exactly the kind of contribution Peter the Great had expected from his academicians, and the information was also of the type and form that Kirilov knew Russia needed if it were to modernize. Müller had honed his skills as a historian and archivist as well, and he developed certain preferences in respect to official documentation. He recognized such sources as invaluable because they were authentic records of state-provincial relations in the past; he also learned of the great variety of other records from which historical information could be inferred. Among those were old coins, religious symbols, grave epitaphs, artifacts, language patterns, customs, and even trade patterns. Müller was now aware that a proper history of the Russian empire, that is, of its many parts, would be of far greater use than a mere account of the Russian rulers. His antiquarian nature still dominated, however, for he assumed that the way to a history lay with the collection of information until everything was known.

During the first months after his return Müller had little opportunity to practise his newly acquired expertise. Perhaps he should have recalled his experiences of 1730–1 when the triumph of his journey through Europe had so quickly dissipated. Almost before he unpacked, Müller once again was caught up in the cross-currents of Academy infighting, jealousies, and rows.

PART THREE

Stormy Decades at the Academy

CHAPTER FOUR

Historiographer
1743–8

Müller was an ignoramus, a living Machiavelli, and
the very first professor to be selected by the Flagellum
professorum.

M.V. Lomonosov on Müller, 1765

Feeling the ill effects of long bouts of sickness and depression, Müller stayed away from the Academy Conference for a full month after his return to St Petersburg in February 1743.[1] A long report to the Senate, which included a register of all items he had posted to the capital during his travels, was not ready until August.[2] Müller's recurring illness had been regarded with some suspicion by Schumacher and others, and descriptions of his symptoms prompted some later writers to speak of his hypochondria. But the degree to which the hardships of Siberia were physically debilitating should not be forgotten. Bitter cold, raging storms, oppressive heat, and swarming mosquitoes had taken their toll. According to Steller, Bering had suffered spells of depression long before his death. De la Croyère died of scurvy aboard ship in 1741; Steller himself died of a "fever" at Tiumen in 1746, aged thirty-seven; Chirikov died in St Petersburg in 1742, shortly after reporting on his trip in the *St Paul* the year before; Krasheninnikov's health was so impaired that he died in 1755 aged forty-two; Gmelin died the same year of "exhaustion" after a long illness.[3] He was forty-six. In his memoir, Gmelin described in some detail the regularity of small-scale epidemics in Siberia, including "a very violent catharral fever which pervaded the whole of Siberia this spring" (1742). Müller had been one of its victims.[4] But the delay between Müller's return and his renewed activity at the Academy may have been more purposeful than he wished known. The atmosphere in St Petersburg had changed dramatically since 1733. He may well have felt it prudent to test the waters before re-entering the volatile sea of Academy life.

It would not have taken Müller long to recognize that the autonomy that the professors assumed they had won in 1733 had been illusory. Repeated requests for an increase in the Academy budget had been ignored, and an annual deficit increased in size each year after 1725. Even Korff's warning to Anna in October 1736 that without further funds the institution "would doubtlessly be destroyed" met with no response. The Academy survived without an increased budget, and its scientists continued to put existing facilities to good use. But the financial stringency and the continued support given Schumacher by the court and the presidents kept the Conference in a state of tension. In fact, the discord and even privation of life at the Academy had reached dangerous proportions by the early 1740s. The situation was described aptly by mathematics professor Christian Goldbach in late 1740 in a detailed response to a request from Brevern that academicians comment on a project for Academy reform put forward by Korff some six years previously – and still languishing in the hands of the Senate. Above all else, Goldbach, who was given permission to leave the Academy for a post with the College of Foreign Affairs in 1742, condemned the stifling bureaucracy which he said hampered scientific initiative and accomplishment. He added that Russia could not hope to attract competent professors unless salaries were increased substantially. Brevern paid little attention to Goldbach's suggestions and within the year was caught up in the turmoil that ensued from the court revolution in November 1741. This, the most spectacular event in St Petersburg during Müller's absence, ended the so-called dark days of Anna and her coterie of Baltic Germans. With Elizabeth's accession, the floodgates of anti-German sentiment in St Petersburg opened.[5]

Ostermann, who had been a sponsor of the second Kamchatka expedition and whom Müller regarded as a patron at court, was himself exiled to Siberia. Russians now dominated the government. The Razumovskiis, led by Alexis, Elizabeth's lover and perhaps even husband, became the leading family. The Shuvalovs, brothers Peter and Alexander, and cousin Ivan, all took on posts of importance. Counts Michael Vorontsov and Alexis Bestuzhev-Riumin were put in charge of state and foreign affairs. The new Russian entourage brought with it a liking for things French, so that even the cultural orientation of Academy members, let alone their politics, came under suspicion.

The most striking consequence of these new trends at court for the Academy was the threat that they posed to Schumacher, who undermined his own position further by making an enemy of A.K.

Nartov. We have seen that Nartov was the founder and director of the Academy workshop, which had become a teaching division with its own staff and students. He had been appointed a councillor of the Academy and was a friend of Joseph N. de l'Isle, the most vociferous opponent of Schumacher among the academicians.[6] Housing laboratories for the study and manufacture of lenses, and for the design of mathematical, navigational, and other instruments,[7] the workshop was an important component of the Academy. In 1741 Nartov was the only Russian who held a position of any significance at that institution. He was incensed when Schumacher failed to list him as a member and flatly refused to pay salaries to his staff, or even to grant him a secretary.[8] Consequently, seven months after Elizabeth's accession, Nartov arrived in Moscow armed with complaints against Schumacher from clerks and copyists at the Academy, most of whom were Russians. Supported by petitions sent separately by three Russian students, an engraver, and a translator, Nartov was able to persuade the court that Schumacher was hostile to the Russian people, that he had embezzled funds from the Chancellery, and that he was working to undermine the very purposes for which Peter the Great had founded the institution in the first place.[9] Such an appeal was bound to have a sympathetic hearing among the new empress's supporters, and Nartov returned to St Petersburg triumphant. Schumacher, the comptroller Hoffman, the manager of the *knizhnaia palata* (N. Preisser), and an academy clerk were all placed under strict house arrest, and Nartov was put in charge of Academy affairs.[10]

To investigate Nartov's charges, a committee of three highly placed officials were formed: Senator-Admiral Count N.F. Golovin; the president of the Commerce College, Prince Boris G. Iusupov; and the Ober-Commandant of St Petersburg, Lieutenant-General S.L. Ignatiev.[11] During the course of their lengthy deliberations (7 October 1742 to 15 December 1743), the committee learned that Schumacher had taken wines from the Academy cellars under false pretenses ("scientific experiment"), had used Academy funds to provide himself with servants and even with a house, and had doctored the accounts to his own advantage on a number of occasions. The committee noted as well that Schumacher "was not comfortable" with the Russian language – a most damning sin at that moment in Russian history.[12]

Schumacher did not bother to deny some of the charges and tried to shift the blame for others on to Blumentrost, who was not asked to testify before the committee. The defendant explained away the accusation that he was anti-Russian by pointing out that it was the job of the academicians to recommend new appointments. But the depositions against him mounted during the first months of the investigation. The translator, Nikita Popov, insisted that Schumacher favoured Germans, paid them a higher wage than he paid Russians doing the same job, and demanded little work from them while overworking Russian students. Popov produced a list of Germans whom he considered superfluous, including a hunter who was paid 200 rubles annually to shoot birds for the zoological division of the *Kunstkamera*. Schumacher responded by saying that the Russians would earn more as they became more skilled and added that most Germans were under contract and often undertook extra duties that were not asked of the Russians. Rather than deny the pay differentials, he said that the Germans were better qualified. The tone of Schumacher's responses seemed to mollify the committee somewhat, but in the end it was the very length of the procedures that saved him. The process lasted just long enough for Nartov to alienate the academicians even more than had Schumacher.

Nartov's regime certainly was a mixed blessing for the Academy. Having access to the Chancellery's finance lists, he was able to demonstrate to the Senate that large sums of money had been directed to the Academy from various sources over the decade of Anna's reign, but that very little of it could be accounted for. He recommended in March 1742 that a president be appointed as soon as possible and that a formal structure, which had been approved in 1735, be given final confirmation. Nartov also dismissed three German teachers from the Academy gymnasium, one of whom was Justus Müller, for not knowing Russian and for appearing only rarely at their posts. In fact, Justus Müller and Christian Hermann were accused of staying home and teaching privately for pay. They were replaced at the gymnasium by V.K. Trediakovskii and Ivan Gorlitskii (one of the complainants against Schumacher), both Russians. Nartov also moved to cut off the pensions being sent to honorary members abroad, and in June 1743 he established the Academy of Fine Arts, which he had proposed in 1724. Financial problems prevented the new unit from becoming a full-fledged Academy for nearly two decades. In the 1740s it was called the artistic department of the Academy of Sciences, and its personnel provided the academicians with drawings, typographical work, and book-binding services. It also began to train young artists and sculptors. Named to the department were Jakob Stählin, who became director in 1757, Johann Jakob Schumacher, an architect and brother to the director of the Chancellery, and two artists.

Nartov's policies pleased most of his Russian associates to a certain extent, but even the strongest advocates of Russianization recognized the essentially international character of science. At any rate, there were no Russians at full professor rank, so Nartov had no natural pool of academic support at the Academy. In the long run, however, Nartov was his own worst enemy. He acted toward all his colleagues, Russian and foreign alike, with a tactlessness that even Schumacher would have known enough to temper.[14] De l'Isle turned against him; the Russian adjuncts, G.N. Teplov and Adodurov, and Trediakovskii, who with Adodurov made up the Russian half of the small Russian Assembly of the Academy, began to speak out on Schumacher's behalf. Shvanvits and Johann-Kaspar Taubert were the foreign members of the Russian Assembly. They also lodged complaints with the commission against Nartov, who appeared even less inclined to pay salaries than had his predecessor.[15]

Schumacher still had friends at court, including Elizabeth's chief physician, J.H. Lestocq, who addressed the commission at length in his favour.[16] Lestocq had been an active proponent of Elizabeth's candidacy for the throne, and so his views carried the weight of an imperial favourite. In December 1742, Schumacher was freed. Shortly thereafter the commission reported that it found him not guilty of any major misdemeanour and limited his punishment to a fine of 109 rubles for misappropriating Academy wines. In December 1743, Elizabeth reinstated Schumacher to his former position with full back pay.[17] He was appointed state councillor early the next year, and his leading supporters at the Academy were promoted. Adodurov, who had been assessor of the government's Heraldmater's Office since April 1741, became a director of the Academy; so did Taubert, who had been an adjunct for history since 1738 and who had the good fortune to become Schumacher's son-in-law in 1750. The bookseller Preisser, who also had been charged with embezzlement, regained his former post in September 1744 – after nearly two years in prison![18]

In March 1744, Schumacher showed his gratitude to Lestocq by naming a newly discovered medicinal herb Herbarium Lestokianum. His antagonists among the students were fined and lost their positions (with the exception of Popov). One of his accusers, Gorlitskii, suffered a lashing and was then exiled with his family to Orenburg. But Elizabeth pardoned him in 1744, and he took up a position as translator at the Academy once again a few years later. Nartov returned to his former duties, but the Academy of Arts was placed directly under the Chancellery and was made Taubert's responsibility. In January 1744, Justus Müller was reappointed to the gynmasium as assessor, a post that he was to retain for nearly forty years.[19]

Gerhard Müller paid little attention to Schumacher's troubles – at least publicly. In a letter to Teplov a few years later, he was less than frank about his reasons for not joining the fray: "On my return from Siberia, I found Mr. Schumacher in such circumstances that he was in danger of losing his position, honour, and perhaps even his life. I was urged strongly to join Mr. Nartov in order to deal Mr. Schumacher the final blow which was needed to overwhelm him. However, I preferred compassion." In fact, Müller preferred to be pragmatic. He stood to gain nothing from Nartov and recognized this as an ideal opportunity to get back into Schumacher's good graces in case the long-time Academy secretary was exonerated. Müller still needed a patron at the Academy and hoped to benefit from the situation without committing himself to one side or the other. Perhaps, too, he was more worried about Nartov's anti-German campaign than he was about the resurrection to power of his old enemy. But his efforts came to nought. In the same letter to Teplov, Müller observed with some bitterness that Schumacher refused to acknowledge his indirect assistance and continued to treat him just as badly as he had done in the 1730s.[20]

However, Müller did take notice of a recently appointed (8 January 1742) adjunct, Mikhail Vasil'evich Lomonosov, who loudly opposed both Schumacher and Nartov.[21] At the time of Müller's return to the capital, Lomonosov was under academic ban for having arrived drunk at the Academy assembly, threating to "readjust the teeth" of member Ch.N. Winsheim, and calling many of his colleagues "swindlers and other foul names" and Schumacher a "thief." This outburst and other alleged "shameless improprieties" were consistent with reports of Lomonosov's conduct as a student in Germany. His behaviour seemed also to have been exacerbated by his dislike of the Germans who dominated the Academy, the fact that he had not received a salary for nearly eight months, and his belief that the Golovin committee mishandled the Schumacher case. He was banned in February 1743 as a result of his actions. Subsequently he came to blows with the Academy gardener, a deed that resulted in an official police interrogation.[22]

The accumulation of complaints lodged with the Golovin committee against Lomonosov led to his arrest in May 1743. The minutes of the Conference suggest that Müller was the leading complainant against him. In contrast to the relatively lenient treatment afforded Schumacher, Lomonosov was kept under strict house arrest until January of the next year.[23] Before he could be freed, he was forced to beg the forgiveness of the professors whom he had maligned, was fined half a year's salary, and was put on probation. On fulfilling these requirements, Lomonosov was pardoned for his "unforgivable error of monstrous dimensions" – but he certainly was not humbled. He confronted Müller and vowed never to forgive him for the prominent part he played in the affair.[24]

Their relationship was strained even further when the Academy Conference asked Müller to judge a short handbook on rhetoric (*Ritorika*) that Lomonosov had sent to J.-G. Stählin in Moscow in late January 1744. Stählin, a professor of elocution and poetry at the Academy since 1735, had been in Moscow since 1742. At Elizabeth's request, he translated French and Italian operas, designed wardrobes and scenes, and planned spectaculars for the coronation. He also served as tutor to the fourteen-year-old duke of Holstein, Elizabeth's nephew, who was designated grand duke and heir apparent in 1742. By dedicating his text on rhetoric to Grand Duke Peter, Lomonosov may have hoped that he would be granted permission to publish it without going through normal channels. Instead, Stählin returned the book to the Academy in St Petersburg. Müller's report of 16 March 1744 suggested that, because of its brevity, there were probably "many things missing in the book which are usually included in a course of rhetoric." He recommended, however, that Lomonosov expand the work, make it "conform more to our century," and present it in both Latin and Russian. Only then should it be printed for use in the gymnasium. Lomonosov had little choice but to agree.[25] The text was rewritten by 1747, but it was not published during Lomonosov's lifetime. Thus began a bitter enmity that embroiled Müller in a clash of wills that went far beyond any contest he was to have with Schumacher.

The last thing Müller needed in 1744 was a new antagonist, not the least because his troubles with Schumacher and the Chancellery were far from over. He continued to have great difficulty in collecting his salary and other monies owed him for expenses incurred during his ten years in Siberia. Müller's regular income had reverted to 660 rubles annually, making him one of the lowest-paid professors at the Academy, even though he had been in service longer than many who received more. On 1 May 1743, Müller was reimbursed in the amount of 480 rubles. In a report to the Senate, however, he calculated that he was still owed 2,270 rubles.[26] It was not until 12 July 1745 that a government *ukaz* awarded Müller and Gmelin back debts. Indeed, almost all the professors claimed to have considerably more money coming to them, in the main because no one had been paid during the crisis of 1742.

Two weeks after Müller and Gmelin were promised compensation, de l'Isle, Gmelin, Weitbrecht, Winsheim, Le Roy, Richmann, and J.-G. Siegesbeck sent a twenty-one-point memorandum to the Senate charging that payments ordered by the government still had not been issued. They blamed Schumacher specifically for the delay. Seven months later they forwarded a second memorandum to the Senate inquiring why there had been no response to their first one.[27] An Academy account sheet for the year 1745 acknowledged that Müller still had 620 rubles owed to him, that is, almost all his salary for the previous year.[28] Later petitions continued to accuse Schumacher, and sometimes Taubert, of mismanaging Academy finances.

Müller and Gmelin clashed directly with Schumacher over a booklet that the Secretary wrote and printed about the personnel and resources of the Academy. The work had been prepared before Elizabeth's successful coup and had been dedicated to Ivan vi's mother, Anna Leopoldovna, whom many expected to act as regent. But the book was slow to appear, and Schumacher was actually saved from a potentially embarrassing publication by Nartov's attack on him in the spring of 1741. In March 1744, the Schumacher book was brought before the Conference once again, this time dedicated to Elizabeth. But Müller and Gmelin accused its author of using political criteria for failing to mention several important acquisitions, among them the materials gathered in Siberia during the second Kamchatka expedition. A furious Schumacher ordered that the discussion of this matter be stricken from the Conference minutes. When the Conference members refused to comply with this demand, Schumacher insisted that Conference secretary Winsheim add a letter (in German) to the minutes in which he accused Müller and Gmelin of "odious comments, made out of a search for glory." He said also that the academicians should spend their time on academic affairs and leave other affairs to him. In their turn, most of the Conference members now charged Schumacher, for example, in a petition to the Senate of 7 August 1745, of behaving even more "despotically" than he had before his trials of 1742–3.[29] One long denunciation of September 1745, signed by nine professors, including Müller, credited Müller with correcting numerous errors and omissions made by Schumacher in the library catalogue that formed part of his controversial booklet.

These accusations affected Schumacher little. His tenure was strengthened even further in May 1746 when Count Kirill Grigor'-evich Razumovskii, the eighteen-year-old brother of Elizabeth's current favourite, was named president of the Academy.[31] The appointment also brought G.N. Teplov, Razumovskii's former tutor, secretary, and travel companion, to a position of prominence at the Academy. Teplov (1711–79), the son of a smelter in Pskov, had been educated in a school at the archepiscopal home of Feofan Prokopovich in Novgorod. He also had studied at the University of St Petersburg and was selected by Elizabeth to be Razumovskii's tutor. In July 1746,

Teplov was named the assessor of the Academy, where he had been an adjunct for botany since 1743. Exactly a year later he was made a full member of the Conference and an honorary member of the Academy. With the blessings of Razumovskii, he allowed Schumacher to have his way with the unruly professors.[32] Nevertheless, Teplov's sudden acquisition of influence at the Academy was bound to undermine Schumacher's absolute control over the Chancellery. Now the academicians had a second bureaucrat of importance in St Petersburg whom they could court and use to offset Schumacher's predominance. In 1748 Teplov seriously considered several long accounts of Schumacher's "despotic" regime sent to him by Müller.[33]

The appointments of Razumovskii and Teplov were in keeping with Elizabeth's policy of Russification and coincided with rumours that foreign professors were agents of European powers. The departure of the Academy's most renowned scholar, Leonhard Euler, for Berlin in 1741 fueled such suspicions. Duvernois also left in 1741. Gottfried Heinsius, Krafft, and Weitbrecht resigned in 1744, embarrassing the Academy still more. In that year, the Senate ordered the transfer of all materials gathered during the Kamchatka expedition to a location safe from prying, foreign eyes. Shortly afterward, guards were deployed around the printing house, the library, and the *Kunstkamera*. Service staff were told not to release any map, book, or document without proper authorization.[34] The Chancellery archives were kept locked.

Russia was almost always at war during the middle decades of the century: in 1733-5 against France, in 1736-9 against Turkey, in 1741-2 against Sweden, and a few years later against Prussia and France during the latter stages of the War of the Austrian Succession. Although Russia remained faithful to its alliance with Austria throughout the period, political intrigue was still rife at court. The new Russian mandarins distrusted the German-dominated Academy.

While continuing to avoid politics as much as possible, Müller laboured over a new map of Siberia, using documentation from the geography department and his own notes. His immediate purpose was to correct errors in earlier charts and also to prepare something for distribution to foreigners who, he wrote, were especially ignorant about Russia's geography: "They know nothing about the divisions [of Russia], its rivers, the location of its towns ... or even of entire provinces."[35] Müller submitted a general geography of Siberia to the Chancellery in late 1745 but was prevented from publishing it when Schumacher allowed the geography department to print a full atlas of Russia (*Atlas rossiiskoi*) instead. The latter had been compiled under the direction of Winsheim and Heinsius, who were left in charge of the department after Euler returned to Germany. Müller, Lomonosov, and several other members of the Academy Conference criticized the Winsheim atlas, but it was too late to resurrect Müller's work.[36]

In March 1746, Müller offered two more maps of Siberia to the Conference, but even this effort proved to be more trouble that it was worth. In April he was ordered to cease all such projects because the government had sanctioned the *Atlas rossiiskoi* and the Chancellery had approved a general map of the second Kamchatka expedition that was based on information gathered by Steller and Chirikov. After seeing the *Atlas rossiiskoi*, Müller requested maps of the Siberian coast and waterways, recently drawn up by naval officers, directly from the imperial cabinet. But when Baron I.A. Cherkasov, head of the cabinet, ordered that the maps be turned over to Müller by the Admiralty College, Vice-Admiral Z.D. Mishukov balked at doing so. It was clear that members of the Admiralty College did not wish to entrust such documents to Germans at the Academy. To avoid making foreigners privy to information the Admiralty considered important militarily, Mishukov stalled Cherkasov for more than a month. He then requested that the map-making task be turned over to the Naval Academy, which had been established in St Petersburg in 1725. The court agreed, and the Academy Chancellery was ordered to gather together all maps created by participants in the Kamchatka expedition and send them to the cabinet. Thirty-six maps and charts were assembled. The general map was then completed by the staff at the Naval Academy. Thus Müller's constructive efforts were short-circuited, and his own maps were not returned to him until 1752.[37]

In the mean time, Müller reworked the manuscript on the peoples of Siberia that he had written in 1734. It was sent to the Conference in April 1745. Müller hoped that it would be printed in the *Commentarii*, but the Conference directed Ivan Golubtsov to translate it into Russian for preservation in the Academy archives. It seemed that Müller's hard-earned knowledge about Siberia was not appreciated very much by his colleagues, or even by the government. The only official attention paid to him by Russia's bureaucracy came in 1744 from a member of the Golovin committee, Prince Iusupov, who commanded him to prepare a report on private trading in Siberia for the Commerce College.[38] But there is no evidence to suggest that Müller's submission was acted on.

Undeterred by the several rebuffs that he met with in 1745, Müller presented Razumovskii with a very detailed proposal on the best means for the Academy to provide Russians with a history and a geography of the Russian empire.[39] In the preamble to the long plan (which the president received on 7 August 1746), Müller echoed

Tatishchev's sentiments in what Pekarskii rightly called a *"profession de foi"*: "It is well-known in what ways every person, no matter his rank, has a need to know history; it is customarily called the mirror of human activity, according to which by looking at the past it is possible to make judgments about the present and the future ... Russian history is very poorly known among the histories of all other European countries. And that which is written in foreign books about it cannot be to the advantage of the Russian Empire, for those foreigners [who write about Russia] are in the country for only a short period of time, do not know the Russian language, [and] do not have the competence to write about important matters."[40] He added, however, that Russian scholars had themselves been very remiss in not providing their nation with a proper history of its own. He admitted that some satisfactory work had been done on a few regions of Russia but complained that nothing was available about the country as a whole and that there was nothing that even remotely touched on modern history. In fact, Müller's experience in the various Siberian archives made him aware of the great value that government decrees held for historians, whereas most of his predecessors among historical writers in Russia tended to rely solely on chronicle materials.

Müller noted that no attempt had been made to integrate the histories of separate noble families and that the period during which the Tatars had ruled Russia had been ignored. To redress these and other deficiencies, Müller recommended that the following collection be organized: (1) all "written historical books, that is, the *Kniga stepennaia*, chronicles, and chronographs, both about Russia generally, and about its different parts"; (2) books on Tatar history in the Tatar, Turkish, and Persian languages; (3) a centralized document depository; (4) the lives of the saints in Church books, many of which belonged to noble families; (5) reports and documents that dealt with the founding of churches and monasteries; (6) grave-site and other inscriptions in Muscovite churches and monasteries and in other Russian towns; (7) genealogical books of princely and noble families and of other families that have had some significance for Russian history; (8) anything from Russian antiquity, no matter how insignificant it may seem; (9) legends and folk-tales, which were not to be taken literally; and (10) foreign books about Russia, Lithuania, Courland, Prussia, Poland, Sweden, Denmark, Germany, Turkey, Persia, and China. This list is perfectly representative of the techniques advocated by the new nationalist historians of the *Aufklärung*.

The gist of Müller's proposal came well into its second section. After trying to persuade his readers of the great national interest that would be served by the preparation of a proper history of Russia, he recommended that a special department be instituted at the Academy and that he, as the senior historian, be named its director with the title of historiographer. Müller could then oversee the collecting process and at the same time complete his history of Siberia. By the time his own work was completed, the department would be in a position to start work on an all-Russian history. He suggested that the bureau be located in Moscow because "that city can be regarded as the centre of the entire empire." Müller felt that the staff should be composed of one adjunct trained in history and, if not a Russian, in the Russian language; a second adjunct, who had to be Russian, who would serve as the department's agent throughout Russia; a translator; two copyists, one German and one Russian; a clerk, with his own copyist; and a custodian. Müller's budget, submitted with his proposal, suggested a 1,200-ruble salary for himself, 1,500 to be divided among the rest of the staff, and about 500 rubles for incidentals.

Well aware of the reluctance on the part of both lay and Church officials to give up documents, Müller recommended that an imperial *ukaz* be issued ordering that all records be sent to St Petersburg but promising to return them once they were copied. He also requested that the College of Foreign Affairs supply translators for special languages on a temporary basis. All in all, this detailed proposition shows that Müller's experiences in Siberia had changed him from a fledgling to an expert in the handling of historical sources and archives.

While awaiting a response to the proposal, Müller worked on his history of Siberia. The first part had already been submitted to Elizabeth in 1744, and in 1746 Razumovskii had assigned to Golubtsov the task of translating it from German into Russian. It was obvious, however, that the Academy intended to watch this German writing Russian history with a vigilant and somewhat suspicious eye. In August the Chancellery asked Müller to outline the "method" he intended to use in writing the history and made it clear that he should attempt "only a history" and should finish it as early as possible.[41] In February 1747, Razumovskii sent Müller a rather curt note telling him that his only concern for the time being must be the completion of the history of Siberia and a geography of Kamchatka. This note can also be taken as a response to Müller's submission about a history department. In fact, Schumacher and Razumovskii interpreted that proposal as an attempt by Müller to escape the restraints of the Academy Conference.[42] Eight months later, Razumovskii reported again to the Senate that Müller's sole occupation should be to complete the work for which he had already been paid, this time in co-operation with Fischer, who returned from Siberia in July 1747.[43]

One of the reasons why Müller's research advanced so slowly was that he was constantly assigned other tasks. In the winter of 1746 he was asked to gather historical material on prominent Russian military leaders and diplomats, as part of a government-sponsored project to build a shrine to Alexander Nevskii and other heroes. In October Razumovskii told him to evaluate a genealogy of Russian princes prepared by Peter N. Krekshin (1684–1763),[44] a collector of historical manuscripts and a persistent glorifier of Peter the Great, on whom he wrote over twenty works of various sizes. Müller had already assisted Krekshin in his genealogy project by sending him manuscripts and short translations from sources written in languages with which Krekshin was unfamiliar. But Müller's assessment, submitted in January 1747, was very unfavourable. The genealogy's ingratiating tone and the fact that Krekshin accepted several legends as fact made it impossible for Müller to approve it. Krekshin took the rebuff personally and sought revenge. He informed the Senate that Müller had given him materials that portrayed Russia in a very bad light. A commission was set up to examine the merits of Krekshin's charges, and the genealogy was turned over to a small committee composed of F.-H. Strube de Piermont, a former secretary to Biron who had been named to the Academy as professor of jurisprudence and politics by Korff in 1738, Trediakovskii, and Lomonosov.[45] Knowing that these men disliked Müller for various reasons, Krekshin expected them to rally to his cause. But even Lomonosov disappointed him.

Lomonosov had been promoted to professor of chemistry in June 1745[46] and had campaigned successfully for a modern chemistry laboratory. He was not then interested in history as an avocation or even as a hobby, but his thirst for knowledge was eclectic. His Russian textbook on rhetoric was an example of the range of his interests.[47] Lomonosov also translated some of Christian Wolff's works, lectured publicly on experimental physics, composed long and flattering odes to the empress and her family, argued with Trediakovskii about Russian grammar, and continued to participate in organized opposition to Schumacher. In short, he was one of the Academy's multipurpose scholars who were logical candidates to be on investigatory committees. He gave Krekshin's history careful thought and supported Müller's criticisms of it. Lomonosov's refutation indicated that he had read the *Sinopsis* and at least parts of the *Kniga stepennaia*. The affair dragged on until December, when the Senate finally ordered the case closed with no decision having been taken. Although the Krekshin episode had little effect on Müller's career in the long run, it serves as one of the many examples of the way in which personal pride and jealousy could undermine the scientific endeavours of the Academy.

The incident also demonstrated in a minor way the importance attributed to genealogy by the court. When Peter the Great decreed that the monarch could choose his own successor, he unwittingly assured that succession crises would plague Russia throughout the eighteenth century. Palace intrigues ran rampant, and the question of legitimacy was a sensitive one to rulers and their supporters. For that reason, when Müller justified his rejection of Krekshin's chart of Russian royalty by referring to his own work on princely genealogy, he received a stiff warning from Razumovskii "not to undertake any genealogical investigations, either of the family of her Imperial Highness, or about particular persons, without a special ukaz to that effect ... under threat of punishment."[48]

In fact, Müller was much too busy to worry about Krekshin's injured pride. In March 1747 he replied to Razumovskii's urging that he finish the Siberian history by complaining that he had too much else to do. Müller's other projects included a geography of Siberia, its provinces, and its districts; a geographical survey of Siberia; and a study of Siberian trade, including data concerning Russian state interests there. He presented a series of lectures on the Tunguses to the Conference and then rewrote the talks for publication in the tenth volume of *Commentarii* (1747).[49] This was Müller's second publication since returning from Siberia, the first being a reworking of his old Kalmyk piece for the *St. Petersburgischer Kalender*, 1744–6, and the last for several years to come.

An abbreviated Russian version of the history and description of Siberia was not ready for printing until 1750.[50] These delays did not trouble Müller in 1747, for within a space of a few months there occurred a series of momentous events for the Academy in general, and for Müller in particular. In July the Academy was granted a charter that carefully delineated the responsibilities of its members. In November Müller signed a new, permanent contract, and early in 1748 his proposal for a historical department was finally acted on.

The crisis of 1742–3 convinced the Russian government to regularize the Academy, and Razumovskii's appointment was part of that process. Ironically, however, the academicians were to have no role whatsoever in the creation of a new order at the Academy, the main authors of which were Schumacher and Teplov. The Regulations of the Imperial Academy of Sciences and Arts in St. Petersburg were made into law on 24 July 1747[51] and called for clear distinctions to be made between the Academy and its university and gymnasium. There were to be only ten academicians, and only they could use that title. Their duties were limited strictly to scientific work and instructing those adjuncts and students assigned specifically to them. All other students were to be taught in the university by university professors. The number of honorary academicians also could not exceed ten. Thus the research dimension of the Academy would still be dominated by foreigners who already held the posts, but room was made for teaching eventually to be the domain of Russians.

The Academy was again divided into specific classes, designated by the disciplines of astronomy, physics, physico-mathematics, and "higher" mathematics. All other forms of study, such as history, eloquence, logic, and jurisprudence – that is, the former concerns of the humanities, or third, class of the Academy – were now assigned to the university. Academicians were paid a base salary of 860 rubles, although three of them received considerably more. The nine adjuncts received only 360 rubles, and university professors 660. Accordingly, the new salary scale discriminated in effect against Russians. The overall Academy budget was doubled, to 53,000 rubles.

Schumacher's and Teplov's part in the preparation of this charter was most noticeable in its revised Chancellery: it now possessed the formal power not allotted to it in 1725. Schumacher – the *Sovetnik* (councillor), or head of the Chancellery – received a salary of 1,200 rubles, decision-making authority in the president's absence, and a staff of twenty-three persons, each of whom held a rank equivalent to his counterpart in a college (ministry) of the government. The assessor – Teplov – was listed as second in command at the Chancellery, with a salary of 600 rubles. A year later, Razumovskii added 600 rubles to Schumacher's salary because, "as a foreigner, he cannot own villages." The president's own authority was made absolute in law, probably to assure that the academics could not go over his head to the Senate.

The Chancellery now tended to act like a forceful bureaucracy. Fines were levied for those who ignored bureaucratic dicta about working hours, decorum in meetings, and teaching duties. The contempt that the scholars had long felt for Schumacher and his minions was now exacerbated into fury by their loss of autonomy and by continual interference in their everyday affairs by the Chancellery office. To add to their frustration, the tradition of late salary payments, equipment failure, and very slow typographical service remained problems that the larger bureaucracy seemed unable or unwilling to solve. Academy members were also annoyed because the Academy now was regarded officially as a branch of the government. Article 34 of the charter stated that any government department could demand the services of academicians and professors by submitting requests to the Chancellery and made it clear that this included summonses from the Admiralty, the police, and the military. The professors (the title generally used by both groups) had no recourse against the new Chancellery.

In March 1748 the Chancellery tried to have all research and teaching personnel confirmed in their new status as bureaucrats by recommending that they be assigned to places in the Table of Ranks. Five classes were proposed: captains (professors, masters of instruments, senior artists, and draughtsmen), lieutenant captains (adjuncts and translators), lieutenants (junior adjuncts and junior translators), second lieutenants (junior artists, geodesists, gymnasium teachers, and senior students), and ensigns (university students). Even though Peter the Great had ordered that professors be granted the rank of captain in 1725, it seems that this practice had not been continued after his death. Nor, it appears, did much come from this 1748 proposal. Müller several times complained in the 1750s that neither he nor most academicians had an official rank.[52]

The place that Russians were to occupy at the Academy was left ambiguous by the charter, which reflected the nationalism of the court while at the same time favouring foreigners with the most prestigious positions. Although the post of academician was still a preserve of non-Russians, the Chancellery was told "to try to select all the adjuncts from among Russians."[53] One can assume that the intention was that the Russian adjuncts eventually would move into academician/professorial positions as they became vacant. All nationalist sentiment aside, it must also have been obvious to the Senate that if the Academy became more and more Russian, it would also become less expensive – at least in terms of salaries – and more naturally subservient, because its members would be subjects of the crown.

Latin and Russian were declared the official languages of the Conference, though such an order could not realistically be enforced at the Academy itself. The great majority of the members still were German-speaking, and so Conference meetings were conducted in Latin or German until the 1770s. At the university, however, the language of instruction was Russian for all courses except Latin. The university was assigned a professoriate of six (one of whom was to be rector), and thirty students who already knew Latin and Russian. The gymnasium was to have eight teachers and twenty students. The fifty students who were selected for study in the two institutions each received annual payment of 100 rubles. Others could enrol, but would have to find their own sponsors. Significantly for Müller, the position of rector at the university was combined in the charter with the new post of historiographer.

The charter of 1747 specified two main tasks for the university: to prepare scholars for the Academy and also persons capable of fulfilling military and civil services for the state. Its professors were "not to teach languages, rather they [are] to teach Science." The main stated purpose of the gymnasium, then, was to provide the university with students fluent in Russian and Latin. In this regard, the charter proved to be overly optimistic. Although there was a surplus of students at the gymnasium in 1747 (there were forty-eight in all), and their numbers actually increased during the next decade, none was qualified to enter the university until 1753. Therefore the university, which had no students in 1747, had to recruit elsewhere. In March 1748, nineteen young men arrived from the Alexander-Nevskii Seminary in Novgorod and the Moscow Slavonic-Greek-Latin Academy – and two of them had to be sent to the gymnasium for further instruction in Latin. Thus the university had to be reorganized practically from scratch, and this onerous task fell to Müller.

On the first day of November 1747, Müller received a note signed by Razumovskii, Schumacher, and Teplov. The three men proposed that he be freed from "all other academic duties" so that he might complete the publication of his Siberian history, "without excuses or further performances." This strident directive was hardly a conciliatory move. The Chancellery and president clearly were anxious that something of consequence be shown for the enormous sum of money spent on the Kamchatka expedition. A few days later, Müller was handed a contract that obligated him to serve the university as historiographer but contained none of the usual restrictions on time, "for the president hopes that he, Müller, will remain in service for the remainder of his life." It also stated that the government would not interpret his signature as an agreement to his naturalization and that his wife and children would be free to go wherever they pleased on his death. Müller's salary was set at 1,200 rubles annually, with an extra 200 for each year since his return from Siberia. A rider to the effect that he would be penalized if he did not fulfil his duties completed the contract.[54]

Müller's response was detailed and bordered on the sarcastic. He noted that he had already served in Russia for a very long time and intended to stay, "if my service was pleasant and if I obtained a salary." Moreover, Russia needed his services more than any other country. He wondered why it was that his signature would enable his family – and himself – to leave Russia only after his death and pointed out that no matter the nature of a contract, his tenure would inevitably be determined by the sovereign, not by the Chancellery. Müller was reluctant to commit himself to one book per year on

Siberia, which was also asked of him. He claimed he had no control over the state of his health or over "other matters," by which he meant censorship and obstructionism on the part of his colleagues. Moreover, he said, such commitments make little sense, because "scientific matters are not determined merely by our wishes." As to the history of Russia, he suggested that the probability of that project being a success was related directly to the degree to which the Chancellery undertook to fulfil the conditions that he had outlined in August 1746. Müller readily agreed to act as historiographer but noted that the charter coupled that position with the post of university rector. He insisted that the task of historiographer was one for the Academy instead. He wished to be regarded as an academician and not to be forced to give time-consuming lectures at the university. Finally, he asked for more money.[55]

It would seem that Müller recognized that Schumacher and Razumovskii needed him more than he needed the position, for these were strong demands to lay before one's superiors in Russia. But Müller hedged his bets, and in a letter sent to Teplov on the same day that he replied to the contract offer he made it clear that he would sign almost anything. He told Teplov that his response was not intended as an ultimatum; rather it was a general statement for Razumovskii's consideration. Assuring Teplov that he planned to sign the contract, he added that if he was granted an increase in salary he would keep the matter secret, so as not to arouse protest among his colleagues.[56] Finally, on 10 November 1747, Müller signed a contract that contained the following stipulations:

1. Müller obligates himself to serve with the Academy of Sciences as professor in the university and for the creation of a general Russian history; for this purpose he is appointed historiographer, in consideration of which he promises in every way to observe the high interests of Her Majesty and the honour and benefit of the Academy.

2. To begin his work, to which so much expenditure has already been granted by Her Imperial Majesty, namely, the Siberian History; in which there shall be an accurate description of the geographical position of all Siberia, its religion, the languages of all its native peoples, and Siberian antiquities, and to produce it together with Professor Fischer so that it be possible to print one book of his travels each year.

3. When the Siberian History is completed, then Müller shall be employed for the creation of a history of the entire Russian Empire in the Department which shall be designated by the Academy according to a plan which shall be prepared by him at that time and approved in the Chancellery.

4. Since Müller is excused from lecturing, he shall occupy the position of

rector at the university according to instructions given when he shall be directed to assume it.

5. The salary granted to Müller by Her Imperial Majesty, with an appropriation from the Imperial Treasury, as of 24 July 1747, will be 1000 rubles per year, and retroactively to that time since he returned from Siberia he shall receive an extra 200 rubles per year, to the day of his new appointment, when that sum will then be added to his regular salary. And if Müller works on his assignment with special diligence, then the Chancellery is free to award him special increments, or rank, on the basis of his merit. But if he works to the detriment of his duties, to which he is assigned as a true subject and servant to Her Imperial Majesty, then he is subject to those penalties which are outlined according to the imperial ukaz.

6. If Müller obligates himself to this document, then he will not be obligated to remain in Russia until his death, but he shall not leave academy service.[57]

Thus the bold front conveyed in Müller's response to Razumovskii's first offer was belied by the fact that he settled for less money than he had originally been offered. Some of the other conditions had been met by the time Müller signed the contract. The first part of his Siberian history was turned over to Fischer on 9 November, and the translator began to work on it. Ten days later, Fischer was promoted to the university as a professor of history and was ordered to do the lecturing that otherwise would have been part of Müller's duties. Fischer also acted as director of the gymnasium. Although the historical department did not yet exist officially, Müller was told to supervise the organization of his and Fischer's Kamchatka materials at the university. Razumovskii had not yielded to Müller's insistence that the post of historiographer be an officer of the Academy, so he was no longer a voting member of the Conference.

Müller's transfer to the university and his acquisition of two important offices was not well received by some of his colleagues. On learning that the two posts were combined in the charter of 1747, Lomonosov assumed that Teplov was now conspiring to push the German to the forefront at the expense of Russians. He exclaimed later that if Müller had been a jurist or a poet, Teplov would have decided that the rector should also be a chief jurist or poet.[58] There may have been reason for Lomonosov to suspect Teplov's motives. Schumacher had used Müller's response of 6 November to suggest that he not be granted the title of historiographer; rather he should be awarded a contract like that given to Gmelin in 1747, which would limit his responsibilities to editing Siberian materials for publication in the *Commentarii*, and to teaching duties.[59] Schumacher's suggestion was ignored, which implies that Teplov may have been acting to spite the councillor of the Chancellery. But Lomonosov was wrong in suggesting that Teplov was trying to undermine the position of Russians at the Academy.

A historical department was set up by decree on 27 January 1748, with Müller as its director and Fischer as his assistant. But it was not the organization that Müller had proposed. The Senate also created a historical assembly of professors to act as an advisory board to the department.[60] The historical assembly included all members of the university who were deemed expert in history and the "humanities," which included poetry, "criticism," and philosophy. Thus, besides Müller and Fischer, the new assembly was joined by P.-L. Le Roy (history), Strube de Piermont (jurisprudence), Jakob von Stählin (rhetoric and poetry), Taubert (history), Trediakovskii (rhetoric), Joseph Braun (philosophy), Lomonosov, and Christian Crusius, who had been appointed professor of antiquity and historical literature in 1745 against Lomonosov's wishes and with Müller's support. Müller was naturally inclined toward Crusius (1715–67), who had studied at Leipzig under Maskov and had helped Mencke with the *Acta eruditorum*.[61] Razumovskii made Teplov the overseer of the department's financial and administrative affairs. Although the charter of 1747 (article 23) assigned to the Conference secretary the additional responsibility of "procurator," or mediator, in the frequent arguments between members, in practice this task also now fell to Teplov. His office employed two translators, Kiriak Kondratovich and Golubtsov, four students, and three copyists. Müller was given two rooms at the Academy, one of which was to house his archival material. He swore an oath of allegiance to the empress on 29 January and assumed, but rarely ever used, the name Fedor Ivanovich Miller.[62]

The historical assembly proved to be a far greater hindrance than help in the publication of Müller's Siberian history. It met on a weekly basis and was ordered to examine carefully anything published in the domain of the humanities. In short, it acted as a censorship board. Fischer checked every page of Müller's work and usually found something with which he could argue. To compound matters, in May 1748 Fischer decided to produce something of his own and offered to write a compendium, or "lexicon," of all materials on the history and geography of Siberia housed at the Academy. Müller immediately appealed to the historical assembly and then to Razumovskii, saying that a student could perform that service because all he had to do was list titles of books and documents, that he would not allow Fischer to enumerate the unpublished items in his own collection, and that according to his own contract, Fischer was supposed to be helping him with the Siberian history. Fischer countered by insisting that a student would not be qualified for such a task, that Müller had no right to keep a fellow Academy historian from his collection, that his own contract said nothing about helping Müller, and that he, as a professor, should not be subordinated to another professor. Fischer decided not to go ahead with the lexicon, but he and Müller remained very cool toward each other.[63]

Shortly afterward, Fischer and Müller had a particularly sharp exchange in the historical assembly over Müller's method in preparing the history of Siberia for publication. Fischer rather rudely suggested that Müller select and edit the great number of documents that he hoped to include verbatim in the study. Müller replied with some heat that Fischer "hopes to turn me into a literary thief" and referred to his erstwhile colleague as a "novelist" and as "Mr. Censor."[64]

Lomonosov did his best to interfere with the printing of Müller's Siberian history as well, challenging any section that he suspected of disparaging Russia's heritage. In April a special commission was organized solely to examine the Kamchatka materials independently of both Müller and Fischer and to report its findings to Trediakovskii, secretary to the historical assembly.[65] Further delays brought accusations that Müller was withholding page proofs, to which Müller responded by criticizing his translator's efforts. In fact, Golubtsov's translating was deemed unsatisfactory even by Lomonosov. Lomonosov was instrumental in having a friend, V.I. Lebedev, assigned to the task in June 1748.[66] On finishing the translation in August, Lebedev turned the manuscript over, for the second time, to Lomonosov, who noted only a few stylistic errors and recommended its publication in Russian.[67]

Now it was Teplov's turn to hold up procedures until Müller agreed to a few minor changes in the Russian suggested by Lomonosov, A. Barsov, and Popov.[68] When the first five chapters were handed over to the historical assembly for approval in June 1748, there arose a wild debate over the role played by Ermak in the conquest of Siberia during the sixteenth century. In describing Ermak's activities, Müller called him a "Räuber" (robber) and accused him of "Verbrechen" (crimes) against the native peoples. Lomonosov was outraged and insisted that "in view of his conquest of Siberia, [Ermak] should not be accused of brigandage." Stählin, Strube de Piermont, and Braun all endorsed Lomonosov in this matter. Teplov agreed with them, albeit for political rather than patriotic reasons. Fischer and Trediakovskii hedged. Their contribution to the discussion was best represented by Trediakovskii, who acknowledged that a historian must never say anything that is untrue, but, "on the other hand, seemliness and some precautions ... suggest that one should not offend readers, and especially Russians, by calling Ermak dishonest."[69]

Lomonosov, who was not yet well versed in Russian historical literature, added: "It is not known whether Ermak conquered Siberia for himself or for the All-Russian autocracy; however, it is true that he turned it over to the All-Russian monarch ... [If the unfavourable items] cannot be changed, then it is better to exclude everything." He said again that Ermak must not be accused of "brigandage." Only Crusius supported Müller. Caught between the Russian patriots and the politically insecure historians, Müller decided to follow Lomonosov's suggestion by omitting most of his description of Ermak's activities in Siberia. "In all truth," Müller said, "it is not possible to call him good."[70]

Thus, when the first five chapters (volume I) of his *Description of the Siberian Kingdom* (*Opisanie Sibirskago Tsarstva*) appeared in print in 1750, it was a much-truncated version of Müller's original manuscript. Even his foreword was eliminated at the request of Schumacher, who told Teplov that "it is intended more to cover him [Müller] with glory than to bring honour to the president and to the Academy. He even makes it sound as if he was the originator of the Kamchatka academic expedition himself." Two chronicles that Müller hoped to include in the book were also removed by Schumacher, who said that too much in them was "false, fables, miraculous, and about church matters."[71] In July 1750 Müller was ordered to submit all further parts of the Siberian history in German to the Chancellery, which would then take full charge of its translation into Russian.[72] This was a blow to Müller. He had written in his introduction that a translator must think in the same manner as the author if he is to do justice to the work.

The second volume was ready in September 1750 but met with still more resistance from the historical assembly. Even Lomonosov became so fed up with the squabbling over the history of Siberia that he asked for and was granted release from the historical assembly in September 1751. He asserted that he wished both to avoid Müller's "usual annoying speeches" and to return to his own scientific pursuits. But Lomonosov agreed to read Müller's manuscripts in the quiet of his home. In October 1751 he submitted a report to the Chancellery on the sixth and seventh chapters of the Siberian history. This time he commented on several relatively minor, but "unseemly," historical interpretations and said that many of Müller's minutiae were "worthless." Lomonosov suggested, among other things, that Müller should give more credit to the Orthodox Church for its missionary work in Siberia. He also offered patriotic terminology to use when describing sixteenth- and seventeenth-century Russian autocracy. Müller actually agreed to a number of slight alterations, and in December the Conference ordered that sample copies of chapters 6–11 be printed. Chapters 12–22 were approved for similar sample printings in 1752. But no regular issue of the second volume was published for general circulation.[73] Lomonosov's report on the second volume of Müller's Siberian history revealed that the Russian had read a lot of history since the episode of Krekshin's genealogy. Indeed, one important by-product of Lomonosov's role as referee of Müller's historical work was a plan for a Russian history of his own, first formulated in 1751.[74]

In recalling these hectic sessions fourteen years later, Lomonosov blamed the slow appearance of the Siberian history on Müller's own "stubbornness."[75] Trediakovskii went so far as to lay the blame for most of the "misfortunes" suffered by the St Petersburg academicians on Müller's "insolence and pride."[76] Although neither Trediakovskii nor Lomonosov can be regarded as impartial witnesses, their recollections of Müller's intransigence have a ring of truth to them. In fact, Müller was beset from all sides during the years 1748–50. He played a central role in a series of minor arguments and major crises that together very nearly ended his career in Russia. Surrounded by political and academic foes, only his dogged stubbornness and sense of his own correctness enabled him to survive.

Although the history and description of Siberia seemed not to be appreciated by his colleagues in the historical assembly, Müller's efforts represented a breakthrough in Russian historiography generally, and in Russian studies of Siberia specifically. In fact, the published volume of 1750 marked the initial attempt to undertake a comprehensive study of Siberia. The first of its five chapters included a summary of all the historical and ethnographical material on the pre-conquest era then available to Müller. Besides the information that he discovered and catalogued himself, Müller outlined the contents of books printed by non-Russian visitors to the east: Abú-al-Gazi (Leyden, 1726), khan of Khiva, who spent nearly ten years in Persia, 1630–9, and wrote genealogies of the Turkmen and Uzbeks; Peter van der Aa (Leyden, 1707), who collected materials on the thirteenth century; Barthelemy d'Herbelot's Bibliothèque orientale, on eastern peoples (Paris, 1697); Antoine Gaubil on Mongolian dynasties (Paris, 1739); Johann Bernard Müller on the Ostiaks (Berlin, 1723); Marcus Paulus Venetus's travels east from Armenia (Amsterdam, 1664); and Strahlenberg.

The second chapter of Müller's book described Siberian history from its "discovery" by Russians to its "conquest" by Ermak and his cossacks. Here Müller employed Russian sources almost exclusively, with some occasional references to Baron Sigismund von Herberstein's *Rerum Moscovitarum commentarii* (sixteenth century) and to Witsen. The *Kniga stepennaia*, the *Razriadnye knigi*, several chronicles, and a quantity of official documents were featured regularly. In the final three chapters, Müller used more official sources to document the organization and administration of the country and its colonization. The volume was therefore fully in the tradition of Maskov, L.A. Muratori, and others of the great document collectors among late-seventeenth- and early-eighteenth-century European historians.

At the same time that Müller was struggling to have his own Siberian history appear in print, he was active in a discussion over the fate of the manuscript on Russian history prepared by V.N. Tatishchev. Tatishchev's interest in Siberia led him to collect and study sources on Russian history. While administering the Urals factory system from Ekaterinburg between 1734 and 1737, Tatishchev had a local teacher translate works by Polish historians on Russia's past. The questionnaire that Müller found in 1740 had been sent to officials throughout Siberia by Tatishchev only six years earlier and had provided him with enough information to compile a report, "General Geographical Description of All Siberia," in 1737.[77] Another questionnaire of over 100 queries served as the basis for a *Russian Geographical Lexicon*, which Tatishchev finished in 1746, but which was not published until 1793. With this information in hand, Tatishchev completed work on the Russian history that he had begun several years earlier.[78]

In 1737, Tatishchev's work in Ekaterinburg was halted so that he could take charge of a geographical expedition to Orenburg. There he helped quell Bashkir revolts by relying on diplomacy rather than on coercion and simultaneously completed the charting of several important rivers. On hearing of Tatishchev's assignment, Korff wrote to him from the Academy and asked him to continue his work on history and genealogy. Tatishchev uncovered a Novgorodian chronicle which he forwarded to the Academy, along with several translations and manuscripts on the Tatars and Scythians. When Müller's work on the Kalmyks appeared in an issue of the *Sammlung* edited by Bayer, Tatishchev read it with care and commented somewhat unfavourably on it.[79] His interests were varied, and his path kept crossing that of the younger Müller.

Back in St Petersburg by 1739, Tatishchev proposed that the Academy create a geography and atlas of the empire and was partially responsible for the establishment of the Academy's geography department in 1739.[80] Euler was its first director. But Tatishchev's efforts to have his own history of Russia published after he submitted it to the Academy in 1740 were stalled when Schumacher was replaced by Nartov. Nothing had been done about the manuscript by 1742, when Tatishchev was reassigned to a newly formed Kalmyk commission and sent to Saratov to help restore peace in that region. There his historical work had to be set aside until 1745. In that year his enemies in St Petersburg forced his retirement from service by having him charged with embezzlement of state funds. Tatishchev settled on his estate at Boldino near Moscow in April 1746 and turned again to historical writing.

In the years between 1745 and his death in 1750, Tatishchev was the most enterprising historian in Russia, even in the light of Müller's activities. Tatishchev's correspondence with other writers within Russia was filled with questions and comments about Russian history and geography. The Academy assigned him five assistants to help him revise his history, and he kept them busy translating and collating documents and tracts by the hundreds. In January 1749 he asked Schumacher to acquire the services of Lomonosov to prepare an author's dedication to Grand Prince Peter Fedorovich. Lomonosov replied that he approved the work without any reservations and that "nothing in it needs corrections."[81] He completed the dedication in two weeks. If Lomonosov had not yet read enough history to disagree with Tatishchev, his views on the purpose of history were already fixed. He took the opportunity to state that history should glorify the deeds of ancient Russians and their rulers.[82] Tatishchev agreed. Lomonosov might not have been so happy to dedicate the work had he known or understood then the significance of a later Tatishchev request to Teplov – for Russian translations of ten of Bayer's articles from the *Commentarii*, including copies of the maps that the German scholar had drawn up of tenth-century Rus' and of ancient Scythia. Much of this information was included verbatim in Tatishchev's history.[83]

Tatishchev also showed a keen interest in Müller's progress. Schumacher sent him a copy of Müller's history of Siberia for evaluation and was probably disappointed when Tatishchev replied in March 1749: "I have read with great pleasure the work on the foundations of Siberian history. This is the first Russian regional history, and there is much that is praiseworthy in it." Müller was shown Tatishchev's remarks and responded with unusual moderation to the minor criticisms and specific suggestions in it.[84] Müller urged the Academy to assure the preservation of Tatishchev's large collection of over one thousand books and documents, either by bringing them to St Petersburg or by having them copied. Tatishchev was old and unwell, and Müller was afraid that the documentation would be lost if its owner died suddenly. The collection included many items that Müller had not seen during his own tour of Siberia, but were noted in Tatishchev's manuscripts. As usual, however, Schumacher and Teplov failed to act on Müller's pleas, and shortly after Tatishchev's death in July 1750, a large part of his library was destroyed by fire.[85]

As if these problems were not enough, Müller also found himself caught in the middle of a minor crisis sometimes referred to as the Gmelin affair. Gmelin had signed a four-year contract with the Academy in July 1747, which included permission to travel to Germany for one year on half-salary. To assure that he would return, Müller and Lomonosov, Gmelin's best friends in the Russian capital, underwrote his contract.[86] When Gmelin gave the impression to several friends of the Academy in Europe, notably Euler and Krafft, that he did not plan to return to Russia, the Chancellery was furious and made it clear to him that such a decision would "ruin those people, namely Professor Müller and Professor Lomonosov," who had guaranteed him. Nevertheless, Gmelin did not honour his contract and instead took a post at Tübingen, where he had begun his academic career in 1723. Thus Müller and Lomonosov were deprived of parts of their income for a short while. Only by 1750, and after careful mediation by Euler, was a compromise reached. Gmelin pledged to reimburse the Academy for funds granted him in 1747–8. He also agreed to have his most famous work, *Flora sibirica sive historia plantarum Sibiriae*, printed in St Petersburg. The first volume had appeared there already in 1747, and Gmelin was promised a stipend of 200 rubles for each subsequent volume.[87]

Although the Academy was satisfied, the affair caused Müller considerable hardship. Gmelin had tried to explain away his own unreliability by accusing Müller of giving bad advice, in that way corroborating suspicions the Chancellery already had of him. It certainly was not hard to persuade Schumacher, who wrote to Euler in April 1750 that "the intriguers [Gmelin and Müller] are hated by God and this world" and that Müller was the real culprit.[88] Müller was still lobbying for payment of items that he had purchased for the *Kunstkamera* in 1743–4, whereas Gmelin was now to be reimbursed for all his expenditures. The final stage in the continuing saga of Müller's struggle for compensation started in 12 January 1748 when he submitted a long list of purchases, including coins, books, manuscripts, idols, Chinese calendars, and a Mongolian book on astrology. This was, in fact, the same list for which he had requested funds vainly in 1744. Müller finally was issued 186 rubles in payment for these items in February 1748. But his financial trials were not yet over.

Little more than a month later he posted a third application for over 100 rubles that he alleged were still due him in unpaid salaries for the middle third of 1743. There is no published record of him ever having obtained this amount. In 1749 Teplov decided that both Müller and Lomonosov should be compensated for monies taken from them to pay for Gmelin's lack of loyalty (630 rubles between them).[89]

While such monetary atonement eased Müller's financial situation, it did nothing to alleviate his very heavy work load. Because he took his position seriously, Müller's duties as rector of the Academy's university proved to be quite onerous. He oversaw examinations, interviewed student candidates, arranged for student housing, organized and recommended curricula, volunteered to be responsible for a student residence (this proposal was rejected by the Chancellery), approved lectures, assigned textbooks, and watched over his teaching faculty to see that they performed their duties properly. He also examined students at the nearby Land Cadet Corps in Latin, history, and geography.[90] In addition Müller took the time to write a chronological table of general history, mainly a list of famous events and people, with extracts from the "best authors," to use as a guideline for lectures. But the Chancellery refused to print it, interpreting the proposal as an attempt by Müller to stay out of lecturing himself. "Besides that," wrote Schumacher in the daily Chancellery journal, "Müller already complains that he has so much to do that he does not know where to begin. Because of that it is impossible for him to do anything well, and he does not remember other things."[91]

With the assistance of Trediakovskii, Müller worked out a detailed prospectus of the duties and responsibilities of both lecturers and students at the university and submitted it to the Chancellery in September 1748. This effort brought him once more into conflict with Lomonosov, who tried to undermine the rector's authority at the university by recommending that an overseer be placed in charge of academic planning. Pointing out that Müller could not expect to be treated differently than any other member of the historical assembly, Lomonosov insisted, ineffectively, that the university should be in the charge of someone who was independent of his colleagues at the Academy.[92]

The fact that Müller held on to positions of responsibility while he incurred such hostility from both colleagues and Academy administrators attests to the equivocal position of the Academy during the first decade of Elizabeth's reign. Dominated by foreigners at a time when the court was wary of espionage, the Academy Chancellery recognized the institution's vulnerability. But Schumacher was aware, too, that the Academy needed a good press abroad if it were to attract skilled scholars to its service. At the same time it must fulfil Russia's needs in order to continue receiving support from the Senate. Ironically, Müller had much to contribute to both requirements, and so Schumacher was more concerned with channelling Müller's energies than he was with replacing him. By 1749, however, the equivocality of the Academy's goals created an atmosphere so charged with mistrust that Müller's very career was imperiled.

The Chancellery's angry and immediate response to the Gmelin incident was provoked partly by apprehension that Gmelin might speak badly of Russia in Europe. J.N. de l'Isle was partially responsible for this anxiety, because he had left St Petersburg in 1747 a very bitter enemy of Schumacher. Rumours that de l'Isle planned an exposé of the Academy reached Chancellery ears in 1748, and Razumovskii issued orders prohibiting anyone in Academy service from corresponding with him. The fact that diplomatic relations between France and Russia were at a particularly low ebb at the time aggravated the situation. De l'Isle was taken off the list of honorary, pensioned members.[93] As was his wont, Schumacher readily assumed that Müller was de l'Isle's agent in the Russian capital.

On 18 October 1748, the Chancellery accused Müller of conspiring with de l'Isle to "abuse the honour of the Academy." Müller's private papers were confiscated, and he was confined to his quarters and told not to contact the president until the matter was resolved. Lomonosov and Trediakovskii were assigned the chore of examining the papers. It seems that de l'Isle had sent Müller a letter from Riga in an attempt to enlist his aid in a campaign of slander against the Academy administration. The letter, which somehow got into the hands of the Chancellery, referred to papers on the history of the Academy that he intended to return to Müller. Although Schumacher took this to mean that Müller had sent proscribed information to the Frenchman, Müller insisted that he had not even replied to de l'Isle and had never sent him Academy-owned materials. A commission was established to investigate the matter, and within a month Müller was cleared of any misbehaviour. But the final report, filed by Lomonosov, left room for doubt in the de l'Isle affair and depicted Müller as a troublemaker within the Academy.[94] Once again, Müller's recently acquired prestige at the Academy was seriously undermined.

CHAPTER FIVE

Debate on "Russian" Origins 1749–55

You, famous author, have dishonoured our nation.

N.I. Popov to Müller, 1749

In March 1749 Müller and Lomonosov's stars had another ill-fated crossing when Razumovskii invited them and Winsheim to read papers at a public meeting of the Academy, scheduled for 6 September. Their selection was by no means a sign of a new goodwill toward Müller and Lomonosov on the part of the Chancellery. It was instead an acknowledgment of their abilities as the Academy's best speakers. Schumacher actually bemoaned the fact that there were no better orators from which to choose. Müller, he said to Teplov, "articulates well enough in Russian, has a loud voice, and a presence of mind which is close to insolence."[1] This comment is the earliest corroboration we have in print for Müller's own statement that he perfected his Russian soon after his return from Siberia. Schumacher also told Teplov that he wished that there were others besides Müller and Lomonosov capable of delivering the speeches, but that "orators must have courage and even a certain insolence in order to have the strength to withstand merciless mockery." Perhaps secretly he hoped that they would fail.

Lomonosov decided to deliver the customary eulogy to Elizabeth, whose nameday was 5 September. Winsheim planned to speak on astronomy, and Müller rather injudiciously chose to lecture on the origins of the Russian nation and its name. Each speaker was expected to submit copies of his paper to the Chancellery for its approval, but as late as 3 August Schumacher complained that only Müller had not delivered anything to him.[2] Twenty days later Müller delivered a trial reading of his dissertation, "Origines gentis et nominis Russorum," to a combined meeting of the Academy Conference and the historical assembly. Lomonosov was present. The meeting decided to print the dissertation in both Latin and Russian, after minor changes were made, even though it contained three contentious assumptions.[3] First, using the Nestor version of the *Primary Chronicle* as his main source, Müller said that the Slavs could not have arrived on the Dnieper from the Danube region before the era of Justinian, that is, before the sixth century AD. Second, he identified the Varangians with "Norman-Scandinavians"; and third, he equated them with the Russes, thereby suggesting that "Norman-Scandinavians" provided the Slavs with their first "Russian" rulers.[4]

In the first week of September the president abruptly postponed the public performance until 25 November on the grounds that it might then coincide with the anniversary of Elizabeth's accession to the throne. But the real reason for the delay seems to have been a series of actions taken by Krekshin and Schumacher, who contacted Teplov and Razumovskii (both then in Moscow) and warned them of some dire political dangers implicit in Müller's paper. The Chancellery was then ordered to send copies of the dissertation to Fischer, Strube de Piermont, Trediakovskii, N.I. Popov, Krasheninnikov, and Lomonosov. These men were asked to decide whether there was anything in it that might be deemed "prejudicial" to Russia. Each reviewer had reservations about Müller's presentation, but Lomonosov, Popov, and Krasheninnikov were especially harsh in their criticisms.[5]

In his first response (16 September), Lomonosov pointed to several of Müller's judgments which he said were "unseemly, ridiculous, and irritating to Russian listeners" and alleged that the German had failed even to read the Russian chronicles thoroughly. Müller rejected the idea that the name Moscow might have been derived from Mosoch and that the Russians took their name from Ezekiel's "Rosh"; he insisted that the ancient Slavs arrived in their present homelands relatively recently. These premises met with Lomonosov's disapproval. More strident, however, was Lomonosov's charge that Müller deliberately insulted Russians by calling the Varangians Normans.

According to Lomonosov, the Varangians were descendants of Slavic Roxolani, spoke a Slavic language, and came not from Scandinavia but from the shores of the Baltic somewhere in the area of Vistula. He was repeating here an assumption held by some eastern Slavic chroniclers since the sixteenth century and based on a descriptive geography of the Mediterranean world compiled by Strabo (64 BC–AD 18), who had identified the Rus' with the Roxolani. Lomonosov also cited the *Sinopsis*, Pliny, and the Dutch humanist Christoph Kepper (Cellarius) in support of his position. In opposition to the Roxolani theory, which he said could not be proved, Müller offered evidence from Jordanes's sixth-century history of the Goths (*De origine actibusque Getarum*), where it was said that the Roxolani were Goths.[7] This argument was the first public exchange in a "Normanist controversy" that goes on in one form or another to this day. On 27 September, the Chancellery ordered Müller's dissertation withdrawn from circulation pending a final decision on its merits.

The subsequent battle was long, dreary, and very bitterly waged – with name-calling and Müller often emphasizing his points by banging his walking-stick on the Conference table. Lomonosov filed a second, more detailed report with the Chancellery in late October. In his introduction, he insisted that he was conducting the investigation "neither out of bias, nor as a result of personal feelings, but as a true son of the fatherland."[8] Müller, who was not likely to be encouraged by Lomonosov's professions of impartiality, submitted a thorough rejoinder after a delay of nearly three months. Discussion of the matter had been postponed in December because Müller said that he was ill, but resumed with a vengeance at the end of January.

Schumacher enjoyed the spectacle immensely and kept Teplov informed of the Conference's proceedings. In a letter of 19 October it was apparent that his own objections to the dissertation had nothing to do with ruffled patriotic sentiment. Like Teplov he was motivated by political concerns, with the additional element of personal malice:

The professors and adjuncts are now working over Mr Müller's dissertation and Mondays begin with a battle. I foresee that this is going to be very difficult because everyone wishes to submit an opinion. I do not know whether you remember, dear sir, that I had the honour to write you about Mr Müller's dissertation. I remember that I maintained that it was written with great scholarship but with little wisdom. This has been proven correct. Mr Bayer, who wrote about this subject in the *Commentarii*, offered his opinions with great prudence ... but Mr Müller, so the Russian professors believe, attempted only to humiliate the Russian nation. And they are right. If I were in the place of the author, then I would have given quite a different twist to my speech. I would expound it in this manner: the origins of peoples are completely unknown. Everything originates from God, and then from heroes. Since I would be speaking about the Russian people, then I would give you, kind sir, the opinions of different writers, then express my own opinion, based on evidence which is – at least in my opinion – quite convincing ... I would also, basing it on evidence preserved by Swedish writers, acknowledge that the Russian state had its beginnings from Scandinavian people. But the Russian people did not come from there, they were already a brave people, distinguished by heroic accomplishments ... Here he could speak of the merits of princes, great princes, tsars, emperors, and empresses. But he wishes to show off his knowledge! Habeat sibi – it is good that he pays for his vanity![9]

Schumacher already had complained to Teplov about Müller's alleged boastfulness, writing in July that "vanity and self-confidence" undermined his judgment and that Müller was surrounded by "parasites" who flattered him and "turn his head."[10]

The long formal investigation was opened by a special committee chaired in absentia by Teplov, who charged that "throughout the entire speech Müller has not shown one event to the honour of the Russian people, but has maintained only what can contribute to their discredit, and especially how they were constantly defeated in war." By the end of October Schumacher was able to write to Teplov: "Professor Müller now sees that he blundered with his dissertation *De origine gentis russicae*, because Popov alone has checkmated him, showing him such serious mistakes that he cannot possibly correct them. They told me that when Popov said to Müller: 'Tu, clarissime autor, nostram gentem infamia afficis [You, famous author, dishonour our nation],' he nearly fainted (tombait presque en defaillance!). Now he claims to be ill and no longer wishes to come into the Conference."[11]

Müller grumbled to Razumovskii that only his enemies had been asked to judge the paper. But not all Russian scholars were upset by the dissertation. Trediakovskii was quite restrained, attributing Müller's "incorrect reasoning" to the fact that so little evidence was available on such questions as the origins of the Russian people and their name. He had reservations about the dissertation and recommended several minor changes, but concluded that Müller had not besmirched Russia's honour. Trediakovskii thought that a revised version should be accepted for publication and even ridiculed Lomonosov's ability to judge the piece.[12] Another Russian, Tatishchev, found little to fault in Müller's scholarship and informed Schumacher that although his opinions differed from Müller's, he did "not wish to condemn" the speech. In May 1750, Tatishchev wrote to Schumacher to say that he was going to ask "Professor Müller, a very well qualified man," to examine and evaluate his own manuscript on Russian history.[13] But Tatishchev's views were not taken into consideration, because the Chancellery long since had made up its mind about Müller's discourse.

To a certain extent the length of the proceedings was Müller's own doing, for it was he who insisted that the matter be turned over to the Academy Conference after he found Teplov's relatively minor suggestions for change unacceptable. After twenty-nine special meetings – from 23 October 1749 to 8 March 1750 – Lomonosov was asked to prepare the Conference's final verdict.[14] Completed by early June, this report showed that Lomonosov (and presumably the Conference) were still most irate over Müller's assertion that the early Russian "princes," that is, the Varangians, were "Gothic," "Norman-Scandinavian," or Swedish. This version of the origins of the Russian dynasty, coupled with Müller's statements that the Varangians "had already subjected Russia to their authority many years before Riurik" and that the Slavs did not have princes of their own (Gostomysl' was an "elder"),[15] could not be accepted gracefully by subjects of a state that warred with Sweden regularly and had so recently been dominated by Baltic Germans at Empress Anna's court (*Bironovshchina*). In fact, Russia had fought Sweden between 1741 and 1743, only a few years before Müller chose to enlighten Russians on the Scandinavian origins of both their state and their name.

Krasheninnikov, Trediakovskii, and Popov all agreed with Lomonosov's insistence that the Slavs had settled in their present habitat long before Justinian's time and that the Varangians were Slavs. But their reasons for such assertions differed. In contrast to Lomonosov's theory that the Slavs were connected with Roxolani, who were alledgedly Slavic and moved from the Dnieper / Don region to mingle with Baltic peoples, Popov said that Riurik was of the "Varangian-Rosses" who lived in Kherson, also on the Dnieper, and were a "Russian people." Trediakovskii used philological techniques to demonstrate – if only to his own satisfaction – that the name Varangian was derived from an old Slavic verb, *variaiu*,[16] which meant "to come before." For his part, Müller did not think that the ethnic origin of the Varangians was an especially important question. The word "Rossiane," he said, had arrived in Russia too recently to be used as evidence that the early Russes and Roxolani were the same people: "One does not see it in ancient books or written memorials," he said in his defence against Lomonosov.[17] One alternative that Müller was willing to consider was Tatishchev's statement that the Varangians were Finns, but that was hardly an improvement insofar as the Russians were concerned. He also said that the name Rus' may have come from the Finnish word for Swedes, *ruotsi*.[18]

Lomonosov was angry about Müller's apparent scorn for the old tale that the Slavs derived their name etymologically from the word for glory. Müller's argument was a little perverse: "Your ancestors, honoured listeners, were named *Slaviane* from their glorious deeds in ancient times," he said, but added that "they lived long ago on the Danube River, where, according to the Russian chroniclers, they were expelled by the Volokhi, that is, the Romans."[19] Müller went on to tell how the Slaviane were driven to the Dnieper and founded Kiev but then were forced once again to move. This time they travelled north, reached Lake Ilmen, and built the city of Novgorod. Lomonosov charged several times that this interpretation by Müller purposely made a mockery of the Slavs' ancient military heroics. He insisted that the Slavs had moved north only to protect their "love for freedom" from the Roman yoke.[20] Müller fired back that his "opponent" wanted him to write "only about glories ... But does he not know the difference between a historical dissertation and a panegyrical speech?" He asked rhetorically whether "Lomonosov, Krasheninnikov, Popov, or Krekshin can charge me with error when I wrote about the ejection of the Slavs from the shores of the Danube? Which tribes were defeated more convincingly?"[21]

These were fighting words, but Müller tried none the less to couch his responses within the context of the historical sciences. He pointed out that all nations began their histories with periods of terrible violence, murders, and other villainous deeds. Such eras should not be hidden by a historian, for they were just as much a part of one's national heritage as were glorious deeds. To strengthen his appeal to scientific integrity, Müller cited other historians of nations: Thucydides (Greeks), Livy (Romans), Muratori (Italians), Mariana (Spaniards), Burnet (English), Thuanus (French), and Maskov (Germans).[22] In doing so, Müller revealed clearly what he saw as history's function. He was dedicated to the study of documents and professed to believe with a passion that rivalled Lomonosov's patriotism that a historian's task was to discover the truth. His references to Thuanus (Jacques de Thou, 1556–1617), whose history described the civil and religious wars in sixteenth-century France, and to Bishop Burnet's (1643–1715) work on the Reformation in England were interesting in that both writers were relatively moderate in their judgments during an age of political and religious partisanship. Burnet wrote on behalf of the Anglican cause but was also one of the first wide-ranging political historians. Both saw the hand of God as a force in history, as did Müller in an equally fatalistic manner. Such a providential viewpoint was also a deterrent against time-consuming analysis and narrative.

Müller's more contemporary models among historical writers, however, were those indefatigable antiquarians who prepared the monumental books of reference from which later historians could draw information for their narrative histories. Lodovic Antonio Muratori (1672–1750) was the author of twenty-five folio volumes of *Rerum italicarum scriptores* (1723–50), an exhaustive collection of documents on Italian history. Johann Jakob Maskov was the erudite antiquarian at Leipzig who was already famous as a historian of medieval Germany when Müller studied there. Maskov and Muratori were products of a tradition that went back to the Bollandist Fathers, a society of Jesuit scholars who in the seventeenth century began to subject the medieval *Acta Sanctorum* (*Lives of the Saints*) to historical criticism. They collected sources, put them in order, and carefully authenticated them. Other religious orders had their scholarly circles as well, among them the French Maurists (Benedictines), whose most famous historical scholar was Jean Mabillon. Müller spoke very highly of Mabillon, author of *De re diplomatica libri VI* (1681), which some see as the founding work of diplomatics and palaeography. Mabillon and others proclaimed the importance of gathering chronicles, biographies of saints, and letters and documents of kings and ecclesiastics and verifying them by collating their style and language to the known characteristics of the age in which they were supposed to have been written. Müller's dissertation of 1749 showed that the previous eighteen years of rather eclectic historical study had brought him – at the age of forty-five – around to where he began in 1731. He had become and was to remain a consummate, and increasingly skilful, antiquarian. In the 1760s, he still awarded his highest praise to the great collectors, among them Gelarius Dobner, whose *Monumenta historica Bohemiae* began to appear in 1764.[23]

Although he applied scientific arguments wherever possible, for example, when he employed philological methods to discard as an "illusion" the idea that the name "Russian" might have come from a word for "dispersed," Müller also knew that there were limits to the kind of conclusions one might draw publicly in Russia. After Lomonosov railed at him for accepting Bayer's denial that St Andrew could have introduced Christianity to Russia, Müller replied: "Bayer did not write or publish anything not approved by the Reverend Feofan. Do you think that he [Prokopovich] would not have apprised the author of anything deemed unlawful by the Church authorities?"[24]

There was little unanimity among Müller's opponents on many parts of the dissertation, but his statement that "Nestor testified clearly that the name of the Russes came to Russia with the Varangians" was unacceptable to each of his accusers. They were also all irate over his contention that the "Varangian princes Riurik and his brothers had power over the Novgorodians not because of an invitation, but because of the force of arms."[25] Lomonosov pointed out that his own ideas were central ones to the *Sinopsis* and recommended that the Academy now move to adopt that work as the official account of medieval Russian history. In the closing short report of 21 June 1750, Lomonosov stressed also the political dangers of an approach such as Müller's, implying that it might forever turn the Russian public against the Academy: "In a public meeting there should be nothing said that could be an affront to a Russian audience which might produce grumblings and hatred against the Academy. But I judge that they, on hearing this dissertation of their new origins, founded on guesses, their naming by the Finns, the contempt for their ancient history, and the new information about the constant defeats, enslavements and conquests by the Swedes over the Russians, they will certainly and rightly be dissatisfied not only with Mr. Müller but with the entire Academy and its directors."[26]

Müller's appeal to the dignity and inviolability of science fell on deaf ears at the Academy Conference and Chancellery. He foretold this himself unwittingly in a furious exchange over Riurik's place of origin: "My opponent [Lomonosov] is maliciously silent about the fact that my account of this is in the dissertation ... He assumes that only his criticism will be read, but my dissertation, which denies the latest incorrect criticism from him and his allies, cannot remain unknown."[27] Müller must have known by this time that he was fighting a losing battle, but he and his opponents alike would probably have been astounded to learn that the *Origines gentis et nominis Russorum* and especially its Russian translation would remain to this day one of the least-studied documents of eighteenth-century Russian historiography and science, while Lomonosov's attack on it became a household word in the history of Russia's historical and cultural heritage.

In September all existing copies of Müller's dissertation were ordered to be destroyed.[28] He was relieved of his post as rector of the university and ordered to lecture there daily on "universal history with chronology, European history and political geography."[29] Russian history was not taught at the university. In October Müller was demoted to adjunct and had his salary cut by nearly two-thirds.[30] He retained the position of historiographer and once again was ordered to expend his energies only on the Siberian history. Müller tried to argue that his contract had freed him from lecturing but was told that because he had ceased being rector, and because he had not published a book on Siberian history annually, the contract was no longer in effect. Aside from the convoluted logic this decision represented, it confirmed the reservations Müller himself had expressed about the contract in 1747. He was also prevented from working on state papers, including those of Prince Alexander Menshikov, Peter I's favourite, who had been arrested on Peter II's orders and exiled to Siberia, that Müller and Strube de Piermont had been preparing for publication.[31]

The charges against Müller were fully outlined in a lengthy evaluation presented to the Conference by Schumacher on 8 October 1750. It was dated 6 October and signed by Razumovskii. The Conference meeting was unusually well attended. Schumacher had not taken part in a meeting since August 1749, and Teplov's participation was the first in nine months. Razumovskii's report raised the question of Müller's relationship with de l'Isle once again. Müller was also reproached for "feigning illness" so as to avoid going to Kamchatka and of malingering in his obligation to finish the history of Siberia. Razumovskii accused Müller of purposely wasting his colleagues' time with his "prejudicial" dissertation of 1749, of falsely charging his colleagues with collusion, and of "abusing" Teplov by calling him a "liar." According to the president, Schumacher also had been a victim of Müller's vilification, and both members of the Chancellery had apologies coming to them.[32] Seemingly fully vindicated, Schumacher wrote to Euler joyfully in December 1750: "Mr. Müller is incorrigible. I thank God that I now have him off my neck."[33] As we have seen, Lomonosov was persuaded by this affair to write his own history of Russia.

But the whirlwind into which his impolitic dissertation had cast him seemed to leave Müller relatively unruffled. He complained vehemently about the daily lectures long after he lost the argument about his contract, arguing instead that his health would not stand up to such rigorous activity, that he had not lectured regularly for nearly eighteen years, and that the lectures would prevent him from working on the Siberian history.[34]

In August 1759, new university regulations, which called for strict control over lecture content, were issued. Insofar as history was concerned, its "professor" was ordered to "conduct the teaching of civil history and political geography cautiously, and in accordance with local religion and civil laws." All lectures had to be submitted to the state chancellery. All subjects were to be treated in a similar manner, so that the university and its gymnasium were much more strictly supervised than the Academy itself. This law was a reflection both of the spirit of the times and of Russian tradition and so is unlikely to have been a product of the current Müller affair. At any rate, Müller had his own way of dealing with the matter.

Although his pleas were ignored, Müller showed that he understood the situation at the Academy much better than anyone else, for he solved his problem simply by not lecturing. Krasheninnikov, who replaced him as rector (with Moderach as an assistant), reported in

October and then again in November that all professors but Müller were performing their duties. Müller had not yet shown up in a lecture hall.[35] Such delaying tactics seemed to work well. On 21 February 1751, Razumovskii demonstrated the whimsical nature of Academy-Senate-court relations with this statement:

Since the adjunct Müller, according to his own admission which he made in a petition to me in his own hand dated 21 February, feels himself to be deserving of that punishment which he brought upon himself, therefore in the hope of his usefulness to the Academy and in an expectation of many accomplishments from him for which not a few expenses have already been provided by her Imperial Majesty, his former rank and professional duties are returned to him, and a salary of one thousand rubles per year will be paid him, as of 21 February; and he is to be freed from all duties other than his work on the history of Siberia, and as soon as it is written by him in the German language, it will be turned over to the Chancellery for translating into Russian.[36]

One of the reasons for this remarkable turnabout in Müller's fortunes was the appearance in early 1751 of the first parts of Gmelin's memoir of his decade in Siberia. Although the Senate's instructions to the Academy in 1732 had included the stipulation that no one was to publish information about the expedition without special permission, at the risk of a heavy fine, Gmelin's work was printed in Göttingen with no consulation whatsoever with the Russians. Schumacher and Teplov were furious about Gmelin's unfavourable comments on the Chancellery's role in the Kamchatka expedition. The Russian government was embarrassed by his vivid descriptions of the drunkenness, harsh living conditions, and official brutality that were part of Siberian life.[37] Gmelin called Peter the Great's treatment of the population of Tara, on the Irtysh, "unreasonably brutal" and blamed "immorality" and syphilis for the fact that "so many people were without noses."[38] He also made derogatory remarks about Ermak's part in the conquest of Siberia, which may have given Müller some private satisfaction, and noted Chuvash and Tatar resentment of Russian occupation.[39] Nevertheless, Müller wondered aloud if he and Gmelin had really been on the same expedition.

The Academy was jolted again the following year. In September 1752 J.N. de l'Isle published in Paris a book with maps and descriptions of the North Pacific that contradicted earlier charts printed by the Russian Academy and awarded himself and de la Croyère credit for discoveries that were not theirs. He went so far as to say that Bering had not reached American shores and insisted that

A.I. Chirikov and de la Croyère were the ones who accomplished that feat.[40] Müller was now called on to act as the Academy's chief defender against Gmelin the memoirist and against de l'isle the map-maker.

To counter Gmelin, Müller suggested in 1752 that Fischer write a single volume on Siberia and its peoples, while Müller undertook a chronicle of his own Siberian travels.[41] Even though Razumovskii was convinced that this was another Müller ploy to procrastinate on the Siberian history ("he begins a great deal and completes nothing"), he agreed reluctantly to the plan. Fischer's book, based mainly on Müller's information, was completed by 1757 but not printed for another decade.[42] In order to refute de l'isle, Müller was allowed to resurrect his old charts, which the Academy once had ignored, work up new ones, and prepare a detailed response for a European audience. In a letter to Müller dated 13 March 1752, Razumovskii insisted that this last task be done "immediately and secretly" and ordered the Chancellery to give Müller the log books of Bering's ship, the *St. Peter*. Müller was ordered to demonstrate "all of Mr. de l'Isle's dishonesties." The rebuttal, "Lettre d'un officier de la marine russienne à un seigneur de la Cour concernant la carte des nouvelles découvertes au Nord de la Mer du Sud, et le Mémoire qui – sert d'explication publié par M. de l'Isle à Paris en 1752," was printed as a pamphlet in Berlin with the assistance of Leonhard Euler. It also appeared in *Nouvelle Bibliothèque germanique* (Amsterdam, October 1753). It was not signed. The essay was translated into English in 1754 and published in London as *A Letter from a Russian Sea-Officer to a Person of Distinction at the Court of St. Petersburg*. This version included observations on both Müller's and de l'Isle's essays by Arthur Dobbs, governor of North Carolina, and also de l'Isle's introduction to his chart. Müller's corrective maps appeared in St Petersburg between 1754 and 1758.[43]

The "Lettre d'un officier," in which Müller used the first person as if he had been on Bering's ship himself, emphasized Bering's accomplishments, including the arrival in America, and scathingly described de la Croyère's failure to contribute anything of substance to the expedition. "Our common sailors deserve much more than Mr de la Croyère," Müller wrote in one place, and in another he charged that almost all of de la Croyère's observations were actually made by Andrei Krasil'nikov, his assistant. Müller was contemptuous as well of J.N. de l'Isle, implying that he had accomplished nothing during his twelve years at the Academy and accusing him of fabricating a Spanish account of these voyages (by an Admiral de Fonte). Müller hinted as well that the French astronomer might now be senile ("Is it to time or to age that we are to impute this error ... ?"). Throughout he defended the honour of the Russian empire and objected strenuously to de l'Isle's implication that foreigners were better able to chart Russia's coastlines than were the Russians themselves.[44]

This outburst of patriotism had very beneficial results for Müller. In February 1754, much to the dismay of Lonomosov and undoubtedly others, Razumovskii appointed Müller permanent secretary to the Academy Conference.[45] Even though he had attended only a dozen of the regular Conference meetings after the charter of 1747 had gone into effect,[46] and was almost a pariah at the Academy after 1749, Müller had so strengthened his position by 1754 that he was able to hold this new and important post for eleven years. In 1755, Müller also was appointed director of the Academy's geography department, with specific orders to assist A.N. Grishov in the revision of the *Atlas rossiiskoi* which had appeared under the Academy's imprimatur in 1745. In fact, he had already been co-operating with Grishov on this project since Winsheim's death in 1751. Once again, however, Müller had so many tasks in hand that he found it nearly impossible to devote sufficient time to each. In this case, it was the atlas that would suffer.

On the private level, Müller served as unofficial source of information for Büsching, who was widely respected in Europe as a geographer. Büsching often was asked by geographers and cartographers to confirm the substance of reports on the Bering expedition published by Gmelin, de l'Isle, and Müller. In his turn, Büsching regularly contacted Müller (between 1751 and 1761) for verification of the accounts. Müller was in this way a regular contributor to Büsching's famous *Neue Erdbeschreibung* (volumes 1–9, Hamburg, 1754–92), which was often reprinted and generally is regarded as the founding work on modern statistical geography.[47] In giving credence to Müller's opinions, Büsching was also providing favourable publicity to the Russian Academy of Sciences.

In 1755 Müller also edited the richly detailed account of Kamchatka and the Kuriles written by Krasheninnikov, who had died before his manuscript was ready for the press. In his introduction, Müller praised the author's thoroughness, congratulated two unnamed "professors of the Academy" for their assistance to Krasheninnikov, and excused those same professors for not proceeding to Kamchatka themselves. In closing, he lauded Krasheninnikov as "one of those who, while not blessed with good birth or good fortune, was the creator of his own good fortune by means of quality, perseverance and service."[48] But Müller's enthusiasm for his own history of Siberia had waned considerably. He had no control over its translation into Russian, and every page was subjected to careful scrutiny by people whom he regarded as enemies. Only when an opportunity arose for him to become independent of the historical assembly did Müller return to his writing about Siberia.

The new Gmelin and de l'Isle crises had provided just such an occasion. As secretary of the Conference, Müller was once more at the very centre of Academy affairs. It seemed that his career had come full circle once again. He recorded Conference minutes, edited the *Commentarii*, and conducted official correspondence with Academy members abroad and on expedition and with foreign learned societies. He was responsible too for the communications with students who were studying abroad at Academy expense and for contacting potential recruits both to Academy service and to the newly established university in Moscow. Among those whom Müller attracted to the University of Moscow were J.G. Reichel and Ch.G. Köllner, both recommended by Gottsched, who was still at the University of Leipzig and by that time one of the most important literary figures in Germany. Reichel and Köllner were both graduates of Leipzig and members of the Leipzig Literary Society, which was dominated by Gottsched. Köllner lectured on general history at the new university in Moscow, and Reichel instructed in German language and literature – using a textbook prepared by Gottsched. They both arrived in Moscow in 1757, as did I.A. Rost, who also was recommended by Müller and who came from the University of Göttingen. In fact, he and Müller were distantly related. Rost taught the English language and mathematics. Büsching put Müller in touch with his cousin, P.H. Dilthey, a doctor of law and a member of the Mainz Academy whom Count Ivan Shuvalov hired in 1756 for the university as a professor of history and law.[49]

Shuvalov was one of the most widely read figures at Elizabeth's court, a patron of the arts and of scientific investigation. He had been Lomonosov's sponsor at the Academy, in part because he was anxious that Russians succeed in creating their own scholarly milieu. It was Shuvalov who presented a project for a university in Moscow to Elizabeth in July 1754. The university was chartered in January of the next year, with Shuvalov as one of its two curators. The former president of the Academy, Laurentius Blumentrost, who had been in charge of a hospital in Moscow since 1738, was the other. But Blumentrost died within a year, leaving Shuvalov to find faculty and to oversee the new institution with its directors. Thus he found Müller's contacts in Europe invaluable. In his turn, when he moved to Moscow himself ten years later, Müller would find a perfectly familiar and congenial community at the university.

On his own initiative, Müller opened discussions with F.U.T.

Aepinus, who came to Russia from the Berlin Academy of Sciences, where he had been a professor of physics, after rather tortuous high-level negotiations between Academy officials in Berlin and St Petersburg.[50] Although he was to take on a number of other tasks, including that of tutor to Grand Duke Paul, Aepinus (1724–1802) enjoyed one of the longest and most distinguished scientific careers in Russia. He attended his first Assembly meeting at the Academy in May 1757 and remained an active member until 1798.

Shortly after his appointment as secretary at the Academy, Müller reopened correspondence with Euler, whom he addressed as "The Honourable, especially praiseworthy Herr Professor! Highly esteemed friend and patron!"[51] Euler, who replied to Müller in a like manner, helped him appoint Aepinus and recruit chemist J.-G. Lehmann, astronomer Georg-Mauritz Lowitz, physiologist C.-F. Wolf, a Spanish lensmaker, Raphael Pacecco, and others to the Academy. Euler also recommended professors for the University of Moscow, among them J.-K. Wilke, who was appointed in 1757 to teach physics,[52] and teachers for the Russian military academies. Three Russian students, S.K. Kotel'nikov, S.Ia. Rumovskii, and M. Safronov were sent to Berlin during the 1750s to study with Euler, who kept Müller informed of their progress. Müller was even able to persuade Euler to contribute regularly to the *Commentarii* during the Seven Years War (1756–63), in which Russia and Prussia were on opposing sides.[53]

Within Russia, Müller began to communicate with provincial archivists and with government administrators who were interested in the history and peoples of the areas to which they were posted. P.I. Rychkov in Orenburg and F.I. Soimonov in Siberia corresponded often with the Academy secretary.[54] So did Adodurov, who was sent into exile in Orenburg in 1758. In the mean time Müller was on better terms with Schumacher, who was in very poor health and at odds with Teplov. This new situation worried Lomonosov, who was now convinced that some insidious relationship existed between Müller and Schumacher's relative, Taubert, at the expense of Teplov. In a disagreeable complaint to Shuvalov, Lomonosov said that Taubert's marriage to Schumacher's daughter could not have been made in Heaven because they "both envied and hated scholarship."[55] But Lomonosov's whining had no effect on Müller's improved status at the Academy. As a result of their mended relations, Schumacher appointed Müller the sole editor of a new Academy publication, *Monthly Compositions* (*Ezhemesiachnyia sochineniia*). Müller eventually selected *Monthly Compositions* from all his own works as the one that "was probably the most beneficial for Russian society."[56] But even those as yet undefined benefits were not to be achieved without further lengthy, acrimonious debate with Lomonosov.

CHAPTER SIX

Monthly Compositions
1755–64

All Russia read this first Russian monthly with joy
and satisfaction.

> Metropolitan Evgenei on
> *Monthly Compositions*, 1821

Soviet writers like to trace the origins of *Monthly Compositions* to a
letter of January 1754 that Lomonosov sent from St Petersburg to
Count Ivan Shuvalov, who was in charge of organizing a new
university in Moscow. In that letter, Lomonosov complained about
the lack of Russian-language books and texts available for use in the
new institution, and he suggested that a new academic journal be
established so that textbook information from foreign and Russian
books could be summarized and distributed relatively easily and
cheaply.[1] But his letter was really no more than a response to a request
from Shuvalov for copies of old *St. Petersburg Gazette* supplements
(*Notes*), which had ceased publication in 1742. As a matter of fact,
Razumovskii had raised the question of a journal himself some six
years before Lomonosov's letter was written. The Academy president
had requested permission from Elizabeth to print a Russian-language
magazine about diverse civil topics, "in which *usefulness* and *amuse-
ment* will be combined with decorum for secular character-building."[2]

Razumovskii's suggestion aside, the connection between Lomonosov's letter and *Monthly Compositions* is obscure. In fact, the matter of
a Russian-language academic journal was not brought to the Conference until 23 November 1754. At that time Müller read a proposal by
Razumovskii that the Academy issue a scholarly periodical in a format
similar to the *Gazette* supplements. The Academy Conference, with
Lomonosov present, was then asked to decide whether the new
publication should be on a monthly or weekly basis, and what sort of
subject matter should be its concern.[3]

The Conference membership unanimously welcomed the idea,
quickly agreed that it should be a monthly, and insisted that all

academicians be obligated to contribute to it. It was also decided that the journal would contain no topics that the Church might consider in its domain and that both critical and argumentative materials should be avoided. Lomonosov raised the issue of control and suggested that the Conference have a pre-publication veto over its content. But Razumovskii's order of 12 December 1754 proclaimed simply that there would be a Russian-language periodical called the *St. Petersburg Academic Supplement* and that Müller would be both editor and arbitrator of its content.[4] The latitude granted Müller was very unusual, and Lomonosov's request reflected the normal practice. In fact, Lomonosov himself had been subjected to strict Chancellery censorship when he was appointed literary editor of the *St. Petersburg Gazette* in 1748.[5] As part of the program that he presented to the Academy Conference on 14 December 1754, Müller noted that Europeans had long recognized the value of such enterprises and cited the *Notes* that he had edited in 1729–30 as the precedent for the current project. Müller emphasized the desperate need for Russian-language summaries of material contained only in books and in foreign languages.[6] In short, he justified the new journal on much the same grounds that Lomonosov had used to propose a new publication in early 1754. But Lomonosov had had a more scholarly audience in mind than the one Müller hoped to attract.

With its highly moral tone and didactic intent, the *St. Petersburg Academic Supplement*, soon to be called *Monthly Compositions*, was in reality a late Russian entry into a Europe-wide trend toward periodicals that began early in the century. More than half of its space was taken up with translations from European journals and from ancient Greek and Roman writers. Müller's own knowledge of such journals was extensive, for he had been educated at a time when moralizing weeklies were the rage in Europe. He was well versed in the tradition of Christian Wolff, the famous philologist, philosopher, educator, contributor to such publications, and one-time tutor in Mencke's home. We have seen that Müller maintained his association with the journalist Gottsched.[7] A list that Müller inserted in the introduction to *Monthly Compositions* provides evidence of his continued familiarity with European journals. The list included five French-language journals, four of which were printed first in the 1750s; seven English-language publications (not including the *Spectator* or *Tatler*, from which he was to draw fourteen and three items respectively); thirty-four German-language works and periodicals; and one each in Italian and Danish. Each of these, Müller said, had goals that conformed to those of *Monthly Compositions*.[8] Non-Academy Russian writers such as A.P. Sumarokov and M.M. Kheraskov were also anxious that Russia have its own journals and co-operated enthusiastically with Müller during the first years of *Monthly Compositions'* existence. Although their interests were mainly literary and they left to set up their own journals at the Cadet Corps typography in 1759, the unhesitating collaboration of these established literati indicate that it was more the spirit of the time than any one person who was responsible for creating *Monthly Compositions*. Neither Lomonosov nor Müller ever claimed credit for founding the journal.

According to Müller's program, printed as a "Foreword" to the first issue (see Appendix B), the journal was to contain "useful" information written in a manner that would make it comprehensible to non-scholars. "For the preservation of good feelings," no criticism or disputatious items would be printed. Contributors could expect that their pieces would be examined before printing by a "special committee," which remained undefined and in practice rarely meant anyone but Müller himself. This may explain why few academicians submitted articles to *Monthly Compositions*. Nearly a month after Müller's "Foreword" was distributed, Lomonosov lodged a complaint against the journal's title, saying that it might lead to the exclusion of poetry. He also said that Müller should not use the expression "uchenye zhurnaly" ("learned journals"), claiming that it was inappropriate in Russian. In this instance Trediakovskii came to Müller's assistance.[9] There followed another vitriolic quarrel between Müller and Lomonosov, during which Müller asked Razumovskii either to allow Lomonosov to take on the duties of editor himself, or to order him to be silent.[10] Razumovskii did neither, but the original title was changed so that the journal appeared in January 1755 as *Monthly Compositions for Profit and Entertainment*.[11] Lomonosov continued to harry Müller for the duration of the periodical's existence. It is not surprising then, though it was not in keeping with Müller's mandate, that Lomonosov was the only well-known contemporary writer whose writing the journal only barely recognized.[12]

In 1851 V.A. Miliutin undertook what is still the most detailed study of the content of *Monthly Compositions* and went so far as to count the articles and categorize them according to their subject matter. Philosophy (94), the natural sciences (57), household economy and technology (42), and medicine (29) had the greatest representation in the journal.[13] But most were short pieces, and the great majority of these were translations from foreign magazines. In total page space and in original work, history and geography far surpassed all other categories. These fields were central to Müller's own interests and career and, along with the eleven articles on education, the ones best suited to fulfil the didactic aims of the journal.

Although literary items played a distant secondary role in *Monthly Compositions*, Müller was delighted to have the participation of several of Russia's best-known men of letters who were outside the Academy, for they could assure him a wider audience. The most prolific of these contributors was the poet and playwright Sumarokov. Müller recommended Sumarokov's poetry so that Russia's youth could read a "multitude of things ... in order not to fall into barbarism."[14] The famous dramatist and poet furnished the journal with 123 poems between 1755 and 1758, and Müller showed his gratitude by arranging through Gottsched that Sumarokov be named a member of the Leipzig Literary Society.[15] Gottsched made a point of announcing the existence of *Monthly Compositions* to his own readers in Leipzig, reprinted poems and essays by Sumarokov and other Russians, in translation, and generally gave Müller and his journal a very good press in Germany.

Sumarokov dissociated himself from Müller in 1759 in order to edit literary magazines on his own. Between that time and 1763, *Monthly Compositions* carried no poetry. Other Russian poets who contributed before 1759 were M.M. Kheraskov (21 pieces) and Trediakovskii, who had three of his works printed. Andrei Nartov, Alexander Demidov, and I.I. Golenishchev-Kutuzov were lesser-known poets whose works also appeared. Of these, only Trediakovskii was associated with the Academy, and it was with him that the first storm over Müller's editorial prerogatives arose.

In 1756 Müller rejected a piece written by Trediakovskii, who then asked Nartov to submit it under his own name. Müller printed it thinking that it was Nartov's work.[16] Needless to say, Trediakovskii was outraged and launched a campaign against the journal, Müller, and Sumarokov, with whom he already had been arguing about poetry. He went so far as to denounce *Monthly Compositions* to the Holy Synod for printing "atheistic" items belonging to Sumarokov, but a Synod request that certain issues be confiscated was ignored by the Senate.[17] The Synod had lost its authority over secular books in Russia in 1743, when Elizabeth assigned that jurisdiction to the Senate. However, Lomonosov was successful in 1757 in preventing the publication of an article by Grigorii Poletika, a College assessor and translator for the Holy Synod; he also had an epigram by Sumarokov banned by appealing directly to Razumovskii. Müller complained to the Chancellery in March, citing the editorial prerogatives granted him by the presidential order of 12 December 1754. He continued somewhat plaintively: "If the Chancellery ignores the presidential decision ... and prevents [*Monthly Compositions*] from going to the press ... then I suggest that it search ahead of time for another editor ... If I cannot act according to my inclination then I know beforehand that soon I will be taken just as before by hypochondriac illness." Schumacher called his bluff successfully by referring to article 50 of the charter which gave the Chancellery the right "to direct everything that belongs to the Academy" in the president's absence. Müller said no more, at least publicly, about the matter.[18]

Lomonosov's limited victory against Müller in 1757 was in part due to the fact that he was appointed to the Chancellery himself in February of that year. Important changes had taken place in that body after 1754, when Schumacher was made a state councillor. His close relationship with Teplov had cooled by then, to the advantage of Müller, and his health was deteriorating rapidly. In July 1756, Müller wrote to Euler that Schumacher was "old and feeble" and in semi-retirement.[19] He died in 1761. But Schumacher's disappearance from the daily scene did not usher in an era of good relations between the Chancellery and St Petersburg's academicians. Taubert and Jacob von Stählin were appointed to the Chancellery along with Lomonosov,[20] and the Conference tended to split once again into feuding factions, this time behind either Lomonosov or Taubert, with Stählin generally caught in the middle.

In an attempt to limit the issues over which Lomonosov and Taubert might quarrel, Razumovskii divided their responsibilities. To Lomonosov went all matters of schools and scholarship; Taubert was put in charge of ancillary services, such as the typography; Stählin was placed in charge of matters concerning the Academy of Arts.[21] This meant that Lomonosov was de facto sponsor of whatever censorship powers the Chancellery might be able to wield over Academy members. Müller recognized that this boded ill for him and wrote to Razumovskii on 13 March that an "ill-wind wished that Mr. Lomonosov be placed in the Chancellery. He will cause difficulties for many of us, and especially for me, although I have not given him the slightest cause for it. He has already attempted to play a decisive role in what is to be printed in the *Monthly Compositions*.[22]

Müller would have been even more concerned had he known that for the previous two years Lomonosov had been compiling notes on all those things that he felt were wrong with the Academy. Müller ("mischievous"), Teplov ("boorish"), and Schumacher ("unscrupulous") figured prominently in Lomonosov's cast of villains. Aside from the somewhat paranoiac assumption that these men were conspiring against him, Lomonosov privately pinpointed several real deficiencies in the operation of the Academy: Razumovskii's distance, which left no check on the authority of the Chancellery; the vulnerability of the professors to spiteful officials; the constant turnover of members; and the complete inability of the learned men of the institution to participate in Academy decisions.[23]

Müller's plea that Lomonosov's appointment be overturned, and especially his assumption of the mantle of innocent martyrdom, fell on deaf ears; but his prophecy soon proved to be accurate enough. The continued and even increased officiousness of the Chancellery without Schumacher was remarked on by a young German who recorded his opinion of the Academy while he lived in Russia during the 1760s: "On the neck of this [scholarly] society sat the Chancellery, in which the president with one or two Councillors, secretaries, clerks, and so on, ruled unchecked. Thus everything was spoiled ... The Chancellery controlled financial matters, concluded contracts, imposed fines, determined raises in salary, and kept officially in contact with the Conference by means of decrees ... No merit was recognized, basic scholarship was ignored, worthy men were reduced to despair ... Despotism gradually spread to all levels of administration; every official, as if in revenge or requital for the evil he had had to suffer from his own superiors, dealt severely and roughly with his own subordinates."[24]

A.L. von Schlözer, whose words these were, was a disgruntled foreigner who felt his merit had gone unrecognized. But he was not alone in his despair at the situation at the Academy. Whereas Schlözer and Müller saw the culprits within the Chancellery, which was dominated by Lomonosov and other Russians by the late 1750s, Russians tended to attribute all crises to the foreigners who were in ascendancy in the academic part of the Academy. A report submitted to the Senate in 1761 by Sergei Volchkov, director of the typography, prolific translator, and long-time secretary in the Chancellery, blamed the "passionate arguments and hostilities between foreign members" for the Academy's difficulties. The occasion of Volchkov's diatribe was the failure of the Conference to approve his translation of Bossuet in good time. "Many of them have no Russian," he said, "and some even no French from which language almost all my books are translated." He went on to complain that the academicians taught very few Russian students and that they "rail and abuse" one another and accomplish "nothing for the benefit of the Russian nation."[25] Still, even Russians complained about Lomonosov. The young astronomer Stepan Rumovskii wrote to J.-A. Euler in 1764 that he supported Academy reform to eliminate "chicanery" and "the despotic power to which Mr Lomonosov aspires."[26] Whatever the cause of such discontent, it was clear that neither the charter of 1747 nor the absence of Schumacher made much difference to the personal dimension of work conditions at the Academy.

Once Lomonosov became a member of the Chancellery he was able to attack Müller and *Monthly Compositions* with impunity. In June 1757, a Chancellery note signed by Lomonosov, Taubert, and Stählin insisted that Müller provide them with a monthly list of everything he intended to print in the journal. They insisted correctly that article 50 of the Academy charter gave the Chancellery rights of pre-publication veto over all manuscripts prepared by Academy members.[27] This set the stage for many subsequent complaints and minor charges culminating in 1761 with another act of censorship against an important article by Müller. Lomonosov demonstrated his new power in other ways as well. Explaining that Müller had no mathematical skills, that only a "natural-born Russian" should be in charge of so delicate a matter as charting the Russian empire, and that Müller was too busy with other chores to do justice to the geography department, Lomonosov recommended that he be relieved of his post as director of that unit. Müller's defence against Lomonosov's charges was half-hearted, for he could not deny that he was busy or even that the department had accomplished very little since it had been ordered to revise the Russian atlas in 1751. He did point out rather stiffly that he was a naturalized Russian subject and could hardly be penalized as if he were a foreigner.[28] Nevertheless, in November 1758 Lomonosov himself replaced Müller as director of the geography department.

Of the twenty-three pieces in *Monthly Compositions* that Miliutin classified as historical, geographical, and statistical, seventeen were written by Müller. Moreover, in 1758 Müller resurrected the *Sammlung russischer Geschichte*, which carried German versions of many of the historical essays appearing in *Monthly Compositions*. On Bayer's death in 1738, the *Sammlung* still had two numbers of its second volume forthcoming. Müller completed that volume before the end of 1758. The resumption of the *Sammlung* was an especially timely event for historical publication in Russia because the new series of *Commentarii* (*Novi Commentarii*), which began to appear in 1750, excluded articles on the humanities and history because they were disciplines of the university. This remained the case even though Müller also acted as its editor from 1758 to 1764.

The importance of history to *Monthly Compositions* was illustrated by the very opening article of January 1755 – 'A Brief Table of the Great Princes of All Russia from Riurik to the Invasion of the Tatars.' Although he did not mention the source of this outline (which was the still-unpublished Tatishchev manuscript on Russian history), Müller suggested that readers keep it as a general reference for pieces scheduled to appear in future issues.[29] Aside from the *Sinopsis* and the much rarer genealogical table usually attributed to Prokopovich, this was the only widely distributed printed chronological list of even a part of Russian history. The chart began with the *Primary Chronicle* tale about Riurik, who "was invited on the suggestion of the Prince of Novgorod, Gostomysl, from the Varangian Russes in 862." No mention was made of the Varangians' homeland, of their nationality, or of the means whereby they maintained and spread their power.

The eighteenth-century pragmatic view of history as a moral and political guide to contemporaries permeated *Monthly Compositions*. In 1757 one of Müller's collaborators, S.A. Poroshin, later to become the tutor to Grand Duke Paul, prepared an essay on learning in which he traced the sequence of study most likely to produce a well-rounded educated person. He advocated that students start with Latin and Greek and then read history. History would bind together all other learning, because it was central to both philosophical and scientific thinking. A historian must look for causes, and his writing must be designed to play an instructive role in society by providing examples from which readers could make judgments on current affairs. History "helps us to see over the expanse of time the theatre of human bravery ... to see PETER's deeds ... to learn about virtues and vices."[30] Müller also constantly pursued the image of the historian as teacher. In an issue of 1761, he wrote that "all history must show us rules and provide examples"; in 1762 he stated that youngsters "must above all be taught to know the *Russian State*, so that they will not be foreigners in their own fatherland. Evidence from History will be combined with moralizing. The light of history will show them the causes for the fall and rise of Great States ... and especially of the Russian State." And in 1763 he wrote that historians should provide "good examples" in order to correct human conduct.[31]

It is true, however, that Müller and Poroshin did not share the same view of history as a science. We saw that in 1749 Müller had responded ironically to Lomonosov: "Does he not know the difference between historical dissertations and panegyric speeches?" A dozen years later, in *Monthly Compositions*, he insisted that a historian must explain everything dispassionately;[32] Poroshin was closer to Lomonosov in his assumption that one should stress the glories of the national past. That Müller remained adamantly opposed to the openly subjective history of the type espoused by Lomonosov was demonstrated well in a private letter written sometime in the early 1760s: "Allow me first to give you my thoughts on how to create such a history. It all may be contained in three words: it must be true, objective, and unpretentious. The duties of a historian are difficult to fulfil: you know that he must seem to be without fatherland, without a faith and without a state. I do not ask that a historian relate everything that he knows, or even everything that is true, because there are things which are not necessary to say and are of little interest ... But everything that a historian says must be strictly true."[33] Müller was the first historian in Russia to advocate such principles regularly and to defend them publicly. Among historians of Russia during the eighteenth century it is usually only Schözer who is credited with such sentiments, and his main works on Russia were written at Göttingen, the most prominent seat of historical studies in Germany. Aside from N.I. Boltin in the 1790s, Müller remained unique among historians in Russia during the century in propagating the method and objectives of eighteenth-century rationalism.

Six of Müller's own historical contributions to *Monthly Compositions* appeared in its first year of publication. They were on rather scattered topics and, compared to later entries, were not of a controversial nature. Nevertheless, most were substantial in length and drew the attention of readers to the great variety of components that combined to make up the history of their homeland. They served as an excellent beginning to Müller's professed ambition of putting on paper more and more bits of Russian history so that eventually there might appear a full historical narrative.

In the second issue, Müller undertook to fulfil one of the promises made in his foreword. He attempted to correct misinformed views commonly held by foreign writers about Russia. In this case he rectified mistakes printed in Europe about marriages contracted between members of the Russian princely families and European royalty in the eleventh and twelfth centuries. In his preamble, Müller criticized foreign writers about Russia generally either for ignoring Russian chronicles altogether or for using poor – or abbreviated – redactions of them. Then he proceeded specifically to find fault with books written by G.S. Treuer in 1733 and J.T. Rönnik in 1753. These authors, Müller said, were completely wrong in their assumptions about the significance of marriages between Kievan princes and German royal houses. He used a number of sources to demonstrate the errors of these writers, among them the Polish chronicler Dlugosh and the *Sinopsis*, but above all the *Primary Chronicle*, the author of which he admitted to having identified wrongly in 1732. Gottsched already had printed this essay in his journal, *Das Neueste aus der Anmutigen Gelehrsamkeit* (July 1754), and J.H.S. Formey had noted it "with interest" in the *Nouvelle Bibliothèque germanique* early in 1755. Two hundred copies were printed as separate pamphlets in St Petersburg (in German) in 1754, and so both its content and its message that one must know the Russian chronicles before undertaking any study about Russia received wide attention.[34]

In a second and shorter essay in the following month's issue of

Monthly Compositions (March), Müller outlined the history of Nyenschanz, the old settlement on the Neva near which St Petersburg was
founded. After describing its foundation by the Swedes in 1300 and
the subsequent struggle for the area between Swedes and Novgorodians, he spoke of it being "returned" to Russia by means of a
protracted siege in 1703. This interpretation repeated the official
Russian version as it was outlined in Shafirov's *Discourses* and
elsewhere. Müller complained that European accounts of the event
ignored "the glorious and brave actions of the Great Victor," Peter the
Great.[35]

The editorial promise to use *Monthly Compositions* to correct images
of Russian history as they were disseminated by non-Russians was
adhered to throughout the journal's existence. In 1757, Müller
addressed the problem directly. "Our Russian youth have been
harmed by this. They do not have books printed in Russian from
which they can obtain basic knowledge about their fatherland." But
just as he had done in 1746 he placed the blame squarely on the
shoulders of the Russians themselves, pointing out that no Russian
had as yet written a national history for his fellow countrymen, let
alone one for foreigners. Foreigners had neither the language skills
nor access to data to enable them to perform the task properly. In this
opinion, Müller echoed the complaints of Lomonosov, but, in contrast
to the Russian scholar, he offered practical solutions to the problem.
He suggested that more extracts from the chronicles and, where
possible, entire chronicles be printed. Five years later Müller published extracts in *Monthly Compositions* from an old chronograph
about the "revolt and villainies" of Stenka Razin. In 1757, he
advocated the publication of existing manuscripts by P.I. Rychkov,
Mankiev, and Tatishchev, each of whom was given further attention
in the journal. He also invited readers to send to the Academy
notations on any errors that they perceived in foreign works about
Russia.[36]

As early as April 1755, *Monthly Compositions* had carried a third
historical essay by Müller which demonstrated that he was anxious to
act on his own suggestions. "About Russia's First Chronicler,
Reverend Nestor," was in fact a reprint and correction of the piece
that he had written for the first volume of the *Sammlung* in 1732.[37] The
new version brought to Russian-language readers their first account
of the early Russian chroniclers. At that time the chronicles were
barely known outside scholarly and monastic circles. The only parts
of the *Primary Chronicle* published as yet were those German-
language extracts printed by Müller in the *Sammlung*. Tatishchev's
still unpublished work referred to Nestor, a monk in Kiev during the

last years of the eleventh century and the first years of the twelfth, as
the author of three chronicles that he used but were later lost.[38]
Müller's article thus represented a revelation of great interest to his
readers. He cited Tatishchev's manuscript this time and appealed for
a full publication of the "Nestor" chronicle both in Russian and in the
leading European languages. The clergy long had opposed the
printing of chronicles, but an increasingly secular attitude at court
enabled Müller to help set in motion a process that saw a sequence of
such publications within the next two decades. In 1758, Razumovskii
set up the *Library of Russian History* (*Biblioteka Rossiiskaia istoricheskaia*),
a publication series in which chronicles and other documents of old
Russia were to be printed by the Academy.[39]

The September 1755 issue of *Monthly Compositions* carried the first
of a detailed six-part series by Müller on trade in Siberia, an
expatiation of the report commissioned by Iusupov in 1744. It was
later printed in an issue of the *Sammlung* in 1760.[40] One hundred
copies of the Russian version were published separately. The series
included a list and description of Siberian cities and trade routes,
enumerated the various goods bartered by Siberian, Kalmyk, Bukharan, and Chinese traders, and noted the main periods of contact
between Russians and the peoples of Siberia. Müller took the
opportunity to advocate the revision of the Treaty of Kiakhta, a trade
agreement signed with China in 1727. He recommended that the trade
monopoly granted to the Russian government by the treaty be opened
up to private Russian merchants. He also insisted that private fur
auctions be allowed, that greater care be taken to avoid the extermina-
tion of rare sables which frequented the Amur region, and that a
colonization program be initiated.

Other essays by Müller carried a wealth of information on the
various peoples of Siberia, on the first Russian travellers to China
(from 1608),[41] on three "heathen" tribles of the Kazan district
(Cheremis, Chuvash, Votiaks),[42] on the whale fisheries of Kamchatka,[43] on gold mining in Bukhara, and on Peter the Great's
fortresses along the Irtysh.[44] Müller also described items found in
grave sites in Siberia and New Russia.[45] Another exhaustive series
in which he depicted Russian voyages in the Arctic and Pacific from
1636 to 1745 appeared in ten parts, 1757–8. This last work was in
part a Russian rendering of Müller's 1753 response to de l'Isle
and also an explanation of changes that were then being made on
maps printed earlier by the Academy. It was translated into English
(London, 1761 and 1764), German (1758), and French (Paris, 1766).[46]
In 1761 *Monthly Compositions* carried the first bibliographical list
of all maps and atlases about Russia. It was compiled by Müller, who

noted all known foreign and Russian works and commented on many of them.[47]

A short essay by Müller on the background to the Nerchinsk Treaty of 1689, which was supposed to delineate the border between Russia and China, appeared in April 1757. Müller was doubtless aware of the fact that the Manchus were then faced with major rebellion by Dzungar Mongols in central Asia and that several Mongolian groups had sought to transfer their allegiance from the Manchu dynasty to the Romanovs. Discussion between Mongolians and Russians had begun already at Selenginsk in 1756, and the next year St Petersburg demanded that Peking agree to a revision of the Nerchinsk agreement. Müller's article explained the Russian case and urged that the easternmost boundary line, then vaguely set somewhere between the Tugur and the Uda, be moved south to Amur. He very carefully described the river system of the region and sharply criticized the former Russian ambassador to China, Sava Vladislavich, for allowing the Chinese to prevail thirty years earlier at Kiakhta. At that time even the Uda was left in doubt in spite of the fact that the Russians already had a fortress and an established trade practice there.[48] The Chinese, however, having crushed the rebellions, were not impressed by Russia's attempts at intimidation.

The long history and description of the Amur River area that Müller had been commissioned to prepare in 1740 was spread over four issues of *Monthly Compositions*, July to October 1757. It was revised and expanded to include another condemnation of the Kiakhta Treaty for giving the Manchus an even firmer grip on the Amur than the Nerchinsk settlement had granted them. The tract was published in French (Amsterdam, 1766) and in German – by Büsching (Hamburg, 1768) and by Ulrich Weiss (Offenbach-am-Main, 1777) – and so became the standard Russian statement on the matter. We have seen that already in 1740–1 Müller went beyond his terms of reference to recommend a revision of the Treaty of Nerchinsk. He repeated this position in *Monthly Compositions* and again in two secret memoranda commissioned by Catherine II in 1763 and 1764. The Amur articles opened with notes on the origins of the existing Chinese-Russian boundary and a charge by Müller that the "cunning" Chinese had duped the Russians at Nerchinsk. The main argument of the long paper, and of his conclusion, was that the Russian state had in fact been the *in loco* lord of the area between the Uda and the Amur before the official agreements were reached with China. Thus his ruler had the right to regain what he had lost. Müller pointed out also that Russia was handicapped in discussions with China because its troops were always out-numbered – a situation for which he was to offer remedies in 1763. The question of the Amur remained a passion with Müller. In the 1770s, while writing memoirs of his Siberian trek, he stressed the importance of charting the entire Amur region in case Russia decided "to assert its just claim" to it.[49]

All in all, Müller's various essays on the Amur represent a substantial precedent for Russia's claims to that area. Indeed, the political component of *Monthly Compositions*, though ignored by Miliutin, was tangible enough to justify a charge that its editor was a proponent of Russian imperial expansion. In June 1755 an article on the renewed dispute between England and France over their colonial possessions was also an implicit rationalization for Russian aggrandizement on the west coast of North America. Müller noted that France, which he saw as an aggressor against England, was ignoring boundary agreements reached at Utrecht (1713) and again in 1749. "It seems," he wrote, "that in several foreign languages the word *eternal* does not have the same meaning as it does for us."[50] The essays on Russian exploration in the Far East that appeared between 1758 and 1760 had similar connotations. Müller was less coy in the article on the gold sands in Bukhara and the construction of fortresses along the Irtysh. Here he praised Peter the Great for opening up central Asia, from which "already for several years there has flowed quantities of wealth and treasure." If Russia maintained Peter's fortresses on the upper reaches of the Irtysh, it might, Müller foresaw, eventually establish a complicated but highly profitable caravan system connecting Astrakhan (at the mouth of the Volga, on the Caspian Sea), Orenburg, Bukhara, India, and China – with Russian settlements slowly spreading to the south and southeast.[51]

Some of Müller's work on Kazan, Siberia, and central Asia had been prepared in the early 1730s, when he wrote his lecture to the Conference on the Kalmyks.[52] The paper on the peoples of the Kazan area was written in 1733 but was augmented in *Monthly Compositions* with corrections of mistakes made by Adam Olearius in the seventeenth-century reports on that region. Müller had compiled more contributions between 1744 and 1747, while he was being thwarted in his attempts to complete the history of Siberia.[53] Because he now had forums of his own in which to publish relatively freely, materials over which the historical assembly had once wrangled rapidly came to light. Ten chapters of the Siberian history were printed in the *Sammlung* over the years 1761–8; and three of the chapters that had not been included in the Russian-language publication of 1750 appeared in *Monthly Compositions* in 1763–4.[54] These long essays thus represented completely new and fascinating reading for the journal's audience.

A spring issue of 1760 contained the first major study published in Russian on the origin and history of the Cossacks, a subject that was bound to catch the fancy of Müller's readers. Gottsched had already printed parts of it in Leipzig in 1756 and told Müller that they had proved very popular.[55] Müller wrote that the "language and law" of the Cossacks "were one with the Russians." Their earliest settlements in "Little Russia" were formed by groups of refugees who fled the Polish conquerors of Volhynia in the 1340s. Müller outlined the Cossacks' history as border guards for the Polish kings and their turbulent relations with the Polish aristocracy, Muscovy, and the Ottoman empire. He spoke very briefly of the uprising led by Bohdan Khmelnitskii – "a man of great wisdom, bravery and skill" – on behalf of Cossack rights and religion, which resulted in the notorious agreement with Muscovy at Pereiaslav' in 1654. He said that the treaty led to the "subjugation" of "Little Russia" (Ukraine) by the tsars of Russia, but he also supported the official opinion that this was Muscovy's "unarguable right," for the area had been taken away from the "ancient Great Princes of Russia by Lithuanian Great Princes."[56]

Here, as in later essays on Novgorod and on modern Russian history, Müller introduced subjects that had political overtones and were not mentioned at all in the *Sinopsis*. The piece included information on Ermak, who was driven into Siberia by Ivan IV, and mentioned with no qualifying judgments the rebellion by Stenka Razin. In this way, Müller brought to light some of the scattered materials on which he had been labouring in the 1740s, but that had been jettisoned from the history of Siberia. Some Cossack-related events of his own century that connected Cossack history to that of the central Russian government were also highlighted. Prominent in this regard was Müller's attempt to trace the tenuous relations between Mazeppa's successors and Russian rulers from 1708 to 1736, when a semblance of conciliation was reached.

The most controversial and most original of Müller's contributions to *Monthly Compositions* was "Essay on the Modern History of Russia," which appeared in the first three issues of 1761.[57] It represented the first endeavour after Mankiev's unpublished effort to carry a detailed narrative of Russian history beyond 1588, where Tatishchev's manuscript had ended. Tatishchev had purposely eschewed modern history, fearing that his bureaucratic career might suffer for it. Müller introduced his essay by calling it a continuation of Tatishchev's history. Mindful of his experiences of 1749–50, Müller began with a long justification for opening the study at the era of Boris Godunov and the "Time of Troubles" (1598–1613), which had been so unsettling for Russia. He noted that all countries have similar dismal periods in their past and said that a description of errors might serve as valuable lessons for the present: "Villainy excites terror when it is forcefully portrayed ... [and] sponsors so much instruction that it seems doubtful whether the presentation of the most pleasing and noteworthy events are preferable insofar as benefits to [the readers'] morals and wisdom are concerned." This strong appeal to the prevailing assumption that history must be didactic was followed by a mollifying assurance that such a history would demonstrate how "God's design brought the Romanovs" to power in 1613.[58]

Equal in importance to the detail of his account was the fact that Müller drew the attention of his readers to a great variety of unpublished records. In an introductory section, he described chronicles that carried accounts to the reign of Alexei Mikhailovich (1645–76), chronographs, the *Kniga stepennaia* and several of its continuations, and Mankiev's *Kernel of Russian History*. Russia had a better collection of chronicles than any other country, he said, and again he singled out Nestor as the greatest recorder of all. The chronographs accentuated the importance to Russian history of Greek accounts. Müller also relied extensively on the *Rodoslovnye knigi*, or books of official precedence, which had ranked all Muscovite officials in a system of preference based on genealogical seniority known as *mestnichestvo* – which had been abolished in 1682; on military registers (*knigi razriadnye*); and on nearly thirty accounts by foreign witnesses, most of whom were ambassadors to the courts at Warsaw and Moscow. Finally, Müller emphasized the importance of "archival papers," which he had located himself in Siberian centres. Among other things, he wrote, such documentation proved that there was a substantial flow of information – in the form of *ukazy* – from Moscow to the outer regions of the empire. He took pains to point out that he was the first to employ such documentation. In closing these prefatory remarks, Müller rather optimistically wrote, "Now I must await whatever approbation my work will have, both outside and within the empire."[59] If he really expected it to draw praise, he was doomed to disappointment.

The complete story as told by Müller, and carried first in the *Sammlung* in 1760, brought Russian history down to May 1606, when Vasilii Shuiskii obtained the throne. Müller's image of Godunov as a man of keen intellect and "great abilities," but also one who was "cunning and perfidious," became a standard interpretation. He took care to warn readers at the outset that his depiction of Godunov might not be to their liking, adding that it was his duty as a historian to explain everthing "dispassionately." Müller then proceeded to laud Godunov for his generosity to foreigners and his own subjects, noted that he brought Russia to a "flourishing condition," and credited him with attempting to sponsor the growth of an active Russian merchant class. He stressed too that Godunov wanted peace with his neighbours even though he was not able to achieve it. But Godunov's faults also were exposed in detail. Müller outlined his harsh treatment of the Romanovs, his helplessness – in spite of efforts to alleviate the crisis – during the terrible famine and concurrent "pestilence" of 1601–3, and the gradual disillusionment on the part of those who had expected great things of Godunov in 1598. Müller continued to grant the devil his due, however, and concluded by saying that Godunov's death was regrettable in that only he might have been able to forestall the chaos introduced by the first False Dimitrii, whom Müller depicted as a pawn of Polish Jesuits and of the papacy.[60]

The "Essay" was one of Müller's most important contributions to Russian historiography on several counts. Although his old friend J.P. Kohl and a Dane, Adam Sellius, had listed Russian and other Slavic literature earlier, this outline by Müller was the first in which the entire question of the sources of Russian history was discussed seriously.[61] Sellius had spent some time in the Alexander Nevsky monastery, where he took vows and the name of Nicodemus. While there he gathered information on chronicles and other sources of Russian history and published a catalogue of them in Latin in 1736. Müller's "correction" of Sellius's list and of several other foreign accounts was in keeping with the purpose of *Monthly Compositions*, and the history itself was thorough enough to serve as the basis for many later studies. M.M. Shcherbatov and N.M. Karamzin were among those Russian historians who relied heavily on Müller's information about the "Time of Troubles." The French historian P.-C. Lévesque also borrowed wholesale from the "Essay" for his controversial *Histoire de la Russie* (1782–3). Indeed, a full century later the famous Russian historian S.M. Solov'ev called it the most influential work on Boris Godunov before his own volumes on that fateful period were published in 1857–8.[62] Unavoidably, however, the tale was replete with the horrors and violence of the "Time of Troubles," and Müller made a conscious effort to present an unbiased picture of the "hatred, cruelties, fear and suspicions" that he said were characteristic of that age.[63] Herein lay his downfall once again.

The Russian translation of the "Essay" began in the January 1761 issue of *Monthly Compositions*. But with the appearance of the third issue in March, Müller received a letter from D.V. Volkov, secretary of Elizabeth's state council, forbidding him to print further instalments.[64] Müller replied that his manuscript had been checked carefully by the Chancellery before publication and asked Volkov to elucidate his "errors." He asked Volkov that he be allowed to print material covering Godunov's reign – which was ready for the April issue. Volkov did not reply. Not surprisingly, it had been Lomonosov who had set the Academy administration against Müller. After reading the *Sammlung* version, he wrote to Razumovskii that "the German ... seeks out stains on the robe of the Russian body" and that Müller intended only to write on the "darkest portions of Russian history, from which foreign readers will draw [wrong] conclusions concerning our glories." Moreover, Lomonosov complained that, "wherever possible," Müller placed "reprehensible ideas about our Fatherland" in *Monthly Compositions*. He reminded the Academy assessor of Müller's "duplicity" in the de l'Isle affair, the "worthless" and "accursed" dissertation of 1749, and both his "boasting" and his "slander of the Russian nation" in the proscribed foreword to the Siberian history.[65] Although Müller wrote Rychkov in June 1761 that Lomonosov's "lies do not hurt me,"[66] no further parts of the "Essay" were printed in Russian. Strangely, this piece of Academy censorship did not affect the *Sammlung*, which meant that foreigners – and some educated Russians – were indeed the main audience for Müller's history of modern Russia. Its author resigned himself to his fate, writing with classic understatement to former Academy president Baron Korff: "My 'Essay on the Modern History of Russia' was not received very graciously here, so I must set it aside and await a better time."[67] He never returned to the project.

Müller should not have been surprised at the official rejection of his work on Russian history. In 1761, Russia was embroiled in the Seven Years' War as an ally of France against Prussia and England. It had been participating successfully since 1757, but at staggering cost to an already depleted treasury and accompanied by dissension and political bickering at court. Court intrigue cost Count Alexis Bestuzhev-Riumin his position as chancellor in 1758, and his successor, Count M.J. Vorontsov, was hostile to Germans generally, and to Prussians in particular. Any writing by a German at the Academy that seemed to denigrate Russia's past would have met the same fate as Müller's "Essay." Even Elizabeth's death in December 1761 made little difference. Her successor, Peter III, who was strongly opposed to war against Prussia, whose monarch he admired, initiated a conflict with Denmark instead. It was still impolitic to attempt to print something that might be perceived as anti-Russian in character, and would remain so. Moreover, D.V. Volkov served as Peter III's secretary during his brief reign and as a member of the monarch's informal ruling council.

Another reason why Müller's attempt at Russian history was

vulnerable to criticism from Lomonosov, Teplov, and others was the fact that Lomonosov's own *Short Russian Chronicle* (*Kratkii Rossiiskii letopisets*) had been published in 1760 and was an immediate success.[68] Three editions were printed between June 1760 and April 1761, and it was translated into German (by Stählin), into French, and English. Lomonosov had turned to historical writing in 1751, shortly after he completed his choleric report on Müller's dissertation of 1749. In spite of his many other pursuits, Lomonosov's historical research progressed so rapidly that his detailed *Ancient Russian History* (*Drevniaia Rossiiskaia istoriia*) was ready by 1758 – though not printed until 1766. In the mean time, however, the appearance of the *Short Russian Chronicle* coincided very neatly with an imperial *ukaz* of August 1760 that asked for more vigilance, loyalty, and, above all, patriotism, so as to assure "order and the national well-being"[69] during this period of war. Lomonosov's text began with a short account of Russian antiquity in which he emphasized the greatness (*slava*) and military prowess of the ancient Slavs, claiming that they were instrumental in defending Troy from the Greeks in the sixth century BC. The Varangians, he asserted once again, had descended from the "Roxolani" or "Rossolani," who were Slavic. Riurik's ancestry was linked to "Prussian Slavs" by means of a philological formula in which Lomonosov derived the name Varangian-Rossii, or "rossov," from "po-russy" or "prussy."[70]

The second part of the book included a list of rulers from Riurik to Peter the Great, with résumés of the important events of each reign. Accompanying the list was a chart showing each prince's connection to the Riurikide family. Riurik was "invited from the Varangian-Rossii by the Slavs ... to be Great Prince of the Novgorodians," Lomonosov wrote. On the death of Riurik's brothers he became monarch (*samoderzhavets*) of all the northern parts of Russia, which received its name from Riurik's tribe. There was no reference to the *veche*, or early electoral assembly, and only a bare mention of the Tatars. Ivan III's subjugation of Novgorod was explained as a result of chaos in that city and the need to retain Moscow's undivided monarchical power. The Romanovs were "unanimously selected" by the "boyars and a *zemskii sobor* of the entire Russian state," and finally, "Peter the Great was the father of our Fatherland."[71] These were the assumptions about Russia's past and present that Russian patriots wanted to hear. They help explain why Müller's next attempt to publish a detailed account of Russian history was also controversial.

A long study on the history of Novgorod appeared in the *Sammlung* in 1761 and in four issues of *Monthly Compositions* that same year.[72] Using chronicles cited in Tatishchev's manuscript, the *Primary*

Chronicle, Procopius, and Scandinavian sources, Müller discussed the origins of the city first. He also returned to those questions that had so angered Lomonosov in 1749. Acknowledging that the theory of Russians descending from Slavic Roxolani was at least conceivable, Müller went on to say condescendingly that "unfortunately" existing evidence strongly suggested that the Roxolani were a Gothic people. He cited the *Kniga stepennaia* and an anonymous geographer of seventh-century Ravenna to support a conjecture that Roxolani – or Varangian Russes – lived around the Vistula, in Prussia, between the sixth and ninth centuries.[73] In this way Müller gave ground on his earlier suggestion that the Russians may have derived their name from a Finnish word for Swedes, but still gave Riurik and the Varangians a Scandinavian origin. He rejected again opinions expressed in the *Sinopsis* about the etymological significance to Russian history of the words for "scattered" and "glory" and discounted abruptly the notion that the name Russian might have originated with a prince of Rosh who was mentioned by the Old Testament's prophet Ezekiel. But in contrast to the very sarcastic tone he had employed in 1749, Müller now seemed almost apologetic for his conclusions and did not depict the Varangians as conquerors: 'The Varangians, from whom Novgorod received its first princes, were called Rossii, and from them the name Russian [rossian] was spread over the Slovenes [slovian], almost in the same way that the Britons took from the Angles or Anglo-Saxons the name English, or that the Gauls were called French after the Franks. The comparison has differences, however, in that the Varangians were not here as conquerors and did not make up an entire nation, which could be transferred from one country to another. The Novgorodians invited only Varangian princes in order to provide them with a government.'[74] According to Lomonosov, who immediately complained about the article to Razumovskii, this piece "demonstrates his [Müller's] maliciousness still further. In his different works he repeats his dingy dissertation and forgets his punishment."[75] This time Lomonosov's allegations could not prevent the series from continuing.

Müller's narrative included a list of all Novgorodian princes from Riurik to Boris Andreevich (d. 1308), the last members of Novgorod's own princely family to govern. Of special interest was his discussion of the events of the 1470s, which resulted in Moscow's subjugation of Novgorod. In writing about Novgorod's traditional freedoms and the *veche*, where "everyone had the right to give his opinion freely," Müller touched on matters that apologists for Muscovite policies consistently failed to mention; he did not apply the *Sinopsis* formula which described all Muscovite territorial aggrandizement in terms of regaining "rightful" Russian lands. But Müller was certainly no renegade when it came to political interpretation. Muscovy's abrogation of Novgorodian freedoms in the fifteenth century was necessary, he argued, because "freedom often caused riots and bad leadership."[76]

The essay contained information about Swedish intrusions into Novgorod in the seventeenth century, a long discourse on Patriarch Nikon, several pages about Feofan Prokopovich in Novgorod, and some scattered material on other church leaders in that city during the 1740s and 1750s. In the August issue, Müller portrayed the administrative apparatus of both medieval Novgorod and Pskov. Power rested with a hierarchy of merchant officials headed by the *posadnik* (mayor), whom Müller equated with an elected "bürgermeister of a German free city-state." References to the *posadnik* as defender of city rights against the tsar's envoy and to the *veche* as a decision-making body were unique in Russian historical writing to that date and for some time afterward. Indeed, for the great majority of his readers this would have been their first introduction to the *veche*.[77]

Besides his own contributions and extracts from works by Tatishchev, Mankiev, and J.-G. Gerber,[78] Müller published studies by three contemporary geographer-historians – Fischer, F.I. Soimonov, and P.I. Rychkov. Fischer contributed three essays to *Monthly Compositions*: a piece on the Tatars and the origin of their name; another on the peoples who lived in the north that appeared in the February and May issues of 1755; and, finally, a historical discussion of the Khans and the names for various Chinese dynasties that was printed in October of the same year.[79] Soimonov's description of the area around the Caspian Sea and parts of its history appeared in all but one issue in 1763 and simultaneously in book form, edited by Müller.[80] The articles contained information about Peter's expeditions throughout the Caspian region, described a Persian tour in which Soimonov was involved in 1722, and outlined the history of caravan trade in the area. Müller was the first to give Soimonov written credit for his contribution to the map-making expedition of the Caspian in 1719–21. As well, in 1764 he reprinted an atlas of the Caspian Sea that F.I. Soimonov had published some thirty years earlier. After Soimonov was appointed governor of Siberia in 1757, he provided Müller with valuable geographical and natural history information. He printed so many reports on Siberia that later writers mistakenly named him the author of Müller's own long essay of 1755 on Siberian trade. Soimonov also contributed a two-part article on Siberia and its history to *Monthly Compositions* in 1764.[81]

In introducing Rychkov's work to his readers, Müller accomplished more than simply making historical and geographical information available. Without Müller's encouragement, Rychkov might never have published his important studies on Orenburg province, where he served the central government. Having published a few minor essays in the 1740s, Rychkov asked Tatishchev for assistance in his efforts to become a member of the Academy. Tatishchev's recommendation that Rychkov be appointed an honorary member was turned down in 1749.[82] An article on the history of commerce that Rychkov sent to the Academy in 1751 was ignored until Müller printed it unsigned in the February and April issues of the first volume of *Monthly Compositions*.[83] In a conclusion, Müller noted that its author should be encouraged to continue his work. Rychkov immediately notified the Academy Conference of his authorship, thanked Müller, and sent him two more pieces, which were duly printed.[84] In 1758 and 1759 Müller nominated Rychkov to the Academy, a proposition that once again embroiled him with Lomonosov. Lomonosov opposed Rychkov on the grounds that he had not yet proved himself as a scholar, did not read Latin, and was not versed in the "literary sciences." Müller won a partial victory in this battle – in 1759 Rychkov settled for a position as the Academy's first "corresponding member."[85]

Rychkov regularly sent Müller information on Orenburg, Astrakhan, and parts of Siberia; he also translated material for *Monthly Compositions* and was the only person to send in answers to a "Problem" ("Zadacha") section that Müller added to the journal in 1763. These "problems," which Müller said were to be "mainly on the history and antiquity of Russia, and the natural history of the Russian Empire,"[86] added to the historical dimension of the journal. Probably the most important of Rychkov's contributions to *Monthly Compositions* was his "History of Orenburg," which appeared in 1759. This work had been completed in a slightly different form and under a slightly different title in 1744 and had impressed Tatishchev, but it was left to Müller to give Rychkov the exposure he needed. When Rychkov's *Topography of Orenburg*, which had been serialized in *Monthly Compositions* in 1762, was printed as a two-volume book, Müller reviewed it and said that it should serve as a model for topographical studies of other Russian provinces. In his turn, Rychkov introduced his *Outline of the History of Kazan* (1767) by recommending that a general history of all Russia be prepared and implied that only Müller was capable of producing it.[87]

In the mean time, Lomonosov refused to let the matter of Rychkov's appointment die. In January 1761, he sent a detailed report to

Razumovskii in which he charged that Müller "not only writes but also prints false and misleading statements; for example, Rychkov is presented as an honorary member." Lomonosov went on to insist that Müller was abusing his position as secretary of the Conference by distorting the minutes and blamed him and Taubert for all the troubles at the Academy.[88] He suggested that the two men be removed from their posts. Taubert showed a copy of the letter to Müller, who rushed to his own defence with a passionate letter to Teplov. After pleading his innocence on the question of the accuracy of the protocols and claiming to have no argument himself with the Chancellery, he wrote: 'M. Lomonosoff cherche en tout occasion à me chagriner par des ordres [from the Chancellery] et quelquefois les autres deux messieurs, voulant seulement montrer par la sa grandeur et ma petitesse ... Croyez-moi, Monsieur, Lomonosoff est un furieux, armé d'un couteau à la main. Il ruinera toute l'Académie, si Son Excell. n'y mettra ordre bientôt. Nous en voyons le funeste exemple de l'université et du Gymnase, dont il a la direction exclusive. Ils n'on jamais été dans un si mauvais état, qu'à present. Il prétendait exercer le même despotisme dans nos conférences. C'est en quoi qu'il m'a trouvé toujours contraire à ses intentions. Hinc illae lacrymae.'[89]

Müller's intense dislike for Lomonosov also was reflected in his correspondence with Euler and, less directly, on the pages of *Monthly Compositions*. In a far from subtle letter to Euler in August 1762, Müller remarked that "Lomonosov is dangerously ill, and Taubert is sick also. To the latter I wish permanent good health, for he is almost irreplaceable at the Chancellery."[90] He said nothing about Lomonosov's recovery.

The arguments between Müller and Lomonosov were not always the result of personal animosity, although their dislike for each other helped determine the vehemence with which they debated. Professional rivalry and Academy politics also coloured their relations. Moreover, there was still the old question of foreign domination of the Academy to rankle the Russian scholars. Thus, when Lomonosov was appointed chief administrator of the Academy university in 1760, his attempts to reform that institution were regarded by Müller and others as part of a scheme to take the university, in which Russians prevailed, out from under Academy control. Lomonosov recommended that special privileges – the right to award degrees, to promote students, to allot vacations, and to have independent access to the Academy budget – be granted to the university. He also asked that university professors be assigned a place on the Table of Ranks.

In fact, Lomonosov's main ambition was to bring some kind of order into the university which was at that time barely functioning as a teaching organization. In 1759 he proposed that the Academy university be modelled after the University of Moscow, that new courses (Russian, law, chemistry, botany, anatomy, and eastern languages) be added to the curriculum, and that an organized program of instruction be established as soon as possible. He was opposed in this by Müller, Taubert, Fischer, and others who did not like the idea of university professors becoming the equal of academicians. At any rate, Lomonosov's illness in 1762 forestalled any effective reform of the university in St Petersburg.

Müller also opposed effectively two geographical expeditions that Lomonosov urged the Academy to sponsor in 1760–1. His opposition was expressed in professional terms, with emphasis on the lack of a detailed prospectus and a statement of purpose in the proposition submitted by Lomonosov. The Russian gained a modicum of revenge in 1763 when he was able to demonstrate the impracticability of a program created by Müller and Taubert to chart the agricultural products and other goods manufactured throughout Russia. Lomonosov persuaded Razumovskii to allow him to incorporate a similar project into the geography department's work on a Russian atlas.[91] Thus, Müller and Lomonosov remained on opposite sides.

When finally he got around to reviewing Lomonosov's *Short Russian Chronicle* in 1763, three years after it had been published, Müller shrugged it off, saying that the text was too brief to be of any use in schools. Only two months earlier, Müller strongly recommended that the *Sinopsis* be reissued "for lovers of history," although he warned readers that it was unscholarly.[92] This proposal was a far cry from sentiments that Müller had expressed in the dissertation of 1749, when he accused the author of the *Sinopsis* of "concluding by means of guesses." Nevertheless, he now preferred that readers go back to the *Sinopsis* rather than read Lomonosov's book.

In the same issue in which he reviewed Lomonosov, Müller singled out Hilmar Curas's *Short Universal History* (*Sokrashchennaia universal'-naia istoriia*), translated from the German by Volchkov and printed in 1762, for criticism. It too was "unscholarly" and lacked references to the role in history of religion, the arts and sciences, customs and morals, laws and political structure, trade and the economy, or military science. "But," he said, "there is no other book which teaches about the first basics of history." He went on to state that the skimpy thirty-four pages devoted to Russia did not lessen the need for a better national history textbook.[93] Lomonosov's was twice as long, but apparently still not long enough. Müller knew, but failed to mention, that the few pages given over to Russia in Volchkov's translation were written by I.S. Barkov, a close associate of Lomonosov's.[94] The Historiographer ended his review of Curas with a suggestion that Voltaire's book on Peter the Great, which Lomonosov had assailed, be used as supplementary reading.

Elizabeth's Russification campaign had not prevented her from agreeing to Voltaire's appointment to the Academy as an honorary member in 1746.[95] She and her favourite, Ivan Shuvalov, then pressed him to write a history of Peter the Great, hoping that Voltaire's name would bring her family some favourable publicity. Even though he resented the idea that such a work be commissioned from someone living outside Russia, Müller yielded reluctantly to Shuvalov's urging that he assist Voltaire. He also recognized that Voltaire's reputation would assure a European reading audience that no Russian author could attract. Thus he sent Voltaire vast amounts of material so as to help shape the final product.

But when the *Histoire de l'empire de Russie sous Pierre le Grand* appeared in two volumes between 1759 and 1763, it infuriated many Russians because the author depicted Russia before Peter as barbaric and violent. Müller was not pleased with the final product either and told Büsching that he had made many suggestions that Voltaire ignored.[96] He immediately took issue with the famous French writer and in 1761–2 anonymously printed a series of very critical reviews of the first volume in a journal published in Hamburg. Nevertheless, a large part of the outcry from Russia's nationalists, who knew only that he had assisted Voltaire, was directed against Müller. In 1761, he wrote Shuvalov: "I hope that in reading [Voltaire's] work, you excuse me from the censure which you directed against it. Certainly, all the shame must fall on its creator; but lamentably, I see myself accused constantly in a cruel way." In June 1762, however, Catherine II became empress. She was anxious to appear enlightened to Voltaire and welcomed his interest in Russia, thereby making it difficult for Russians to attack the French writer in print. Müller ventured to write sarcastically about those who saw Voltaire as "the greatest man of the century," in a review that appeared in *Monthly Compositions* in 1764, but his earlier recommendation of the book on Peter the Great was a sign that he preferred to curry Catherine's favour.[97]

Müller was not quite so prudent when it came to publishing outside Russia. He challenged Voltaire's interpretation of Russian history in 1769 and again in 1782 by sending articles for Büsching to print anonymously in the *Magazine für die neue Historie und Geographie*.[98] He and Lomonosov had been the most prolific critics of the work in the year (1759–60) during which sample copies were examined by members of the Academy. Voltaire shrugged off much of the criticism by telling Shuvalov that his detractors contradicted each other. One familiar dissonance occurred over Voltaire's suggestion that the name of "les anciens Slaves, ou Slavons," derived from the word "esclave," or slave. Lomonosov reacted sharply saying that it came from *slava* and that this could be demonstrated by the fact that many early "princes had names which ended with 'slav,' for example, Sviatoslav, Vseslav, and others." Müller agreed this time that the name came from *slava*, but added that this "signifies nothing."[99]

Generally, however, Müller's main concern in the early 1760s was to protect the integrity of *Monthly Compositions*, and the squabbles with Lomonosov over other matters were more time-consuming and irritating than they were of serious consequence. After 1762, somewhat to his surprise, Müller was drawn away from his favourite work more and more because his special skills were suddenly in demand at court.

The accession of Catherine II, who was known to have far stronger leanings toward the world of learning than the four rulers whom he previously served, was greeted enthusiastically by Müller. The short and erratic reign of Peter III generally had unsettled the country and endangered the careers of Elizabeth's favourites in government and at the Academy, among them her close friend Razumovskii. But the important part that he and Teplov (who had been placed under arrest briefly in 1761) played in the conspiracy that brought Catherine to the throne assured their continued dominance of the Academy.

The apparent guarantee of the status quo at the Academy suited Müller perfectly. Indeed, most of the academicians and Russia's men-of-letters were immensely relieved at Catherine's success. Her German origins and her known asociation with European "enlighteners" promised an end to the rather erratic anti-foreign outbursts that had characterized Elizabeth's reign. Her reputation as a friend of learning, her current popularity (at least in the capital city), and her professed desire for peace all augured well for enlightenment in Russia. Ruled by incompetents since 1725 and subjected to a series of succession crises, useless and expensive wars, and the uncertainties of court machinations, educated Russians anxiously looked forward to a period of stability. Even the Russian nationalists were appeased by Catherine's tendency to draw analogies between her projects and those of Peter the Great.

The new empress demonstrated an interest in the affairs of the Academy by attending a public assembly on 2 July 1763. Accompanied by "noble people of both sexes," she listened to lectures by Aepinus (in German) on his meteorological observations, by J.-E. Zeiger (in German) on the manufacture of telescopes, and by Rumovskii (in Russian) on the history of optics. Müller presented her with a volume of the *Commentarii* on behalf of the academicians.[100]

Catherine's visit to the Academy was by no means a symbol of mere polite interest in the world of learning. She was anxious to examine the institution at first hand in order to discover what services it was best able to render to her. She had already taken the first steps toward the reorganization of all the agencies of education in Russia and looked to the Academy for experts to guide her in that and other grandiose schemes for reshaping the Russian empire. In that sense her ambitions for the Academy were much like those of Peter the Great.

Müller had conversed with Catherine while she was still grand duchess, and later events suggest that she was impressed by his awareness of the needs of the Russian empire. The fact that his former student, Adodurov, had been Catherine's Russian teacher and was appointed curator of the university in Moscow in 1762 helped further to bring him to her attention.[101] Adodurov had been arrested at the time of Count A.P. Bestuzhev-Riumin's disgrace in 1758 and exiled to Orenburg. He had corresponded with Müller from there. Catherine's accession saw him returned with considerable prestige. Besides the university post, Adodurov was appointed president of the College of Manufacturers. He asked Müller for proposals on the structure of the university and probably recommended him to Catherine for consultation on a variety of matters. The Adodurov connection may also have brought Müller to the attention of Count Nikita Panin, *Oberhofmeister* (1760–73) to Grand Duke Paul and Catherine's adviser on diplomacy. Panin and Adodurov had been friends since the 1730s. The memoranda on China that Catherine commissioned from Müller in 1763 and 1764 must have gone to Panin before they reached the empress. They were addressed to vital national issues and the degree to which Müller felt secure is reflected in the fact that he touched on questions that went well beyond her instructions, that is, on serfdom, the Russian social system, and economic development.

Catherine's concern for China was in part a consequence of the dire circumstances of the Russian economy at the time of her accession. Relations with China were so poor that customs revenue from the East had dropped drastically since the mid-1750s. This, coupled with a report that she received from Teplov in 1762 criticizing both the system of monopolies and tax farming persuaded her to eliminate most crown and private monopolies. The lucrative China caravan trade was officially opened to everyone in October 1762, but since all diplomatic and commercial relations between the two countries were broken off in 1764, the central treasury benefitted very little from her

decision. The empress requested from Müller background information for meetings undertaken in St Petersburg in October 1764, at
which the likelihood of war with China was discussed. The tone of his
reports indicates clearly that Müller saw war as a possibility.

In 1763 Müller recommended that the large area stretching from the
Irtysh to the Argun' be settled by Russian peasants and serfs, whose
owners should be forced to release them if they volunteered to serve
as colonists. Although he suggested that some form of compensation
be offered the landed gentry, the adoption of such a plan would have
shaken the traditional relationship between landowner and serf.
Müller's reasoning was shaped by practical consideration in the light
of potential conflict with China. He hoped to build up the population
of Siberia "in such numbers that after the first advance against the
Chinese, settlers can be moved from there immediately to newly
acquired places."[102] His primary concerns were strategic and economic; he had been advocating the colonization of Siberia with free
peasants since 1741. Müller long had been convinced that they would
provide both a market and an entrepreneurial spirit that would allow
for the rapid development of Siberia's rich resources. But it would be
unrealistic to assume that Müller was unaware of the broad social
implications of his proposal. In fact, at this very time Catherine was
acting to strengthen the hold that members of the nobility had over
their land and serfs. In 1760, Elizabeth already had granted landowners the right to banish serfs to Siberia as settlers. Catherine allowed
this practice to continue and by 1767 made it difficult to protest the
actions of landowners.

In order to bolster Russia's position against China further, Müller
recommended that the government cater to the Mongolians, who
were then subject to Manchu authority, by offering to act as their
patron. To allay Mongolian suspicions, he proposed that Catherine
issue a manifesto to promise them the sanctity of their own laws and
religion and to remind them of their own greatness during the era of
Genghis Khan.[103] In the memorandum of 1764, Müller ventured into
the field of diplomacy and told Catherine that if she wished to be
successful in her negotiations with the Chinese, she should appoint
an envoy who would "show manly firmness, dignity, wisdom,
calmness, virtue and honesty." The Chinese respect such qualities,
he said, even though they are "liable to many vices themselves." Her
envoy must also be well informed about China's government structure, its economy, and its way of life. His immediate staff must also be
suitably prepared, conversant in Chinese, and well equipped with
maps and charts.[104] In fact, there were few people in Russia better
qualified for such a post than Müller himself. But, although we know

that by 1764 he wanted to leave St Petersburg, it is not clear whether he would have taken on such a post – if he had been asked. At any rate, Catherine finally opened up negotiations with China in 1768, and an agreement was signed that amended somewhat the Kiakhta treaty of 1727. Customs barriers were removed by Russia, and trade was resumed. It would seem that Müller's concerns had been realistic, for Russia had little real strength from which to deal with questions on the Chinese borders.

Müller's satisfaction with the new regime in 1762 was revealed in the same letter to Baron J.A. Korff in which he had bemoaned the fate of his "Essay on the History of Modern Russia":

Now it appears that a favourable period has opened, because her Imperial Majesty, our gracious Empress, expressed kindly satisfaction with my work. I only regret that I have too many academic duties. The minutes of meetings, domestic and foreign correspondence, publication of the *Commentarii*, and our Russian journal on which I, having no assistance, am now working for the eighth year, take from me an extraordinary amount of time: but meanwhile my strength is failing, and I am scarcely able to stand work until twelve or one at night. The historian of a country about which so little has been written must be occupied with this work alone. I was worried as to how this work would be maintained after my death, and therefore invited from Göttingen an adjunct, to whom I might give the necessary directions and show the use of my extensive collection of data. This succeeded quite happily. Herr Schlözer, of whom I speak, is by no means a novice. Some years before this he spent in Sweden and became known by his article on the contemporary state of learning there and by his Swedish biographies. I decided to do what someone else may not have done. I invited Herr Schlözer without consulting anyone else. His journey here was made at my own expense. I gave him lodgings with me and, in addition, one hundred rubles salary on condition that he should help in my work. Finally, when he became well accustomed to the Russian language, he entered academic service and I count the money expended well spent, because in this way I served society and laid the foundations of success for a man full of promise.[105]

The reality of Müller's relationship with Schlözer was not quite like that which he depicted to Korff. Now earning about 1,700 rubles annually, Müller had the means to advertise in the *Königsberg Zeitung* for a young German to serve both as an assistant to him and as a tutor to his children.[106] On the advice of Büsching, he hired twenty-six-year-old August Ludwig Schlözer, who arrived in St Petersburg in November 1761. At Göttingen in 1754, Schlözer had studied with the famous theologian, orientalist, and historian Johann David Michaelis, who recommended him to Büsching. After spending some years in Sweden, where he mastered a number of languages, including Swedish, Danish, and Arabic, Schlözer had returned to Göttingen to study philology, jurisprudence, and political economy – so Müller was blessed with a highly skilled assistant. Schlözer's decision to take up Müller's offer was prompted in the main by his need for money and an assumption that only in Russia would he find the means to attain his real goal, which was to reach the Far East. Müller had encouraged him in this, having written that anyone "who wishes to travel will find no better occasion for it except in the Russian Empire" and promising that it would be relatively simple for Schlözer to arrange transportation to Turkey, Persia, or China, if he so desired.[107]

Schlözer was greeted warmly by Müller, lived in his home for three months, and worked hard to learn Russian. Even though they were soon to become estranged, Schlözer later recalled his first impressions of Müller thus:

He was handsome as a picture, impressive on account of his size and strength ... He could be extraordinarily cheerful, come upon witty, whimsical thoughts and give caustic answers; a satyr looked out of his small eyes. In his manner of thinking there was something great, just and noble. In relation to the merits of Russia, which had neglected him to that time, he was a warm patriot, and in expressions concerning the faults of the contemporary government, which no one knew better than he, he was extremely restrained. And this worthy man, who had contributed so much to Russia, after thirty-six years was only a professor ... He was himself an untiring worker, circumspect and exact in every way, and he wished to make others exercise the same qualities in the same degree.[108]

Schlözer noted that the atmosphere in Müller's large home on the shore of the Neva was a "pleasant contrast to the stiffness, pomposity and aloofness" that one found "in small towns" everywhere and that five languages (German, Russian, Finnish, Swedish, and French) were spoken there regularly. He marvelled at a fourteen-year-old serf boy who spoke the first three "freely and correctly" and at the "crowds" of foreigners who came to visit the "famous Müller."

It was from Schlözer that we get a rare glimpse of Müller as a family man. Schlözer also praised Müller's wife, Kristina, as a "beautiful woman in all respects, without pretension, and a perfect mistress of the house," handicapped only by deafness which kept her outside many conversations. The Müller home life was astonishingly full and active. Besides Müller's stepdaughter, his own daughter, and his two sons (Karl and Jakob), three young students lived there. One of them,

H. Condoidi, the son of the gymnasium student whom Müller had tutored in 1728 and who had passed away in 1760, was a ward of Count Nikita Panin, who himself was in charge of Grand Duke Paul's education. Condoidi had his own tutor with him, who also stayed in the Müller household. Another student had come from Holstein and helped instruct Müller's children while attending a *pension* himself. A third young man was German, but Schlözer could remember neither his name nor what he was doing in St Petersburg. H.L.Ch. Bacmeister, a long-time friend of Schlözer's, also lived with the Müllers in 1761, helped to tutor Condoidi and Müller's sons, and assisted with the *Sammlung*.[109] It seems, in fact, that Müller's home became an oasis for young Germans who arrived in St Petersburg in the hope of finding some gainful employment in Russian service. Müller interviewed them, fed them, and did what he could to find them positions.

Also in the house were servants of various nationalities – a Russian coachman, a Swedish housekeeper, a Finnish serf, and several Russian women, some of whom had children of their own. According to Schlözer, foreign-born citizens could not own Russian Serfs (although some manufacturers did), but they could own Finns. At any rate, Müller presided over a veritable assembly of nations with a paternal kindness and generosity that Schlözer continued to admire long after the two men came to dislike each other professionally. According to both Schlözer and Büsching, members of the household ate well and were entertained well – as Schlözer put it, "he kept a good German table." But Müller and his wife were thrifty, and, in contrast to many of his professional colleagues, Müller never went into debt.

Schlözer's admiration of Müller as a person was by no means unqualified, because he also wrote of his employer's "unusual irascibility ... which he did not try to contain." Moreover, having been the victim of an official misinterpretation of such actions once already, Müller was very hesitant about granting Schlözer access to his vast collection of material on Russian history. Schlözer's remark that Müller "had grovelled – but who, at the time, did not grovel in order to move up?" suggests that he recognized the awkwardness of Müller's position. This situation was eased somewhat when Taubert, who was put in charge of preparing the *Library of Russian History* for publication in 1761, brought Müller several parts of the *Primary Chronicle* for evaluation. Müller showed this material to Schlözer and had him compare it with other redactions of the chronicle. Schlözer's ability in studying the chronicles inspired Müller to propose his admission to the Academy for five years as an adjunct for Russian history. But for Schlözer this proposal in the winter of 1762 was not an honour; rather it was the last straw in his increasingly strained relations with Müller. Schlözer now reminded his mentor of the "promise" to arrange a trip to the Orient. A quarrel ensued, and Schlözer moved out of Müller's home. Mutually incompatible temperaments cost Müller a valuable assistant and Schlözer a valuable patron.

After rejecting Müller's offer of an adjunct post, and then spending some months searching for a position as private tutor, Schlözer accepted a slightly more favourable contract at the Academy from Taubert as an adjunct with no obligatory time of service. He was also to tutor Razumovskii's children. In spite of their differences, Müller gave Schlözer glowing references in a letter to Razumovskii and even suggested that if he progressed sufficiently in Russian history Schlözer might soon be eligible for appointment as professor. Razumovskii thereupon named Schlözer an adjunct to the historiographer, to work on Russian history and "in the case of [Müller's] death to continue his activities."[110] To all intents and purposes, Schlözer was right back where he had started. But even though Müller had acted honourably in his dealings with Schlözer, he soon found that the young man had no intention of assisting him in the normal sense of the word. In fact, the very first time Müller asked him to index a volume of the *Sammlung,* Schlözer replied that such a task was beneath his dignity as an adjunct of the Academy. After that, Müller ignored Schlözer, who then applied himself to the study of Russian history on his own.

With no further assignments forthcoming from Müller, Schlözer became a de facto assistant to Taubert, who gave him Tatishchev's manuscript and a German translation of one of the chronicles to read. He then began research on the connection between the early Russian princes and Byzantium. He also applied to Michaelis for a posting to Hanover and twice turned down offers to teach in the Russian Cadet Corps. In April 1764 Schlözer asked the Academy for a three-month leave of absence in order to travel in Germany. At the same time, he submitted for approval a *Periculum,* in which he proposed a detailed study of Greek and other foreign sources of Russian history, with special attention to word derivations. Taubert suggested that Schlözer be invited to a general assembly so that members might discuss his proposals and decide upon his potential as an Academy or university professor.[111]

Taubert's associates in the Chancellery, including Lomonosov, agreed to the general meeting, but Müller persuaded the Chancellery to request a detailed written plan from Schlözer beforehand. In response, Schlözer submitted two propositions: one in which he recommended a method for examining ancient Russian documents and history, the other a plan for making historical information better known. All in all, his ideas were quite like those that Müller had been advocating and practising for years. Schlözer proposed to collect and collate chronicle texts and then to publish short pieces about Russian history in a style suitable for popular reading.[112] But his suggestion in the *Periculum* that "the Russian language was not only filled with a great number of Greek words, but changed under the influence of Greek speech so much ... that in reading your ancient writers one might think that he is reading not Russian, but a Greek text" attracted Lomonosov in the way that a bull is excited by a red cape.[114]

Lomonosov tried to prevent Schlözer's appointment, saying that the *Periculum* demonstrated that the German was "unacquainted with the Russian language." Noting also that Müller and Fischer were already professors of history and that his own study of ancient Russia was already in the press, Lomonosov declared that there were no openings for Schlözer. In other words, there was no need to hire more foreigners to do a job that was best left to Russians. Even though he and Müller had a common goal for a change, Lomonosov could not miss an opportunity to discredit Müller, and so he warned Razumovskii that it would again be folly to appoint a professor of Russian history who at first could not read Russian properly. He then pointed out, not particularly accurately, that Schlözer had not even been elected as an adjunct, rather he had been presented by one person only, Müller, "a man who himself has been brought before two commissioners ... suspected of writing and speaking improper opinions about Russia."[114]

In his statement to the Conference, Müller lauded Schlözer's potential but said that the young man was not yet qualified to write Russian history. "If Mr Schlözer intends to spend all his life working on Russian and in the service of the Russian state, I would be very pleased, for that is why I invited him from abroad," Müller said, while making it plain that he did not think that that was what Schlözer had in mind. Müller urged that the Conference not allow Schlözer to take Russian historical documents to Germany with him, implying that he might not return to St Petersburg.[115] Years later Schlözer was to write: "Only two opposed me; they were also opponents of Taubert. One was a Russian, Lomonosov; the other my fellow countryman, Müller. The first cursed rudely in wild fury; the second praised and played the hypocrite, and so was more dangerous."[116]

But even the combined energies of Müller and Lomonosov could not override the fact that the majority of the Academy had already voted in favour of Schlözer. As a last resort, Lomonosov turned to the tactic he had employed against Müller in 1749 – he told the Senate that Schlözer's appointment might prove politically dangerous because he had asked to take confidential archival material to Europe with him. In typical Academy fashion, Schlözer's private papers were seized, but this time by Taubert, who was acting to protect him.[117] Because Taubert and Lomonosov could not possibly agree on the issue, the Senate assigned to Razumovskii the task of investigating Schlözer's papers. Confusion reigned throughout the summer of 1764. Razumovskii was a friend of Taubert and was furious at Lomonosov for interfering in the matter. But Lomonosov had the ear of the Senate, to which Razumovskii was responsible. Compromise was reached only when the father of one of the boys Schlözer tutored in the Razumovskii home was persuaded by Teplov, by now a close associate of Panin's at court, to use his influence to bring the matter directly to Catherine II.

Using Teplov as a go-between, Catherine requested proposals from Schlözer and, after examining them, agreed in December that he be appointed a member of the Academy as a professor of history. In January 1765, Schlözer signed a five-year contract, was allowed full access to books and manuscripts on Russian history, and was granted permission to take a three-month leave of absence abroad. Schlözer's salary was set at 860 rubles, and he was given permission to publish all his works on Russian history, under the supervision of the empress herself.[118] On the face of it, Catherine's decision marked a major victory for the foreign component of the Academy and a shattering blow to those Russians who resented having their national history written by foreigners. Lomonosov blamed Taubert for praising Schlözer "almost limitlessly" and for allowing him to take manuscripts from collections supposedly "preserved especially from foreigners."[119] But Catherine's decision was by no means a rejection of Russian national consciousness. In fact, she was motivated above all else by a desire that a Russian national history be written and had taken care that she had control over the content of any history book that Schlözer might publish. She was also even more acutely conscious than Elizabeth had been of the importance of a good press in Europe. As her own historical writing of the 1780s would demonstrate, she saw history as a medium through which Russia might be placed in the mainstream of European cultural development and as a means to enhance her own image as the heir to both real and imagined ancient Russian glories.

Müller and Lomonosov had been pressing each other during the early years of Catherine's reign. Lomonosov very nearly left the Chancellery in July 1762, when he applied to Catherine for a discharge from service with a pension.[120] The empress was not happy with Lomonosov anyway. He had not greeted her coup with the glowing odes she expected from Russia's men-of-letters – in the main because he was very ill at the time – and his patrons, Count Ivan Shuvalov and Count M.L. Vorontsov, had been close to Peter III. It was nearly a year before Catherine asked one of her officials to find out from Razumovskii whether it was possible to pension Lomonosov. The investigation resulted in an imperial order that Lomonosov be awarded the rank of state councillor and be retired from service at half-pay for the remainder of his life. On hearing this news, Müller was overjoyed. He gleefully wrote to Hebenstreit that "*finally* the Academy is free of Lomonosov."[121] For some reason, however, Catherine changed her mind on both counts in August 1763, and Lomonosov continued in his former capacities.[122]

The change in monarchs in 1762 emboldened Taubert and Teplov. Teplov had helped Catherine achieve the throne and was rewarded both with a large sum of money and with a post as her secretary. Thus he wielded considerable authority. The two men persuaded Razumovskii in late 1762 to reassign Müller to the Academy's geography department as its director, replacing Lomonosov. In his letter to the Chancellery, which in fact had been prepared for him by Taubert, Razumovskii charged that the department had done nothing "for several years" toward the correction of a Russian geography and that its members wasted too much time in arguments and administrative confusion. Lomonosov was enraged. Müller, who had been an indifferent member of the department since he lost the directorship to Lomonosov in 1758, was not anxious to take the job. He notified the Chancellery that he would do so only with a clear mandate, in writing, that he be able to put the department in order as he saw fit and that he could resign the post whenever he wished. In January 1763, Lomonosov outlined in a long memorandum the actual accomplishments of the unit while under his leadership, which included the preparation of nine maps for the revised *Atlas rossiiskoi* and topographies of various towns. He attributed the delays in their publication to Müller's "malicious conduct." While Lomonosov's terminology may have been too harsh, it is true that Müller had been of very little assistance to the geography department. In October 1759 and again in February 1760, the Chancellery, at the behest of Lomonosov, sent sharp reprimands to both Müller and Grishov for not attending departmental meetings.[123]

Lomonosov blamed Taubert for the lack of necessary astronomical equipment and for the fact that the typography had not printed works that the department had completed. Finally, he told Razumovskii that the decision to make Müller director had been based on completely false information provided by Lomonosov's detractors. Although neither Razumovskii nor M.L. Vorontsov, to whom Lomonosov also appealed, would help him, he won this round against Müller anyway. Lomonosov simply continued to run the affairs of the department as if nothing had happened. Müller was too busy with other matters to challenge him.[124]

Müller's concern still lay primarily with the fate of *Monthly Compositions* and his own future in St Petersburg. He had no interest whatsoever in further battles with Lomonosov or with the Chancellery. He was, after all, sixty years old. The final issue of *Monthly Compositions* appeared in December 1764. Four months later, Müller took up residence in Moscow. Officially he went there at the request of Ivan Betskoi, Catherine's adviser on education, on a two-year contract as director of Catherine's new Foundling Home, with the title of college councillor and at the rank of colonel ("*Oberst*").[125]

In February 1765, Müller asked the Conference to decide the fate of *Monthly Compositions*, noting inaccurately that Lomonosov was "disputing" its continuance.[126] Lomonosov wrote to Euler in the same week that Müller was an "ignoramus and the very first professor to be chosen by the flagellum professorum [Schumacher], the living Machiavelli."[127] Within two months, both long-time combatants were gone from the Russian capital, and the final direct confrontation between them was a draw. The Chancellery petitioned the opinion of every Academy member on the fate of *Monthly Compositions* and on a proposal by Lomonosov that a special supplement for economics and physics be issued. It was decided that *Monthly Compositions* would not be reissued, and Lomonosov's suggestion was allowed to die with him in April 1765.[128]

Müller had offered to supply any new editor of *Monthly Compositions* with a full year's content and then to assist him the next year if the journal was revived. He urged its rebirth again in 1766, but the Academy seemed not to be interested. Thus, Müller could start his new career in Moscow with a clean slate and avoid the acrimonious atmosphere of the Academy at his discretion. The remarkable degree to which he was able to complete his myriad projects during the next eighteen years in Moscow is a sad commentary on the futility of Academy life.

Whatever the cross-currents of animosity and respect surrounding Müller as editor, his historical contributions to *Monthly Compositions* survived all debates to become an important part of subsequent Russian historiography and even folklore. Prince M.M. Shcherbatov adopted broadly from Müller's essays on modern Russia and Novgorod and from his extracts from the *Primary Chronicle*. Shcherbatov also cited often from Rychkov's contributions. Nicholas Karamzin included over one hundred citations from Müller's "Essay" and other pieces in each of the first (1818) and ninth (1821) volumes of his *History of the Russian State*, and his heroic tale "Martha Posadnitsa" (1803) was based in part on Müller's study of Novgorod.[129] As we shall see, articles from *Monthly Compositions* were frequently reprinted in European magazines.

Lomonosov's consistent opposition and general lack of support from Müller's fellow academicians did not prevent *Monthly Compositions* from becoming the most popular journal of its time. Its first issues were printed in lots of 600 to 700 copies, but by 1759, 1,250 copies of each number were turned out.[130] This was more than double the number sold of any other Russian-language journal until Karamzin's *Messenger of Europe* (*Vestnik evropy*) appeared in 1802. Karamzin himself wrote in 1801 that *Monthly Compositions* was "incomparably useful to the Fatherland" because it spread "historical" and other information widely throughout the empire.[131] Although Metropolitan Evgenii's description of its readers' reaction may have been too glowing, his comment of 1821 that all literate Russians "read the first Russian monthly with joy and satisfaction"[132] was a sign of the journal's great success.

PART FOUR

Calm and Creativity in Moscow

CHAPTER SEVEN

Educator and Academy Deputy 1765–8

Yesterday I received an unexpected kindness: Her
Imperial Majesty requested my presence for about an
hour [and] talked pleasantly with me about different
matters.

Müller to Taubert, from Moscow, 1764

The final eighteen years of Müller's life were considerably calmer than
the four decades he had spent in Russia's capital city. Now in his
sixties, he was indulged by the court and treated with respect by the
Academy. He was financially secure and was even granted assistants
to help him fulfil the goals he had set for himself many years earlier.
Above all, the contentiousness of which he had been both victim and
sponsor regularly for forty years was no longer a deciding factor
either in his professional career or in his personal life.

The initiatives that led to Müller's association with the Foundling
Home in Moscow came from A.F. Büsching, who arrived in St
Petersburg in the summer of 1761 to serve as pastor in a newly
instituted Lutheran church school. Although he and Müller had been
corresponding for some time, this was the first opportunity for them
to become close friends. Early in 1764, Ivan Betskoi asked Büsching to
be director of the Foundling Home in Moscow. This was an invitation
of considerable significance, because the Foundling Home was the
centre-piece of a wide program undertaken by Empress Catherine
and Betskoi to disseminate knowledge among her people. During the
1760s, Catherine called for the reform and reorganization of the
University of Moscow, the Cadet Corps, and the Academy of Fine
Arts. She also established educational institutions for noble and
burgher girls and sponsored a comprehensive network of public
schools.

Betskoi (1704–95), president of the Academy of Fine Arts and
director of both the St Petersburg Cadet Corps and the school for
noble girls at Smolny, was Catherine's chief agent in this sweeping

attempt to enlighten at least part of Russia. He believed with passion that the main emphasis in schools should be on moral training. In this he echoed the ideas of John Locke, who also stressed character-building as the chief function of schools. In Betskoi's regular boarding-school system, children entered at age five or six and remained in the school until they reached eighteen or twenty. They were almost completely isolated from outside society to give the school an opportunity to inculcate into them ideals that Betskoi and Catherine wanted their new generation of citizens to have. In the Foundling Homes, however, children were registered as infants and were therefore even more suitable subjects for Betskoi's educational experiments. In short, the Foundling Homes were intended as incubators for a new type of Russian subject. "The main purpose of our education system," Betskoi announced in 1764, "is to produce healthy, strong, cheerful foster-children who are able to serve the fatherland in art and trade, to create in them wisdom and heart so that they will not only be useful to themselves, but good Christians and true citizens."[1]

Büsching recognized the honour that Betskoi's invitation to him implied, but he did not wish to commit himself to such an important task. In fact, already in 1764 he was planning to return to Berlin. In his stead he proposed Müller. In Büsching's own words, "[Müller's] skill in Russian, his forty years of familiarity with the Russian people, and his considerable practical knowledge, together mean that there is no person better suited to the position." Betskoi agreed, and together they persuaded Müller to go to Moscow. According to Büsching, Müller's reluctance was overcome by Betskoi himself, who stressed the importance Catherine attached to the undertaking. Büsching told Müller that it was time for him to be "free from the Academy Chancellery, from Lomonosov and people like him."[2] These were compelling arguments.

Müller's seemingly precipitous move to Moscow took his colleagues by surprise. Schlözer wrote: "The news shocked me. A man of 60 years ... commanded to a completely new kind of work. This was terribly cruel ... When I went to visit him that day ... he did not deny that he could not adjust to this unnatural change, which he saw as a punishment."[3] Others suggested that Schlözer had actually replaced Müller as professor of history, and this may have seemed to be the case when Lomonosov's death left Schlözer's friend Taubert in control of the Chancellery. But Müller's own notes make it clear that the decision to leave St Petersburg was entirely his own and that he had professional as well as personal reasons for doing so. In his 1746 proposal that there be a history department established at the

Academy, he had recommended Moscow as the logical place in which to write a history of Russia. Acknowledging, in his autobiography, that he would not "normally be inclined" to take on a position such as that of "Chief Supervisor" of a Foundling Home, he added that it was an opportunity to bring him closer to the "archives for Russian history in Moscow."[4]

Büsching's high praise for Müller was not a mere reflection of their close friendship, for Müller's credentials as an educational administrator were quite impressive. With the exception of his ten years in Siberia, he had been involved directly with education from the time of his arrival in Russia until his disgrace of 1749-50. Müller returned to school-related duties in April 1757 when Elizabeth issued a decree that demanded that all foreign tutors in Russia have their qualifications certified. Examining boards were established at the University of Moscow and at the Academy of Sciences. In St Petersburg, Müller joined Fischer, Braun, and Strube de Piermont on a committee charged with assessing the qualifications of all foreigners who taught in *pensions* (private schools) or in private homes.[5] The tone of Elizabeth's decree suggested that this was a matter not to be taken lightly. Fines of 100 rubles could be levied against employers who failed to comply with the new regulations, and the offending teacher could be expelled from the country. The law was enforced sporadically, and complaints about the incompetence and prevalence of foreign tutors increased during the remainder of the century.

During the 1750s and early 1760s, Müller's interest in education was reflected on the pages of *Monthly Compositions*, which contained eleven articles (mainly translations) on pedagogy. Their emphasis was upon the usefulness of education, the value of instruction for both sexes, a concern for health and hygiene, and the avoidance of harsh punishments. More important, however, was their contention that schools must inculcate good morals, strong character, religious faith, and loyalty to the state. These notions were fully in keeping with educational views held by Betskoi – and Locke – and were to be the guiding principles of his Foundling Homes. Thus, Müller's pedagogical principles made him a logical participant in the sweeping educational reforms of the 1760s by which Catherine and Betskoi hoped to modernize Russia.

Since Müller's selection of material on education for *Monthly Compositions* all appeared before Betskoi's theories were made known publicly, they are worth examining in some detail. They bear witness to Müller's desire to keep abreast of current pedagogical theories. In the very first year of the journal, an article entitled "Rules for Educating Children" was translated from the German moralizing weekly *Der Patriot*. The word "usefulness" was its keynote, but it also urged that sons and daughters be educated with equal zealousness, that harsh punishments be avoided, that good health be a special concern, and that both parents and teachers set impeccable examples for children to emulate.

The majority of the articles on education were translated extracts from the works of Aristotle and Plato, especially the dialogues of Socrates about the duties of citizens, methods of teaching, and the nature of human morals. Typically, an essay on the education of children in the Roman Empire, which was spread over four issues, stressed that Roman instruction had as its main objective the training of good citizens and that a heavy onus lay on parents to set the stage for such training. Further notices, all in translation from the classical writers on the education of children in Sparta, Athens, and Persia, carried similar messages. In each case, the inculcation of virtue, good morals, and patriotism was considered more important than general learning. In 1759 another essay was taken from a current German magazine to demonstrate the importance of the physical well-being of children, who were compared to "young sprouts" or seeds that had to be very carefully nurtured from infancy. The next year a writer was quoted as saying that man is naturally good (a sentiment with which many Christian teachers disagreed), but that youngsters must be "always overseen by parents lest they accidentally learn things that will incline them to evil."[6] In this way ideas that resembled those of Wolff, Locke, Montaigne, and Prokopovich appeared as food for thought in Russia before Catherine II opened her campaign for a new system of education.

In the review section that he added to *Monthly Compositions* during its final two years, Müller regularly noted new textbooks and other publications that might benefit the education of Russia's youth. Etiquette and moralizing works by Madame le Prince de Beaumont, which happened also to be favourites of the empress, were singled out as mandatory for young girls; Dilthey's universal history ("for noble youth") was recommended for boys; and tracts by John Locke were singled out as valuable guides to parents and instructors of both sexes. Locke's *Some Thoughts Concerning Education* (1693) was translated into Russian in 1759. Müller followed Catherine's example by casting some doubt on Rousseau's *Emile, ou de l'éducation*. Although Rousseau was "one of the most famous writers of our time, and has great talent," Müller wrote, "he is not always right and … sometimes has quite unfounded opinion … against the law of God and the duties of a citizen."[7] Catherine banned *Emile* in 1763 for religious reasons, and she continued to disapprove of Rousseau's ideas on education.

Nevertheless, *Emile* and most of Rousseau's other works (except *Du Contrat sociale*) were translated into Russian with her permission in the 1770s.

The July 1764 issue of *Monthly Compositions* carried a review of Louis René de Caradeuc de la Chalotais's *Essai de l'éducation nationale, ou plan d'études pour la jeunesse*, which had been presented to the parlement at Rennes in 1763 and then published. La Chalotais long had been involved in controversy in France over the role of the religious community in schools. When royal decrees closed Jesuit schools in 1762 and then drove the Jesuits from France itself in 1764, La Chalotais's proposals were among those that helped to provide the basis for a new national school system. He suggested that educational activities should be a prerogative solely of the state, that it be secular, and that its purpose should be to create useful, loyal, and skilled citizens. His essay was translated into Russian seven years later as *Opyt narodnago vospitaniia, ili chertezh nauk* (St Petersburg, 1770). Müller would not have accepted La Chalotais's idea that education should be a monopoly of the upper strata so as not to tempt the less fortunate into dissatisfaction with their lot in life. The Frenchman's advice that religious instruction be replaced altogether by lessons about ethical "Truths" (one of which was to be nationalistic indoctrination) also was too extreme for Russian educators. But his plea for state control of education, lay teachers, more science, and a practical curriculum found a receptive audience. "We should examine this work very carefully, it is worth considering," was Müller's pronouncement on it.[8] Müller's published viewpoint on education coincided almost exactly with opinions expressed by Betskoi in March 1764.

Although Betskoi's first choice to head his Foundling Home in Moscow was Büsching, other government officials already had recognized Müller's special talents even before Catherine ascended the throne. In 1761 the Admiralty College requested his services on behalf of the Naval Cadet Corps, offering him a free hand to investigate its curriculum and to make recommendations for change. While seeking permission to do so from Razumovskii, Müller noted that he had been proffered an extra 200 rubles annually for the task, on which he expected to spend "a couple of hours per day." He insisted that this would not prejudice his work at the Academy, for he was "accustomed to working not only in the day, but also for the good part of the night." Müller ended this letter (in French) by "modestly" informing the Academy president that his contributions to knowledge recently had earned him full membership in the Stockholm Academy of Arts, and that the Académie des sciences in Paris had invited him to serve as a corresponding member.[9]

A few years later, in 1764, Catherine asked Müller to join a commission on educational reform that she established in St Petersburg. Teplov chaired the commission, which, besides Müller, was composed of P.H. Dilthey, T. Klingstedt (vice-president of the College for Lithuanian, Estonian, and Finnish Affairs), and Daniel Dumaresq (chaplain of the English Factory in St Petersburg). Müller and Dumaresq submitted a report to Teplov in April 1764, which contained some criticisms of Betskoi's famous "General Statutes for the Upbringing of Youth of both Sexes," which Catherine had enacted into law in March.[10] Betskoi had proposed that children be segregated from their parents at the earliest possible age – five or six – and educated in state boarding-schools "to fear God and to love moral virtue." The Statutes emphasized primary schooling, on which, its author said, "all subsequent education depends, for it is from the first level that the *new order* will arise."[11]

Neither Müller nor Dumaresq wished to argue against the principles of the Statutes; indeed, the last two essays in *Monthly Compositions* fully endorsed them.[12] But they both questioned the practicality of Betskoi's proposals. Dumaresq had reservations about the usefulness of a curriculum based on a "dead language" (Latin) and that seemed to give pride of place to the humanities. He felt that Russians needed practical training in mathematics, the sciences, and vocational skills. Müller agreed and made more specific suggestions which Teplov summarized for Catherine. In a rare compliment to Müller, Teplov wrote that his ideas were, "it seems to me, ... the most appropriate for the Russian state."[13] Müller urged that three types of schools be established, each attuned to the needs of one of the divisions of state service – military, civil, commercial – and each with its own syllabus. He added that arrangements should be made so that youngsters from all "free" classes might have the opportunity to attend schools to which their abilities recommended them.[14] Thus, Müller's tracts on education echoed the utilitarian motif that filled his writings on trade in Siberia and Russo-Chinese relations.

Dilthey's report to the commission was much more detailed than Müller's and Dumaresq's and stressed above all the need for more qualified teachers. He opposed Betskoi's boarding-school (hothouse) concept and even suggested that domestic servants be trained to act as teachers to the very young in the homes of the gentry. Dilthey went on to say that middle schools should be divided according to estates, that is, separate schools for children of the nobility, for children of merchants, and "for those of other classes." His scheme coincided with Catherine's and Betskoi's only when he acknowledged the primacy of moralizing lessons, which he felt should be passed on to pupils through the agency of courses in ancient history, taught in the Russian language.[15] To this end, Dilthey had already completed a first volume of his *Fundamentals of Universal History (Pervyia osnovaniia universal'noi istorii)* in 1762. Müller reviewed it very favourably in *Monthly Compositions* and recommended that it be adopted for use at the University of Moscow. Dilthey's book was written especially for the edification of "young nobles" and made ample use of Bossuet's *Discours sur histoire universelle* (1681), for which Müller congratulated the author. Nevertheless, the university conference asked Kh.A. Chebotarev to translate H. Freyer's *Vorbereitung zur Universal-historie* (1763) for use at the university. This assignment was concluded by 1769 and included a long section on Russian history prepared by Chebotarev himself but based mainly on Lomonosov's history of medieval Russia.[16] Thus, the work of Dilthey, Müller, and the other members of the commission on educational reform came to nought. By the time the commission actually forwarded its recommendations to the empress, Betskoi already had started the process of reform. In fact, Müller moved to Moscow nearly a year before the report was submitted.

Even though it was not implemented – Catherine may not even have read it – the very detailed plan that Catherine's commission on education produced warrants examination because it included several rather innovative proposals. It therefore reveals yet another dimension of Müller's versatile thinking on the question of enlightenment for Russia. The plan's authors proposed that four types of gymnasia be established: one for especially talented students, who would be expected to advance to university, and the other three to provide trainees for the military, civil, and commercial branches of society. Most striking, however, was the recommendation that the schools be open to "all Russian subjects of the Orthodox faith (except serfs) ... without any regard to rank."[17]

The curriculum was to be the same for all schools during the first eight years of instruction and then would change for the final four years according to the purpose of the gymnasium. For example, students in the advanced gymnasium would study Latin and Greek, rhetoric, ancient and modern history ("which must be accompanied by chronology"), geography ("in more detail than in the other schools"), and basic mathematics. Moral philosophy was also deemed important, as it was for all branches of education. Military students would spend less time on Latin, none on Greek, and much more on Russian, German, and French. Their ability to write reports clearly was stressed above most other subjects. Students within the civil branch were expected to pay more attention to "state affairs" and the intricacies of Russian grammar. Students of commerce were assigned more mathematically oriented courses than were those in the other gymnasia. In geography, they were to trace trade routes, and they alone were to be asked to study manufacturing. The principal of class-free schools, the emphasis on skill training, and a recommendation that schools be compulsory for all males were characteristics more reminiscent of education projects under Peter the Great than they were of Betskoi's. The commission's insistence that moral training be the starting point for all education was a feature that it shared with Betskoi. Its secular tone was common to both eras of educational reform.

Müller's interim predecessor at the Moscow Foundling Home was I.A. Rost, who had been invited to the University of Moscow (from Göttingen) by Müller in 1757 to serve as an instructor in the English language and in higher mathematics. Rost had held the position of director from the Home's inception in 1764 but had not been an active administrator. As well as being occupied with university matters, he was seventy years old at the time of his appointment. However, he did give Müller a written statement on the school's purpose and its problems and discussed the institution with him several times. Rost was Müller's cousin by marriage and spoke quite frankly with him about difficulties he might encounter when dealing with Betskoi.[18]

During his short term of office, Müller fashioned regulations in order to place the institution on a firm administrative footing. His rules included instructions for the physical well-being of the children and for proper household management on the part of the Home's mistresses. They also detailed his own responsibilities and those of the Home's council of trustees. According to P.M. Maikov, Betskoi's biographer, Müller's instructions formed the greater part of the second and third sections of the "General Plan of the Moscow Foundling Home," which became law in Agust 1767.[19]

While at the Moscow Foundling Home, Müller also prepared a syllabus for the Imperial Corps of Pages in St Petersburg. He proposed that a special home be established for the corps, with a resident housemaster and a curriculum including mathematics, philosophy, ethics, national and international law, history, geography, Latin and Russian, as well as character-building and moral training. Müller's program marked a decided improvement over the existing one, which had not included Russian and had left all instruction in the hands of one rather incompetent foreigner who knew no Russian.[20]

Müller took the time in 1764 to prepare a detailed evaluation of another educational institution as well. He was asked by his friend

Adodurov, who had returned from exile to be appointed curator of the University of Moscow by Catherine in October 1762, to examine the structure of that academic organization. Müller suggested that the curator and the professors be closely associated, perhaps in the person of a rector who would be elected by the professors from each faculty in turn and who would act as liaison between the curator's office and the university's instructors. He agreed that the professors' salaries should be relatively high and recommended that they be granted high ranks in state service. By this device, Müller hoped that professors might be attracted from Russia's *dvorianstvo*, thereby uniting practices of scholarship with a traditional concept of service, notions that he felt were absent in other classes.

In spite of Betskoi's eloquently expressed ambitions, Catherine's financial support, and Müller's energy, things did not go well for the Foundling Homes (another was established in St Petersburg in 1770) during their first few years. Müller complained regularly to Betskoi about the ineptness of his staff, financial stringencies, and problems with individual children. Betskoi's responses ranged from attempts to placate Müller to suggestions that he was complaining too much and administering too little. Although Müller had been given carte blanche in the appointment of personnel, Betskoi had to warn him several times that he was ignoring the animosities and jealousies developing between those who had been with the Home under Rost and new appointees who were given authority over them. The problem lay with Müller's notorious inability to deal with people at the professional level for any protracted period of time. Betskoi, who in contrast to Müller was well known for his patience, expressed his concern in a letter of 23 June 1765: "Your letter, Sir, filled with sourness, offends me, especially since you explain only the bad side of things; be persuaded that this troubles me. I refer once more to what I said last time, that is, that all commencements are difficult and that only with time and patience will everything work out properly."[21]

Betskoi had reason to worry, for a lot was expected of the Foundling Homes. Thus, grateful as he may have been for Müller's administrative accomplishments, Betskoi was probably just as relieved as Müller when the historian applied for a position elsewhere. A letter to Vice-Chancellor A.M. Golitsyn, dated 9 January 1766, indicated that Müller had been negotiating the move for some time and that he hoped soon to be placed in charge of the archives of the College of Foreign Affairs: "My only purpose in soliciting a place in the archive was to perform a significant service to the state which I have served for more than forty years. I have devoted myself primarily to the treatment of Russian history – an occupation which I had to give up, but which is too hard for me to abandon altogether. If I am employed in the archives, I flatter myself with the hope of returning to that occupation and to that work for the Academy from which I am receiving support."[22] Müller received word of his appointment as director of the archives one month later.

Müller's new post with the College of Foreign Affairs represented a significant step toward personal financial security and finally allowed him to engage in whatever historical research he wished without interference from a chancellery or a historical assembly. It came at a particularly opportune moment, because he had suffered through a very unhappy half-year. His wife and family had not accompanied him to Moscow, he was soon disillusioned with his work at the Foundling Home, and he did not receive the salary that he expected from the Academy.[23] Pekarskii cited from a letter written by Müller sometime in 1765 in which Müller admitted to having applied for the position of governor in the province of Voronezh.[24] His mood improved immeasurably when his family joined him in August, only to be dealt a shattering blow when his youngest and favourite child – his only daughter – died.

The new directorship carried with it a salary of 1,000 rubles above his previous income from the Academy, which he now also started to receive. Müller was obligated to serve directly only Golitsyn and Count Nikita Panin, Catherine's adviser on foreign affairs since 1763. Even more significant, Müller was now manifestly in favour at court. Besides asking for the memoranda on China, in 1763 Catherine personally had asked Müller to assist the elderly Count Münnich in the preparation of his memoirs. Münnich had been field marshal, president of the War College, and governor of St Petersburg for Empress Anna, but was arrested and exiled to Siberia during the palace revolution of 1741. He had been allowed to return to St Petersburg by Peter III. Müller's work was timely, because Münnich died in 1767. Catherine even granted him ready access to the J.A. Korff library of some 36,000 volumes, which she purchased in 1764 for her son, Grand Duke Paul. In 1767, Catherine gave Müller 6,000 rubles to buy a stone-house in Moscow.[25] In that same year Müller wrote Taubert: "Yesterday I received an unexpected kindness: Her Imperial Majesty requested my presence for about an hour [and] talked pleasantly with me about different matters. Among other things, she asked me about the continuation of the *Sammlung russischer Geschichte*, and, knowing that the ixth part is now being printed ... asked that in future a copy of everything that comes into print and in which I am involved, should be sent to her."[26]

Müller's good relations with the empress in the 1760s were due more to his contribution to her educational projects, which were a consuming passion with her at the time, than to her concern for Russian history. But she was keenly interested in the preparation of a national history as well and readily acceded to Müller's proposal in 1767 that Prince M.M. Shcherbatov replace him as historiographer,[27] so that "a younger person" could complete what he had begun. This was the same argument he had used to bring Schlözer to Russia a few years earlier. At any rate, Catherine granted Müller audiences seven times in 1767, when she wintered in Moscow. She also approved the Academy's nomination of him as its delegate to the legislative commission that she opened with great fanfare that year. His long friendship with State Councillor Aepinus gave him another – with Adodurov – personal link to the court. Aepinus – a bitter opponent of Lomonosov – was especially favoured by Catherine, who appointed him tutor to Paul in 1765 and head of the cipher department at the College of Foreign Affairs in 1769.[28]

When Lomonosov died, both Büsching and Stählin asked Müller if he would return to the capital. Müller replied to Büsching, in April 1765: "Not all the evil-mindedness has died with Lomonosov. What could possibly convince me to return to that struggle when here I can live in peace and calmness?"[29] Neither rumours of impending reform at the Academy nor the much publicized return of Leonhard Euler to St Petersburg in July 1766 could induce Müller to leave Moscow. Even a letter from Euler in August, addressed to his "oldest and dearest friend," failed to overcome the hostility Müller felt then toward the Academy community. His pent-up antipathy was reflected in a note to Stählin in which he congratulated him on his new post as Conference secretary. Müller cautioned him, however, to watch out for those who "already have hooks in their hands." He spoke of being out from under the "yoke" himself and admonished Stählin to "do well! ... Be a patriot!"[30]

Euler's return may not have impressed Müller, but the long and rather tortuous negotiations that persuaded the Berlin Academy and the Prussian government to grant him leave prompted Catherine to sponsor reforms at the Academy in order to make the institution attractive again to internationally known scholars. Euler involved himself in this reform almost immediately upon his arrival. At his first meeting with the Conference he outlined a reorganization project that he then submitted to the empress.[31] He strongly recommended that the number of professors be left open so that "superior" people might be offered contracts whenever they became available. He also urged that all of Europe's research academies work more closely together.

Another of Euler's suggestions had ominous implications for the autonomy of the professoriate. He agreed that Academy members should always be available for regular state service when their expertise was needed and tactfully cited the case of Aepinus as one worthy of emulation. In order to assure the best interests of science, Euler recognized, academicians should enjoy some immunity from political pressures. This, he said, could best be achieved if the scholars were given ready access to high civil ranks. He also advocated opening the Academy to more honorary members under less rigid qualifications, increasing the number of adjuncts, and making annual salaries available to "learned foreigners" who would work actively on behalf of the Academy in Europe. Finally, he offered plans for improving the financial circumstances of the Academy and put forward names of foreign scholars who should be invited to take over various departments.

Although Müller wrote Euler that he "entirely approved" of Catherine's general proposals, he was not likely to be much impressed by the flurry of reformist activity at the Academy.[32] The Senate had invited members to submit ideas for Academy reform as far back as 1754. At that time Müller had recommended that a "Historical Class" be created, and Lomonosov argued vociferously with Teplov over the degree to which the Conference could be autonomous from the Chancellery. No changes had taken place.[33] A full decade later Razumovskii ordered Taubert and Lomonosov to prepare new rules for the Academy, "together, or if [you] cannot agree, separately," in consultation with all the Academy members.[34] The degree to which real consultation took place is not known, but Lomonosov did submit several detailed proposals of his own without bothering to discuss them with Taubert. Simultaneously, he wrote a very long "Short History of the Conduct of the Academic Chancellery,"[35] in which he again blamed all the ills of the Academy on the machinations of Schumacher, Taubert, and Müller. Other Lomonosov reports called for power to be taken away from the Chancellery and placed directly in the hands of the president, who must be a Russian and knowledgeable about the sciences; and he insisted that the duties of the Conference secretary, that is, Müller, be taken over by a vice-president selected from the regular members and put in charge of all scientific affairs. Lomonosov also proposed that the Academy be divided into three classes – mathematics, physics, and history[36] – and that the academicians be the sole arbiters of recruitment. Latin and Russian were recommended as the languages of the Academy, and he offered the services of all members to the state whenever their expertise was required. This last point is the one area in which his and

Euler's recommendations coincided. Finally, Lomonosov insisted that all future academicians be appointed from native-born Russians, a hope that was dashed only a few months later when Catherine raised Schlözer to the rank of professor.

Lomonosov and Euler might have spared themselves their effort. The *ukaz* promulgated on 5 October 1766 provided few safeguards for the academicians. Razumovskii, who lost his position in Ukraine when the Hetmanate was abolished in 1764, remained an absentee president until 1798. He was more active as a member of Catherine's state council and as an envoy to Sweden. V.G. Orlov, the twenty-five-year-old brother of Catherine's current favourite, was named to the new office of director.[37] In theory, the professoriate was now to have control over scholarly affairs, and an academic commission consisting of Stählin, the two Eulers, Lehmann, Kotel'nikov, and S.Ia. Rumovskii replaced the Chancellery on 30 October. Taubert was not included and no longer had any real influence at the Academy. A sentiment common to most of the professors was expressed well in a letter from Stählin to Müller in which he gloated, "The Babylon of the Academy, the Chancellery, has fallen; the dragon has disappeared, or has been shoved aside."[38]

Their glee was short-lived. Orlov received a letter from the Senate saying that since conditions at the Academy were chaotic, he was to "have the same authority as the Charter of the Academy gives to the President."[39] The institution now had less real autonomy than it had enjoyed under Schumacher, for the office of director signalled a close affiliation with court circles. Müller heard about these matters from Stählin and Euler. H.L.Ch. Bacmeister, inspector of the Academy gymnasium (1766–78), who was still living in Müller's St Petersburg house, also sent complaining letters regularly.

Two weeks after the Academy reform was announced, Müller wrote the following to Euler:

But when will I hear that there is a substantial improvement at the Academy? About this, I certainly feel very strongly; I sigh as much as anyone who has the occasion to see the present circumstances on a daily basis. Will I soon have cause to send you hearty congratulations? The matter is not limited to the Academy alone, but also in a decisive reorganization of the so-called university and gymnasium, and especially of the latter so that highly placed people might send their children there. The first objective should be a preparatory school in which translations of useful books might be prepared. The present insufficiences in that are unbelievable, inasmuch as I tortured myself over the last ten years editing a Russian journal! Doubtless, in this case, no one wishes to undertake its continuation.

TABLE 2
Election Results for Academy Delegation to the Legislative Commission 1767

Field Marshal Count Razumovskii	4
Professor Euler the elder	2
State Councillor Stählin	6
State Councillor Taubert	2
College Councillor Müller	7
Professor Fischer	1
Professor Braun	4
Privy Councillor Popov	1
College Councillor Aepinus	5
Professor Kotel'nikov	4
Professor Schlözer	3
Professor Euler the younger	4
Professor Rumovskii	4
Professor Extraordinary Protasov	2
Honorary Members	
State Councillor Teplov	5
State Councillor Kruse	3
Privy Councillor Model	5
College Councillor Kositskii	5
Assessor Mothonis	2

Signed: J.D. Stählin, J.E. Fischer, Braun, N. Popov, S. Kotel'nikov, J.-A. Euler, S. Rumovskii, A. Protasov

Source: Protokoly, 2 (19 February 1767): 593.

Four months later, in February 1767, Müller wrote Stählin: "The circumstances at the Academy are certainly lamentable. All one can hope for is the best. A good president would be able to direct people along the right path."[40] His lack of confidence in the reform movement had proved prophetic.

One of Orlov's first tasks was to select an Academy delegate to the legislative commission that Catherine was organizing in Moscow. To do so, he called an election in which he and eight academicians took part. The rather striking division of interests among the professoriate was well illustrated when nineteen people, including the president and five honorary members, received votes, with Müller the highest at seven. Stählin and Aepinus were next, with six and five (see Table 2).[41] In April 1767, Orlov, N.I. Popov, Kotel'nikov, Braun, Samuel Gmelin, Fischer, and Stählin began to prepare the Academy *nakaz* to the legislative commission. Müller sent his submission from Moscow.[42]

The academicians first drew up a *nakaz* that reflected their concern about the new administrative system at the Academy. They called for freedom from censorship for those books that they published outside the Russian empire, licence to travel freely across the borders, and the right (with the University of Moscow) to censor all books, other than religious ones, printed in Russia. They also asked that they be granted positions on the Table of Ranks and that their living conditions and salaries be improved. But Orlov refused to accept this document. Since the Academy was in a state of flux and its own committee was still drawing up plans for further reforms, he felt its *nakaz* should be limited strictly to academic matters. Thus, the instructions finally sent to Müller told him flatly to "concern himself generally with the benefits which arise from science."[43]

There followed a strong argument for a substantial increase in higher- and lower-school facilities in Russia, with the judgment that the lower schools must be expanded first in order to provide skilled students for higher education. The tendency of well-to-do Russians to rely on foreign tutors to train their children at home was sharply criticized, because most of the tutors were "worthless." To remedy this situation, the Academy asked that the law of 1757, which made it illegal for any foreigner to teach in Russia without some accreditation from the Academy or University of Moscow,[44] be revived and reinforced. The *nakaz* also called for more co-ordination of effort between book publishers and asked that the Academy have the right to print books without censorship. It seems, however, that this *nakaz* had no impact on the legislative commission, and Müller never spoke in its defence. He may not even have approved of it. In a memorandum prepared by Orlov in April it was said that "a work by Mr Councillor Müller, written by him for the *nakaz* to deputies ... has nothing in it that the Academy can adopt."[45]

Whatever the reasons, Müller's zeal for both education and the work of the legislative assembly had so dissipated by December, when sessions were prorogued, that he did not accompany the commission when it shifted its venue to St Petersburg in February 1768. Complaints about the absence of school facilities were heard often during his five-month participation, but the Academy *nakaz* was not discussed in the assembly during that time. Müller did not sit on the sub-commission on education that was established in 1768. His one recorded statement to the assembly was a pronouncement on procedures. In the long run, then, Müller's only real contribution to the work of that remarkable gathering was his collaboration with Klingstedt and Count Ernst Münnich on a translation of Catherine's own *nakaz* into German.[46]

The Academy Conference was reminded by Orlov of its commitment to education a year later. But only Leonhard Euler and his son, Johann-Albrecht, who had joined the Academy in July 1766 as professor of physics, remained concerned enough to prepare and present a statement on education to the Conference in January 1768.[47] The sub-commission on schools continued to meet after the legislative commission itself was adjourned in October because of the outbreak of war with Turkey. One of its members was Baron G.F. Asche, curator of the Hermitage and an honorary member of the Academy. But his participation did not prevent the sub-commission from foiling an Academy proposal that a governing agency of nine people, preferably well-known scholars, be organized to administer education in Russia. The sub-commission countered what it probably interpreted as an Academy bid to monopolize education by recommending that the Senate oversee all schools. Neither suggestion seemed to have had any real influence on Catherine or Betskoi. Nothing further came of either the Academy's or Müller's interest in Catherine's projections of a school system for Russia.

CHAPTER EIGHT

Archivist, Historian, Publicist 1769–83

All the scholarly world now regards you as the premier
Historical writer of the century.

V.G. Ruban to Müller, 1774

Even though he did not return to St Petersburg, and his post as its
representative to the legislative commission seemed of little practical
consequence, Müller remained closely associated with the Academy.
In fact, he acted as its agent in Moscow, where the Academy
maintained an official residence,[1] and kept in constant touch with
Johann-Albrecht Euler, who was appointed Conference secretary in
February 1769. Among Müller's assignments was the role of corresponding geographer and adviser to Academy-sponsored expeditions. These included expeditions by P.S. Pallas and J.P. Falk to
Orenburg; Samuel Gmelin (J.G. Gmelin's nephew), K.I. Hablitz
(whom Müller recommended to the Academy in 1769), and J.A.
Güldenstädt to Astrakhan; and J.G. Georgi to the Lake Baikal
regions.[2] Pallas set out in 1768 armed with the instructions compiled
by Müller for Krasheninnikov in 1737. As middle-man for the
Academy, Müller often took possession of collections sent by
expeditionary scientists, including a large botanical collection forwarded to Moscow by Güldenstädt from Tambov in 1769 and a
detailed map of the Caucasus from the same explorer in 1773. In
January 1771, Pallas sent Müller fifteen boxes of material from one of
his expeditions. In turn, Müller forwarded scientific equipment,
charts, and general information to the travellers and relayed whatever he learned from them to the Academy. Müller's contribution was
acknowledged by Pallas in a foreword to his *Reise durch verschiedene
Provinzen des russischen Reiches* (volumes 1–2, St Petersburg, 1773–6),
which became the standard reference work on Siberian natural
history.[3]

The information received by Müller included accounts of the dangers to which Gmelin and Güldenstädt were exposed from rebellious tribesmen. Indeed, an entire series of Müller's letters to Euler in 1773 displays worry and then a growing horror about the fate of Gmelin, who had been imprisoned by a rebel Turkmen khan and died from dysentery after a long internment and seemingly bungled negotiations on the part of the Russian government. The very next year Müller had to inform the Academy of the death of G.-M. Lowitz at the hands of Pugachev's rebels in the area of Astrakhan. That Müller's knowledge and experience proved valuable was illustrated in a letter from the most famous of the expeditionary leaders, Pallas, to Euler in 1769, in which he noted the "unusual accuracy" of Müller's correspondence with the Academy about the affairs of his troupe.[4]

In 1770 Müller was visited in Moscow by T.I. Shmalev, a captain in service at Okhotsk and Kamchatka, who had accompanied several Aleuts to St Petersburg for presentation to Catherine. Their lengthy discussions persuaded Müller once again to gather documentation for a history of all Russian ocean voyages after 1743. He wrote to State Secretary S.M. Koz'min to suggest that Shmalev be sponsored in an exploratory trip to the Aleutian Islands so that information could be gathered to augment his own earlier publications in *Monthly Compositions*. The association with T.I. Shmalev and his brother, Vasilii, proved very fruitful. They continued to send Müller up-to-date accounts from Okhotsk, one of which he edited in 1774 for publication in the *Trudy* of the Free Russian Assembly.[5] Müller also corresponded regularly with European scholars, sent them maps, answered queries on geographical matters, and reviewed works sent him by foreign editors and authors.

During these years, Müller's reputation as a geographer and ethnographer began to outstrip his renown as a historian. Even the Russian military took advantage of his expertise, requesting and receiving new maps of Moldavia and Wallachia in which special care was taken to delineate the Russian position on the borders of Poland and the Ottoman Empire. Müller also made meticulous charts of the Russo-Persian boundaries.[6] The wide exposure given to many of his earlier reports on Siberia, the Caucasus, the Cossacks, and the peoples of Siberia and the Amur region in journals edited by Büsching and Gottsched, and in several English translations of his essay on Russian voyages, made Müller's name better known in Europe than that of any other member of the Russian Academy. Consequently, he was besieged by requests for information, copies of papers, and invitations to review books and manuscripts.

Müller's own ambition, however, was still to prepare the way for a full narrative of Russian history. When he asked the Academy in February 1765 to determine the fate of *Monthly Compositions*, he had also requested immediate decisions on assorted other matters: that he be allowed to take to Moscow a copy of the *Primary Chronicle* and some books from the Academy library; that he be accompanied to Moscow by his translator, Samson Volkov; that his own work now be published by the university typography in Moscow; that his vast collection of materials from Siberia be sent to Moscow so that he could complete the Siberian history; and that the Conference decide upon his replacement as secretary.

Knowing full well the tendency of the Conference to procrastinate and of the Chancellery to be difficult, Müller decided not to wait for an answer from the Academy. In the spring of 1765 he used the Moscow typography to print the ninth volume of the *Sammlung* and to reprint several natural history essays that had appeared in supplements to the *St. Petersburg Gazette* between 1729 and 1740. He intended that these reprints, which included information mainly on geography and astronomy, be used as texts at the University of Moscow. Letters from "patriots" were inserted as well, so as to provide "moral" instructions to readers. Müller defined his patriots as those who were "zealots" for the well-being of the fatherland.[7]

Most of Müller's later works, however, were published in the capital city. His other requests of the Academy had a mixed reception. He was denied a copy of the *Primary Chronicle* but was allowed to keep Volkov as his translator – somewhat to Volkov's dismay. Eventually, most of the Siberian collection was housed in a special room in the library of the College of Foreign Affairs.[8] When it came to replacing Müller as secretary, Lomonosov, who had long been arguing that the Conference did not really need a permanent secretary, now spoke loudly for the appointment of someone who was "wise, hardworking, and willing to publish our works." He recommended either Braun or Fischer, but in March 1765 the Conference selected Stählin, one of Müller's choices.[9]

By that time the internal affairs of the Academy were no longer of much concern to Müller anyway. He soon was settled comfortably in his post as director of the archives of the College of Foreign Affairs and at last was free to act upon those grandiose schemes that had been proposed under his name in 1732. As archivist, Müller paved the way for every historian who attempted to write a history of Russia in the latter half of the eighteenth century and much of the nineteenth. He trained young scholars in archival work, the most important of whom was N.N. Bantysh-Kamenskii. Bantysh-Kamenskii, who was already with the archives as a translator when Müller arrived, became chief assistant and replaced him as director in 1783.[10] Müller organized and catalogued the resources of the College archives, found a new and safer location for them in 1766, provided other historians with documents and books, and published important documents and chronicles.

He continued to build his private collection as well, at considerable cost to himself. One addition was a thirteen-volume collection of Peter the Great's letters which Müller found in the archives and arranged according to years.[11] In 1779, S.G. Domashnev (director of the Academy after 1775) made it known that he expected Müller to bequeath his personal library to the Academy of Sciences. But long and complicated negotiations between Müller and Prince Grigory Potemkin, mediated by Shcherbatov, resulted in the empress purchasing the collection instead for 20,000 rubles. Müller had insisted that it not go to St Petersburg, repeating to Shcherbatov his sentiments of 1746: "Moscow is the centre of the empire, where one can locate all information necessary for history and geography." As part of his arrangement with Potemkin, Müller was granted an assistant to help catalogue his materials. He requested specifically J.-G. Stritter, "a very capable man and perhaps after my death he will replace me." Müller also asked that his family be assured of financial security and that Büsching be given 200 rubles to purchase books to send to Moscow. These wishes were readily granted. In October 1779, Catherine named Stritter "Aide-Historiographe et Archiviste de l'Empire" at the rank of College assessor. The Academy then elected him adjunct in history.[12] Müller's wife was guaranteed a pension of 3,000 rubles,[13] which was just as well, for Müller spent most of his money on new additions to his library. Müller's collection remained in his possession until his death; only then was it turned over to the College of Foreign Affairs. Müller also tried to persuade Prince A.D. Golitsyn to leave the large Golitsyn family library, which contained many important historical works (catalogued by Müller in the 1760s), to the College of Foreign Affairs. But he did not succeed.[14]

Among the historians Müller assisted directly were Shcherbatov, N.I. Novikov, I.I. Golikov, Schlözer, Stritter, and P.-C. Lévesque. In the foreword to the first of his seven-volume *Russian History* (*Istoriia Rossiiskaia*, 1770–91), Shcherbatov wrote, "I cannot state well enough how much I am grateful to Mr Councillor Müller, who is so well known for his many works on Russian history, for the great assistance he has given me toward the success of this work ... I must admit that he instilled in me the desire to know the history of my fatherland ... and convinced me to undertake this work."[15] Golikov credited Müller with providing him with some 500 "pieces" for his multi-volume *Deeds of Peter the Great (Deianiia Petra Velikago,* volumes 1–12, 1788–9).[16] According to Metropolitan Evgenii, Müller gave Novikov the very idea to publish the *Old Russian Library (Drevniaia rossiiskago Vivliofika,* volumes 1–7, 1773–5), which may or may not have been the case. At any rate, Novikov credited Müller for delivering many documents for publication.[17] In spite of their many differences, Schlözer praised Müller's archival work in his own *Nestor,* which appeared first in German (1802–5) and then in Russian (1809–19).[18] He also printed several of Müller's documents and reports in his journal, *Beylagen zum Neuveränderten Russland.* Ulrich Weiss went a step further, increasing Müller's audience by publishing an abridged version of the *Sammlung* in Offenbach-am-Main in 1777. Printed in five volumes, the Weiss selection included Müller's essays on modern Russian history, the origins of Novgorod, the study of the Amur region, and the complete history and description of Siberia.[19]

Büsching's several journals also benefited from the essays, documents, and reports sent him by Müller,[20] as did a number of organizations and societies that were interested in Russian history and geography. Among those groups listed by V.S. Ikonnikov for extensively using Müller's collections was the Free Russian Assembly (*Vol'noe rossiiskoi sobranie*), organized in 1771 by I.I. Melissino, curator of the University of Moscow. The aim of the enterprise was to improve and enrich the Russian language, to compile a correct Russian dictionary, and to publish and preserve literary relics of Russia's antiquity. The six volumes of the Assembly's collected works (1774–83) carried numerous items from Müller, including three essays on the youth of Peter the Great. Along with Novikov and Shcherbatov, Müller helped to make the group the centre of an extremely active historical community in Moscow. Just as it had been in St Petersburg, Müller's home in Moscow was constantly open to short- and long-term visitors who also played a part in the lively Moscow intellectual circles. J.M.R. Lenz – poet, Freemason, and later literary instructor to the young Nicholas Karamzin – lived with the Müllers from 1781 to 1783.[21]

There was a certain irony to the fact that Müller seemed to have taken the historical discipline to Moscow with him, leaving the Academy to flounder insofar as historical writing was concerned. Schlözer left Russia for Göttingen again in September 1767 and did not return. Fischer and Taubert both died in 1771, leaving only Moderach as professor of history until Stritter and J.-F. Hackmann (1782) were appointment adjuncts.[22] Indeed, after Fischer and Taubert's death, only Stählin of the original ten members of the historical assembly remained in St Petersburg. Le Roy and Crusius had been dismissed sometime during 1748 and 1749; Strube de Piermont was released from the Academy in 1757 and took a post in Moscow with the College of Foreign Affairs; Lomonosov, Braun (1768), and Trediakovskii (1769) had also died.

The Academy continued to print Russian historical sources, including, in 1767, the first issue in the *Library of Russian History*. This was the Königsburg (Radziwill) redaction of the *Primary Chronicle*, edited by I.S. Barkov. Schlözer and Taubert wrote a long introduction stressing the importance of the publication for nurturing Russian national consciousness:

All European countries enlightened by science have for two hundred years and more worked indefatigably in order to bring to light the circumstances and, as much as possible, the underlying causes which account for a description of their situation through past centuries. Only we, even with our wealth of good chronicles, have brought almost nothing to light. Our ancient history ... from the beginning of the monarchy to the present time ... has been hidden in chronicle manuscripts ... Our youth who undertake instruction in schools and at home pore over the names of rulers of Assyria, Persia, and the Roman monarchies, but about Founders, Enlighteners, and Protectors of their Fatherland they hear hardly anything. The main science for man is based on self-knowledge; and for *citizens* is understanding their Fatherland.

This refrain could easily have been written by Müller, who, Schlözer and Taubert acknowledged grudgingly, had explained all this in *Monthly Compositions* – "fairly well."[23]

Later that same year Semen Bashilov, with help from Schlözer and A.Ia. Polenov, edited the Niconian Chronicle collection. Polenov was a translator at the Academy who submitted an award-winning essay on the Free Economic Society in 1766, in which he opposed many of the regulations that bound serfs to their status. He had studied jurisprudence in Strasbourg and Göttingen and so brought considerable acumen to the study of old documents. Schlözer and Bashilov, who was both his student and a translator for the Academy, also prepared copies of the *Russkaia pravda* and the *Sudebnik* of Ivan III for printing in 1767–8. These were reprinted in 1786 along with Tatishchev's discussion of them.[24]

Müller, Fischer, Stritter, and Shcherbatov prepared many other documents for the Academy typography, but aside from Lomonosov's *Ancient Russian History*, which was printed in 1766 with a foreword by Schlözer,[25] and Shcherbatov's fifteen-part *History*, there were no historical monographs prepared at the instance of the Academy while Müller was in Moscow. Shcherbatov resided in Moscow, where

Novikov was also active in publishing documents. Stritter, who compiled his famous *Memoriae populorum* with Müller's assistance, moved there in 1779.[26] Rychkov, another active historical writer associated with the Academy, lived in the provinces. F.A. Emin's *Russian History (Rossiiskaia istoriia)* was published in three parts by the Academy in 1768–9, but he was neither a member nor a historian. The work was sponsored directly by the empress.

Bacmeister remarked upon this situation already in 1766 when he wrote Müller that "Russian history has entirely left St Petersburg and has been taken to your place in Moscow."[27] Bacmeister undertook a number of historical tasks himself. He translated Lomonosov's last historical work into German in 1768 and during the 1770s translated Shcherbatov's edition of Peter the Great's journal. His famous *Russische Bibliothek* was initiated in 1774 with Müller's help, and in 1789 he translated the letters of Peter the Great to Count Sheremetev, which Müller had first edited in 1774. But Bacmeister's work was directed toward a German audience and was published in Riga and Leipzig. Only the *Russische Bibliothek* was also issued in St Petersburg.[28] His affiliation with the Academy was as librarian and inspector of the gymnasium. Even a Russian history textbook that Catherine ordered from Stritter in 1783 for use in her new public schools did not appear until 1800.[29]

Perhaps the most important book on Russian history to appear in the 1760s was Schlözer's *Probe russischer Annalen*, which he worked on throughout 1767 while still an Academy professor and published in Göttingen in 1768. In it Schlözer singled out the *Primary Chronicle* as the first written record of Russian history, treated it as the effort of one individual (Nestor) rather than as a compilation, and insisted on its reliability. He was unequivocal in his declaration that the Varangians were Germanic, and he tried to trace the "Russes" to the non-Slavic and non-Germanic Cumans. Schlözer's unhappy experiences in Russia were reflected in his claim that Bayer and Tatishchev were the only two in Russia ever to write real history and in his statement that Müller "also devoted himself originally to ancient Russian history, as can be seen from the advertisement printed in 1732 in which he announced the *Sammlung russischer Geschichte*. But ... his ten years in Siberia, and other concerns after his return, diverted him from it."[30] Lomonosov was not mentioned.

Müller's health was constantly impaired during the early 1770s. Indeed, already in 1766 he had such trouble with his eyes that he was afraid that he might lose his sight. Müller was bedridden by pneumonia for much of the winter of 1770, was confined to his home for several months in 1771 because of a "plague" epidemic (from which one of his maids died), and suffered debilitating strokes in 1772 and 1773. The last attack apparently was stimulated by a fire that destroyed nearly 1,000 homes in his neighbourhood.[31]

But Müller continued to work long hours on Russian history and geography. One of the most important products of his labour was his book *On the Peoples Who Have Lived from Olden Times in Russia* (*O narodakh, izdrevle v Rossii obitavshikh*). Printed anonymously by Novikov in 1773, it had a second edition fifteen years later. In this study Müller assailed the interpretation of ancient and medieval Russian history as it was elaborated in the posthumous Lomonosov publication of 1766. Lomonosov's introduction to the *Ancient Russian History* finally clarified the real difference between his and Müller's understanding of the purpose of historical writing. For Lomonosov, history was a means whereby the heroic deeds of Russia's past might be recorded. Books should accentuate only those activities that were worthy of emulation by contemporary readers. History "gives to rulers examples of government; to subjects – obedience; to warriors – manliness, judgment and justice; to the young – wisdom of their elders; to the old – special fortitude; to everyone – unforgettable strength and unlimited benefits."[32] In this way Lomonosov hoped to stimulate national pride, a quest that unwittingly he shared with Müller.

To counter Bayer and Müller's contention that the "Varangian-Russes" were Scandinavians and that the Slavs had little in the way of organized society before the ninth century, Lomonosov turned to Procopius, Jordanes, Ptolemy, Tacitus, and many others to demonstrate that the Slavs had a sophisticated community life long before Riurik arrived in Novgorod. Moreover, he insisted again that the "Russes" were really Slavic Roxolani, a sub-tribe of the Sarmatians, who were themselves Slavic. The "Russes" moved north from the steppes and mingled with the Baltic peoples, including the Prussians, to form "Varangian-Russes" – a heterogeneous group of tribes, with several languages, whose livelihood was based on plunder. Riurik could not have been Scandinavian, Lomonosov said; rather he was Prussian and Slavic.[33]

Lomonosov's book was a success of sorts. It was translated into German (by Bacmeister) in 1768 and into Italian in 1772 and had three French editions in Paris between 1769 and 1776. In Russian it had a large printing of over 2,000 copies, but it was not reissued in the eighteenth century.[34] Although the book had a relatively large audience, it failed to achieve one of its author's main aims, that is, to alter the generally accepted perspective on the origins of the Russians and their state system. In fact, its credibilty as scholarship was undermined almost immediately by the Academy of Sciences itself. In 1767 the Academy typography published three of Bayer's books that had been translated into Russian by K. Kondratovich twenty years earlier. These included a book on the Varangians, a study of the geography of "Russia" and its neighbors in the tenth century, and an essay on Constantine VII Porphyrogenitus's views on Russia. A second edition of Bayer's book on Azov was issued by the Academy in 1768. In that same year Schlözer published his *Probe russischer Annalen* and wrote a very strongly worded introduction to the Latin text of Müller's *Origines gentis et nominis Russorum* which appeared in Gatterer's *Allgemeine historische Bibliothek*. Schlözer emphasized that "Riurik was a Norman!" and chastised Müller for hedging on the question in the *Sammlung* in 1761.[35] Therefore, Müller's *On the Peoples* merely helped reconfirm what most historians of Russia already believed.

In *On the Peoples*, Müller connected the Roxolani to Prussians. He insisted again, however, that their dominant stock was "Gothic" and that they and the Varangians came from Denmark, Norway, or Sweden. Müller concurred with Tatishchev's suggestion that "Iani" was probably a Finnish suffix to a word for Swedes but disagreed with his opinion that the Sarmatians were Finns. Müller drew his arguments from the *Primary Chronicle* from which he quoted extensively, as well as from Bayer, Mankiev, Tatishchev, and the *Kniga stepennaia*.[36] On the derivation of the name for Russians, he wrote: "Thus, the Varangians were different people, i.e., the word referred to several tribes, and those from whom Riurik was called into Novgorod as Prince were called Rossolani ... Although there may be reasons to argue against the idea that Russia received its name from the Varangians, it cannot be denied that the *Russian name* appeared at about that time ... We intend to defend the authenticity of the Russian chronicles, but ... recognize that 'Rossii' were here before Riurik."[37]

Once again Müller debunked as fables those accounts that said that the name Slav was derived from "glory" and that the name Russian came from "scattered," and he ridiculed Lomonosov's assumption that the ancient Slavs had been involved successfully in the Trojan Wars.[38] Müller's first references to Lomonosov were oblique, for he twice mentioned a "book of 1766" that had attracted far too much "glorification" and "about which it is not really necessary to say anything."[39] He reminded readers of his own controversial dissertation of 1749, noting that Catherine II "now honours truth in science." As a parting gesture, however, he wrote that he did not intend to "impugn the name of a talented man. *Lomonosov* commanded respect until his final days because of the merits of his Russian writing, but in history he did not show himself to be a skilful and truthful narrator."[40] His very longevity allowed Müller the last word in his long and bitter dispute with Lomonosov. This work was widely circulated in Russian and in German, appearing in Büsching's *Magazin für die neue Historie und Geographie* in 1782 and was noted by Bacmeister in *Russische Bibliothek*.[41]

The effects of Müller's illnesses on his capacity for work during the early 1770s were only barely perceptible, and in 1774 his health was so good that he told Büsching that he had not felt better since leaving St Petersburg. He was elated in July 1775 when he was appointed state councillor and informed Büsching that he was filled with "glory and thanks" for his good fortune.[42] He continued to participate in the affairs of the Free Russian Assembly, and he spent many hours compiling material for a new serialized publication, *Treasure of Russian Antiquity* (*Sokrovishche rossiiskikh drevnostei*), which was announced in March 1775. The idea for the magazine came from Novikov, who proposed it to Catherine II as a collection similar to his *Old Russian Library*. Novikov intended to act both as its editor and publisher. The *Treasure* was scheduled to appear six times annually and include descriptions of Russian cathedrals, monasteries, and churches, with a historical account of each and a list of their great treasures. Portraits and brief histories of Russian tsars, information on Russian-language books of history and geography, and notes on the provinces were also planned. Unfortunately, however, Müller's labour went for nought. Only the first issue was printed, and that was a limited edition financed by the empress.[43]

Even more remarkable for a man of Müller's age and health was a project initiated by him in 1778 – a geographical and archival study of the entire Moscow region. Sponsored by the Academy, Müller prepared a series of new geographical accounts of Kolomna, Mozhaisk, Ruza, Dmitrov, Zvenigorod, Pereiaslavl'-Zaleskii, as well as lists of the archival holdings in various monasteries. These were printed in the *S.-Peterburgische Journal*, the *Trudy* of the Free Russian Assembly, and later in *New Monthly Compositions* (*Novyia ezhemesiachnyia sochineniia*, 1786–96). The essays seem to have made a lasting impression on Nicholas Karamzin, who commented on them at length in his *Vestnik evropy* in 1802. Although he corrected Müller on several minor points, Karamzin – who became the official historiographer less than a year later – wrote very favourably of Müller's interviewing methods and echoed his conclusions on Godunov, Poland, and Muscovy. Müller came in for some glowing tributes in his own time as well. While he toured Moscow and its surroundings he acted as an adviser to V.G. Ruban, who was writing a general history of the same area. He may have been gratified by Ruban's gushing gratitude – "all the scholarly world now regards you as the premier historical writer of the century" – but his only material reward for all this effort was the promotion to state councillor.[44]

In the same year, Domashnev commissioned Müller to write a history of the Academy of Sciences for the celebration of its fiftieth anniversary. This work proceeded very slowly, however. Müller was occupied with matters he regarded as more important, and the empress continued to request specific tasks of him. Among other things, he was convinced that Catherine's legislative commission was about to be reconvened in Moscow and wrote the Conference for copies of all its deliberations and documents that reflected on the work of the commission. Conference members agreed to comply on the condition that Müller accept a new set of instructions from them. Meanwhile, Catherine pressed him to complete his description of Russian sea voyages to the Arctic and Kamchatka. Although he began to compile new information and sift through materials that he had not used in 1758, this project was still unfinished by the time of Müller's death. Ten years later Pallas edited and published Müller's compilation separately and also serialized it in several issues of *Neue Nordische Beiträge*.[45]

Müller seems to have had his fill of Far Eastern geography anyway. The arguments of the 1750s over the de l'Isle map had been enervating at the time and had continued to plague him intermittently during the 1760s. But they came back with a vengeance in the next decade when he was swept unwillingly into a bitter dispute with an eminent Swiss geographer, Samuel Engel. In 1765, Engel published a detailed French-language geographical description of the Pacific and contradicted some of Müller's earlier conclusions. A few years later he wrote Müller a letter asking for some response. Müller ignored the request. But when Engel's book appeared in German translation in 1772, Büsching persuaded Müller to take some action. The Swiss writer had criticized him for making Siberia appear much larger than Engel believed it to be. He implied that Müller was merely trying to curry favour with the Russian government by increasing the size of its empire. Müller's answer to Engel's charges appeared in Büsching's *Wöchentliche Nachrichten von neuen Landkarten* in 1773; Engel retaliated in 1777 with a biting personal attack on Müller and a general denigration of all discoveries claimed by Russian explorers. Once again Müller used Büsching's good offices to reply, albeit quite cautiously and with no invective. According to L. Breitfuss, who described this argument, the dimensions that Müller attributed to Siberia were much closer to reality than were Engel's; but Müller was unsure of his facts and preferred that the controversy be laid to rest. Büsching was aggressive in Müller's defence, however, and wrote several very harsh reviews of Engel's work. Pallas also enthusiastically endorsed Müller's position.[46]

As if there were not enough demands on Müller's time, in February 1776 the general procurator of the Senate, Prince A.A. Viazemskii, presented him with orders from Catherine that obliged him to prepare a report on the origins and legal evolution of the Russian *dvorianstvo*. The empress had been concerned with the privileges held by the nobility since her succession. As early as February 1763 she established a commission to examine the implications of Peter III's manifesto of 1762 that freed the nobility from obligatory service. Nothing conclusive came from the commission, although Catherine did issue decrees in the late 1760s that rather tentatively confirmed her late husband's manifesto. The issue was kept alive by means of the legislative commission, the Pugachev rebellion, and the sweeping administrative reforms that were finally enacted in 1775.

Müller's study, which he submitted to Viazemskii in 1777, was in response to clear directives issued by the empress: to seek out the judicial foundation of the *dvorianstvo*, to clarify its obligations, and to gather documentation on leading families. When the book was finally published in 1790, slightly more than one-fifth of its 500 pages were taken up with genealogical tables. It included as well documentation on Muscovite officials, their early duties, their control over villages, and proof of their and their progeny's noble status. Catherine's interest in Müller's report and a similar one drawn up by A.T. Kniazov, a member of the Land Survey Chancellery, was part of the long process that culminated in the enactment of her own Charter of the Nobility in 1785.[47]

Müller's research on the origins of the Russian *dvorianstvo* may well have been the catalyst for an essay that he wrote sometime in the late 1770s on serfdom: "Uber Herrn Linguet, die Knechtschaft überhaupt, und die Russische insonderheit" ("On Mr Linguet, about Slavery in General and Especially in Russia"). Büsching published it in his *Magazin für die neue Historie und Geographie* one year after Müller's death.[48] Müller challenged the position taken by the radical French publicist S.N.H. Linguet, who wrote facetiously that as long as the conditions under which hired labourers worked were worse than those of slavery, then it might be better to reintroduce slavery. Linguet edited a journal, *Annales politiques, civiles et littéraires* (1777–92) in which he attacked social abuses and property laws for turning free men into paupers and beggars, and even predicted a sweeping class war in France. Müller, who called Linguest "notorious," thought it wiser to ease the restrictions of serfdom by going over completely to the *obrok* (payment in kind or money) system and abolishing those laws that prevented peasants from leaving the land. In this way peasants would be encouraged either to grow surpluses or to move eastward as colonists.

Müller also cited two cases in Poland where noblemen had emancipated their serfs to "the great benefit" of both peasant and landowner. Rather than risk referring directly to the Russian situation, he outlined the evolution of serfdom in Russia and tempered whatever criticism his readers might perceive in the article by claiming that peasants were better off in Russia than they were in Poland, Bohemia, "and other states" – and claimed that the worst conditions for "serfs" were in America. But he stated his real position clearly enough by quoting at length from a French-language work of 1773 about serfdom in Poland. "The natural effect of slavery is to render men indolent and slothful," he cited from the French author, and he then went on to describe the two enlightened Polish noblemen. In both cases peasants were emancipated, given small plots for their personal use, and allowed to rent buildings and farm lands for cash rather than for labour. As a result, both peasant and landowner became "wealthier and happy."

Müller had touched on the question of serfdom already with Catherine's blessing in 1764 when he published an article in the *Sammlung* that compared conditions of the Livonian peasantry unfavourably to that of Russian serfs.[49] The piece ostensibly was the work of J.G. Eisen, a Lutheran pastor who advocated the abolition of serfdom in Livonia, part of the territory acquired by Peter the Great from Sweden in 1721. According to Schlözer, Eisen was a regular visitor to Müller's house in 1761. Eisen was introduced to Catherine in 1763, and it was she who commissioned the account. But his report had been concerned only with the peasantry in Livonia, and so the comparison with Russian serfs probably was added by Müller. In another essay, which was not printed until 1789 (in *New Monthly Compositions*), Müller went so far as to suggest that landowners be deprived of the right to raise peasants' obligations arbitrarily or to take back lands in lieu of rent payment; he also recommended a gradual introduction of small-scale land ownership for serfs. As his authority, Müller cited an essay on peasant property ownership that had been awarded a prize in 1766 by the Free Economic Society.[50] Catherine had approved that award.

Müller's essays, and the memoranda of 1763–4, illustrate his continuing interest in economic issues and also demonstrate his disregard and even contempt for those parts of Russia's caste system that acted to retard the government's attempt to modernize. They suggest too that in economic thought Müller was close to the physiocrats (who were angrily opposed by Linguet), who believed that both agricultural production and trade should be free of government regulation. Müller's observation of the hardships imposed on Siberian merchants, whether Russian or indigenous, by direct involvement of the state in commerce had inclined him in that direction. At any rate, such objections to the existing landholding order were futile, even though Catherine had been influenced by physiocratic ideals when she founded the Free Economic Society in 1765. The realities of Russian absolutism, exacerbated as they were after the Pugachev revolt of 1773–4, dictated that Müller keep such notions to himself.

Catherine's own curiosity about Russia's past was by no means a matter of simply "searching for the truth," as Müller had phrased it in 1773. That she fully intended historical writing to serve state interests was revealed in 1773 when she ordered Shcherbatov to prepare a historical justification of her treatment of Pugachev.[51] It was Catherine, too, who forced the delay in publication of Stritter's textbook, because she did not approve of its interpretation. But her motivation was of little concern to Müller. He benefited from the funds she released to pay for the publication of Tatishchev's manuscript and to sponsor Novikov's *Old Russian Library*. Shortly after Müller's death, the empress established a historical commission in Moscow to continue work he had started. It consisted of two University of Moscow professors, A.A. Barsov and Kh.A. Chebotarev, who had been associated with Müller in the Free Russian Assembly. In 1782–3, Müller had helped them collect information for Catherine. The empress used it to compile a work of her own entitled "Notes on Russian History" ("Zapiski kasatel'no Rossiiskoi istorii"), which appeared in serialized form in a journal she edited together with Princess Catherine Dashkova and O.P. Kozodavlev in 1783–4.

The "Notes" consisted mainly of excerpts from chronicles, but they were extensive, taking up some 1,300 pages of *Companion of Lovers of Russian Literature* (*Sobesednik liubitelei rossiiskago slova*) and were intended to accomplish some of the goals Müller had aimed at in *Monthly Compositions*. Catherine opened the study by defining history as "a description of all those deeds which teach one to create good and to avoid evil" and by insisting that "all people need to know their own history and geography." In fact, she undertook the project specifically for the edification of her grandsons. Like Müller, she professed to be correcting foreign versions of Russia's past, but her actual picture was eclectic and often closer to Lomonosov's view than it was to Müller's. She portrayed the Varangians as a Slavic people and the ancient indigenous population of the northern part of her empire as Russians. Further, she altered the traditional picture of Gostomysl' by calling him a Great Prince. Like Tatishchev, she believed that Riurik was the offspring of one of Gostomysl''s daughters and a Finnish king. Although she admitted that the old assumption that Riurik had descended from Augustus Caesar was "clearly a fable," the empress accepted as fact the opinion that the name of Slavs derived from the word *slava*.[52] Catherine used a mere twenty-nine pages to dispose of the pre-Riurikide years, however, so that the similarity between her work and Lomonosov's was more by accident than by design. Catherine's interest lay in espousing the merits of autocracy. In her version the national historical development after Riurik was credited to wise and prudent rulers, who were all above reproach. Republican institutions such as the *veche* and other old Slavic freedoms were ignored, and autocracy was demonstrated to be the only possible form of government for Russia. Indeed, no other kind was even mentioned.

Müller could not have exerted much influence on Catherine's presentation of Russian history, but she consistently relied on him for historical information. In the mid-1770s, when the empress was tightening her control over the Dnieper and Don Cossacks, Müller was asked to compose papers on the *Zaporozhskaia sich'* and the rights that were purported to be theirs under the terms of the treaty signed by the tsar of Muscovy and hetman Khmelnitskii in 1654. Müller submitted two long essays on the "malorussians," historical information on various Cossack centres – especially the *Zaporozhie*, lists of government documents on Ukraine, and charts of Ukrainian hierarchies. He also answered questions about Ukraine sent to him by several government officials. Throughout these papers, Müller made it clear that he believed that the Pereiaslavl' agreement of 1654 made legal the complete subservience of Ukraine to Muscovy and that later Russian policies were soundly based in law and tradition. Müller's *O malorossiiskom narode i zaporizhe* (1775–6) was the first detailed Russian history of the Cossacks and Ukraine. He emphasized the events of 1665, when the hetman Ivan Briukhovets relinquished Ukrainian autonomy to the Muscovite tsar. When all was said and done, however, Müller justified Russian centralizing practices on the grounds that the territory of Ukraine belonged to the imperial order by "ancient legal rights."

It is quite likely that Müller's reports had some bearing on Catherine's decisions about Ukraine. She had begun to reorganize Ukraine in 1764, when Razumovskii's hetmanate was abolished and replaced by a new office, the Little Russian College, under a Russian governor-general. Her actions were inspired in large part by a long memorandum from Teplov, Razumovskii's long-time assistant in the hetmanate and now secretary to the empress. Teplov urged that Little Russia be integrated directly into the Russian administrative system, arguing that the area was tied to the Russian dynasty historically and so should have no unique privileges. Müller's subsequent support probably was welcomed in that it gave prestigious historical substantiation to her policy of destroying all autonomous institutions in Ukraine.

The turning point in these affairs, of course, was the revolt of the Cossacks and the peasant war of 1773–4. In 1775, the Zaporozhian Host was condemned and abolished; and between 1779 and 1782, Little Russia was divided into three Russian provinces. In 1846 the secretary of the Imperial Society for the History and Antiquity of Russia gathered together Müller's diverse papers on Ukraine (which he found in Müller's files) and printed them in a single volume under the society's imprimatur.

Other Russian notables requested information from Müller, among them Potemkin, who asked questions about Russian military history. Sumarokov (who in 1760 had begged I.I. Shuvalov to free him from the control of Müller and others in literary matters) now regularly required general information and sources for his historical drama and poetry. An especially persistent petitioner was Count A.R. Vorontsov, who had served as Russia's ambassador to the Court of St James in 1762–3 and later was president of the College of Commerce. Vorontsov's continued interest in Britain was reflected in queries about Russian-British relations, which Müller answered at some length.[54] In 1783 Vorontsov asked about the origin of the word *duma*, to which Müller replied that it referred to special assemblies convoked on the initiative of tsars. Only in the time of Peter the Great, he said, could such meetings take place in the tsar's absence. Vorontsov also asked and received answers about marriages between British and Russian aristocratic families. After Müller's death, Vorontsov agreed to act as patron to his children.[55]

While Müller researched these and other queries, Domashnev badgered him about the Academy's history. Having tried flattery unsuccessfully in the spring of 1777, when he told Müller that only he had the experience, skill, and length of tenure to complete such an important work, Domashnev turned to vague threats by early November. In a letter that must have reminded Müller of his days in St Petersburg, the director wrote that several members of the Academy were grumbling that Müller was not earning his salary and should be forced to complete the history: "It is my duty to remind you of your obligations to the Academy if only to shut the mouths of those who speak against you."[56] This tactic seemed to work, for Müller sent Domashnev a partial manuscript in January 1778. The historiographer insisted, however, that he needed more help if he was to complete the project. In the summer of 1780 he proposed that Stritter be put in charge of the history. The Conference assented to the suggestion, but it seems that Müller tended to divert Stritter's attention toward archival work. After Dashkova, Vorontsov's sister, replaced the incompetent and probably venal Domashnev as director in January 1783, she reminded Müller of his obligation. His response had a familiar ring to it:

Your Grace is kind to acknowledge my first letter with your customary grace; for that I am humbly grateful and I will be most pleased to end my career under your gracious directorship. In that regard I should say that, because of my late years and sporadic attacks of ill-health, I have not been able to work so diligently and heartily as I had hoped to do in order to fulfil all my obligations to the Academy, and for that I beg to receive [your] forgiveness ... However, I do not despair of finally ending my history of the Academy, if only I continue to receive the necessary supply of information. For that reason, I ask you Highness to order the Academy Conference to send to Mr Assessor Stritter not only the Conference protocols, but also all the supplements which are cited in them. Similarly, I would like from the Academy Chancellery all its Protocols, ukazes, announcements, reports, and notes about books which it receives and issues, correspondence with scholarly people, that is everything.[57]

Ill or not, Müller still believed in doing things thoroughly. Indeed, his sense of organization had been remarked upon with some awe a few years earlier by Archdeacon William Coxe, a well-known Englishman who toured Russia in 1778. Coxe visited Müller twice and later was to write a major study of Russian voyages in the Pacific. Müller's memory, he wrote, "is still surprising, and his accurate acquaintance with the minutest incidents of the Russian annals almost surpasses belief ... His collection of state papers and manuscripts is invaluable, and arranged in the exactest order."[58] Coxe's praise notwithstanding, the history of the Academy was never finished. A first draft, covering the years 1725 to 1743, was submitted to Dashkova in 1782, the last ten years of it being mainly the work of Stritter.

In many ways, the history of the Academy represents a summary of Müller's *Weltanschauung*. Scattered through it are his own recollections of Schumacher, the early days of the Academy and his first friends (Mencke, Kohl, Euler), a memoir of his ten years in Siberia, and his first battles with Lomonosov. To cite but one example of his tendency to use the history to raise once again opinions of his own, here is a paragraph from a section in which he describes his travels along the Chinese border in 1734:

In my view this achievement of easy access to the Kamchatka Sea would be attained with or without Chinese approval along the Amur River. However, the opportunity should not be missed to prepare an exact map of a large and still unknown piece of land which no surveyor had undertaken to describe. It was also necessary to get to know better a land which in the Nerchinsk Treaty of 1689 had remained very undefined along the border of both empires. It contains the best sables of all Siberia. Since it is not otherwise inhabited, the area is used by hunters regularly from both sides of the border. It could be cause for future strife if one decides that on behalf of shipping to the American and Kurile Islands, to Japan or to India, just claims were made by us to the whole Amur region. It was thus patriotic duty and a desire to expand geographical knowledge that drove me energetically to push this task to completion.[59]

In this way, Müller preached once again a project that he first espoused actively in 1741.

Müller published other essays during the 1770s, including the correspondence between Peter the Great and Field Marshall Count Boris Petrovich Sheremetev.[60] His introduction to this collection, which was reissued in German by Bacmeister in 1789, included an account of Sheremetev's life and details about his family. Since Sheremetev was a member of one of Russia's old aristocratic families and also a successful commander of Peter's armies against the Swedes in Livonia and Estonia, and against Cossack rebels in Astrakhan, these papers represent important documentation of Peter's reign.

It may well be that Müller's greatest contribution to subsequent historical studies during those years was the publication of invaluable manuscripts and documents pertaining to Russian history. Especially gratifying to Müller himself was the appearance in 1768–9 of the first two parts of Tatishchev's History of Russia from Ancient Times. A second book was printed in 1773 and a third in 1774. Although Müller had been campaigning on behalf of this project for years, the immediate stimulus for its completion came from actions taken by Schlözer. In 1767 Schlözer proposed to the Academy that he and Stritter, who had come to St Petersburg with Schlözer in 1766, publish Tatishchev's historical work. Taubert rushed to inform Müller of the proposal, which included the statement that "Tatishchev is a Russian, he is the father of Russian history, and the world should know that it was a Russian not a German [Müller?] who broke the ice in Russian history."[61]

Müller then acted to keep the project in his own hands. Although Russians from Taubert to more modern ones may well be right in designating Tatishchev the founder of modern Russian historiography, one would not be far off in saying Müller made even that possible. In December 1782, Müller was commanded by Catherine to prepare the remaining parts of Tatishchev's manuscript for publication, and he was still working hard on this project a few weeks before illness, and then death, ended his many years of intense labour. Müller's regular correspondence with Catherine's secretary, A.V. Olsufiev, shows that he even tried to speed the process up by requesting that a special typography be assigned to his own archives. But this request was not acted upon in time. The fourth volume of Tatishchev's work was not printed until the 1840s, after M.P. Pogodin found it among his own manuscript papers.[62]

Simultaneously, Müller edited for publication the sixteenth-century Sudebnik of Ivan IV (1768) and Mankiev's Kernel of Russian History (1770), which he wrongfully attributed to Prince Khilkov. The continuing significance of Mankiev's work to eighteenth-century historians is indicated by the fact that it had four reprintings before the turn of the next century. In 1773 Müller edited a geographical lexicon of the Russian empire that had been compiled by the voevoda of Vereia, Fedor Polunin. The manuscript had been sent to the University of Moscow by its author in 1770. Polunin had asked for Müller's participation, saying that much of the information in the lexicon had been gleaned from publications by Müller and Büsching on Russian towns. In a foreword to the work, to which he added new data of his own on the Cheremis and other Siberian peoples, Müller stressed its importance as the first book to synthesize information on all facets of the Russian Empire.[63] Müller also wrote the entries for "Rossiia," "Moskva," and "Peterburg." The book served as an important complement to his own publications in Monthly Compositions, to an abridgment of Büsching's general geography of Europe and Russia which Müller had published in Russia in 1766[64] and to Krasheninnikov's description of Kamchatka. Müller was working on a second, much expanded edition of the Polunin lexicon at the time of his death.

Finally, Müller published the Kniga stepennaia in two volumes in 1775. Using the methods advocated by Maskov and other accumulators of documents, Müller sought out the oldest and most complete copy available. He then collated that version, a manuscript from Ivan

IV's reign loaned to him by Ambrose, metropolitan of Moscow, with a later one. He changed nothing from the earliest copy, so that the printed book might be as accurate as possible. In his long introduction he noted that the emphasis in the *Kniga stepennaia* was on religious history, but said that its authors "wrote according to their profession. We can recognize the spirit of their own times from their writing ... which, after all, is the main purpose of historical writing."[65]

Altogether, Müller's editorial and publicist activity proved invaluable to a community where historical studies were still in the preliminary stages – but also a community in which there was an increasingly strident demand for a record of the national heritage. What is more, Müller's contribution did not end with his death. A number of his tracts appeared posthumously as entries in the *Geographical Dictionary of the Russian State*, edited by A. Shchekatov and L. Maksimovich in 1788–9.[66] The tenth volume of the *Sammlung*, edited by Gustav Ewers and M. Engelhardt and published in 1816, also contained many Müller papers. The Archeographical Commission of Moscow printed many more of his reports and documents in the 1830s and 1840s, and, as we have seen, his essays on Ukraine and the Cossacks appeared in the *Studies* produced by Moscow's Society for the History and Antiquity of Russia.

In a letter written to Vice-Chancellor A.M. Golitsyn in December 1765, Müller had proposed that he "prepare a collection of treaties, conventions, alliances, and other official acts concluded between Russia and foreign states to be used by those who are destined for ministerial positions. If it is agreeable, I shall add to each document of this collection an historical introduction and notes, in which I will explain everything that needs explanation. Perhaps it would also be well to publish the correspondence of the old embassies, as is regularly done in many other countries."[67] The first parts of this enterprise were not ready for presentation to the empress until April 1780, when Müller handed her a collection of documents pertaining to the diplomatic relations (1486–1519) between Muscovy and the Habsburg emperors. Subsequent collections (Muscovy and Prussian Brandenburgs, 1517–1700; Muscovy and Denmark, 1493–1562), which Müller and Bantysh-Kamenskii gathered for Catherine II in the early 1780s, were all printed in various sets during the nineteenth century.[68]

The second edition of Novikov's *Old Russian Library* included many more items from Müller's apparently inexhaustible supply. In fact, the entire part VII (1789) and most of part XVII (1791) were composed of Müller's edited papers, and in 1791 Novikov printed a previously unpublished original essay by Müller on the Kiev Academy.[69] *New*

Monthly Compositions contained more than twenty papers from Müller's files; and in the 1790s A.N. Radishchev drew information for a short tale on the conquest of Siberia entirely from Müller's history of that region.[70] A special series of documents and works from the era of Peter the Great, edited by Fedor Tumanskii in 1787–8, included reprints of Müller's essays on Peter's youth.[71] Müller's articles on Russo-Chinese relations along the Amur proved even more resilient. In introducing some materials on the Russian conquest of the Amur to readers of his *Moskovskii telegraph* (*Moscow Telegraph*) in 1832, N.A. Polevoi praised Müller for making known information held in the Iakutsk archives. He noted that the essays on the Amur that Müller had printed in *Monthly Compositions* had figured prominently in articles on China placed in Russian journals during 1821 and 1830.[72]

When Müller (and Bayer) predicted in 1732 that it would take "twenty years or more" to gather all the documents necessary for the preparation of a "full Russian history and a geographical description of the Russian Empire," they probably did not think that the emphasis should be on the "or more." But fifty years later there was still no full history and geography of the Russian empire. Yet Müller had done everything in his power to achieve the goal. He provided the material and even brought forward likely candidates for the task: Schlözer, Shcherbatov, Stritter, and Rychkov. Unhappily, factors well beyond his control had militated against the endeavour. Nevertheless, the less ambitious promise, "to perform a significant service to the state which I have served for forty years," which Müller had made to A.M. Golitsyn in 1766, was much more than fulfilled.

Müller and Russian Historiography

[Müller] will always be considered as the Great Father
of Russian history, as well from the excellent specimens
he himself produced as from the vast fund of information which he bequeaths to future historians.

William Coxe in *Travels in Poland,
Russia, Sweden and Denmark* [1778]
(London, 1802)

Gerhard Friderich Müller died on 11 October 1783. Catherine II noted his passing with regret in letters to Baron Melchoir von Grimm and said that he was the most praiseworthy historian among her subjects.[1] Müller had earned many honours during his long and often stormy life in Russia: most recently, actual state councillor (August 1783) and cavalier of the Order of St Vladimir, 3rd class (September 1783). He was among the earliest recipients of the Order of St Vladimir, which was initiated to honour those who contributed to Russia's enlightenment,[2] Betskoi having been the first in 1782. Thus, formal recognition from Russia's government came only at the very end of Müller's career. He was honoured abroad earlier, by the Royal Society in London, the Swedish Academy in Stockholm, the Académie in Paris, and the Göttingen Learned Society. Moscow's Free Russian Assembly and the Free Economic Society awarded him certificates of merit as well.[3]

Leonhard Euler also died in 1783, and with the death of these two old scholars an era in the history of the Academy of Sciences came to an end. It is fitting perhaps that the same year witnessed a sharp turn in the administrative affairs of the Academy. The decree that appointed Dashkova director in January also called for the abolition of the academic commission. It was replaced by two councillors, O.P. Kozodavlev and V.A. Ushakov, and a treasurer, an army general named M. Riabov. Kosodavlev was at the same time co-editor with Dashkova of the journal *Sobesednik liubitelei Russkago slova* and a member of the Commission for the Establishment of Public Schools that Catherine set up in September 1782. Ushakov joined the board of the new Russian Academy of Letters which the empress founded in

September 1783 with Dashkova as its first president. The new Russian Academy took under its wing the Commission for the Translation of Foreign Books (established in 1768) and the Free Russian Assembly, with which Müller had been closely associated during his years in Moscow. The decree that appointed the new administration of the Academy of Sciences made it clear that the Academic Commission was deemed a failure and that the professors were now to "remain members of the Conference and fulfill the duties for which they are paid."[4] In short, Müller and Euler died the very year that Catherine began seriously to centralize all the cultural institutions of Russia. Thus, the Academy of Sciences lost the last vestige of its collegial autonomy, for which Müller and Euler had fought for so long, and became instead a direct agency of the government.

Ironically, these were the very years when Catherine was most anxious to find a historian to prepare a history text that could be used in her proposed public school system. It has been noted already that her own "Notes on Russian History" was serialized in the *Sobesednik* (1783–4). In December 1783, Catherine instituted a new "Historical Assembly," supervised by Count A.P. Shuvalov for the purpose of compiling extracts about ancient history generally, and early Russian history specifically. A few years later this group sponsored Catherine's "Notes" for publication in book form. Her intention to maintain control over the interpretation of Russian history was signalled in 1783 when she ordered that the textbook commissioned from Stritter be held up because of the disparities between it and her own work.

Even Dashkova was moved to bemoan the lack of good national history in her opening address to the Russian Academy: "The different memorials of antiquity spread over the vast surface of the Russian Empire, our numerous chronicles, those precious records of past actions of our ancestors, of which few of the nations of Europe now existing can boast an equal number, present a vast field for our exertions, upon which we are led to advance under the guidance of the enlightened genius of August Protectress. The lofty deeds of our princes, the exploits of the past and present ever memorable age, present an almost boundless range of subjects worthy of our labour."[5] These sentiments had been expressed regularly by Müller in one form or another since 1730 – but he was no longer in a position to benefit from Russia's new public schooling system's need for textbooks of the national history.

There can be little doubt about Müller's remarkable capacity for hard work, which moved S.M. Solov'ev in the 1850s to call him a "tireless worker for the vast machine of Russian civilization," and Paul Miliukov to explain in 1897, "Tel homme, tel oeuvre!"[6] Nor, in spite of claims to the contrary by his enemies, could Müller's loyalty to Russia be questioned. Schlözer and Büsching both said that Müller worked tirelessly in Russian service and expected his colleagues and subordinates to do the same. Bacmeister thanked Müller for persuading him "always to be a good Russian" and to scorn those foreign scholars who failed to take into account Russian national sensibilities.[7]

As far as Müller was concerned, history was a matter of straightforward fact-finding. He assumed, naïvely perhaps, that eventually enough written documentation would be discovered to make a "truthful" account merely a matter of someone taking the time to write it down. The outburst of anti-German patriotism at the Academy in 1749–50 had left him relatively unscarred and could be set aside as yet another example of the volatile and unpredictable cross-currents of Russia's intellectual milieu. The sharp division between those who admired and those who despised Müller in his lifetime was not an unusual one, for the Academy was constantly divided into warring factions. By the 1760s he was a senior member, so more than anyone else he was both a target and a sponsor of shifting loyalties within various cliques. There were always academic, personal, or national circumstances to colour opinions on Müller's scholarship and publicist activities.

The fate of his interpretation of old Rus' during the past two centuries would not have surprised Müller very much, for he was accustomed to being a focal point in contentious matters. He would have been startled, however, to see himself portrayed sometimes as the initiator and at other times as a main propagator of something called a "Norman theory." In fact, Müller can neither be blamed nor credited for the resilience of the Norman theory as an explanation for the origin of the Russian state and its name. After Lomonosov's death, the patriotically inspired assault on the idea that the Varangians were Scandinavian remained dormant for nearly a century, and the assumptions that were later referred to as "Normanism" were sustained in one form or another in the eighteenth century by Shcherbatov, Stritter, Strube de Piermont, N.I. Boltin, and, above all, Schlözer.

Strube's position had the distinction of being the strangest. In 1785 he published a book entitled *Dissertation sur les anciens Russes*. It had a Russian translation in 1791. Strube said in a foreword that he had been gathering information on the subject ever since the great debate of 1749–50. But his pretension to serious research was belied somewhat by his conclusion that the Varangians were Gothic Roxolani who lived "somewhere" between the Baltic Sea and the

Arctic Ocean! They were, he said, the most northern of the northern peoples. Another contemporary, Timofei Mal'gin, wrote a short textbook in which he accepted Tatishchev's version by giving Riurik a Finnish heritage.[8] Everyone else followed the example of Bayer, Müller, and Schlözer – who themselves relied on the best-known Russian sources of the time. Schlözer's *Nestor* carried the theory to its most extreme position: "Russian history began with the calling of Riurik: and the founding of the Russian monarchy ... the Novgorodians (Slaviane), the Chud (Finns) and Russes (Normans) united together to create one nation ... Not intending to anger patriots [I must say that] ... their history is even more recent than that of the Germans and Swedes ... Before this epoch [calling of the Varangians] everything was in darkness in Russia as well as in the neighbouring regions. Certainly there were people there, but God knows from what lands they came; they were a people without a government, living like animals." Elsewhere in the exhaustive study, Schlözer said that "the Varangians were Normans, and mainly Swedes."[9]

Schlözer extended the Normanist explanation much further in *Nestor* than he had forty years earlier in the *Probe russischer Annalen*, but it had become the standard version of Russia's origins anyway. Even Catherine, who wrote in her "Notes on Russian History" that the Varangians were Slavs, could not check the predominance of Normanism among historians of Russia. In 1799 the first textbook of Russian history to be officially accepted for use in schools hedged somewhat about the Varangians. They were described as a mixture of many warlike Baltic tribes who lived as sea-raiders but were not referred to as Scandinavians or Normans. Indeed, the question of their place of origin was ignored altogether. Nevertheless, the Varangians were differentiated clearly from the Slavs and were credited with founding the Russian state.[10] There were a few attempts to revise opinions on pre-Riurik Russia expressed by Schlözer, but they were isolated. In 1808, J.P.G. Ewers called for a re-examination of existing assumptions about ancient Russia and suggested that the Russes may have been southern Slavs. Shortly afterward, N. Brusilov also challenged the consensus in an article prepared for *Vestnik evropy*. Neither of these works was persuasive enough to have much effect on contemporary historiography. By 1821, according to church historian Metropolitan Evgenii, "the opinion that the Varangians were Normans, or Swedes, is now generally accepted without argument."[11]

The strongest Russian devotees of Schlözer's methods, who are often referred to collectively as the "Sceptical School" of historians (M.T. Kachenovskii, N.S. Artsybashev, N.A. Polevoi), disseminated

Normanism actively in the first half of the nineteenth century. In 1809, Kachenovskii acknowledged that there were written sources for Russian history before the *Primary Chronicle* but believed that the formal history of the Slavs and northern Europe could begin only with the advent of Christianity and the introduction of writing skills. Thus, no credible native corroboration existed to support contentions that the Varangians were Finns, Roxolani, or Prussians. One must accept the obvious, he said, and agree with the *Primary Chronicle* that the Varangians were Scandinavian. Elsewhere Kachenovskii disputed Karamzin's argument that historians must be patriotic in their writing by saying that he was not embarrassed to admit that he owed his knowledge of ancient Russia to "Bayer, Müller, Stritter and especially to the famous A. Schlözer."[12]

The "Sceptics" accepted the *Primary Chronicle* as authentic because they believed that a study of history was possible only where written native sources were available. They adopted the "historians' law" as it had been expounded by Schlözer in the *Probe*: "Ne quid falsi dicat!" It is better to write "a short history of 600 years," Schlözer had written, "than a long one of 3,000 years of fables."[13] Given the chance, Müller would not have argued with either of these criteria for writing history.

Ironically, the very historians whom the "Sceptics" treated most scornfully – Karamzin, M.P. Pogodin, N.G. Ustrialov – were the most effective promulgators of Normanism among the general reading public. Karamzin's twelve-volume *History of the Russian State* (1818–29) was by far the most widely read multi-volume history before Solov'ev's began to appear in the 1850s. It was abridged for use in Russian schools, translated into nearly every European language (except English), and had fourteen editions in Russia during the nineteenth century. Not only did Karamzin regularly refer to the Varangians as Normans, but he named and rebuked the academicians who opposed Müller in 1749. "Now it is difficult to comprehend the persecution suffered by the author of that dissertation of 1749," Karamzin wrote in his first volume.[14]

Ustrialov prepared the official Russian history text for schools in the 1830s, and Pogodin went so far as to turn the Norman theory into a nationalistic one on behalf of Nicholas I's doctrine of Official Nationality. Ustrialov and Pogodin consistently referred to the Varangians and Riurik as Normans and insisted that Russian history started in 862.[15] Although Normanism increasingly was called into question during the second half of the nineteenth century, it remained the foremost, if often modified, interpretation until Soviet historians made it their special *bête noir*. The greatest of Russian historians during the nineteenth century, Solov'ev, and his equally famous student, V.O. Kliuchevskii, themselves leaned toward the Normanist viewpoint. Aside from his monumental history of Russia and a number of individual essays where both sides of the debate were accorded space, Solov'ev wrote a textbook for schools in which his Normanism was unqualified. Kliuchevskii's commitment was more reserved, and he reacted angrily to a review by N.I. Ilovaiskii that accused him of Normanism in 1882. Nevertheless, Kliuchevskii gave Riurik a Scandinavian origin and said that Lomonosov's diatribe against Müller in 1749 was "not so *convincing* as it was *cruel*." Solov'ev, Bestuzhev-Riumin, and even the Slavophile M.O. Koialovich took Lomonosov and the Academy to task for their treatment of Müller in 1749. Although Koialovich had harsh words for Bayer, Schlözer, and Normanism in general, he separated Müller from the other German scholars in Russia and credited him with valuable contributions to Russia's historical sciences.[16]

There were some scholarly challenges to the traditional scheme during the later nineteenth century, but Normanism continued to reign supreme in the world of school texts and therefore in the popular mind. To cite but a few late-century examples: in texts written for the middle and lower school in the 1880s by V.A. Abaza, the *Primary Chronicle*'s "invitation" to the Varangians (whom Abaza called "Germans") from "across the sea" was repeated just as it had been 200 years earlier in the *Sinopsis*. This practice was so common that it was still followed in 1919 by Russian missionaries in Peking who prepared a history textbook for distribution there. But there was a very important exception to this rule. One of the most reprinted history texts was Ilovaiskii's *Short Guide to Russian History* – which had thirty-six printings between 1860 and 1912. Ilovaiskii said that the *Ros'* or *Rus'* were a native people and blamed Bayer and Schlözer (not Müller) for the widespread acceptance of the notion that they were Scandinavians. In his opinion, the *Rus'* were an indigenous nation whose original home was the region between the Dniepr and the Azov Sea and who were known to the Greeks as "a Sarmatian people named Roxalon or Rossalon." These people eventually mingled with the Slavs and founded a "strong state with Kiev at its centre."[17] Ilovaiskii's text was widely adopted for use in seminaries. In nineteenth-century Russian historical writing, then, Müller generally was neither blamed nor praised for Normanism; nor was he charged even with being its main proponent. The most tangible element of Müller's contribution to the argument over the origins of the Russian state and its first leaders was the simple fact that it was he who first expressed, documented, and defended Bayer's thesis, which became known as the Norman theory, before a Russian audience.

Since the 1920s, Müller's image as a historian has been subject to the vicissitudes of state-directed policy on historical perspectives. His labour as an archivist, geographer, and ethnographer of Siberia has been studied and properly commended by Soviet scholars. We have seen this already in the work of A.I. Andreev, L.S. Berg, and M.O. Kosven. But as a historian, his clash with Lomonosov and his Normanism have hung like an albatross around his neck. Nevertheless, in the first Soviet book on Siberian history, written by V.I. Ogorodnikov in 1920, Müller was introduced as the "father" of Russian and Siberian historiography. Shortly afterward, in keeping with the moderation of Lenin's New Economic Policy (1921–8), V.I. Picheta acknowledged the important influence of Müller's publicist activity and noted that Lomonosov's attacks on him were prompted by the latter's patriotic sentiments. But Picheta made no qualitative judgments about Müller's work; and an article published in the Academy of Science journal in 1926 referred to Müller as the "father of Russian historical sciences."[18]

In 1937, after Stalin had subordinated the discipline of history completely to state controls, the first volume of Müller's Siberian history was printed with much accompanying publicity and complimentary introductory essays by leading Soviet historians. S.V. Bakhrushin, for example, wrote that his "significance in Russian historiography was considerable. In the person of Müller, Russian historical science broke with the naïve and undocumented methods of feudal historiography and moved towards the more completely scientific practices." Bakhrushin added, however, that Müller's notion of causality was a product of "antiquated feudal ideology"; that is, he explained Russia's conquest of Siberia by referring to Providence and the hand of God. The editor of a collection of Radishchev's work repeated Bakhrushin's judgment in 1941. But in the same year, after the second volume of the Siberian history appeared, N.L. Rubinstein credited Müller with being the first to illustrate the value and multiplicity of documentary sources for Russian history.[19]

Just as Miliukov had done in the 1890s, Rubinstein saw Müller as a predecessor of Schlözer, Shcherbatov, and Karamzin. But in 1948, M. Tikhomirov condemned Rubinstein's book for describing Müller as a "representative of a completely new stage in the growth of Russian historical sciences." Müller was not a historian at all, said Tikhomirov. He was, rather, an "archeographer" and made useful contributions only in that capacity. Tikhomirov's viewpoint reflected the quite understandable anti-German feeling of the post–Second World War Soviet Union. But his observation that the "German academics of the eighteenth century ... left their mark on Russian historical sciences, but ... Russian historiography in the eighteenth century was created by Russian hands, for Russians," also was typical of the Stalinist rewriting process.[20]

The 1950s saw more mixed reviews of Müller's part in the evolution of Russian historical writing. While M.O. Kosven marked the 150th anniversary of Müller's birth with a favourable evaluation of his geographical and ethnographical work, the editors of the four-volume *Outline of the Historical Sciences in the USSR* (1955–6) strongly condemned his Normanism. They also made sweeping judgments about foreign writers in eighteenth-century Russia, saying that they had done more harm than good for Russian national consciousness and historical writing.[21] These were the very years in which new collected works by Herzen and Chernyshevskii, in which Müller was highly esteemed,[22] were published. Herzen's evaluation of the early foreign historians of Russia – Müller, Schlözer, Lévesque, and Ewers – was exactly opposite to the one presented in the *Outline*.

The editors of the *Outline* grudgingly acknowledged Müller's usefulness as a collector of Siberian materials, as did V.K. Iatsunskii in 1955 and D.M. Lebedev and L.V. Cherepnin in 1957. Iatsunskii, who was also one of the contributors to the *Outline*, published a book on historical geography in which he said that the "historico-geographical investigations" of both Bayer and Müller were beneficial to later Russian investigators. Two years later Cherepnin took issue, albeit very cautiously, with the editors of the *Outline* for the blanket denigration of the eighteenth-century German historians of Russia. He rehabilitated some of Rubinstein's conclusions about the overall contribution by Bayer and Müller to the evolution of Russian historiography. Cherepnin's re-evaluation may have been a by-product of the cultural "thaw" stimulated by Khrushchev's anti-Stalin campaign, but party and Russian shibboleths about Lomonosov's heroics and anti-Normanism remained firmly in the deep-freeze. Cherepnin and his colleagues still all treated Müller mainly as a foil for their unabashed praise for Lomonosov as a historian, and they remonstrated with him, and with Bayer, for making Normanism so long an integral part of Russian historiography.[23]

During the 1960s, S.L. Peshtich, M.I. Radovskii, and V.G. Mirsoev redressed somewhat the consistently unfavourable post-war Soviet version of Müller as a historian. Peshtich took exception to the *Outline*'s charge that Müller was an apologist for Russia's *dvorianstvo*. Citing the historical essays in *Monthly Compositions*, the Soviet historian said that Müller's "method and socio-political views ... inarguably evolved towards the bourgeoisie direction, although it is true that his references to the hand of God testify to the dependence of his opinions upon artificial historiography and ideology."[28] It was Mirzoev, however, who in 1963 introduced a decidedly revisionist approach to Müller's historical writing.

In an article that purported to outline the nature of the literature on Müller from the eighteenth century, Mirzoev quietly resurrected the view that Müller contributed to all aspects of the development of historical studies in Russia. He stressed works on Müller as a historian of Siberia and therefore was able to ignore the question of Normanism. By accentuating the very favourable picture of Müller presented in pre-Soviet writings, and by singling out Bakrushkin's interpretation above most other Soviet commentators, Mirzoev was able to present a balanced and fair assessment of the German's work. In general, however, Mirzoev's position has not been taken up by other Soviet writers, who still relentlessly focus on Müller as a Normanist and continue to laud Lomonosov at his expense.

Authors of the two most widely used Soviet textbooks on historiography published in the 1960s confined their observations on Müller and other foreign historians of Russia in the eighteenth century to chapters on either Tatishchev or Lomonosov. Both books attribute great scholarship and foresight to Lomonosov's criticisms of Müller, and in one of them, by V.I. Astakhov, the polemics of 1749–50 are described as "the beginning of a decisive struggle with the German falsifiers of Russian history. Müller, who was one of the most important German historians who worked in Russia, was supported by the Germans who sat in the Academy of Sciences, and also by numerous and often influential Russian noblemen – enemies of Lomonosov."[26] The degree to which Astakhov exaggerated the importance of Lomonosov as a historian is equalled only by the degree to which he underestimated the significance of Müller in the evolution of the historical sciences in Russia. A book on ancient "Rus'" and Scandinavia, which appeared in Moscow in 1978, reiterated Astakhov's premise.[27]

It is still often assumed in Soviet writing that Müller was anti-Russian, an apologist for both autocracy and serfdom, and a leader of the predominantly foreign professoriate of the Academy against a small but progressive and patriotic Russian faction. A glaring example of this habit appeared in another recent Soviet monograph on Russian education in the eighteenth century that depicted Müller as one of Schumacher's "henchmen" and as an "enemy of the Russian enlightenment."[28] Such absurd interpretations fail to account for the unusual events of Müller's oath of allegience to the Russian monarchy, his advocacy of the use of Russian in schools, his persistent lobbying for the completion of a national history in order to correct foreign misconceptions about Russia, and his disputes with foreign as well as Russian members of the Academy.

Mirzoev made these very points again in 1970 when he contrasted Müller with Fischer in a book on the historiography of Siberia. "Müller served Russia honourably, made it his second homeland, studied the Russian language, and undertook Russian history," Mirzoev wrote, adding that Müller's collection of "facts" about Siberian history was a "colossal" accomplishment.[29] Kopelevich's very interesting book of 1977 on the first two decades of the Academy of Sciences in St Petersburg, to which reference has been made above, treats the entire foreign contingent objectively and is free of ideologically inspired polemics. Events after 1747 – and sensitive questions of historical writing – were, however, outside Kopelevich's chronological and subject frame of reference. Such acknowlegment of the intrinsic merits of Müller's historical work (even if only on Siberia), his posture as a loyal subject to the Russian monarch, and his important public relations and administrative contributions to the Academy in its early years remain rare in Soviet scholarship. Those writers about Siberian history, geography, and ethnography who praise Müller's technique and his labour in gathering information generally say nothing about Russian history or about his role as Russian citizen. A.I. Andreev delivered two papers on Müller in the 1950s (1950, 1954) that lauded his geographical contributions, but these remain unpublished. Nevertheless, the material that Andreev collected in the late 1930s and that was published posthumously in 1965 as *Ocherki po istochnikovedeniiu Sibiri* reflects very favourably on Müller as ethnographer, cartographer, and geographer. Apparently Andreev hoped still to edit the final two volumes of the Siberian history, but his death in 1959 and lack of official sponsorship meant that the project remains in limbo.[30]

The authors of a five-volume history of Siberia that was published in Leningrad during 1968–9 regularly drew information from Müller's reports, publications, and archives for their descriptions of eighteenth-century Siberian towns and trade. They also praised him as the first scholar to attempt a serious study and classification of Siberian documents and enthused over the way in which he applied ethnographical and linguistic data to problems of history and population movements. They called his own history "state oriented" – quite rightly but perhaps irrelevantly – and said nothing about the likelihood of further volumes going to press.[31]

The discovery of new materials and the application of modern historical research methods made passé much of what Müller and Lomonosov argued over so bitterly in the eighteenth century. But the degree to which subsequent discussions of their views were partisan changed very little. It was this dimension of his professional heritage that would not have surprised Müller; he would have been somewhat non-plussed, however, at the importance that later historians assigned to what undoubtedly he considered to be insignificant historical events.

Although he spoke of writing a history of Russia as early as 1732 and again in 1749, and compiled historical essays throughout his career, there is little evidence in Müller's works that he was influenced to any extent by his illustrious contemporaries Voltaire, Hume, Robertson, and Schlözer, or by other prominent writers whose works he knew well. In fact, Müller once voiced disapproval of Hume's study of James I as "very free-thinking, especially against religion."[32] The literary artistry, rationalist interpretation, and critical analysis of sources, traits that were represented in varying degrees in the works of such authors, were not completely absent from Müller's myriad studies. But he rarely brought together the disparate trends of modern historical writing as they were known in his time.

Müller's essays embraced the history of indigenous peoples, commerce, and social customs; and he attributed causative force to such factors as climate and geography much in the manner of Montesquieu. He also stressed often the importance of truth in historical writing, the value of official documentation, the universal context of historical growth, and the need to authenticate sources. In general, his assumptions about historical investigation, which went beyond the theological, nationalistic, or strictly annalistic interpretations that were still common to Russian writers in his day, were more the result of his own learning experiences in Siberia than they were a reflection of trends among European historians. If his historical description of Siberia was to be compared to Hume's first volume on the Stuarts, which also appeared in 1750, or to Voltaire's work on the age of Louis XIV (1751), it would seem unsophisticated, disjointed, with little criticism and only barely a narrative. It was a collection of documents, and that is exactly what Müller intended it to be.

It was, indeed, as a collector of documents on Russian geography, ethnography, statistics, linguistics, the natural sciences, and, above all, history that Müller was unsurpassed. Even his opponents admit that he was the first published writer in Russia to emphasize the importance of official documentation for historical studies. His reliance on documents and his insistence on historical accuracy stimulated further large-scale archival gathering, which provided starting points for many later historians. Not to be discounted either, in judging Müller among his peers, is the fact that he was by far the best-known and most respected writer of Russian history and geography among western European intellectual circles before Schlözer came to dominate the field.[33] At the popular level, his exposition of a number of topics hitherto unknown to his Russian readers could not help but contribute to the growth of a historical consciousness in Russia. Whether he willed it or not, his contentiousness drove opponents to delve further into Russia's past.

Insofar as the immediate uses of history were concerned, Müller was typical of most eighteenth-century men-of-letters who saw history as the ideal instrument for instruction. In a review of an English publication of extracts from Plutarch's *Lives*, he wrote: "If it is true, and there is no doubt that it is, that good examples accomplish more in correcting human morals than do the best laws ... [and if it is] true as well that the main end of all history is to provide wise rules for all circumstances in human affairs, then the best way to instruct in character-building is to depict the lives of great men, especially their characters."[34] The review section of *Monthly Compositions* was replete with commentary on classical reprints and character-building texts, and also lexicons, geographical compendia, and universal histories.

Müller had been quick to pick up the trend toward world histories that gathered momentum in Europe during the 1760s. Classical antiquity was attractive to the humanist scholars of the eighteenth century; the religious conflicts of the two preceding centuries already had promoted the study of the history of Christianity; and the discovery of the vastness of the world outside Europe had brought a world-wide scope to historical perspective. Müller himself had first-hand experience away from the eurocentric world during his decade in Siberia. Universal histories were a natural outgrowth of rationalistic examinations of the historical process. The earliest multi-volume enterprise in universal history was the English *Universal History from the Earliest Account of Time to the Present*, the first volume of which appeared in 1736. Müller reviewed several of its later issues, 1763–4, and stressed their importance.

He had some reservations, however, about the tendency of universalists to divide early history into the "four great [biblical] monarchies." "It is much more logical," he said, "to know about the history of empires." He gave pride of place in his own reviews to single-volume world histories that were written in Russia for a Russian audience. These included the previously mentioned books by Curas and Dilthey, and also an *Abrégé de l'Histoire universelle* (2 volumes, 1764), written "for Russia's youth" by a University of Moscow professor of French, Jacques Préclos de Lery.[35]

Emphasis on critical method and debate over a philosophy of history did not take root in Russia until the second quarter of the nineteenth century, when the "Sceptics," Kachenovskii (1755– 1842), Artsybashev (1773–1841), Polevoi (1796–1846), and Kachenovskii's students at the University of Moscow (V.V. Shenshin, S.M. Stroev, N. Sazonov, O.M. Bodianskii, N. Strekalov, N.I. Nadezhdin, and N.V. Stankevich) dominated briefly the historical profession.[36] Although they were self-styled protégés of Schlözer, and admirers of both Müller and N.I. Boltin, the "Sceptics" drew their main inspiration from the first two volumes of B.G. Niebuhr's *Römanische Geschichte*, which appeared in 1811–12.

According to Kachenovskii, who came late to Niebuhr whereas Polevoi started with him, that work represented a milestone in the evolution of source criticism, a major step beyond Schlözer's "elementary" critical method. Niebuhr had drawn a scholarly mass of material and facts from the myths and legends that dominated previous studies of ancient Rome. In a review of Niebuhr's work, Kachenovskii wrote in 1830 that "there is nothing more suitable for science than scepticism – that is, neither superficial nor thoughtless, but founded on the collection of texts, on critical evidence. Investigate, doubt, explain yourself, if you have enough fortitude."[37] This was certainly well beyond the demands made on historical researchers by Müller, but Kachenovskii respected him as a predecessor to his way of thinking.[38] The Sceptics had forums of their own. Kachenovskii edited the *Messenger of Europe* (*Vestnik evropy*) between 1809 and 1830, Polevoi founded and edited the *Moscow Telegraph* (*Moskovskii telegraf*, 1825–34), and Nadezhdin edited the ill-fated *Telescope* (*Teleskop*, 1834–6).[39] These journals carried many historical articles and served as media for wide-ranging debate between proponents of various interpretations of Russia's past. Nevertheless, all historians in Russia were overshadowed by the success of Karamzin's monumental *History of the Russian State*, which relied on eloquent narrative and national sentiment to remain the model for history writing in Russia until mid-century.[40]

In the years between Müller's death and the efforts of Kachenovskii and his colleagues, history in Russia remained a matter of collecting documents on the one hand and of writing panegyrics on the other. Shcherbatov's seven-volume *History of Russia from Ancient Times* was an exception in that he included a large cross-section of new documents, amassed considerable detail, and tried to place Russia in the context of world affairs. His account began with Riurik and carried on to the early seventeenth century. But he accepted most of the chronicles uncritically, ignored economic or social considerations, and selected sources to suit his assumption that the aristocracy should be the leading force within Russia's government. In 1790–1 Shcherbatov was assailed by N.I. Boltin (1735–92), who was a more striking exception among the normal historical practitioners of the time. Boltin took a much broader view of societal developments, that is, such crucial considerations as the general consequences of the Petrine reforms and the growth of Russian national consciousness. Boltin was the first to attempt an organic picture of Russian history by explaining the nature and development of the institutions, including serfdom, and the customs of medieval Russia. His four volumes of historical commentary were all directed against Shcherbatov and the French historian Nicholas G. LeClerc, whose *Histoire physique, morale, et politique de la Russie ancienne et moderne* (volumes 1–6, Paris, 1783–94) offended his patriotism.[41]

Boltin challenged LeClerc's statement that Novgorod and the Slavic tribes inhabiting it in the ninth century were more barbaric than the peoples of western Europe before the Varangians arrived to civilize them. He supported his remarks by means of an analysis of the historical process itself, with careful attention paid to documentation, rather than with the type of blind patriotism that had driven Lomonosov against Müller a half-century earlier. Like Müller, Boltin insisted that history could not be written properly until all relevant documents were gathered from within Russia and abroad and put into some systematic order. The Sceptics included Boltin among their predecessors, with Müller and Schlözer, but treated Shcherbatov as a precursor to Karamzin, whose work they scorned.

In fact, there had been very few attempts by Russians to write a full history of their homeland. In 1792 Karamzin complained with justification that Russia still had no adequate history of its own. The best history of Russia ("despite its faults"), he said, was P.C. Lévesque's *Histoire de la Russie* (volumes 1–5, Paris, 1782–3), which had been translated into Russian in 1787. Karamzin went on to say that Russian history was every bit as fascinating as that of western Europe and, if written with "intelligence, taste, and talent," would be attractive to both Russians and foreigners.[42] Karamzin's own twelve-volume *History of the Russian State* (*Istoriia gosudarstva Rossiiskago*, 1818–29) was to be the first attempt to fill that gap.

Shcherbatov, Novikov, and even Karamzin had continued one Müller tradition by editing valuable historical documents for publication. In fact, owing in large part to the efforts of Count N.P. Rumiantsev (1754–1826), minister of foreign affairs and state chancellor, archivists and publicists predominated in the field of historical activity well into the first quarter of the nineteenth century. Rumiantsev oversaw the preparation of documents for publication by a group of scholars at the Moscow archives of the College of Foreign Affairs. Among them were Müller's former assistant, Bantysh-Kamenskii, K.F. Kalaidovich, A.F. Malinovskii, P.M. Stroev, and Bishop (later Metropolitan) Evgenii. The last-named wrote a very complimentary biographical essay on Müller for *Syn otechestva* (*Son of the Fatherland*) in 1821.[43] This group printed the first volume of the *Collection of State Documents and Treaties* (*Sobraniia gosudarstvennykh gramot i dogovorov*) in 1813. Three more large volumes appeared by 1826.

The same individuals, along with Karamzin and Schlözer, were members at one time or another of the Society of History and Antiquities that was founded by Rumiantsev at the University of Moscow in 1804. Stroev and Kalaidovich eventually undertook an exhaustive expedition over most of northern and central Russia, gathering materials in the real tradition of Müller, Gmelin, Pallas, and others of the previous century. They examined libraries and archival holdings and copied thousands of official documents and chronicles. Among the many important consequences of this five-and-one-half-year (1829–1834) expedition was the establishment in December 1834 of an Archeographical Commission, which was granted a permanent charter in 1837. It was assigned the task of publishing the documents collected by Stroev's expedition, and in 1846 it began the systematic publication of the Russian chronicles. The Archeographical Commission, which existed until 1922, also printed many of the papers gathered and edited by Müller, whose archival work, Stroev wrote in 1817, was "incomparably more important" for subsequent historians than were the written products of any other historian to that time.[44]

Thus Müller was prophetic when he wrote in 1764 that Russia had "enough material ... chronicles, chronographs, books of rank, genealogies, embassy records, military and ceremonial papers, and other lists ... When all of this is carefully prepared in printed productions, only then, and not before, will historical writers be in a position to create a proper history of Russia."[45] But it was still nearly a century before the great multi-volume histories of Russia, above all S.M. Solov'ev's, and the important juridical-historical works by K.D. Kavelin, B.N. Chicherin, and others, could demonstrate the full maturity of historical writing in Russia. And these men looked to Müller as their most important predecessor among historians whose careers were made in Russia.[46]

Appendix A

THOMAS MÜLLER'S ADVICE TO HIS SON 1725

My son, as you are about to set forth to distant lands, read these words with a mindful heart. Let honesty be in your heart, let not deceit be on your tongue, and worship God with true piety. Make sure that others everywhere approve of your way of life and manners – that you please the good and displease evil men. Hurry home and, my adored son, keep your foot firmly on the toilsome path of honour. On one side pleasure will aim her hostile shaft at you and the siren's mouth will sing her alluring song. On another, sloth, fearful of the journey in the harshness of Aonia [i.e. part of Boetoia, home also of the Muses], will strike its tardiness into you. Elsewhere the maliciously persuasive wickedness of a cunning acquaintance will, with unseen treachery, lay snares and traps for you. My adored son, with these monsters you must then do battle with mind and heart strong and brave. You must be humble of spirit and countenance and you must labour to help someone, if you can, and hurt no one. Be careful of your own, leave what is not yours to others, and wisely see that you keep faith with him with whom it should be kept. Hear much, say little, keep confidence, and learn to spare the weaker, yield to the stronger, and endure your equal. Remember to be sober, wakeful, and truthful, ready to love the good and tolerate the evil. Above all, revere God who sees and learns everything, whom in the end no one can deceive. Acting thus, you can

Translated by Roger C. Blockley of the Classics Department, Carleton University, from the original Latin in Büsching Beyträge, 3 (1785): 8–9.

everywhere live safe among strangers and in the heart of barbary. Thus no inconvenience of an unknown land will befall you, and you will be a dear and welcome guest to all. Here we shall not cease to belabour our Supreme Father with our endless prayers and vows, that he restore you to us safe and sound. Meanwhile live happily, and farewell for a long time.

Appendix B

FOREWORD TO *MONTHLY COMPOSITIONS* 1755

There is no need it seems to praise the benefit derived from learned journals and similar transactions, published on postal days weekly and monthly. All European nations agree on that, and prove it by innumerable examples. To this day, many are those who still read with pleasure the notes by some members of our Academy of Sciences, which were published by the gazette from 1729 to 1742. The reader is not taught in a perceptible way when at a given time he receives a small number of leaflets at once; and this teaching usually becomes rooted more solidly in him than the reading of large and lengthy books. At the same time his curiosity always increases when the time comes for the publication of a new leaflet or of a new instalment of such a work. Rare is the person who will not want to read it; and because of its brevity, it cannot bore anyone; and hardly anyone will put it down without reading it from beginning to end. What more could one wish if each time every reader will be satisfied in finding something for his curiosity and interest in Sciences?

To everybody's satisfaction, such useful business has been set up again under the praiseworthy patronage of His serene and noble Grace, the Grand Lord and Hetman of the Ukraine, President of the Academy of Sciences. Members of the Academy will apply all their efforts to try to deserve the praise of their readers through their works, desiring nothing as much as to be of real

Translated by George Melnikoff of the Russian Department, Carleton University, from the original Russian in *Monthly Compositions*, 1, no. 1 (January 1755): 3–12.

benefit to the Russian state and people, and to induce in everybody, as far as possible, the pleasure derived from a knowledge of Sciences. Moreover, they will provide space in these Compositions for other lovers of Sciences, who might wish to acquaint the world with their writings.

In an enterprise such as this, we do not set ourselves exact limits; but taking into account the variety of readers, one must always change the subject matter, so that each may use something according to his inclination and desire. Thus we shall be offering here any kind of writing that could be useful to society, namely: not only discourses on the so-called Sciences proper, but also some that will show any new discoveries in Economics, Trade, Mining, Manufacturing, Mechanical handiwork, Architecture, Music, Painting and Sculpture, and other fields, or that might lead to the correction of any kind of mistake in anything.

The only writings that will be excluded from our purpose are those that, on account of their deep meaning, are not clear and intelligible for everybody: for we have adopted as a rule to write in such a way that anyone, regardless of his rank or understanding, can understand the matters we are offering. In order to preserve decorum and to prevent any adverse consequences, we will not include here any obvious controversies or sensitive objections to the writings of others, nor anything written in resentment against anybody.

Should any subject matter be questionable and interpreted differently by various writers, each of them in all justice should be allowed [to express himself] as long as he keeps to the heart of the matter and does not refute with bitterness the opinions of another, but leaves it to the reasoning of the reader which opinion he choses to accept as true or probable.

And just as we equally desire that poets should submit to us their works, some of which may also be amusing, we do hope that their authors will not get personal with anybody. For the sake of which we ask all those who will start sending us their works not to deviate from our purpose.

Should any piece included in our Compositions unexpectedly displease anybody, we hope that the blame will not be put on us, for it is impossible to foresee everything.

Writings in verse we accept mostly because there is a lot in them that is expressed more forcefully and pleasantly than in simple speech: moreover we consider it our duty to write not only for the benefit but also for the entertainment of our readers. Poets such as the ones Russia possesses at present deserve to be set up as an example for posterity; and especially we must not pass over in silence those works that contain well-deserved praise for the greatest queen regnant in the world, and the most gracious Writer and Patroness of sciences.

There are also other poetical works that do not require to be written in verse, namely moralizing parables, dreams, narratives, and similar accounts. Works of poetic fiction rendered in such simple speech are no less useful or pleasing. Because of this, we intend from time to time to publish such works; we also expect, at the same time, that translations of various useful and interesting matters, taken from foreign books, will not be disagreeable to the readers. It is sufficient that our main purpose be observed, and that everything taken from those books will be of obvious benefit.

What a multitude of other material we also have when we undertake to give our readers some excerpts from the most reliable Russian chronicles, copies from ancient charters and archival records, descriptions of ceremonies and of festivities held at the court of HER IMPERIAL MAJESTY, imperial statutes and decrees concerning the well-being of the whole nation, and which, because they are to remain in force for ever, deserve more than others to be preserved; and when moreover we will announce new and interesting books printed abroad and here, as well as the most notable political events of each month. Given such a great abundance, we do not think that there could ever be a lack of subject matter, and, given its variety, we fear even less that it could bore anyone.

But will there not be difficulties in selecting from this abundance of materials the best and most useful? Some pople might not like it when they notice a difference in style when dealing with a different subject matter; but this is quite impossible to avoid, given such an enterprise where various authors are at work. Also not all translations may seem to them of equal quality, for at times they will be the work of young people who could not suddenly achieve the same excellence as the one required from a skilful translator. However, all this notwithstanding, we expect no less benefit from our enterprise and a favourable opinion of it from our readers.

One more point remains to be mentioned. All writings included herein must be examined by a special committee before printing. We justly hope that nobody will request to be exempted from such scrutiny. For this commission will not examine words or style, even if something in need of correcting could be found; but only the matter itself, i.e. that nothing in our selected works is contrary to the law, the state or good behaviour, or reprehensible and injurious to the honour of the author himself. However, each author himself is left responsible to answer for what may sometimes seem either doubtful or insufficiently demonstrated to the reader; the commission will not take any part in it.

It has already been indicated in the title that our benevolent reader can expect a sequel to our selected works every month.

Abbreviations

Arkh. ezheg.	*Arkheograficheskii ezhegodnik.*
Chteniia	*Chteniia v Imperatorskom obschchestve istorii i drevnostei Rossiiskikh pri Moskovskom universitete* (Moscow 1846–1918).
Der Gottschedkreis	*Der Gottschedkreis und Russland. Deutsch-russischer Literatur-beziehungen im Zeitalter der Aufklärung.* Ed. Ulf Lehmann (Berlin 1966).
Die Berliner	*Die Berliner und die Petersburger Akademie der Wissenschaften im Briefwechsel Leonhard Eulers.* 3 vols. (Berlin 1959–76).
ES	*Ezhemesiachnyia sochineniia,* 20 vols. (St Petersburg 1755–64).
Lomonosov, PSS	M.V. Lomonosov, *Polnoe sobranie sochinenii,* 10 vols. (Moscow-Leningrad 1950–9).
Materialy	*Materialy dlia istorii Akademii nauk,* 9 vols. (St Petersburg 1885–1900).
MERSH	*Modern Encyclopedia of Russian and Soviet History,* 30 vols. (Blacksburg, Va., 1976–85)
Protokoly	*Protokoly zasedanii Konferentsii Imperatorskoi Akademii Nauke s 1725 po 1803 goda.* 4 vols. (St Petersburg 1898–1911)
PSRL	*Polnoe sobranie russkikh letopisei.*
PSZR	*Polnoe sobranie zakonov Rossiiskoi imperii s 1649 goda.*
SIRIO	*Sbornik imp. Russkago Istoricheskago obshchestva,* 148 vols. (St Petersburg 1867–1916).
Uchenaia korresp.	*Uchenaia korrespondentsiia Akademii Nauk XVIII veka. Nauchnoe opisanie. 1766–1782 gg.* (Moscow-Leningrad 1937).
Zapiski IAN	*Zapiski Imperatorskoi Akademii nauk.*

Notes

Short-form references are used in the notes for works cited in the Bibliography. Works not included in the Bibliography are cited in full at their first mention.

CHAPTER ONE

1 Anna Maria Bodinus, Gerhard Friderich and Heinrich Justus's mother, was Thomas Müller's second wife. He had four other children from an earlier marriage.

2 A.F. Büsching, *Beyträge* 3 (1785): 4–5. Büsching was related to Müller by marriage, see ibid. 6 (1789): 20, 167. Information on Müller's youth and student days is very scarce. For a few more details about Müller's early years, see Müller, "Avtobiografiia," 145–56. The one English-language study of Müller is the unpublished PHD dissertation completed by S.H. Cross for Harvard in 1916, "The Contribution of G.F. Mueller to Russian Historiography," but its biographical content relies very heavily on Pekarskii, *Istoriia*, 1:308–430.

3 Büsching, *Beyträge*, 3:5–6.

4 J.D. Schumacher to Peter I, 1721. The letter is contained in full in Pekarskii, *Nauka i literatura*, 1:533–58, cited here, p. 557.

5 The full testament is contained in Büsching, *Beyträge*, 3:8–9 and is translated from Latin. See above, Appendix A.

6 See V.I. Guerrier, *Sbornik pisem i memorialov Leibnitsa otnosiashchikhsia k Rossii i Petry Velikomu* (St Petersburg 1873), and A. Vucinich, *Science in Russian Culture* 43–8.

7 See Alexander V. Muller, trans. and ed., *The Spiritual Regulations of Peter*

the Great (Seattle 1972), 30–1. See also James Cracraft, *The Church Reforms of Peter the Great* (Stanford 1971).

8 On this see Pekarskii, *Nauka i literatura*, 1:47–9; Iu.Kh. Kopelevich, *Osnovanie peterburgskoi Akademii Nauk*, 48–50; and E.S. Kuliabko, "Pervye prezidenty," 144–5.

9 E.A. Kniazhetskaia, "Nauchnye sviazi Rossii i Frantsii pri Petre I," 92.

10 *PSZR*, 7, no. 4443 (22 January 1724): 220–5. The plan can be found also in *Istoriia Akademii*, 1:429–35.

11 Kuliabko, "Pervye prezidenty," 145.

12 V.O. Kliuchesvskii, *Sochineniia*, 8:341–2. See also Rudolph Daniels, *V.N. Tatishchev*, 17–23.

13 *Materialy*, 1:47.

14 Müller, *Materialy*, 6 (1890): 64. S.H. Cross suggested that Müller may also have learned about cases like those of John Perry, who fulfilled contracts for Russia and then was refused payment. In his *The State of Russia under the Present Tsar* (London 1716) [reprinted 1967], Perry described how Scottish schoolmasters were also refused payment and referred as well to the harsh punishments meted out to Russians (see especially 214–15).

15 Letter cited in Kopelevich, *Osnovanie*, 78. Pekarskii, *Istoriia*, 1:310, includes the entire letter.

16 Schumacher to Blumentrost, 30 April 1724, cited in Pekarskii, *Dopolnitel'nyia izvestiia dlia biografii Lomonosova*, 8. This book also appeared as an appendix to volume 8 of *Zapiski IAN*, no. 7 (1866).

17 *Materialy*, 1:139.

18 Müller, *Materialy*, 6:64.

19 *PSZR*, no. 4443 (28 January 1724): 20.

20 *Protokoly*, 1:2. Vucinich, *Science in Russian Culture*, 75–82; V. Boss, *Newton and Russia*, 102–3.

21 Müller, *Materialy*, 6:69–73, 184–5, 193; Kopelevich, *Osnovanie*, 83.

22 *Materialy*, 1:1; Kopelevich, *Osnovanie*, 93.

23 *Materialy*, 1 (2 February 1725): 89; (23 February 1725): 91–2. Golovkin was praised by Bülfinger as the most important proselytizer of the Russian Academy in Europe; see Kopelevich, *Osnovanie*, 96.

24 The *ukaz* did not mention Schumacher; see *Materialy*, 1 (20 November 1725): 158–9. It was received in the Senate on 7 December.

25 Müller, *Materialy*, 6:20, 22, 73–4; *Protokoly*, 1:4; Kniazhetskaia, "Nauchnye," 92–3.

26 *Istoriia Akademii*, 1 (1958), "Plan," 429– 35.

27 *Materialy*, 1:76–9.

28 On this generally, see Müller, *Materialy*, 6:92, and Kopelevich, "V dni osnovaniia Akademiia," 122– 4.

29 Bayer's and Goldbach's enthusiastic recommendations were printed in Mencke's *Neue Zeitungen von gelehrten Sachen*, 37 (1726): 382–4; cited in

Kopelevich, *Osnovanie*, 87–8. See also J. Tetzner, "Die Leipziger neuen Zeitungen," 97–8. *Materialy*, 6:68–9

30 *Materialy*, 1 (2 August 1727): 266–9. The Academy had been granted a budget of 24,912 rubles (273).

31 *See Materialy*, 1:173, for salary lists. Students received 200 rubles annually, and those who were both students and teachers, like Müller, were given 266 rubles.

32 Cited in Kopelevich, *Osnovanie*, 116.

33 Schlözer, "Obshchestvennaia," 33.

34 See documents in Pekarskii, *Dopolnitel'nyia ... Lomonosova*, 10.

35 *Materialy*, 1 (January 1729): 445–8.

36 See, for example, Lomonosov, *PSS*, 10:26–64.

37 See Pekarskii, *Istoriia*, 1:15–65; *Dopolnitel'nyia*, 1–17.

38 *Dnevnik Kamer-iunkera F.V. Berkhgol'tsa, 1721–1725*, part 3 (Moscow 1902): 61; part 4:16.

39 Pekarskii, *Dopolnitel'nyia*, 4–7. See also Kopelevich, *Osnovanie*, 32–64. Müller and Lomonosov were among the first to attribute prominent roles in the founding of the Academy to Leibniz and Wolff, but both were long-time enemies of Schumacher. See Müller, *Materialy*, 6:80; Lomonosov, *PSS*, 10:267–8.

40 *Materialy*, 1 (22 October 1722), undersigned by Peter I, regarding the museum, 7; (1 January 1724): 14 (Schumacher's contract signed by Blumentrost). See also Büsching, *Beyträge*, 6 (1789): 166; Pekarskii, *Nauka i literatura*, 1:59–61.

41 *Materialy*, 1 (4 January 1728): 345.

42 Bülfinger and Beckenstein were recommended as the other two assistants for the first year. The Hermann letter is quoted by Müller in *Materialy*, 6:147–8; on the "Chancellery," see 149.

43 Ibid. 172.

44 D.A. Tolstoi, "Akademicheskaia gimnasiia," appendix 2, p. 10. The gymnasium opened in 1727 with 112 students. It had only 74 in 1729 and 19 by 1737.

45 *Materialy*, 1:217–18, 226, 228.

46 *Protokoly*, 1:5; Müller, *Materialy*, 6:6.

47 *Materialy*, 1 (6 January 1728): 346. On the various moves by members, the relocation of the *Kunstkamera* and library, and the inauguration of the new press, see 36–7, 107, 116, 122, 170, 205.

48 On the founding of the *Gazette*, see ibid. (1 December 1726): 207, 210, 213, 346, 353–4, 699; 6:110, 353; *Svodnyi katalog*, 4 (Moscow 1967): 51–2.

49 See *Primechaniia na Vedomostiam*, in *Svodnyi katalog*, 4:171–3; *Protokoly*, 1:354–5, 603; 2:22, 122; 6:110–11; A.V. Zapadov, ed., *Istoriia russkoi zhurnalistiki*, 22–5.

50 Müller, *Materialy*, 6:110; "Preduvedomlenie," *Ezhemesiachnyia sochineniia*,

1, no. 1 (January 1755): 1. V.K. Trediakovskii and M.V. Lomonosov were translators for *Notes* to the *Gazette* by 1741. Generally, the German version included articles that Academy translators had converted into Russian from their original German.

51 Gary Marker, *Publishing, Printing ... Russia, 1700–1800*, 66, 154–55. For the *ukaz* of 1727 that closed most of the presses in Russia, see *PSZR*, 7, no. 5175 (16 October 1727): 873–4. *Notes* was exempted from Church censorship on the orders of I.K. Kirilov in January 1728; see *Svodnyi katalog*, 4:172.

52 Kopelevich, *Osnovanie*, 181–3; see also Tetzner, "Die Leipziger neuen Zeitungen."

53 *Materialy*, 1:602; 6:149, 173. Unofficially, Müller was referred to as vice-secretary of the Conference. Goldbach was its secretary from 1725 until 1741.

54 The Russian translations for *Kratkoe opisanie Kommentariev Akademii* were very awkwardly done because Russia did not yet have a scientific vocabulary, and the translators were not trained in the scientific disciplines. For its content, see Neustroev, *Istoricheskoe rozyskanie*, 11–12.

55 Müller, *Materialy*, 6:142: Pekarskii, *Istoriia*, 1:312.

56 Müller, "Avtobiografiia," 148. The lexicon was printed in 1731; see *Materialy*, 2:252; *Protokoly*, 1:71, 78, 425.

57 Schumacher report to Blumentrost (27 December 1729), *Materialy*, 1:595, 600. Müller was ordered to send all important matters to Moscow, "without delay." See also Müller, "Avtobiografiia," 148.

58 Lomonosov, "Kratkaia istoriia o provedenii akademicheskoi kantseliarii," (1764) In Lomonosov, *PSS*, 10:268–9; Biliarskii, *Materialy dlia biografii Lomonosova*, 050, 051.

59 Müller, *Materialy*, 6:250; see also Kopelevich, *Osnovanie*, 116–17.

60 See series of letters about the Bülfinger/Bernoulli affair in Pekarskii, *Dopolnitel'nyia* 12–16; *Materialy*, 1 (Müller report of 1 July 1729): 501–4; see also 539–42; 574; 6:186–7 (on the committee). V. Boss, *Newton and Russia*, 102–11; and Lomonosov to Euler, 1763, in V.I. Lamanskii, comp., "Lomonosov," 81.

61 Kopelevich, *Osnovanie*, 111–13; Müller, *Materialy*, 6:149; Lomonosov, *PSS*, 10:268.

62 Schumacher recalled this in 1745 in response to a denunciation of him by Müller and other academicians; see Pekarskii, *Istoriia*, 1:312–13; Müller, *Materialy*, 6:221.

63 For a copy of Müller's contract, see *Materialy*, 2 (1 January 1731); see also *Protokoly*, 1 (22 January 1731): 36.

64 Müller, *Materialy*, 6:251.

65 Mencke died in 1732, and Müller later noted with regret that his "very full library, especially in historical items," was sold by his wife to

booksellers; *Materialy*, 6:200. For the "testimonials" from Herman and Bülfinger, see ibid. 1:685–6.

66 Kopelevich, *Osnovanie*, 48; Schlözer, "Obshchestvennaia," 25–6. For Müller's own description of the "great disorder" at the Academy, see "Avtobiografiia," 148.

67 These instructions are included in Iu.Kh. Kopelevich, ed., "Pervaia zagranichnaia," 47–52. For Müller's "passports," see Golitsyn, *Portfeli*, 469; *Materialy*, 2:631.

68 Müller then referred to Kohl, Martini, Buxbaum, Hermann, and Bülfinger; see Kopelevich, ed., "Pervaia," 48; see also Müller, *Materialy*, 6:202–3.

69 *Materialy*, 6:202.

70 Kopelevich, ed., "Pervaia," 50–1. See also A.G. Cross, *'By the Banks of the Thames'*, 95–6.

71 Letter quoted by Pekarskii, *Istoriia*, 1:313–14.

72 Müller arrived in Herford on 21 January. His recollections of the German part of the trip are included in *Materialy*, 6:196–216, from which the following is summarized.

73 Besides Müller's memoir (*Materialy*, 6:206–9, 294–5 [Ammann]), see Pekarskii, *Istoriia*, 1:313–14; *Materialy*, 10:70, 73 (Hebenstreit).

74 J.P. Kohl, *Introductio in historiam et rem literarium Slavorum* (Altona 1729). On this, see Riccardo Picchio, "La 'Introductio … ' " 3–28.

75 Letter quoted in Pekarskii, *Istoriia*, 1:315. Anna's sister Catherine had married Charles Leopold, duke of Mecklenburg, in 1716.

76 Ibid. 315–16; Müller, *Materialy*, 6:37–9, 212–14.

77 *Materialy*, 3 (9 July 1736): 107–8; see also Golitsyn, *Portfeli*, 469–70.

78 Müller to Teplov, 25 October 1748, quoted at length in Pekarskii, *Istoriia*, 1:26.

79 Schumacher letters to Blumentrost, cited from the Müller papers at the Academy of Sciences of the USSR by Kopelevich, *Osnovanie*, 118–19.

80 *Materialy*, 2 (6 September 1732): 168–9. Justus Heinrich Müller was granted a salary of 200 rubles.

CHAPTER TWO

1 *Materialy*, 2 (21 March 1732): 121.

2 See Müller, *Materialy*, 6:250–2.

3 Müller, *Ob'iavlenie*; *Neue Zeitungen von gelehrten Sachen* (10 November 1732): 735–9, cited at length in Tetzner, "Die Leipziger neuen Zeitungen," 108–11; *Bibliothèque germanique*, 16 (1732): 186–9; see also Kopelevich, *Osnovanie*, 183.

4 Tatishchev to Schumacher, 19 September 1732, *Materialy*, 2:180. For Bayer and Müller's association with Tatishchev, see R. Daniels, *V.N. Tatishchev*, 23.

5 October/November 1730, nos. 80–3, cited by A.I. Andreev, "Trudy V.N. Tatishcheva po istorii Rossii," in Tatishchev, *Istoriia Rossiiskaia*, 1: 11–12.

6 *Protokoly*, 1 (15 January 1728): 11; Tatishchev, *Istoriia Rossiiskaia*, 1:368–9, 371–6.

7 For an English translation of Tatishchev's proposal, see Paul Dukes, ed., *Russia*, 20–7.

8 C.H. von Manstein, *Contemporary Memoirs*, 244.

9 *PSRL*, 1 (1926), 2nd ed., 19–20. The Lavrentius text of this chronicle was translated into English, with detailed commentary, by S.H. Cross and Olgerd P. Sherbowitz-Wetzor, and published by the Medieval Academy of America in 1953.

10 *PSRL*, 1 (1926): 1, 8.

11 *Kniga stepennaia tsarskago rodosloviia*, part 1, *PSRL*, 21 (1908): 2, 5, 7, 78.

12 S.L. Peshtich, *Russkaia istoriografiia*, 1:45–53. On early historical writing in Russia, see also A.M. Sakharov, "Iz istorii istoricheskoi mysli v Rossii nachala XVIII, v.," *Vestnik Moskovskogo universiteta*, no. 3 (1972): 70–86.

13 *Fedora Griboedova Istoriia o tsariakh i velikikh kniaz'iakh zemli Russoi*, ed. S.F. Platonov, V.V. Maikov (St Petersburg 1896): on Prussus and Augustus Caesar, 6–7; on Romanov and Ivan IV, 36–7.

14 On the "Historical Book," see "Predislovie k istoricheskoi knige," in E. Zamyslovskii, ed., *Tsarstvovaniia Fedora Alekseevicha*, 1 (St Petersburg, 1871): xxxv–xlii; and A.S. Lappo-Danilevskii, "Ocherk razvitiia russkoi istoriografii," *Russkoi istoricheskii zhurnal*, book 6 (1920): 16–17.

15 *Sinopsis, ili kratkoe opisanie ...* , 9th ed. (St Petersburg 1810): 4–5, 10–11, 17; on Rosh and Mosoch, see Ezekiel (38.2, 3; 39.1). For the *Sinopsis* as part of the official historiography, see J.L. Black, "L'histoire au service de l'Etat: le *Synopsis* du XVIIe siècle et son heritage historiographique," *Laurentian University Review*, 10:1 (November 1977): 7–16.

16 On this generally, see William E. Butler, "P.P. Shafirov and the Law of Nations," introduction to Butler's edition of Shafirov, *A Discourse ...* (New York 1973); T.S. Maikova, "Petr I i 'Gistoriia Sveiskoi voiny'," in N.I. Pavlenko, ed., *Rossiia v period reform Petra I* (Moscow 1973): 103–32; Peshtich, *Russkaia istoriografiia*, 1:74–5, 87–8, 154–76.

17 L.N. Maikov, *Raszkazy Nartova o Petre Velikom* (St Petersburg, 1891): 34; Jakob Stählin, *Original Anecdotes of Peter the Great* (London 1788; reprint 1967): 166–7.

18 Peshtich, *Russkaia istoriografiia*, 1:83, 110–12. See *Pis'ma i bumagi imperatora Petra Velikogo*, 7, issue 2 (Moscow 1951): 939, for Musin-Pushkin's letters to Polikarpov.

19 Kurakin, "Gistoriia o tsare Petre Alekseevicha i blizhnikh k nemu liudakh, 1682–1694 gg.," *Arkhiv kn F.A. Kurakina*, ed. M.I. Semevskii, 1 (St Petersburg 1890): 41–78; see also his "Vedenie o glavakh v Gistorii," ibid. 79–94. See also Peshtich, *Russkaia istoriografiia*, 1:113–19. On

Kurakin in English, see James Cracraft entry in *MERSH*, 16 (1980): 168–70.

20 For the doubts about Prokopovich as author, see James Cracraft, "Did Feofan Prokopovich Really Write *Pravda Voli Monarshei?*" *Slavic Review*, 40, no. 2 (Summer 1981): 173–93; see also Cracraft, "Feofan Prokopovich," in J.G. Garrard, ed., *The Eighteenth Century in Russia* (Oxford 1973): 75–105.

21 See *The Spiritual Regulations of Peter the Great*, trans. and ed. A.V. Muller (Seattle 1972): 30–45. All citations were taken from this translation of the *Ecclesiastical Regulation*.

22 See "Propozitsii Fedora Saltykova," in *Pamiatniki drevnei pis'mennosti i iskusstva*, 83, no. 5, series 4 (St Petersburg 1891): 22, 24.

23 On the *Podrobnaia letopis' ot nachala Rossii* ... , 4 vols. (St Petersburg 1798–99), ed. N.L. L'vov, see A.N. Nasonov, *Istoriia russkogo letopisaniia. XI–nachalo XVIII veka* (Moscow 1969): 496–7.

24 *PSZR*, no. 3693 (20 December 1720): 277; no. 3908 (16 February 1722): 511–12. See also Pekarskii, *Nauk i literatura*, 1:317–18.

25 "Dlia general'noi istorii i opisaniia Rossiiskago gosudarstva" is printed in *200-letie Kabineta ego imperatorskago velichestva, 1704–1904* (St Petersburg 1911).

26 Mankiev, *Iadro Rossiiskoi istorii* (1770), 2nd ed. (St Petersburg 1784): 384. See also 22–3, 13–14. Mankiev rejected specifically the idea that the name Slav came from the "Italian *schiavo* or *sclavo*, for slaves" (13). Mankiev spent fifteen years of internment in Sweden.

27 See A.I. Rogov, "Stryikovskii i russkaia istoriografiia pervoi poloviny XVIII v.," in *Istochniki i istoriografiia slavianskogo srednevekov'ia. Sbornik statei i materialov* (Moscow 1967): 145–57; and Peshtich, *Russkaia istoriografiia*, 1:105–7.

28 Mankiev started his history, however, with the statement: "Adam, from whom all people descend, ... "; *Iadro Rossisskoi istorii*, 1. On Peter, see 373–85.

29 Tatishchev, *Istoriia Rossiiskaia*, 1:79–81, 288–9, 371.

30 Cited in Likhareva-Bokii, "Iz istorii pedagogicheskoi mysli," 447.

31 Kopelevich, *Osnovanie*, 91–2; for Bayer's contract, *Materialy*, 1 (18 October 1725): 150; see also 84–5, 163.

32 For biographical and other information on Bayer, see Müller, *Materialy*, 6:44–8; Pekarskii, *Istoriia*, 1:180–96.

33 "I say that the Varangians referred to by Russian writers were from Scandinavia"; Bayer, *Sochinenenie*, 2; on "Normans," see also 21, 30–1. For the original articles, see "De Varagis," *Commentarii*, 4 (1729): 331–69; "De russorum prima expeditione ... ," 6 (1731): 365–91; "Origines Russicae," 8 (1736): 388–436.

34 Tatishchev, *Istoriia Rossiiskaia*, 1:184–207, 208–31, 292–310.

35 Ibid. 290–1, 311, 372.
36 Cited in E. Winter, "I.–v. Paus," 322. See also G. Moiseeva, "Iz istorii," 130–7, and Müller, *Materialy*, 6:101–2, 251.
37 Müller, "Auszug Russischer Geschichte nach Anleitung des Chronici Theodosiani Kioviensis (860–945)," *Sammlung russischer Geschichte*, 1, no. 1 (1732): 9–27.
38 Müller, "Nachricht von einem alten Manuskript," ibid. 1–18. For the comment on the Varangians, see 4.
39 Witsen, *Noord en oost Tartaryen* (1672), reviewed by Müller in *Sammlung*, 1 (1732): 196–222. See "Neuste Historie der östlichen Calmuckei," ibid. no. 2 (1733): 123–53, for extracts from Müller's speech on the Kalmyks. The diary on the Kalmyk communities was written by Ivan Unkovskii and covered the period between October 1722 and June 1723; see "Auszug aus dem Reise Journal des Herrn Ober-Kriegs-Commissarii Johann Unkowski von der Calmueckey," ibid. no. 1 (1732): 141–66. For Müller's own "Consilium et conspectus operis edendi de rebus Calmycieus," see *Protokoly*, 1 (6 February 1733): 63, and *Materialy*, 2:301, 415.
40 Müller, "Leben des Heiligen ... Nevsky," *Sammlung*, 1, no. 3 (1733): 281–314. The chronicle continuations appeared as follows: no. 2 (1733): 93–113; no. 3 (1733): 171–95. Kramer edited more extracts left him by Müller when the latter went to Siberia, for issues 4–6 of volume 1 (1734–5).
41 *Sammlung*, 1, no. 1 (1732): 1–2; he referred to this again in *ES*, 17 (April 1763): 365.
42 Müller, *Materialy*, 6:250; Golitsyn, *Portfeli*, 529–31; Pekarskii, "Materialy," 390–1.
43 Kopelevich, *Osnovanie*, 119.
44 *Protokoly*, 1 (1 December 1731): 53; Müller, *Materialy*, 6:225–6.
45 Keyserling was named vice-president first and then took the position as president in June. See *Materialy*, 2 (19 July 1733): 340–1. On the death of Princess Catherine Ivanovna and its effect on Blumentrost, see Pekarskii, *Istoriia*, 1:13.
46 *Protokoly*, 1 (7 January 1732): 64; *Materialy*, 2 (12 January 1732): 95.
47 *Materialy*, 2 (3 August 1732): 160–1; (2 November 1732): 187–8, 189–94, 200; for Schumacher's reports on the typography and the gymnasium (3 March 1732): 111–18; (7 September 1732): 169–75. See also Kopelevich, *Osnovanie*, 121–2.
48 This report was signed by de l'Isle, Gmelin, Bayer, Weitbrecht, Beckenstein, de l'Isle de la Croyère, D. Bernoulli, Müller, Duvernois, and Weitman; *Materialy*, 2 (1 December 1732): 199–202.
49 Ibid. 226–45. They proposed that all professors be paid 900 rubles annually. At the time salaries ranged from 400 to 1,800 rubles.
50 Ibid. (22 January 1733): 258–61.

51 Francesco Locatelli, *Lettres moscovites*, 18; *Materialy*, 205–7, 310–11.
52 *Protokoly*, 1 (10 July 1733): 69–70; *Materialy*, 2 (19 July 1733): 340–1.
53 Müller, *Materialy*, 6:297, 299–302; Pekarskii, *Istoriia*, 1:500.
54 *Materialy*, 2 (18 December 1733): 409–14; see also 344, 367–77. Müller, *Materialy*, 6:299–302, 309–14.

CHAPTER THREE

Parts of this chapter are reprinted from my article "G.-F. Müller and the Russian Academy," 235–52.

1 V. Ger'e [V.I. Guerrier], *Sbornik pisem i memorialov Leibnitsa otnos-iashchikhsia k Rossii i Petry Velikom* (St Petersburg, 1873): 360.
2 John Perry, *The State of Russia* (London, 1716), 61; "Propozitsii Fedora Saltykova," 28–30.
3 Messerschmidt had a difficult time gaining compensation for his collections and lived in near-poverty before his death in 1735; see *Materialy*, 1 (28 September 1727): 288–9, and Walter Kirchner, *A Siberian Journey*, 14–15. Strahlenberg's book had an English translation in 1738 and appeared in French in 1757. Messerschmidt's account of his travels was printed in Berlin in four volumes, 1962–8. On Strahlenberg and Messerschmidt, see E.P. Zinner, *Sibiri'*, chapters 4 and 5.
4 The two geodesists, Fedor Luzhin and Ivan Evreinov, were students of the Naval Academy in St Petersburg; *PSZR*, 5, no. 3266 (2 January 1719): 607. Sokolov, "Severnaia ekspeditsiia," 199–200.
5 On the Tatishchev proposal, see L.V. Cherepnin, *Russkaia istoriografiia do XIX veka*, 165.
6 *PSZR*, 6, no. 3534 (29 February 1720): 141–60, cited here, 157; no. 3788 (22 May 1721): 394–5. On the Soimonov expedition, see especially L.A. Gol'denburg, *Fedor Ivanovich Soimonov (1692–1780)*.
6 See I.K. Kirilov, *Tsvetushchee sostoianie vserossiiskogo gosudarstva* (Moscow 1977), and M.G. Novlianskaia, *I.K. Kirilov i ego Atlas Vserossiiskoi imperii* (Moscow 1958).
8 On this especially see R.H. Fisher, *Bering's Voyages*; see also P. Lauridsen, *Vitus Bering*; F.A. Golder, *Bering's Voyages*; L.S. Berg, *Otkrytie Kamchatki*.
9 The notice is reprinted in Fisher, *Bering's Voyages*, 12–13.
10 On the question of Bering's motives, see ibid. 114–16.
11 The order can be found in V.F. Gnucheva, ed., *Materialy ... ekspeditsii*, 40; see also *PSZR*, 8, no. 6023 (17 April 1732): 749; no. 6041 (2 May 1732): 770–4. A full Senate report can be found in *PSZR*, 8, no. 6291 (28 December 1732): 1002–14. Bering's proposals can be located in Sokolov, "Severnaia ekspeditsiia" 426–36.

12 Müller, *Materialy*, 6:252–3; for de l'Isle's long explanation of his map, see Sokolov, "Severnaia ekspeditsiia," 437–45.

13 On this see Fisher, *Bering's Voyages*, 120–2; Golovin was appointed president of the Admiralty College in April 1733; for Müller's praise of Kirilov, see *Materialy*, 6:113, 253.

14 Müller's work on the Samoeds was gleaned from the writings of Witsen and the Englishman John Fletcher; *Sammlung*, 1, no. 3 (1733): 196–221; on the material in the *Notes*, see A.I. Andreev, *Ocherki*, 74. Johann Gustav Gerber's notes on the Caucasus (1728) and Bayer's historical study of Azov appeared in the second volume of the *Sammlung* (2:36–280), the first three issues of which were edited by Bayer.

15 Müller, *Materialy*, 6:253; [Müller], *A Letter*, 11–12. On Schumacher's order to Müller of 28 February 1733, see Golitsyn, *Portfeli*, 531.

16 Müller, *Materialy*, 6:270. In 1748 Müller wrote Teplov that he was forced to go to Siberia "to escape persecution" by Schumacher (25 October 1748), but that must have been only a secondary issue. See letter in Pekarskii, *Dopolnitel'nyia*, 15–16.

17 Müller, "Opisanie morskikh ... ," *Ezhemesiachnyia sochineniia*, 4 (January 1758): 11–12; Müller, *Materialy*, 6:270.

18 *Protokoly*, 1 (3 July 1733): 69; *Materialy*, 2 (16 April 1733): 326–7; Müller, *Materialy*, 6:270–1.

19 *Materialy*, 2:326–7, 346–7; *Protokoly*, 1:65. Gnucheva, *Materialy ... ekspeditsii*, 40–2.

20 Gmelin, *Reise*, 1, introduction, x. For the instructions to Müller, see Gnucheva, *Materialy ... ekspeditsii*, 42–4. The instructions are also published in Müller, *Istoriia Sibiri*, 1:460–1.

21 See M.O. Kosven, "Etnograficheskie," *Sibirskii etnograficheskii sbornik* 3 (1961): 120; Lauridsen, *Vitus Bering*, 77; Berg, *Otkrytie Kamchatki*, 129. A full list of participants in the second Kamchatka expedition, aside from service personnel, can be found in Sokolov, "Severnaia ekspeditsiia," 444–7.

22 On Locatelli, see Müller, *Materialy*, 6:278–9. For lists of students, technicians, and their salaries, see ibid. 326–7, 446–7; and Gmelin, *Reise*, 1:3–4

23 *Materialy*, 2:446; 6:272–3; see also 5 (7 January 1742): 4, where the academicians' salaries are still listed as 1,260 rubles.

24 De la Croyère was in his early forties and was probably selected for the trip through the good offices of his half-brother. See Pekarskii, *Istoriia*, 1:150.

The following account of Müller's part in the Kamchatka expedition is synthesized mainly from Müller, *Materialy*, 6:270–1, 179–87, 340–66, 393–422; Müller, "Opisanie morskikh ... ," *ES* (1758); Müller, *Voyages from Asia to America*; Müller, *Conquest of Siberia*; *Materialy*, 2–3; Gmelin,

Reise, 1, and *Voyage*, 1–2; Büsching, *Beyträge*, 3:25–42; S.P. *Krasheninnikov v Sibiri; neopublikovannye materialy* ed. N.N. Stepanov; and Sokolov, "Severnaia ekspeditsiia."

25 Müller, *Materialy*, 6:270–1; Lauridsen, *Vitus Bering*, 79–80. One verst = 0.66 miles.

26 See especially *Materialy*, 2 (21 September 1733 [Tver']: 383–90.

28 Müller report to Senate, 7 August 1746, *Materialy*, 8:195.

29 Müller, *Materialy*, 6:280, 401; Gmelin, *Reise*, 1:43–4.

30 Müller, *Materialy*, 6:281. The town of Makariev referred to by Müller was located on the Volga below Nizhnii Novgorod. Another, larger, town by the same name lay farther north on the Unska River.

31 Büsching, *Beyträge*, 3 (1785):25; Gmelin, *Reise*, 1:80–1.

32 For reprints of some of these drawings, see V. Radlov, "Iz sochinenii," appendix xv, *passim*. On the dictionary, see Müller, *Materialy*, 6:285.

33 See chapter 6, below, 247 n42, 248 n53; Müller, *Materialy*, 6:285.

34 *Materialy*, 2:394–5; *Protokoly*, 2:130– 1.

35 Lauridsen, *Vitus Bering*, 72.

36 See Z.V. Bashkatova, "Sibirskaia," 30–3; Gmelin, *Reise*, 1:113; Locatelli's book was printed in three languages: *Lettres moscovites* (Königsberg 1736), *Lettres moscovites: or, Muscovian Letters* (London 1736), and *Die so gennante Moscowitische Brieffe* (Frankfort 1738).

37 Müller, *Materialy*, 6:343; Gmelin, *Reise*, 1:117–19.

38 Müller, *Materialy*, 6:344–5. On Pleshcheev's book, see Andreev, *Ocherki*, 76.

39 Müller, *Istoriia Sibiri*, 1:331–6.

40 *Protokoly*, 2:247–9.

41 Gmelin, *Reise*, 1:131–2, 135–6, 157, 162; *Voyage en Sibérie*, 1: 53–4, 56–7, 70–7.

42 Outlined in detail in a report submitted to the Senate by Müller, 7 August 1746, *Materialy*, 8:196–7.

43 Gmelin, *Reise*, 1:314–15; *Voyage en Sibérie*, 1:156–9. On the 20 Cossacks and cannon, see Müller, *Materialy*, 6:351.

44 Ibid. 346–7; Gmelin, *Reise*, 1:256–7, 260.

45 The travel information contained in the last two paragraphs has been synthesized from Gmelin, *Reise*, 1:264–5; *Voyage en Sibérie*, 1:95–8, 181–2, 240, 327–8. Müller mentions only that the governor gave them a difficult time, but that they "finally obtained horses"; *Materialy*, 6:395. On A.G. Pleshcheev (no relation to A.L.), see Pekarskii, *Istoriia*, 1:324, and Radlov, "Iz sochinenii akademikov," 42–4.

46 *Materialy*, 6:404. On the question of Müller's attitude to the Amur, see L. Maier, "Müller's Memoranda." For Müller's report on the Tungus language, see "De scriptus Tanguticis in Siberia repertis commentatio," *Commentarii*, 10 (1747): 420–68. In this essay Müller acknowledged information already gathered by Messerschmidt and Tatishchev.

The Amur River region really was controlled by the Tungusi Jurchens, whose leader, Abahai, adopted the name Manchu for his people in 1635. The Manchus defeated Chinese forces in 1644 and placed Abahai's son, Fu-lin, on the Chinese throne in Peking – as Emperor Shun-chih. In the same year, the Manchus extended their tribal dominion from their own homeland, Manchuria, to the Amur River, which originally had been Tungus land. The Manchu dynasty, then, was not Chinese, and the Amur River was associated with China only through the Manchus. Müller, however, always referred to China when speaking of this area, which was correct in the diplomatic sense. On this generally, see O. Edmund Clubb, *China and Russia. The 'Great Game'* (New York 1971).

47 Gmelin, *Voyage en Sibérie*, 1:244–5, 256, 283–5, 290–1.

48 Ibid., 325–6. Elsewhere he said that the *sluzhivye* were lazy, "uncivil and a little officious" (311).

49 Sokolov, "Severnaia ekspeditsiia," 328.

50 Gmelin, *Voyage en Sibérie*, 1:356– 7.

51 Müller, "Opisanie morskikh … ," *ES*, 4 (July 1758): 14–15; Berg, 132.

52 Müller to Euler in *Die Berliner*, 1:40. Gmelin, *Voyage en Sibérie*, 1:381–2; see also 181–2, 258–89, 352.

53 For the fire that destroyed Gmelin's material, see *Materialy*, 3 (report to Korff, 9 March 1737): 391; and Gmelin, *Voyage en Sibérie*, 1:381.

54 Gmelin, *Voyage en Sibérie*, 2:2, 6.

55 For Krasheninnikov's reports to Müller and Gmelin, see *S.P. Krasheninnikov v Sibiri: neopublikovannye materialy*, ed. Stepanov, 175–93. Müller, "Geographie und Verfassung von Kamtschatka," was reprinted as an introduction to G.W. Steller, *Beschreibung von dem Lande Kamtschatka …* (Frankfurt 1774): 1–58.

56 Büsching, *Beyträge*, 3 (1785): 34–5; *Protokoly*, 1 (17 April 1738): 472–3; *Materialy*, 3:686–9.

57 Müller, "Opisanie morskikh … ," *ES* (January 1758): 8–9, 21–2. The full text of the Dezhnev report can be found in Golder, *Russian Expansion in the Pacific 1641–1850* (Cleveland 1914), 282–9. On the authenticity and nature of the Dezhnev document submitted by Müller, see B.P. Polevoi, "Nakhodka podlinnykh dokumentov," 145–52.

58 Gmelin, *Reise* 2:79–81, 99, *Voyage en Sibérie*, 2:18–19, 23.

59 See ibid. 159. Müller, "Morskikh opisanie … ," *ES*, (February 1758): 3. On Steller, see the detailed biography by Leonhard Stejneger referred to in the bibliography below. The book contains much general and interesting information on the Academy and on the Kamchatka expedition.

60 On Lindenau, see especially Kosven, "Etnograficheskie rezul'taty," 201–5; on Fischer, see *Materialy*, 3:688, 793–94, *Protokoly*, 2:272–3, 477, 478, and Stejneger, *Georg Wilhelm Steller*. For Gmelin's praise of Steller,

see *Reise*, 3:175–83, and Otto Gmelin, *Johann Georg Gmelin* ... , 114–17. A later printing of Steller's *Reise von Kamtschatka nach Amerika mit den Commander Captain Bering* (St Petersburg 1793) was translated and contained in full in Golder's *Bering's Voyages*, 2 (1925).

61 *Materialy*, 3:793–4; 4 (16 April 1739): 95– 7.

62 Ibid. 4:317–18, 477–8. Fischer and Steller were both committed to a five-year contract at 660 rubles annually (3:688).

63 Müller, "Opisanie morskikh ... ," *ES* (August 1758): 116–17; Lauridsen, *Vitus Bering*, 117–26; Golder, *Bering's Voyages*, 2:14.

64 *Protokoly*, 1 (11 November 1734): 118; (12 September 1736): 310. Korff was highly regarded by most of the academicians; see Büsching, *Beyträge*, 3:198–209; Lomonosov, *PSS*, 10:146.

65 *Materialy*, 2:692–3, 770–1; 3:64–8, 311, 544–5, 840–1; *Istoriia Akademii nauk SSSR*, 1 (1958): 66–9.

66 For Brevern's appointment, *Protokoly*, 1 (25 April 1740): 607–8; and his dismissal (17 April 1741), 675. The notice of Brevern's dismissal was written into the Conference minutes in German; subsequent entries once again were in Latin. On this generally, see Neuschäffer, *Katherina II*, 173–5.

67 Korff had recommended Schumacher and Goldbach as directors in September 1737; see *Materialy*, 3 (23 September 1737): 480; *Protokoly*, 1 (7 February 1738): 457.

68 Golder, *Bering's Voyages*, 1:33–4.

69 Ibid. log books of the *St. Peter* and the *St. Paul*, 230, 311, 329; Müller, "Opisanie morskikh ... ," *ES* (September 1758): 228–30.

70 Gmelin, *Voyage en Sibérie*, 2:55–6, 70– 1.

71 Ibid. 101–2, 126.

72 Gur'ev, "Istoriograf Miller v Tomsk," 65.

73 See Pekarskii, *Istoriia*, 1:328–9.

74 Ibid. 618–20. Fischer was accompanied to Siberia by his wife and three children. Gmelin's portrayal of Fischer to Müller was very uncomplimentary.

75 Parts of Müller's very detailed guide can be found in Radlov, 106–14. For Tatischev's questionnaire, see Tatishchev, *Izbrannye*, 77–95.

76 Müller to Gmelin, January 1741, in Plieninger, ed., *Gmelini*, 188, 194.

77 Müller to Euler, 21 June 1740, in *Die Berliner*, 1:43. Müller's letter from Tobol'sk is cited from Pekarskii, *Istoriia*, 1:329. Müller complained again to the Senate about Siberian officialdom in March 1741.

78 Gmelin, *Voyage en Sibérie*, 2:186–8.

79 Cited in Pekarskii, *Istoriia*, 1:330.

80 Büsching, *Beyträge*, 3 (1785): 41–2. A.L. von Schlözer and Büsching both later spoke very highly of Müller's wife; see Büsching, above, and Schlözer, "Obshchestvennaia," 27.

81 Müller implied this himself in a report to the Chancellery in 1746, *Materialy*, 8:212.

82 Gmelin, *Voyage en Sibérie*, 2:254.

83 Stejneger, *Georg Wilhelm Steller*, 458–9, 464–6.

84 *Protokoly*, 1:731

85 *Materialy*, 4 (20 February 1740) 318; 6:516.

86 Müller, ibid. 6:516. The Amur River study was printed in 1757 (*ES*, 3 [July 1757]). For its submission to the Senate, see *Materialy*, 7:529; Maier, "Müller's Memoranda," 219, 224.

87 Müller, "Izvestie o severnom morskom khode Rossiian iz ustei nekotoryk rek, vpadaiushchikh v ledianoe more, dlia provedyvaniia vostochnykh stran," *Primechaniia k Vedomostiam*, parts 50–60 (1742), 197–228. This was printed anonymously, but was established as Müller's by V.F. Gnucheva; see *Materialy ... ekspeditsii*, 65–6. *Protokoly*, 1 (31 October 1740): 305–6; 8:198–205.

88 Müller, *Materialy*, 6:450. On this, see Andreev, *Ocherki*, 83–4.

89 *Materialy*, 8:211–12.

90 Müller, *Materialy*, 6:253, 2:673; Gmelin, *Reise*, 1, "Foreword."

CHAPTER FOUR

1 *Protokoly*, 2 (14 March 1743): 731.

2 This report can be found in *Materialy*, 3 (7 August 1743): 183–213.

3 Müller, "Opisanie morskikh ... ," *ES* (October 1758): 333–4; Pekarskii, *Istoriia*, 1: 453; Golder, *Bering's Voyages*, 2 (1925), from Steller's journal, 37, 51, 155–7. Steller may have died because of problems related to alcohol consumption, ibid. 4; see also Stejneger, *Georg Wilhelm Steller*, 484–6. In 1752 Müller wrote that Bering died of an "excess of grief that he could not recover [find his way back to] Kamchatka" and implied that de la Croyère was weakened by "the great quantity of brandy which he swallowed everyday"; *A Letter*, 19, 21.

4 Gmelin, *Voyage en Sibérie*, 2:172–7, 186, 204–6, *Materialy*, 2:244–5, 381–2, 490–92; 3:109– 10.

5 On this, see Rogger, *National Consciousness*, 25–34. For Korff's warning of 22 October 1736, see Pekarskii, *Istoriia*, 1:liv; for Goldbach's memorandum, Müller, *Materialy*, 6:528–33.

6 F.N. Zagorskii, *Nartov*, 11.

7 *Istoriia Akademii nauk SSSR*, 1 (1958): 66–9.

8 See *Materialy*, 4 (22 June 1741): 701 (Schumacher on Nartov's salary). See also Zagorskii, *Nartov*, 46–50.

9 Nartov's fellow complainants were translators Ivan Gorlitskii and Nikita Popov, Commissioner Michael Camer, clerk Dmitrii Grekov, copyist Vasilii Nosov, and students I. Pukhort, P. Shishkarev, and M. Kovrin.

See Pekarskii, *Istoriia*, 1:33–42, for another general account of the affair. Volume 4 of *Materialy* has a full complement of documents for this affair.

10 Nartov replaced Schumacher officially on 4 November 1742; see *Materialy* 5 (1 December 1742): 439–40.

11 Ibid. 5 (7 October 1742): 376–80. For further documentation on the Schumacher case, see P.I. Ivanov, "Sledstvennoe," 64–122.

12 *Materialy*, 5:703–7; see also reports from the Committee, ibid. 446–8, 466–71, 504–7, 561–80, 581–94, 741–63.

13 On the Academy of Arts, ibid. 724; see also S.M. Solov'ev, *Istoriia Rossii*, Book 11, vol. 22:539–41; *Materialy*, 5 (31 May 1743): 703–4. Christian Hermann was no relation of Jacob Hermann.

14 *Materialy*, 5:439–40, 472–5, 418–19, 639–43, 835–6.

15 The Russian Assembly (*Rossiiskoe sobranie*) was established by Korff in 1735 "to meet in Conference twice a week ... to study everything that is translated and carefully correct the Russian language"; *Materialy*, 2:63. The unit had an official existence of only three years, but its members – mainly translators – continued to meet irregularly and discuss their common interests. On the complaints against Nartov, see *Materialy*, 5 (August 1742): 329–35; see also 504–7, 526–56, 697–701. Taubert was born in St Petersburg in 1717 and was among the first students at the Academy gymnasium. His father, who was not a Russian, was employed by the Admiralty. When Taubert took a post at the Chancellery in 1732, he was designated a foreigner.

16 See Lomonosov's far from impartial version of this, "Kratkaia istoriia ... kantseliarii," Lomonosov, *PSS*, 10:278.

17 See *Materialy*, 5 (24 December 1742): 470 (freed from house arrest); (5 December 1743): 981–82. The final decision on the Schumacher case was initialed by members of the Imperial Senate, 10 May 1744; see *Chteniia*, Book 3, section 5 (1860): 122.

18 *Materialy*, 5:376, 468; 7:123, 140–1.

19 Ibid. 5 (7 December 1743): 985. On the "Herbarium Lestokianum," see Pekarskii, *Istoriia*, 1:43. On Justus Müller, see *Protokoly*, 3 (9 January 1744): 1. Gorlitskii returned to St Petersburg in 1745.

20 Müller to Teplov, 25 October 1748, in Pekarskii, *Istoriia*, 1:336–7.

21 For Lomonosov's attack on Schumacher, see Lomonosov, *PSS*, 10:171–2; and on Nartov, Biliarskii, ed., *Materialy ... Lomonosova*, 39, 41; *Materialy*, 5:450–1.

22 See the Golovin committee report on these events, which took place 27 April 1742; *Materialy*, 5 (27 May 1743): 697–701; (11 October 1742): 386–7. For Lomonosov's fight with the gardener, whose wife he allegedly had insulted, see ibid., 696–701; see also *Protokoly*, 1:729–30, Biliarskii, ed., *Materialy ... Lomonosova*, 9–13, includes the entire police report.

23 Lomonosov, *PSS*, 10:331–2; *Materialy*, 5:700–1, 729–30, 795, 842;

Protokoly, 1 (29 April 1743): 737. See lists of complaints that date back to November 1742 in Biliarskii, ed., *Materialy ... Lomonosova*, 33–9.

24 "Lomonosov told me himself one day that he could not forgive me because I acted against him with the other professors during the time of his arguments with Winsheim"; Müller to Teplov, 25 October 1748, quoted in Pekarskii, *Dopolnitel'nyia*, 20; *Materialy*, 5:583–4; for Lomonosov's address of apology to the Conference, see *Protokoly*, 2 (27 January 1744), 4.

25 Lomonosov, *PSS*, 7:19–79, 790–800; *Protokoly*, 2 (13 February 1744): 8, (16 March), 13. *Letopis' ... Lomonosova*, 70, 78, 80.

26 *Materialy*, 7:384. Even in 1747 Müller's salary was still only 660 rubles, the same as Lomonosov, P.-L. Leroy, Gmelin, and Trediakovskii. The only professor who drew less was G.-W. Richmann, a professor of physics since 1741, who was paid 500 rubles. De l'Isle and Schumacher (early 1748) both received 2,400 rubles. See *Materialy*, 8:720.

27 Ibid. (31 July 1745), 490–1; 8 (19 February 1746): 34–5.

28 Ibid. 563.

29 Ibid. 418–24; see also 214, 383, 453, 461–2; 8:34–5, 131–2; *Protokoly*, 1 (15 March 1744): 11–12; Pekarskii, *Istoriia*, 1:44–6.

30 *Materialy*, 7:640; Pekarskii, *Istoriia*, 1:45.

31 *Protokoly*, 2 (28 May 1746): 146.

32 Teplov (1711–79) was made an honorary member of the Academy Conference, 28 July 1747. See *Istoriia Akademii nauk SSSR*, 1 (1958): 156–7, 456.

33 See especially the long letter, Müller to Teplov, 25 October 1748, contained in Pekarskii, *Istoriia*, 1:336–8.

34 *Materialy*, 5:634–7. See also 321, 323, 643.

35 Ibid. 185.

36 For Müller's detailed criticism of Winsheim's work, see Büsching, *Beyträge*, 3 (1785): 116–21; *Protokoly*, 2 (22 November 1745): 97; (20 December): 103–4; (10 January 1746): 106–7.

37 *Protokoly*, 2 (3 March 1746): 121; (7 March): 122; (10 March): 124; *Materialy*, 7:706–7; 8:78–80; 106–8. See also Pekarskii, *Istoriia*, 1:344–5, 424–6. On the Naval Academy's map of the second Kamchatka expedition, see M.I. Belov, "O sostavalenii," 131–45.

38 On the peoples of Siberia, see *Protokoly*, 2 (22 April 1745): 55–6; see also 51, 97; *Materialy*, 8:212. On Iusupov's order, see Büsching, *Beyträge*, 3:46. Both of these papers were expanded upon later for publication.

39 Pekarskii reported that this proposal was ready on 16 March 1744 and referred to an original copy signed by Müller which he found in the archives of the Academy Conference (Pekarskii, *Istoriia*, 1:338). But there is nothing to suggest that it was actually presented to the Academy at that time. It was not mentioned in the Conference minutes. The copy

included in *Materialy* (8:183–94) is dated 7 August 1746 and is directed to Razumovskii, who was not president in 1744. The following information is summarized from the *Materialy* version.

40 *Materialy*, 8:183.

41 Ibid. 211–13.

42 Ibid. 302, 331; for Razumovskii's note to Müller, 19 February 1747, see 384–5.

43 The report was signed by Razumovskii, Schumacher, and Teplov, 1 November 1747, shortly before Müller signed his new contract.

44 The Krekshin work was printed later as *Rodoslovie vysochaishei familii gosudaryni imperatritsy Elizavety Petrovny* ... (St Petersburg 1883). See *Materialy*, 8:323–4, 368, 399–400, and *Protokoly*, 2 (3 October 1746): 158, for documentation of the argument over this work. On Krekshin, see James Cracraft "Krekshin, P." in *MERSH*, 16 (1980): 58–60.

45 *Protokoly* (18 March 1747): 408; for Müller's report to Razumovskii (17 January 1747): 360–61; see also 514, 517; Biliarskii, ed., *Materialy ... Lomonosova*, 891–93; Müller, "Avtobiografiia," 150. Although he was not involved in this controversy, Tatishchev once called Krekshin a reckless "storyteller"; see *Istoriia rossiiskaia*, 1:371.

46 *Protokoly*, 2 (1 July 1745): 67.

47 Lomonosov read a manuscript on rhetoric to the Conference in March 1744 (*Protokoly*, 2 [16 March 1744]: 13). See Lomonosov, *PSS*, 7:88–378, for its published version.

48 Razumovskii's warning to Müller can be found in K.S. Veselovskii, "Zapreshchenie," 626; and *Materialy*, 9 (6 February 1748): 58; Lomonosov, *PSS*, 6:9–12 (Lomonosov's first report to the Senate, July 1747); see also Lomonosov, *PSS*, 541–5, and Biliarskii, ed., *Materialy ... Lomonosova*, 88–93.

49 "De scriptus tanguticis in Siberia repertis commentatio," *Commentarii*, 10 (1747): 420–68. Müller read this paper to the Conference during the winter of 1744–45; see *Protokoly*, 2 (3 December 1744): 42; (1, 4, 15 February 1745): 49–50; *Materialy*, 8:404–6; Andreev, *Ocherki*, 94–5, 100–1. The Conference called for the printing of fifty extra copies of the Tangus treatise.

50 *Materialy*, 8:499; 7:297.

51 *Istoriia Akademii nauk SSSR*, 1 (1958): 436–53.

52 Pekarskii, *Istoriia*, 1:53; *Materialy*, 9 (3 September 1748): 393–6.

53 *Istoriia Akademii nauk SSSR*, 1 (1958): 439.

54 *Materialy*, 8 (6 November 1747): 587–8.

55 Müller to Razumovskii, 6 November 1747, ibid. 588–91.

56 Müller to Teplov, 6 November 1747, ibid. 591–2.

57 Ibid. (10 November 1747): 595–6, 607–9. The contract was signed by Razumovskii, Schumacher, Teplov, and secretary Peter Khanin. Müller

was ill at the time and did not actually sign it. He invited Razumovskii to bring it to his house, but Teplov declined in the president's name.

58 Lomonosov, "Zapiski, 1758–9," Lomonosov, *PSS*, 10:50; Biliarskii, ed., *Materialy ... Lomonosova*, 446.

59 *Materialy*, 8 (10 November 1747): 597.

60 Ibid. 9 (24 March 1748): 125–6; M.I. Radovskii, *M.V. Lomonosov*, 69–72.

61 *Materialy*, 7 (28 November 1745): 710. Crusius filled the spot left vacant by Bayer in 1738. Eight professors, all foreign, supported Crusius's nomination in a letter of recommendation to the Senate. Pierre-Ludwig Le Roy (1699–1774) went to Russia in 1731 to act as tutor to the elder son of Biron. He was assigned to the Academy as an extraordinary member for modern history in 1735, but when Müller and Fischer obtained new contracts as professors of history in 1747, Le Roy's position became redundant. He was released from the Academy in August 1748; Pekarskii, *Istoriia*, 1:569–72; on Crusius, 690–6. Von Stählin was appointed an adjunct in 1735 and was named professor in 1737.

62 Pekarskii, *Istoriia*, 1:346; *Materialy*, 9 (26–27 January 1748): 41–3.

63 Müller report to the historical assembly, 29 April 1748; Fischer to Razumovskii, 4 May 1748; in "Akademiki Miller i Fisher ... ," *Chteniia*, Book 3, section 5 (1866): 16–21.

64 Exchange contained in the Müller portfolios, cited by V.G. Mirzoev in *Istoriografiia Sibiri*, 86–7.

65 *Materialy*, 9 (14 April 1748): 150–1.

66 Ibid. 8:361, 405, 594–5, 610–11 (on translators); 9:63–4 (on Lebedev).

67 Lomonosov, 12 August 1748, Lomonosov, *PSS*, 9:620; Biliarskii, ed., *Materialy ... Lomonosova*, 112; *Materialy*, 8:499.

68 Ibid. 9 (10, 14 October 1748): 460, 480. Teplov to Müller 14 October 1748, *Chteniia*, Book 3, section 5 (1866): 22–3.

69 "Protokoly Istoricheskago sobranie peterburgskoi Akademii nauk" (3 and 6 June 1748), *Bibliograficheskie zapiski*, 3:17 (1861): 515–18. In fact, Ermak defeated native peoples, led by Khan Kuchum, at the behest of the Stroganov family; Sibir' lay just west of the Urals. These territories were offered to Tsar Ivan iv by the victors, but the "conquest" of Siberia was still to come.

70 "Protokoly Istoricheskago sobranie," 517; Biliarskii, ed., *Materialy ... Lomonosova*, 105–6. On "brigandage," see *Letopis' ... Lomonosova*, 121.

71 Schumacher report to Teplov, 16 March 1749, in Müller, *Istoriia Sibiri*, 1:462–3; Schumacher report to Teplov, 14 June 1749, *Chteniia*, Book 3, section 5 (1866): 23–4. See also *Materialy*, 10 (13 June 1749): 17–18.

72 19 July 1750; see Pekarskii, *Istoriia*, 1, 361; *Materialy*, 10:487–8. See also 10:443 (19 June 1750).

73 Pekarskii, *Istoriia*, 1:406; for Lomonosov's report on the second part of Müller's history of Siberia, see Lomonosov, *PSS*, 6:81–4, 559–62. *Materialy*, 10:484–5, 489, 524–6. For Lomonosov's request that he be

released from the historical assembly, see *PSS*, 10 (4 September 1751): 347–8, and Biliarskii, ed., *Materialy ... Lomonosova*, 155–6.

74 Lomonosov, *PSS*, 6:85: Lomonosov to I.I. Shuvalov (10 September 1751), ibid. 10:471–2; in his polemical essay on the Chancellery written in 1764, Lomonosov said that he had been collecting works on history for "around twelve years"; Biliarskii, ed., *Materialy ... Lomonosova*, 163, 187.

75 Lomonosov, *PSS*, 10 (4 September 1764): 287.

76 Cited in Solov'ev, *Istoriia Rossii*, 13 (1965): 542.

77 See Tatishchev, *Izbrannye trudy po geografii Rossii*, 14–16, 43–76; Andreev, "Trudy," in Tatishchev, *Istoriia Rossiiskaia*, 1:5–38; Daniels, *V.N. Tatishchev*, 49–65.

78 Conrad Grau, *Der Wirtschaftsorganisator*, 209–15; Daniels, *Tatishchev*, 52–5; Tatishchev, *Leksikon rossiiskoi, istoricheskoi, politicheskoi, i grazhdanskoi ...* , 3 vols. (St Petersburg 1793).

79 *Materialy*, 3:682, 683, 128, 396, 397, 863.

80 Ibid. 4:228; Radovskii, *M.V. Lomonosov*, 114.

81 Lomonosov to Tatishchev, 27 January 1749, *PSS*, 10:461–2.

82 See generally Andreev in Tatishchev, *Istoriia rossiiskoi*, 1:5–38; Tatishchev to Razumovskii, 30 September 1746, in *Istoricheskii arkhiv*, 6 (1951): 255–6; Lomonosov, *PSS*, 6:13–16, 545–6. The dedication did not appear in the first volume when it was published in 1768, perhaps because Müller edited it.

83 Tatishchev to Teplov, 16 May 1749, *Istoricheskii arkhiv*, 6 (1951): 288, 289; *Istoriia rossiiskaia*, 1:184–207, 208–31, 261–6, 292–309. Most were translated by Kiriak Kondratovich in 1747.

84 Tatishchev to Schumacher, 30 March 1749, *Istoricheskii arkhiv*, 6 (1951): 285; *Materialy*, 10:52.

85 Pekarskii, *Istorii*, 1:347–9; Müller, *Materialy*, 6:249.

86 *Materialy*, 9 (27 September 1748): 427–32, outlines the official Academy position. For the letter of guarantee signed by Müller and Lomonosov, see ibid. 430, and Lomonosov, *PSS*, 10 (July 1747): 342–3. On the "Gmelin Affair," see Lothar Maier in *Jahrbücher für Geschichte Osteuropas*, 26 no. 3 (1979): 219–40.

87 Euler to Teplov, 9 May 1750, in *Die Berliner*, 2 (1961): 202–3. *Flora Sibirica* appeared in four volumes, 1747–69.

88 *Die Berliner*, 2:199. See also 202, and Euler to Schumacher, 9 May 1750, 204; Schumacher to Euler, 23 and 30 May 1750, 208, and [Euler], *Leonard Eiler*, 199–200; *Materialy*, 10:336–7, 582.

89 *Materialy*, 9 (12 January 1748): 11–13; (12 February): 68–9; (30 March): 142. For Müller's and Lomonosov's reimbursement, ibid. 10:194; Biliarskii, ed., *Materialy ... Lomonosova*, 121–2, 128.

90 *Materialy*, 9 (3 February 1748): 52; (26 February): 80; (4 April): 148, 156; (16 May): 210–13, 347, 615–20; 10 (10 March 1749): 699; (5 August): 353. On the Cadet Corps, 9:80.

91 Ibid. 10 (13 July 1749): 45.
92 Lomonosov to Trediakovskii, 12 October 1748, in Biliarskii, 115–16. Lomonosov's objections were discussed in the historical assembly on 25 October; *Materialy*, 9 (3 August 1748): 347, 396.
93 Ibid. 9:273–6.
94 For Lomonosov's report of 18 November 1748, see *PSS*, 10:178–86. For further information on the de l'Isle affair, see *Materialy* (19 November 1748): 556–7; see also Pekarskii, *Istoriia*, 1:349–52; Biliarskii, ed., *Materialy ... Lomonosova*. 498; *Dopolnitel'nyia* 32–4.

CHAPTER FIVE

1 Schumacher to Teplov, 9 February 1749, quoted by Pekarskii from the Schumacher archives, *Istoriia*, 1:51.
2 *Materialy*, 10 (2 August 1749): 65; parts of Müller's dissertation were given to Schumacher on the 17th. See Schumacher to Teplov, 17 August 1749, in Biliarskii, 130. It was translated into Latin by Moderach only on the 14th; *Materialy*, 10:71.
3 *Protokoly*, 2 (23 August 1749): 206. Lomonosov is noted as present. See Lomonosov, *PSS*, 6:42–78, for Müller's responses to Lomonosov's later criticisms. Since this is a key point in the chronology of the controversy, I will repeat the entry (23 August 1749 o.s.) from the Conference minutes here in its entirety: 'Dissertatio Cl. Mulleri in hodierno Consessu proposita et postquam non solum quae mandato illustrissimi Praesidis emendandam sed et ea quae ab Academicis notata erant, loca mututa essent, judicatum fuit, eam ita comparatam esse, ut publici juris fieri possit.' (The dissertation of Müller was offered at today's session, and it was decided that, after changes had been made, both those corrections that were to be made at the order of our illustrious president and those that were noted by the academicians, it was prepared in a manner adequate for publication.)
4 Müller, "Origines gentis et nominis Russorum" [1749], *Allgemeine historische Bibliothek*, 5 (1768): 291, 294, 304–8. Some time after the initial draft for this work was prepared, I was able to obtain a copy of the original Russian version, which was printed by the Academy in 1749. It was sent to me on microfilm by the library of the Academy of Sciences in Leningrad, through the good offices of Mr Alexei Makarov of the Embassy of the Soviet Union in Ottawa. I have added references from the Russian version to the Latin ones, rather than eliminate the latter, which are more readily available. The Russian-language version was entitled *Proiskhozhdenie naroda i imeni Rossiiskago* (St Petersburg 1749). On the actual events of 1749, see Dimitri Obolensky, "The Varangian-Russian Controversy," 322–42.

5 For individual reports, see Biliarskii, ed., *Materialy ... Lomonosova*, 131–2, 763–4, 144–5; *Materialy*, 10 (12–13 September 1750): 553–5.

6 Müller, "Origines ... russorum," 288–9 (on Mosoch), 299, 304–5, 330–1 (on defeats); Müller, *Proizkhozhdenie*, 7, 11, 13–14.

7 Ibid. 9–10; Lomonosov, *PSS*, 6:19–25; in the *Sinopsis* it was said in one place that the Varangians spoke a Slavic language, but Lomonosov failed to mention that the *Sinopsis* also said that they came "from across the Baltic" and that Riurik and his brothers were "German" (*Sinopsis*, 23–6). On the Normanist controversy, see, among many others, A.V. Riazanovsky, "The Norman Theory"; Hans Roggers, *National Consciousness*, 208, and *passim*; S.R. Tompkins, *The Russian Mind*, 197–202; O. Pritsak, *The Origin of Rus'*; Henry Paszkiewicz, *The Origin of Russia*, 107–25.

8 Lomonosov, *PSS*, 6:25, 33; *Letopis' ... Lomonosova*, 152–53. Lomonosov's second report was prepared sometime between 24 October and 3 November.

9 Schumacher to Teplov, 19 October 1749, in Pekarskii, *Dopolnitel'nyia*, 51–2.

10 Schumacher to Teplov, 3 July 1749, quoted from the Müller archive by Pekarskii, *Istoriia*, 1:55.

11 Schumacher to Teplov, 30 October 1749, in Pekarskii, *Dopolnitel'nyia*, 52–3; see 43–53 for an entire series of letters from Schumacher to Teplov on the subject.

12 Trediakovskii's report of 13 September 1749 can be found in Biliarskii, ed., *Materialy ... Lomonosova*, 756–8. See also the essay by Karen Rosenberg, "The Norman Theory," 37–49.

13 Tatishchev to Schumacher, 30 May, 30 June 1750, in *Istoricheskie arkhiv*, 6 (1951): 295–7.

14 Lomonosov, *PSS*, 6:21–2, 42. See *Letopis' ... Lomonosova*, for notations about the special Conference meetings on the Müller affair. See also *Protokoly*, 2 (20 October 1749): 214; (4 December): 215; (8 January 1750): 218; (9 March): 224; (24 September 1750): 243.

15 See extracts from Müller's defence, cited in Lomonosov, *PSS*, 6:551; "Origines ... russorum," 330–1; Müller, *Proizkhozhdenie*, 44–5, 52.

16 See Rosenberg, "The Norman Theory"; Peshtich, *Russkaia istoriografiia*, 2:225–30. Peshtich cites from a Müller journal that was unavailable to me.

17 *Proizkhozhdenie*, 11; Lomonosov, *PSS*, 6:42–3.

18 *Proizkhozhdenie*, 51–2.

19 Ibid. 13–14.

20 Lomonosov, *PSS*, 6:37, 67.

21 Ibid. 67, 69–70. Müller quoted the *Primary Chronicle* in his defence.

22 Lomonosov, *PSS*, 6:69.

23 For Müller's praise of Dobner, see *ES*, 20 (July 1764): 92.

24 Lomonosov, *PSS*, 6:56–7. *Proizkhozhdenie*, 12 (on "dispersed").

25 "Origines ... russorum," 294, 322, 332; *Proizkhozhdenie*, 44–5.
26 Lomonosov, *PSS*, 6:41–2, 25–6, 37, 80; see also Biliarskii, ed., *Materialy ... Lomonosova*, 770–1.
27 Lomonosov, *PSS*, 6:75.
28 *Protokoly*, 2 (28 September 1750), 243, M.M. Gurevich and K.I. Shafronovskii ("Ob izdanii 1749," 282–5) pointed out that many of the copies were not destroyed. They refer to a report of 1751 that noted the existence of 6 manuscript copies, 491 printed Latin texts, and 488 printed Russian versions. The Latin edition of the dissertation was published in Gatterer's *Allgemeine historische Bibliothek* (1768), with an introduction by A.L. von Schlözer, who sent it to Gatterer from St Petersburg in June 1767.
29 *Materialy*, 10 (18 June 1750): 438; (8 October 1750): 588–9; *Protokoly*, (9 July 1750): 235.
30 *Materialy*, 10 (6 October 1750): 581–97. *Protokoly*, 2 (8 October 1750): 244. Müller's salary was set at 360 rubles.
31 *Materialy*, 10 (13 September 1750): 555; see also 488.
32 Ibid. (6 October 1750): 581–6.
33 Schumacher to Euler, 12 December 1750, in *Die Berliner*, 2:227.
34 Pekarskii, *Istorii*, 1:262.
35 *Materialy*, 10 (31 October 1750): 614–65; (17 November 1750): 636.
36 Quoted at length in Pekarskii, *Istoriia*, 1:365. Müller did not receive this notice until four days later, see Schumacher to Müller, 25 February 1751, in *Chteniia*, Book 3, section 5 (1866): 25.
37 Gmelin, *Reise*, 1:46–7, 52, 101–2, 131–2. Pekarskii, *Istoriia*, 1:452. On the Senate's order for secrecy, see *PSZR*, 8, no. 6291 (28 September 1732): 1012–13.
38 Gmelin, *Reise*, 1:148, 177–8; *Voyage en Sibérie*, 1:34–5, 156–9.
39 Gmelin, *Reise*, 1:138–9.
40 On this see A.I. Andreev, "Trudy," 5–6. J.N. de l'Isle, *Explication de la carte des nouvelles découvertes au nord de la mer du sud.* (Paris 1752).
41 Pekarskii, *Istoriia*, 1:366–8; Andreev, "Trudy," 7–8.
42 Fischer, *Sibirischen Geschichte von der Entdeckung Sibiriens bis auf die Eroberung dieses Lands durch die russische Waffen*, parts 1–4 (St Petersburg 1768). A Russian translation appeared only in 1774. See *Protokoly*, 2 (13 November 1766): 581–2, 620–1; (11 August 1768), 648. In a foreword to the German edition, Müller's predominant role in the work is mentioned, but his name does not appear in the Russian version. A letter from Schumacher dated 13 March 1753 gave full support to the project (see *Chteniia*, Book 3, section 5 [1866]: 25–7) in spite of Razumovskii's reluctance.
43 *Nouvelle Bibliothèque germanique* 13 (1753): 46–87. See Schumacher to Euler, 10 April 1753, in *Die Berliner*, 2:306; Müller, "Opisanie morskikh ... ," *ES*, 8 (November, 1758): 393–4. On the maps see Gnucheva, ed.,

Materialy ... ekspeditsii, 62. An abbreviated version of Müller's letter was printed in Gmelin, *Voyage en Sibérie*, 2:263–304. Parts of this letter to de l'Isle were rewritten from Müller's memorandum which had appeared in the *Notes* in 1742. Müller also prepared a detailed account of his own travels, which was not published; see V.V. Radlov, *Sibirskiia drevnosti*, 1:9–101. On the argument, see L. Breitfuss, "Early Maps of North-Eastern Asia," 87–99. Golder incorrectly attributed the "Lettre" to Sven Waxell; see *Bering's Voyages*, 1:362.

44 Müller, *A Letter*, 3–5, 11–12, 26–9, 31.

45 *Protokoly*, 2 (11 March 1754): 295 (the protocols still sometimes used Western chronology). Lomonosov insisted in 1758 and again in 1761 that the Chancellery did not need a secretary. He later accused Müller of falsifying the Conference minutes; see Lomonosov, *PSS*, 10:66, 81.

46 If the Conference minutes, which list those present at meetings, are accurate, then Müller attended meetings only twice between 1747 and 1749, three times in 1750, not at all in 1751, once in 1752, five times in 1753, and once in 1754 before he became secretary.

47 See Hoffmann, "O perepiske," 290–5. Eleven volumes of *Neue Erdbeschreibung* were to appear before Büsching died in 1793.

48 Krasheninnikov, *Opisanie*, 17–22. The work was translated into English in 1764 by James Grieve and reprinted in 1962 as *The History of Kamtschatka and the Kurilski Islands, with the Countries Adjacent* (Chicago 1962).

49 See *Biograficheskii slovar' professorov i prepodavatelei imp. Moskovskago universiteta ...* , 1 (St Petersburg 1855): 403; 2 (1855): 340–1; Müller to Gottsched, 21 December 1756, in *Der Gottschedkreis*, 97–8; see also 108. Gottsched had shown an interest in Russia as early as 1725, when he published an ode on the death of Peter I. See H. Grasshoff, "Gottsched," 189, 200.

50 *Die Berliner*, 2 (21 May 1757): 380–1. On Büsching's connection with Dilthey's appointment, see *Biograficheskii slovar' professorov*, 1:301. R.W. Home, Introduction, *Aepinus's Essay on the Theory of Electricity and Magnetism* (Princeton, NJ, 1979): 27.

51 Müller to Euler, 29 March 1754, *Die Berliner*, 1:48–50. Müller's earlier correspondence with Euler had broken off in 1741.

52 Euler to Müller, 27 May 1757, ibid. 141.

53 See, generally, E. Winter, A.P. Iushkevich, "O perepiske," 479, 486–7, 488–9; and *Die Berliner*, 169, 172, 58–9, 164, 167, 232, 107–8.

54 See Pekarskii, *Zhizn' i literatura perepiska Petra Ivanovicha Rychkova*, 68; S.L. Peshtich, *Russkaia istoriografiia*, 2:265–95.

55 Lomonosov to Shuvalov, 1 November 1753, in Biliarskii, ed., *Materialy ... Lomonosova*, 229; Pekarskii, *Istoriia*, 1:62, 369–70; Lomonosov, *PSS*, 10:292, 299.

56 Müller, "Avtobiografiia," 151.

CHAPTER SIX

1 Lomonosov to Shuvalov, 3 January 1754, Lomonosov *PSS*, 10:498. Still the most detailed Soviet discussion of *Monthly Compositions* in the context of the history of Russian journalism is that in P.N. Berkov, *Istoriia russkoi zhurnalistiki XVIII veka*, 77–107. He begins by saying that the "idea" for *Monthly Compositions* belonged to Lomonosov and goes on (77–82) to refer to the letter of 1754 and to an essay written by Lomonosov on the responsibilities of journalists, which was printed in a European magazine in the same year. But when it came to actually pinpointing the credit for the journal's founding, Berkov had to rely on an "it is possible" and "probably" (83). Berkov denies categorically that A.A. Kunik ("Ob uchenykh," *Zapiski IAN*, 1 [1853], i–cxxx) had any proof for his claim that Müller founded *Monthly Compositions*. Berkov ignored another writer from that century, A.P. Piatovskii, who said that Müller provided the idea because of his experience as editor of the *Gazette* and its various supplements (*Iz istorii*, 31). In *Istoriia russkoi zhurnalistiki XVIII–XIX* (Moscow 1966), 26, A.V. Zapadov also credits Lomonosov with having the original idea for *Monthly Compositions*. The most important nineteenth-century study on the journal, by V.A. Miliutin, refers to Lomonosov's letter of 1754 but attributes little significance to it other than as evidence of a widespread feeling that Russia needed a scholarly Russian-language journal. See Miliutin, "Ocherki."

  ES had two subsequent titles: *Sochineniia i perevody k pol'ze i uveseleni sluzhashchiia* (January 1758 to December 1762); *Ezhemesiachnyia sochineniia i izvestiia o uchenykh delakh* (from January 1763).

2 Razumovskii to Elizabeth, 27 January 1748, in Biliarskii, ed., *Materialy ... Lomonosova*, 277.

3 See *Protokoly*, 2 (23 November 1754): 318; Pekarskii, "Redaktor," 4.

4 Ibid. 5; *Protokoly*, 2 (14 December 1754): 320; Biliarskii, ed., *Materialy ... Lomonosova*, 324 (Müller report to Chancellery, March 1757).

5 See Prikaz of 3 August 1749 in *Materialy*, 10:63; 9:197–9.

6 Miliutin, "Ocherki," *Sovremennik*, no. 1:10. The program was printed later as a foreword to the first issue of the journal; see "Preduvedomlenie," *ES*, 1 (January 1755): 1–16. For a translation, see Appendix в, above.

7 Büsching, *Beyträge*, 3 (1785): 5. *Der Gottschedkreis* contains copies of twenty-one letters between Gottsched and Müller.

8 *ES*, 1 (January 1755): 13–16.

9 Pekarskii, *Istoriia*, 2:562; Pekarskii, "Redaktor," 8.

10 Müller report to Razumovskii, 12 January 1755, in Lamanskii, "Lomonosov i Peterburgskaia Akademiia nauk," *Chteniia*, Book 1, section 5 (1865): 134–6.

11 For official approval of the title, see *Protokoly*, 2 (13 January 1755): 320–1.

12 On Lomonosov's constant criticism of *Monthly Compositions*, see P.N. Berkov, "Polemika," 147–94; Lomonosov, *PSS*, 10:192–5, 203–4, 213–14, 228–33. A Lomonosov poem, "Pravda nenavist' razhdaet," was printed anonymously in January 1755 (p. 68), and Berkov attributes to Lomonosov an essay on poetry, "O kachestvakh stikhotvortsa rassuzhdenie" (ES, 1 [May 1755] 371–98). It too was printed anonymously. See Berkov, "Polemika," 154–6.

13 Miliutin, "Ocherki," *Sovremennik*, 26, no. 3 (1851): 1–4.

14 Müller, "Avtor pervyi list'," *ES*, 2 (July 1755): 83, 87. In that article, Müller referred to Sumarokov as a 'friend' of the journal.

15 Miliutin, "Ocherki," *Sovremennik*, 26, no. 3:21. *Der Gottschedkreis*, 66; Grasshoff, "Gottsched," 200.

16 Nartov [Trediakovskii], "Veshnee Teplov Oda," *ES*, 3 (May 1756), 469–77. Note that the first letters of the title are "V.T.," for Vasilii Trediakovskii. On this argument, see Pekarskii, "Redaktor," 16–17.

17 See "Doklad sviateishago Sinoda Imperatritse Elizavete Petrovne o Knigakh, protivnykh vere i nravstvennosti," *Chteniia*, part I, no. 1 (1867): 7–8. *Protokoly*, 2 (1 November 1755), 343; Berkov, *Istoriia*, 97–8; Pekarskii, "Redaktor," 43–5. For a general outline of the literary squabbles of the time and Müller's role as middle man in many of them, see Moiseeva, "K istorii," 56–64. See also Papmehl, *Freedom of Expression*, 6–8.

18 Schumacher to Müller, 30 April 1757, in Biliarskii, ed., *Materialy ... Lomonosova*, 331. For full details on the Poletika case, see 321–33. See also Lomonosov, *PSS*, 10 (report of 13 March 1757), 131–92; (14 March 1757), 193–4; Pekarskii, "Redaktor," 45–7; Pekarskii, *Dopolnitel'nyia*, 79. For article 50 of the charter, see *Istoriia Akademiia Nauk SSSR*, 1 (1958): 446.

19 Müller to Euler, 13 July 1756, in *Die Berliner*, 1:116.

20 *Protokoly*, 2 (2 May 1757): 379 [Stählin]; (18 May 1758): 407 [Taubert]; Biliarskii, 316–19 [Lomonosov].

21 *Protokoly*, 2 (27 March 1758): 404.

22 Müller to Razumovskii, 13 March 1757, quoted in Pekarskii, *Dopolnitel'nyia*, 79.

23 Lomonosov, "Zametki" (February 1755 to February 1757), Lomonosov, *PSS*, 10:189–91.

24 Schlözer, "Obschchestvennaia," 69–70.

25 "Zhaloba ... Volchkova," *Chteniia*, Book 2, section 5 (1859): 153–62; cited here, 155–6.

26 Quoted from the Academy of Sciences archives by R.W. Home in *Slavonic and East European Review* (January 1973), 76–7.

27 Lomonosov, *PSS*, 10 (from the Chancellery journal, 2 June 1757), 194–5.

28 Radovskii, *M.V. Lomonosov*, 97–9; Biliarskii, ed., *Materialy ... Lomonosova*, 394–402; Lomonosov, *PSS*, 10:207.

29 Müller, "Kratkaia rospis' velikim kniaz'iam vserossiiskim," *ES*, 1

(January 1755), 1–16. The "Foreword" had the same pagination, but preceded this piece. On Miliutin's categories of historical subjects, see *Sovremennik*, 25, no. 2 (1851): 154.

30 Poroshin, "Pis'mo o poriadkakh v obuchenii nauk," *ES*, 5 (February 1757): 125–51; cited here, 134–6. Emphasis was Poroshin's.

31 *ES*, 13 (January 1761): 6; 16 (August 1762): 145, emphasis was Müller's; 17 (April 1763): 463.

32 Ibid. 13 (January 1761): 6; (February 1761): 147; Lomonosov, *PSS*, 6:67.

33 This letter was sent in French to an unknown recipient who apparently had told Müller that he hoped to write a history of Moscow; quoted in Pekarskii, *Istoriia*, 1:381.

34 Müller, "Rassuzhdenie o dvykh brakakh ... ," *ES*, 1 (February 1755): 83–97; on Gottsched's printing of the piece, see Müller to Euler, 30 July 1754, in *Die Berliner*, 1:56.

The books that Müller reviewed were G.S. Treuer, *Abstammung des allerdurch-lauchtigsten Russisch-Kaiserlich Hauses und der durch-lauchtigsten Brauschweig-Lünebergischen Hersoge von einer deutschen Stamm-Mutter* (Wolfenbuttel 1733), and J.T. Rönnik, *Versuch einer zuverlassigen geneologisch-historischen Nachricht von dem ersten Gemale der Gräfen Kunigunde von Orlamünde einem Könige der Russen* (Göttingen 1753).

35 Müller, "Izvestie o byvshem gorode Nienshantse," *ES*, 1 (March 1755): 179–87. It also appeared in *Sammlung*, 5 (1761): 573–84, and was noted in the *Hannoversche nutzliche Sammlung* in 1756; see Gert Robel, "Der Wandel," 414. The tale of Nyenschanz was not taken up again by a Russian historian until A.I. Nikitskii published a paper on it in 1884.

36 Müller, "Predlozhenie tak ispravit' pogreshnosti nakhodiashchiesia v Inostrannykh pisateliakh pisavshikh o Rossiiskom gosudarstve," *ES*, 5 (March 1757); 224–31, cited here, 226. On Stenka Razin, see "Isvestie o bunte i o zlodeistviiakh Donskago Kozaka Stenki Razina," ibid. 18 (November 1763): 409–25.

37 Müller, "O pervom letopisatele rossiiskom prepodobnom Nestore, o ego letopisi, i o prodolzhateliakh onyia," *ES*, 1 (April 1755): 275–98. On the early *Sammlung* article, see above, Chapter 1. Müller blamed Paus for the error in the 1732 essay by attributing his mistake to the translation; see *ES*, 1:281.

38 Tatishchev, *Istoriia Rossiiskaia*, 1:119–21; *ES*, 1 (April 1755): 276–7, 298.

39 Its first publication came only in 1767, when Taubert and Barkov edited the list of the *Primary Chronicle*, which had been found in Königsberg in 1758. See Ikonnikov, *Opyt*, 1:123–5; Neustroev, *Istoricheskoe rozyskanie*, 124–6.

40 Müller, "Isvestie i torgakh Sibirskikh," *ES*, 2 (September 1755): 195–250; (December): 525–37; 3 (February 1756): 180–91; (March): 195–226; (April): 339–60; (May): 387–421. "Nachrichten von den Handlung Sibirien," *Sammlung*, 3 (1760): 413–612.

41 Müller, "O pervykh Rossiiskikh puteshestviiakh i posol'stvakh v Kitai," *ES*, 2 (July 1755): 15–57. *Sammlung,* 4, part 6 (1760): 473–553.

42 Müller, "Opisanie trekh iazycheskikh narodov v kazanskoi gubernii," *ES*, 4 (July 1756): 33–64; (August): 119–45. This was reprinted after Müller's death, as a book, *Opisanie zhivushchikh* ... (1791).

43 Müller, "O kitovoi lovle okolo Kamchatki," *ES*, 5 (May 1757): 470–9. This piece had already appeared in 1740 in a German magazine edited by Büsching, see *Beyträge*, 3 (1785): 151–2. According to Kosven, it was printed again in 1759 in *Beyträge zum Nutzen und Vergnugen* (Hanover).

44 Müller, "Izvestie o pesoshnom Zolote v Bukharii, o chinennykh dlia onago otpravleniiakh, i o stroenii krepostei pri reke Irtysche," *ES*, 11 (January 1760): 3–55; (February): 103–42. *Sammlung* 4, parts 1–2 (1760): 183–274. This article was reprinted in the *Zapiski Russkago geograficheskago obshchestva*, 11 (St Petersburg 1886).

45 Müller, "Iz'iasnenie o nekotorykh drevnostiakh v mogilakh naidennykh (v Sibiri i Novorossiiskam krae)," *ES*, 20 (December 1764): 483–515.

46 Müller, "Opisanie morskikh puteshestvii po Ledovitomu i po Vostochnomu moriu s Rossiiskoi storony uchinennykh," *ES*, 7 (January 1758): 3–27; (February): 99–120; (March): 201–18; (April), 299–334; (May): 405–26; 8 (July): 9–34; (August): 99–124; (September): 195–232; (October): 309–36; (November): 393–425.

Müller, "Nachrichten von Seereisen und zur See gemachten Entdeckungen die von Russland aus langst den Kusten des Eismeeres und auf dem Ostilichen Weltmeere gegen Japan und Amerika geschehen sind. Zur Erlauterung eine bei der Academie der Wissenschaften verfertigten Lankarte," *Sammlung*, 3, parts 5–6, (1758): 1–381; Müller, *Voyages from Asia to America*; *Voyages et découvertes*.

47 Müller, "Izvestiia o landkartakh, kasaiushchikhsia do Rossiiskago gosudarstva s pogranichnymi zemliami, takshe i o morskikh kartakh tekh morei, koi s Rossiei granichat," *ES*, 14 (November 1761): 387–488; (December): 483–527. *Sammlung,* 6, part 1 (1761): 1–108.

48 Müller, "Iz'iasnenie sumnitel'stv nakhodiashchiksia pri postanovlenii granits mezhdu Rossiiskim i Kitaiskim gosudarstvami 7197 (1689) goda," *ES*, 5 (April 1757): 305–21, cited here, 317–18, 319–20. Copies of the Nerchinsk and Kiakhta treaties can be found in Mark Mancall, *Russia and China. Their Diplomatic Relations to 1728* (Cambridge, Mass., 1971): 280–3, 302–10.

49 Müller, *Materialy*, 6:404–5; "Istoriia o stranakh, pri reke Amure lezhashchikh, kogda onyia sostoiali pod Rossiiskim vladeniem," *ES*, 6 (July 1757): 3–39; (August): 99–130; (September): 195–227; (October): 291–328. For Müller's declaration that the area had been Russian, see especially 328. He also included a full copy of the Nerchinsk agreement in Russian (317–31); *Sammlung*, 2, parts 5–6 (1758): 293–448. On this entire question, see, above all, Maier, "Müller's Memoranda." Büsching

printed the shorter original essay, of 1741, in 1768; see Müller, "Nachrichten von dem Amur-Flusse," *Magazin fur die neue Historie und Geographie*, 2 (1768): 483–518. See also Müller, *Voyages et découvertes*, and "Geschichte der Gegenden am Flusse Amure," in Müller, *Sammlung russischer Geschichte*, 5:329–472.

Two secret reports on the Amur to Catherine of 1763–64 can be found in N.N. Bantysh-Kamenskii ed., *Diplomaticheskoi sobranie*, 378–93, 396–8.

50 Müller, "Izvestie o ssorakh anglichan i frantsuzov v amerike," *ES*, 1 (June 1755): 539–48, cited here, 539. Emphasis was Müller's. In 1937, S.V. Bakhrushin charged that Müller's aim was to assist the "feudal empire" in enriching itself; *Istoriia Sibiri*, 1: 11.

51 Müller, "Izvestie o pesoshnom zolote v Bukharii, o chinennykh dlia onago otpravleniiakh, i o stroenii Krepostei pri reke Irtyshe," *ES*, 2 (January 1760): 5, 12–13.

52 See *Materialy*, 2 (6 February 1733): 301, 415; *Protokoly*, 1:63.

53 The essay on the Kazan region was received by the Academy in 1745; that on Siberian trade was commissioned by Prince B.G. Iusipov in 1744; see *Protokoly*, 2:51; Müller, "Avtobiografiia," 149.

54 *Sammlung*, 6 (1761): 109–564; 8 (1768): 1–458; "Kratkoi perechen' Sibirskoi istorii," *ES*, 18 (October 1763): 354–68; "Sibirskaia istoriia," chapter 6, *ES*, 19 (January 1764): 3–42; (February); 99–135; chapter 7 (March): 195–237; (April): 291–324; chapter 8 (May): 387–418; (June): 483–528. The work was printed in this century; see Müller, *Istoriia Sibiri*. Two further volumes were promised then but have not appeared.

55 Müller, "O nachale i proizkhozhdenii kozakov," *ES*, 11 (April 1760): 303–48. *Sammlung*, 4 (1760): 365–472. "Von dem Ursprung der Kosaken," *Das Neueste aus der anmuthigen Gelehrsamkeit*, nos. 5–7 (1756), 386–439; see Müller to Gottsched, 26 February 1756, in *Der Gottschedkreis*, 95; see also 107, 328, 380–92, 431–41, 489–502. Büsching printed an abbreviated version of it in his *Neue Erdbeschreibung* in 1774. An article on the Zaporozhian Cossacks was printed in *Monthly Compositions* in 1760; see *ES*, 11 (May 1760), 403–60.

56 Ibid. (April 1760): 314–15. The *Sinopsis* failed to mention Khmelnitskii and ended a list of Ukrainian *voevody* at 1651. Since the *Sinopsis* was written only two decades after the momentous events of 1654, they were described as follows: "With the help of God and because the people wished it, Ukraine once again opted to place itself under the aegis of God's elect, the Russian tsar"; 9th ed. (St Petersburg 1810): 202–8.

57 Müller, "Opyt noveishiia istorii o Rossii," *ES*, 13 (January 1761): 3–63; (February): 99–154; (March): 195–244. *Sammlung*, 5, nos. 1–2 (1760): 1–180; no. 3 (1761): 181–264; no. 4 (1761): 265–380.

58 *ES*, 13 (January 1761): 4–6.

59 Ibid. 7–20.

60 Ibid. 27, 37; (February): 99–100, 105–6, 114, 135–42 (on the Romanovs). *Sammlung*, 27, 209–11, 249–50.

61 On Sellius's book of 1736, which was printed in Russian only in 1815, see P.N. Berkov, "Burkhard-Adam (Nikodim) Sellii i ego 'Katalog pisatelei o Rossii' (1736 g.)," *Vestnik Leningradskogo universiteta*, no. 20 (1966): 98–109.

62 Solov'ev, *Istoriia Rossii*, 26 (1965): 544; Lévesque, *Histoire de la Russie*, 8 (Paris 1812); 3rd edition, 220–73; on Shcherbatov and Karamzin, see above, 180–1, 186.

63 *ES*, 13 (January 1761): 31.

64 See Müller's letter to Volkov (20 April 1761) contained in Pekarskii, "Redaktor," 53–4; and "Goneniia na 'sochinenniia'," *Ezhemesiachnye sochineniia*, 244–5.

65 Lomonosov to Razumovskii, January 1761, *PSS*, 10: 228–33; and to Teplov (30 January 1761): 547–62; Biliarskii, 491–2.

66 This letter of 14 June 1761 is contained in Pekarskii, *Zhizn' ... Rychkova*, 47.

67 Müller to J.A. Korff, 1 September 1763, cited in Pekarskii, *Istoriia*, 1: 387–8.

68 Lomonosov, "Kratkii Rossiiskii letopisets s rodosloviem" (St Petersburg 1760), *PSS*, 6: 588–89. Over 6,000 copies were sold.

69 *PSZR*, 15, no. 11.092 (16 August 1760): 498–9.

70 Lomonosov, *PSS*, 6: 293–4, 295.

71 Ibid. 297, 303, 319–20, 332–4, 345.

72 Müller, "Kratkoe izvestie o nachale Novagoroda i o proizkhozhdenii Rossiiskago naroda, o Novogorodskikh Kniaz'iakh i znatneiskikh onago goroda sluchaiakh," *ES*, 14 (July 1761): 3–50; (August): 92–158; (September): 195–240; (October): 291–323. *Sammlung*, 5, parts 5–6 (1761): 381–572.

73 *ES*, 14 (July 1761): 6–10. The reference to a geography of Ravenna was Ravenna Anonymus, *Cosographus*, edited by J. Shvnetz, *Itineraria Romana*, 2 (Leipzig 1940).

74 *ES*, 14 (July 1761): 10–11, 12; Müller used the analogy about the Saxons and Gauls in 1749, but at that time had said that the Russians took their name from conquerors; *Proizkhozhdenie*, 51.

75 Biliarskii, 492.

76 *ES*, 14 (August 1761): 129.

77 Ibid. 126–31. On Nikon (October, 291–4); the work was translated into French by one Lizakevich, who printed an abridged version in Copenhagen under his own name in 1767 and failed to acknowledge Müller's authorship. See Solov'ev in *Sovremennik*, 10: 123–6.

78 Müller printed biographical information on Johann Gustav Gerber, who died unpublished in 1734; *ES*, 12 (July 1760): 3–10. Gerber's "Izvestie o

nakhodiashchikh s Zapadnoi storony Kaspiiskago Moria ... sostianii v 1728 godu" appeared in the next four issues: (July): 3–48; (August): 99–140; (September): 195–232; (October): 292–308. It also appeared in *Sammlung,* 4 (1760): 1–148.

79 Fischer, "O narode i imeni Tatarskom, takzhe o drevnikh Mongol'tsakh i ikh iazyke," *ES*, 1 (May 1755): 421–50; "Razsuzhdenie I.E. Fishera o Giperboreitsakh ili o narode za severom nakhodiashchimsia," 1 (February 1755): 123–38; "Razsushdenie o raznykh imenakh Kitaiskago gosudarstva i o khanskikh tutulakh," 4 (October 1756): 311–27.

80 Soimonov, "Opisanie Kaspiiskago moria i chinennykh na onom Rossiiskikh zavoevanii iako chast' istorii Petra Velikago," ibid. 17 (January 1763): 7–35. A continuation appeared as the lead article in each issue thereafter, to and including the November number. Müller's review of Soimonov's book praised it; see ibid. 18 (December 1763): 557.

81 "Drevnaia poslovitsa Sibir zolotoe dno," ibid. 14 (November 1761): 449–67; 19 (January 1764): 44–59. On Soimonov's relationship with Müller, see L.A. Gol'denberg, *Soimonov,* 170–4, 177–82, 199–202. See D.N. Bantysh– Kamenskii, *Slovar' dostopamiatnyk liudi russkoi zemli,* 3 (St Petersburg 1847): 279, for a writer who credited Soimonov with a work prepared by Müller.

82 See "Perepiska V.N. Tatishcheva za 1746–1750 gg.," *Istoricheskii arkhiv,* 6 (1951): 290.

83 Rychkov, "Perepiska mezhdu dvumia priiateliami o komertsii," *ES*, 1 (February 1755): 105–22; (April): 307–38. They were printed in the form of a letter to the editor and signed "N.N."

84 Ibid. 338; 2 (December 1755): 493–515; 5 (January 1757): 50–60.

85 "Zapiski P.I. Rychkova," *Russkii arkhiv,* Book 3, no. 11 (1905); *Protokoly,* 2 (29 January 1759): 420. Lomonosov to Razumovskii, 21 January 1759, Lomonosov, *PSS,* 10: 76–7; see also Pekarskii, *Zhizn' ... Rychkova,* 42–4.

86 *ES*, 17 (January 1763): 93. The questions appeared in most subsequent issues. They did not all have to do with history; the first query was for information on the roots of "vich" as a suffix in the Russian language.

87 Rychkov, "Istoriia Orenburgskaia po uchrezhdenii Orenburgskoi gubernii," *ES*, 9 (January 1759): 3–30, and in each of the following issues to and including November; Tatishchev, *Istoriia Rossiiskaia,* 1: 234–40; Rychkov, "Topografiia orenburgskoi gubernii," *ES*, 14 (January 1762): 3–70, and in each of the following issues to and including November. For Müller's review of the book, see ibid. 17 (March 1763): 269–70. Rychkov "Predislovie," *Opyt Kazanskoi istorii drevnikh i srednikh i vremen* (St Petersburg 1767),

88 Lomonosov, *PSS,* 13 (January 1761): 288. Biliarskii, ed., *Materialy ... Lomonosova,* 488. For the reference to Rychkov in the Conference minutes, see *Protokoly,* 2:420, 441.

89 This letter of 12 March 1761 is carried in full in Lamanskii, *Chteniia*, Book 2, section 5 (1865): 141.

90 Müller to Euler, 23 August 1762, in *Die Berliner*, 198–9.

91 Biliarskii, 409, 465–6, 604–13.

92 This was the fifth Academy edition of the *Sinopsis*. See *ES*, 17 (February 1763): 175. On Lomonosov's book, see ibid. 9 (May 1763): 461. For Müller's 1749 comment about the *Sinopsis*, see *Proizkhozhdenie*, 22.

93 "Sokrashchennaia rossiiskaia istoriia," in Curas, *Sokrashchennaia univer-sal'naia istoriia* (St Petersburg 1762): 357–90; see *ES*, 17 (May 1763): 459–61. Curas's book was translated by Volchkov first in 1747. The edition of that year and another in 1750 did not carry the section on Russia. Müller's reviews were carried in a new section that he introduced in January 1763 called "Information on Scholarly Affairs." It was Russia's first book review section.

94 Barkov had been collaborating with Lomonosov on the latter's historical work since 1754; see *Letopis' … Lomonosova*, 232, 245, 256, 306.

95 *Protokoly*, 2 (24 February 1746): 119; (17 March): 126. The proposal was made to the Academy by de l'Isle.

96 Büsching, *Beyträge*, 3 (1785): 157–8. Müller's many suggestions and protests to Voltaire are detailed in A.F. Shmurlo, *Voltaire et son oeuvre*; see especially 6–13, 129–30, 239–55. See also "Pis'mo Vol'tera k G.F. Milleru" [1746], *Moskovskii telegraf*, no. 2 (1825): 105–7.

97 Müller's first series of reviews appeared in the second and third volumes of *Neues Gemeinnutzige Magazin fur die Freunde der nutzlichen und schönen Wissenschaften und Kunste* (Hamburg 1760–1); see Shmurlo, *Voltaire et son oeuvre*, 7–8. Writing nearly fifty years later, M.T. Kachenovskii noted that "everyone" blamed Müller and that the French historian Pierre-Charles Lévesque even accused Müller of sending Voltaire poor documentation; see *Vestnik evropy*, no. 21 (1809): 61–8. For Müller's review in 1764 of a book called *Les erreurs de Voltaire*, 2 vols. (Paris 1763), see *ES*, 19 (March 1764): 268.

98 Müller, "Nachrichten von dem Zarewitsch Alexei Petrowitsch," *Magazin für die neue Historie und Geographie*, 3 (1769): 195–200 (this article was unsigned); Müller, "Eclaircissemens sur une lettre du roi de France, Louis XIII au tzar Michel Fedorowitch de l'annee 1635," ibid. 16 (1782): 349–54 (this article was signed). Müller to Shuvalov, 14 July 1761, quoted by Pekarskii, *Istoriia*, 1:386–7.

99 Shmurlo, *Voltaire et son Oeuvre*, 280–1.

100 *Protokoly*, 2 (2 July 1763): 504; *ES* 18 (July 1763): 73.

101 Adodurov had been placed under house arrest in 1758, as an alleged plotter against the throne. He was sent the next year to Orenburg, whence he began regular correspondence with Müller.

102 Müller, "Razsuzhdenie o predpriiatii voiny s Kitaitsami" (1763), in Bantysh-Kamenskii, *Diplomaticheskoe Sobranie*, 380.

103 Ibid. 283–4.

104 Müller, "Razsuzhdenie o posol'stve v Kitai" (1764). On this question (of the Amur), see Maier, "Müller's Memoranda," 238–40.

105 Müller to Korff, 1 September 1762, quoted in full in Pekarskii, *Istoriia*, 1: 387–8.

106 *Schlözers öffentlichen und Privatleben*, 1 (1828): 83; Schlözer, "Obshchestvennaia," 4–5.

107 Büsching, *Beyträge*, 3 (1785): 61–2; Schlözer, "Obshchestvennaia," 5, 7, 337; Pekarskii, *Istoriia*, 1:375.

108 Schlözer, "Obshchestvennaia," 25–6.

109 Ibid. 27–8, 160. Bacmeister wrote an article on the university in Dorpat, where he had been an instructor; see *Sammlung*, 9, nos. 1–2 (1764): 95–262; see also Annelies Lauch, *Wissenshaft*, 25–30, 367.

110 Razumovskii to Chancellery, 4 July 1762, in Biliarskii, 696–7; Müller to Razumovskii, May 1762, *ibid*. 685–96.

111 Schlözer, "Obshchestvennaia," 100; "Periculum antiquitatis Graegis collustratae luminibus," ibid. 393–418; see also notice in *Protokoly*, 2 (10 May 1764): 516.

112 Schlözer, "Obshchestvennaia," 188–9; for the two reports in Russian, see ibid. 287–301. They can also be found in Schlözer, *August Ludwig v Schlözer und Russland*, 49–64.

113 Lomonosov, *PSS*, 9 (29 July 1764): 420; (25 June): 410–11; (26 June): 411–13; (10 May): 409; see also *Schlözers offentlichen und Privatleben*, 1 (1828): 85–6; "Periculum," 407.

114 Lomonosov, *PSS*, 9 (25 June 1764): 410–11; (26 June): 411–13; (29 June): 420.

115 Müller's opinion ("Gutachten") can be found in *August Ludwig v. Schlözer und Russland*, 66–8.

116 Biliarskii, ed., *Materialy ... Lomonosova*, 702; Schlözer, "Obshchestvennaia," 193–5, The Periculum did not appear in print for more than a century, that is, until it was included with the Russian edition of Schlözer's memoir; see note 111 above.

117 Schlözer, "Obshchestvennaia," 211–12, 312–13; Biliarskii, ed., *Materialy ... Lomonosova*, 729; Lomonosov, *PSS*, 9 (January 1765): 433–4.

118 See Schlözer, *Schlözers offentlichen und Privatleben*, 1: 86; and Schlözer, "Obshchestvennaia," 264– 5, 324–5; see also Ikonnikov, *Shletser*, 25–7.

119 Lomonosov, "Kratkaia istoriia ... Kantseliarii," *PSS*, 10 (August 1764): 268.

120 Ibid. (July 1762): 251–2.

121 See Biliarskii, ed., *Materialy ... Lomonosova*, 603–4; Pekarskii, *Dopolnitel'nyia*, 86–8. The order was dated May 1763.

122 Lomonosov, *PSS*, 10 (7 August 1763): 353. By August 1763, Lomonosov was involved in a major project to create a statue in honour of the new empress. Biliarskii, ed., *Materialy ... Lomonosova*, 613–15.

123 Lomonosov, *PSS* 9 (11 February 1760): 220–1. Lomonosov had reported to Razumovskii as early as 18 October 1759 that Müller was "indifferent" to his duties within the geography department; see *PSS*, 9: 206; see also 209–10, where a Chancellery report of 21 October 1759 complained that Müller did not bother to attend geography department assembly meetings. Müller himself admitted as much to Euler.

124 Biliarskii, 574–9; Radovskii, *M.V. Lomonosov*, 105–9. For the initial Razumovskii order of 31 August 1762, see Biliarskii, ed., *Materialy ... Lomonosova*, 574.

125 *Protokoly*, 2 (7 January 1765): 530; Müller, "Avtobiografiia," 153; Müller to Gottsched, 15 March 1765, in *Der Gottschedkreis*, 106.

126 Müller report to the Chancellery, 27 February 1765, in Biliarskii, ed., *Materialy ... Lomonosova*, 737. This report was found in Lomonosov's papers, and beside Müller's reference to him Lomonosov had pencilled in, "Again slanders and lies!"

127 Lomonosov to Euler, 21 February 1765, *PSS*, 10: 595. He had used this term for Schumacher in a report submitted to the Chancellery in 1764; see note 40 to chapter 1.

128 Twenty years later, the Academy issued a *Novyia ezhemesiachnyia sochineniia* (St Petersburg 1786–96), which included a number of Müller's still unpublished archival and archaeological findings. For Lomonosov's proposals of 28 January 1765, see *Protokoly*, 2:532; see also Lomonosov, *PSS*, 10: 317–18, 737–78.

129 Shcherbatov cited liberally from *Monthly Compositions* in his discussion of Riurik's arrival in Novgorod (*Istoriia rossiiskaia*, 1, part 2, 367–8), and even repeated Müller's error in attributing the *Kernel* to Prince Khilkov rather than to Mankiev. See also *Istoriia rossiiskaia*, 1:136; 2:294, 279, 391, 427, 3:710, 783, 825. He used Müller's Siberian history as well: 3:562–6, 718, 732, 738, 778, 792–4; and Müller's publications of Rychkov, 2:255, and elsewhere. Karamzin's citations from Müller are too numerous to list. For "Marfa Posadnitsa," see Karamzin, *Izbrannye sochineniia*, 1 (Moscow-Leningrad 1964): 680–728.

130 See *Svodnyi katalog*, 4:131.

131 *Sochineniia Karamzina*, 1, ed., A. Smirdin (St Petersburg 1848): 365–6.

132 Evgenii, *Slovar' russkikh svetskikh pisatelei*, 2 (Moscow 1845): 67. This was serialized first in *Syn Otechestva* (1821). On Müller, see no. 22 (1821): 49–74; no. 23: 97–117.

CHAPTER SEVEN

1 Betskoi, *General'noe plan Imperatorskago Vospitatel'nago doma v Moskve*, part 1 (St Petersburg 1763), 2nd issue (1767): 4–6. On Betskoi in general

see P.M. Maikov, *Ivan Ivanovich Betskoi*; see also David Ransel, "Ivan Betskoi," and David M. Griffiths, "The Early Years."

2 Büsching, *Beyträge*, 3 (1785): 67–8.

3 Schlözer, "Obshchestvennaia," 267.

4 Müller, "Avtobiografiia," 153.

5 The decree and committee of 1757 can be found in Biliarskii, ed., *Materialy ... Lomonosova*, 338.

6 On the essays about education in *Monthly Compositions*, see J.L. Black, *Citizens for the Fatherland*, 58–9.

7 Catherine included *Emile* among books published by the Academy of Science in the 1760s that met with her disapproval because they were "against law, good morals, and the Russian nation itself." See Catherine to General Procurator Glebov, 5 September 1763, *SIRIO*, 7 (1871): 318. For Müller's remarks about Rousseau, especially in reference to *Emile* and also to *Du Contrat social*, see *ES*, 17 (April 1763): 278–9; on Madame le Prince de Beaumont (January 1763): 83; 20 (July 1764), 90; on Locke, 89; on Dilthey, 19 (January 1764): 265–6.

8 Ibid. 20 (July 1764): 91. On La Chalotais see H.C. Barnard, *Education and the French Revolution* (Cambridge 1969): 17–28.

9 Müller to Razumovskii, 22 October 1761, *Chteniia*, Book 3, section 5 (1866): 27–8.

10 Betskoi, "General'noe uchrezhdenie o vospitanii oboego pola iunoshestva," *PSZR*, no. 12, 103 (22 March 1764): 668–71.

11 Ibid. 670. Emphasis was Betskoi's.

12 See "Perevod' iz Merkuriia Frantsskago" [July 1764], *ES*, 20 (December 1764): 537–44; and "O uchenykh delakh," ibid. 546–7.

13 "Nachal'noe razsuzhdenie o plane dlia uchrezhdeniia publichnykh uchilishch," in S.V. Rozhdestvenskii, ed., *Materialy*, 7.

14 Ibid. 5–9.

15 Dilthey, "Plan o uchrezhdenii raznykh uchilishch dlia rasprostraneniia nauk i ispravleniia nravov," ibid. 10–81, cited here, 12, 22.

16 For Müller's review of Dilthey's text, see *ES*, 19 (March 1764): 265–7. For the university's adoption of Freyer's book, translated by Chebotarev as *Kratkaia vseobshchaia istoriia ...* (Moscow 1769), see *Dokumenty i materialy po istorii Moskovskogo universiteta*, 1 (Moscow 1960): 254; 2:207–8.

17 "General'nyi plan gimnazii ili gosudarstvennykh uchilishch" in Rozhdestvenskii, *Materialy dlia istorii uchebnykh reform*, 103.

18 *Biograficheskii slovar' professorov i prepodavatelei imp ...* , 2: 367; Büsching, *Beyträge*, 3 (1785): 66.

19 "General'nyia plan Moskovskago Vospitatel'nago dlia prinostnykh mladentsov Doma," 2 parts, *PSZR*, no. 12.957 (11 August 1767): 290–326. Maikov, *Betskoi*, 170. Müller's "Regulations" can also be found in a somewhat different form, as a response to specific questions from

Vice-Chancellor Prince A.M. Golitsyn, in Büsching, *Beyträge*, 3 (1785): 82–97.

20 See Pekarskii, *Istoriia*, 1:390–1; A.N. Radishchev was then a student at the Corps of Pages; see D.M. Lang, *The First Russian Revolutionary: A.N. Radishchev* (London 1959): 27. Müller's contribution to the Corps of Pages is not mentioned in G.A. Miloradovich, *Materialy dlia istorii pazheskago ego imperatorskago Velichestva Korpusa, 1711–1875* (Kiev 1876).

21 See letters from Betskoi to Müller in *Chteniia*, Book 4, section 5 (1863): 102–16.

22 Quoted by P.N. Miliukov from the Müller archives; see *Glaynyia techeniia russkoi istoricheskoi mysli*, 1: 60. Miliukov said that in 1765 Golitsyn gave Müller verbal assurances that he would be named director of the archives.

23 Büsching, *Beyträge*, 3 (1785): 74–6, 46–7.

24 Pekarskii, *Istoriia*, 1:393.

25 Golitsyn, *Portfeli*, 515; on the Münnich memoirs, see Pekarskii, *Istoriia*, 1:288–9. The memoir was printed in French in 1774; Pekarskii, *Istoriia*, 1:395.

26 Quoted in Pekarskii, "Redaktor," 56. Volume 9 of the *Sammlung* was printed in 1764 and was very favourably reviewed in *Allgemeine deutsche Bibliothek*, Book 8, issue 1 (Berlin 1768): 157–70.

27 See A. Lentin, ed., *Shcherbatov On the Corruption of Morals in Russia* (Cambridge 1969): 55.

28 Aepinus contributed several articles on electricity and magnets to *Monthly Compositions*; see *ES*, 6 (October 1757); 8 (November 1758); 9 (January 1759); 12 (September 1760). See also R.W. Home, "Introduction," *Aepinus's Essay on the Theory of Electricity and Magnetism*, 53–4.

29 Büsching, *Beyträge*, 3 (1785): 74.

30 Müller to Stählin, undated, in *Der Gottschedkreis*, 171; Euler to Müller 9 / 20 August 1766, in *Die Berliner*, 263.

31 *Protokoly*, 2 (31 July 1766): 566. The report is carried in its entirety, in French, in Pekarskii, *Istoriia*, 1: 303–8.

32 Müller to Euler, 1 September 1766, in *Die Berliner*, 1: 264.

33 See Lomonosov, *PSS*, 10:11–23, 24–6, 32–70. Müller report to Teplov, in Lamanskii, *Chtenniia*. Book 1, section 5 (1865): 132–4.

34 Razumovskii to Chancellery, March 1764, in Biliarskii, 637.

35 Lomonosov, "Kratkoe istoriia o ... Kantseliarii," *PSS*, 10: 267–316.

36 Ibid. 85–92, 93–131, 132–70.

37 *Protokoly*, 2 (6 October 1766): 574–5; *PSZR*, 17, no. 12.750 (5 October 1766): 1015–16.

38 Stählin to Müller, 1 December 1766, in *Der Gottschedkreis*, 201.

39 Letter contained in V.P. Orlov-Davydov, "Biograficheskii ocherk grafa V.G. Orlova," 352.

40 Müller to Euler, 20 October 1766, in *Die Berliner*, 265–6; Müller to Stählin, 6 February 1767, in *Der Gottschedkreis*, 177. This must have been in response to information sent him by Stählin. Bacmeister's letters can be found in Lauch, *Wissenschaft*, 35–7. See also Euler to Müller, 26 October 1766, in *Der Berliner*, 266–8; and 15 January 1767, 268–9. The house in which Bacmeister resided was retained by Müller until 1771, when Stählin arranged its sale for him; see *Der Gottschedkreis*, 823.

41 *Protokoly*, 2 (19 February 1768): 592–3.

42 On this generally, see S.V. Rozhdestvenskii, "Akademiia," 637–42; *Akademiia nauk SSSR*, 1, 142–7.

43 The Academy *nakaz* is printed in *Protokoly*, 2 (20 August 1767): 612–14. The first set of instructions was also recorded in the Conference minutes, but was not sent to Müller; see *ibid.*, 615–16. Müller's instructions can also be found in *SIRIO*, 43 (1885): 371–3. See also Papmehl, *Freedom of Expression*, 58.

44 *PSZR*, no. 10.724 (5 May 1757): 765.

45 Orlov's letter of 23 April 1767 is contained in full in Orlov-Davydov, "Biograficheskii," 365–6, but the editor does not say to whom the memorandum was directed.

46 On Müller's participation in the translation of Catherine's *Nakaz*, see Neuschäffer, *Katherina II*, 2: 184; for Müller's one comment to the assembly, *SIRIO*, 4 (1869): 75.

47 *Protokoly*, 2 (22 December 1768): 661; (12 January 1769): 662; (23 January 1769): 664. See also Rozhdestvenskii, "Akademiia," 640–2. Johann Albrecht Euler's appointment is recorded in *Protokoly*, 2 (4 August 1766): 466.

CHAPTER EIGHT

1 See *Uchenaia korresp.*, 223, where Müller asks for funds in 1772 to repair the house.

2 Ibid. for example, 120, 124, 136–7, 144, 152, 233; and Stählin to Müller, 9 March 1769, in *Der Gottschedkreis*, 279–80.

3 *Uchenaia korresp.*, 145, 234, 240; *Protokoly*, 3 (21 January 1771): 4. On this generally, see Kirchner, *A Siberian Journey*, 28–30.

4 Pallas to J.A. Euler, 21 September 1769, *Uchenaia korresp.*, 153. On S. Gmelin, see *Protokoly*, 3 (23 May 1774): 131; see also 12–21, 136, 140, 142, 149; on Lowitz's death see (8 December 1774): 165; on Güldenstädt, who was attacked by local mountainmen on his way to Mozdok, *Uchenaia korresp.*, 230.

5 Müller, ed., "Kratkoe opisanie o Kamchatke, uchinennoe v Iune mesiatse 1773 goda Kamchatkim Komandirom Kapitanom Timofeem Shmalevym," *Opyt Trudov Vol'nago Rossiiskago Sobranie*, part 1, no. 8. (1774):

195–212. Müller left a full volume of reports from the Shmalevs covering the years 1762–75 in his private papers; see Golitsyn, *Portfeli*, 440. For the letter of 1770 to S.M. Koz'min, see Kosven, "Etnograficheskie" (190–1), where it is reprinted in full.

6 *Uchenaia korresp.* (3 May 1770): 182; (8 April): 178. These were paid for by the Academy.

7 *Istoricheskiia Genealogicheskiia i Geograficheskiia Primechanii v Vedomostiakh* (Moscow 1765). Müller edited a second volume in Moscow the next year. Information about Kamchatka was also included; see 98–106.

8 Biliarskii, ed., *Materialy … Lomonosova*, 737–8; Pekarskii, *Istoriia*, 1: 391–2.

9 Lomonosov's speech to the Assembly, 28 January 1765, Lomonosov, *PSS*, 10: 317–18; *Protokoly*, 2 (28 January 1765): 532; (7 March): 533.

10 See K. Kalaidovich, "Zapiska," 117–18. Müller's other assistants, who worked with Bantysh-Kamenskii, were Stritter and M.M. Sokolovskii. See also Miliukov, *Glavnyia techeniia*, 61–2, 68.

11 Golitsyn, *Portfeli*, 412.

12 The Conference had appointed Stritter aide to Müller already in April 1779; Catherine's *ukaz* confirmed it; see *Protokoly*, 3 (26 April 1779): 407; (7 October): 429. On the fate of Müller's library, see Pekarskii in *Zapiski IAN*, (1867): 92–8; Golitsyn, *Portfeli*, 404–7, 413–14; Büsching, *Beyträge*, 3 (1785): 115–22.

13 Apparently this money was not enough for the Müller family to live on. After his death, Kristina Müller had to divide the sum equally among her children. She was forced to appeal to A.R. Vorontsov, her patron, for support; see *Arkhiv … Vorontsova*, 30 (1884): 390.

14 Golitsyn, *Portfeli*, 491–2. On the Golitsyn family library, which was founded in 1712 by D.M. Golitsyn, see Ikonnikov, *Opyt*, 1:1078–82.

15 Shcherbatov, *Istoriia Rossiiskaia*, 1: 24–5.

16 Golikov, *Deianiia Petra Velikago*, 1 (St Petersburg 1788), vi.

17 Novikov, "K chitateliu," *Drevniaia rossiiskaia Vivliofika*, 1 [January 1773], 2nd ed. (1788): ix–x; "Pis'ma mitropolita Kievskago Evgeniia Bolkhovitinova k V.M. Anastasevicha," *Russkii arkhiv*, no. 5 (1889): 43 (letter of 28 March 1815). See also I. Gurliand in *Chteniia*, Book 3, section 5 (1899): 20–4.

18 Schlözer, *Nestor*, 1: rma–rmv.

19 *Sammlung russischer Geschichte des herrn Collegienraths Müllers in Moscaw*, parts 1–5 (Offenbach-am-Main 1777).

20 See, besides those already mentioned above, Büsching's *Magazin für die neue Historie und Geographie*: part 2 (1768), "Nachricht von den Umständen der Erhebung des Zaars Michael Fedrowitsch aus den russischen Thron," article by Büsching based on papers sent him by Müller, 401–6; part 3 (1769), "Beschreibung der Moldau von Demetrio Kantemir," with

an introduction from Müller, 1–12; part 15 (1781), Müller, "Izvestie o Khristine Sofii" [Moscow 1777]: 221–44; part 16 (1782), Müller, "Eclaircis-semens sur une lettre du roi de France, Louis XIII, au Tzar Michel Fedrowitch de l'année 1635," 349–54. P. Hoffman ("O perepiske G.F. Millera i A.F. Bushinga," 293) suggests that an article with documents on Pugachev (part 18 [1784]: 3070) may also have been based on papers sent by Müller to Büsching.

21 On Lenz in Müller's home, see Neuschäffer, *Katerina II*, 344. See *Opyt trudov*, part 1 (1774): 58–66, 195–212; part 4 (1778): 1–106, 107–44; part 5 (1780): 87–118 (three essays on the youth of Peter the Great) and 186–214. In 1783 the Free Russian Assembly was absorbed by the new Russian Academy which was founded in that year by Catherine, with Dashkova as its president.

22 Taubert had been appointed adjunct for history in 1738, but (outside the Chancellery) his Academy position had been mainly with the Academy library. Moderach was adjunct of history from 1749 to 1759, when he was made professor. He left Russia in 1761 but returned two years later. Stritter was appointed adjunct for history in 1779, but left as honorary member in 1787; Hackman became adjunct for history in 1782, and he too left as an honorary member in 1784.

Johann-Heinrich Busse was the next appointment as history adjunct – in 1795! Three years later Jean-François Vauvillier was appointed academician in history and antiquity.

23 *Biblioteka rossiiskaia Istoricheskaia*, part 1 (St Petersburg 1767), Introduction, 32.

24 Schlözer, *Nestor*, 1, "Vvedenie," part 5: rmo–rn.

25 Lomonosov, *PSS*, 6:163–286, 572–88. Lomonosov's manuscript was handed to Razumovskii in 1758 but taken from the typography by Lomonosov himself in 1759. It was returned to the Conference only in 1766 after its author's death and Müller's departure from St Petersburg.

26 The *Memoriae populorum ad Danubium et Pontum Euxinum inclentium e scriptoribus historiae Byzantinae erutae*, 10 vols. (St Petersburg 1771–79), was a compilation of extracts from Byzantine sources that were related to Russian history. An abridged Russian version, translated by V.P. Svetov, appeared in four volumes, 1770–5.

27 Letter from Bacmeister cited in Lauch, *Wissenschaft*, 72.

28 The *Russischer Bibliothek, zur Kenntnis des gegenwärtigen Zustander der Literature in Russland*, 11 vols. (St Petersburg / Riga / Leipzig, 1772–89), was the first bibliographical journal in Russia. On its origin and character, see Lauch, *Wissenschaft*, 71–8; on Müller's advice to Bacmeister, 97–101, 456.

29 Stritter, *Istoriia Rossiiskago gosudarstva*, 3 vols. (St Petersburg 1800–3). It had been completed in German, 1794–7.

30 Schlözer, *Probe russischer Annalen*, 149; on the Varangians as Germanic, see 84; on the "Ruses" and the Cumans, 87; on Tatishchev and Bayer, 148–9.

31 Büsching, *Beyträge*, 3 (1785): 91–6; on Müller's eyesight, see letters to Euler, September and October 1766, in *Die Berliner*, 264–5.

32 Lomonosov, *PSS*, 6:171.

33 Ibid. 205–13.

34 Ibid. 572, 578: G.E. Pavlova, ed., *M.V. Lomonosov*, 211–19; Pekarskii, *Istoriia*, 1:196.

35 *Allgemeine historische Bibliothek*, 5 (Halle 1768): 282–3. Schlözer was referring to Müller's suggestion in his article on Novgorod that Riurik might have lived in Prussia. Bayer, *Sochinenie; Geografiia rossiiskaia i sosedstvennykh s Rossieiu oblastei okolo 947 godu* (St Petersburg 1767); *Feofila Sigefra Beera, ... Geografiia rossiiskaia iz Konstantina Porfirogenite* (St Petersburg 1767); *Kratkoe opisanie vsekh sluchaev kasaiushchikhsia do Asova* ... (St Petersburg 1768).

36 Müller, *O narodakh*. Translated from the German by Ivan Dolinskii. I have used the second edition, (1788): 107–8; 21–2. Schlözer said that no Goths ever lived in Prussia; *Allgemeine historische Bibliothek*, 5 (1768): 282.

37 Müller, *O narodakh izdrevle*, 93–5; Müller's emphasis.

38 Ibid. 30–2.

39 Ibid. 112, 133.

40 Ibid. 122, 127.

41 *Russische Bibliothek*, 4 (1776): 548. Müller, "Abhandlung von den Volkern, welche vor Alters in Russland gewohnt haben," *Magazin für die neue Historie und Geographie*, part 16 (1782): 287–384; Büsching's journal had a very large circulation and was cited in 1802 as one of the models for the *Vestnik evropy* (*Messenger of Europe*) edited by Nicholas Karamzin; see Karamzin, "O knizhnoi torgovle i liubvi k chteniiu v Rossii," *Vestnik evropy*, no. 9 (1802): 61.

42 Büsching, *Beyträge*, 3 (1785): 98.

43 *Svodnyi katalog*, 5 (1975): 49–50. See also S.R. Dolgova, "'Sokrovishche rossiiskikh drevnosti' N.I. Novikova." Dolgova does not mention Müller's participation.

44 Ruban, *Opisanie imperatorskago stolichnago goroda Moskvy* (St Petersburg 1782). Apparently Ruban also acted as go-between for Müller and Prince Potemkin. For Müller's essays on the Moscow region, see, for example, "Eine reise von Moscau nach Kolomna, im Jahre 1778, und Beschreibung der Staat Kolomna," *S.-Peterburgische Journal*, 2 parts (1782). Parts of this piece were also printed in *Opyt trudov*, part 4 (1778): 107–47; see also *Novyia ezhemesiachnyia sochineniia*, Book 2, part 41 (November 1789): 3–52 (on Sviatotroiskii Sergeius monastery); Book 4, part 42 (December 1789): 3–34 (on Pereiaslavl'-Zaleskii); Book 2, part 46 (April 1790): 41–91

(Mozhaisk, Ruza, and Zvenigorod). See also list in Hoffmann, "Müller als Geograph," 55–6. For Ruban's praise of Müller, see Peshtich, *Russkaia istoriografiia*, 3:88.

For Karamzin's long article of 1802, "Istoricheskiia vospominaniia i zamechaniia na puti k Troitse, i v sem monastyre," *Vestnik evropy*, no. 15 (1802): 207–26; no. 16, 287–304; no. 17, 30–47.

45 Müller, "Nachrichten von den neuesten Schiffahrten im Eismeer und in der Kamtschatkischen See seit dem Jahr 1742, da die zweite Kamtschatkische Expedition aufgehört hat. Ein Stück aus dem Regierungs-Geschichte der grossen Kayserinn Katherin II," *Neue Nordische Beiträge*, 5 (1793). See also Andreev, *Ocherki*, 133–4. For Müller and the legislative commission in 1775, see *Protokoly*, 3 (6 February 1775): 170; (2 March): 173.

46 See Breitfuss, "Early Maps," 98; the Engel/Müller argument is outlined in Andreev, "Trudy," 9–13.

47 Müller, *Izvestie o dvorianakh rossiiskikh*. For Catherine's commission of 1763, see *PSZR*, 16, No. 11.751 (11 February 1763): 167. On the connection between these reports (especially those of Kniazev) and Catherine's Charter of the Nobility, see A.N. Filippov, in *Izvestiia Akademii nauk SSSR* (1926): 423–44. On Kniazev, see N. Barsukov, "A.I. Kniazev," *Russkii arkhiv*, book 2 (1885): 462–74.

48 *Magazin für die neue Historie und Geographie*, 18 (1784): 71–82.

49 "Eine liefländischen Patrioten Beschreibung der Leibeigenschaft, wie solche im Liefland über die Bauern eingeführt ist," *Sammlung russischer Geschichte*, 9 (1764): 491–527. The work was unsigned. See Neuschäffer, *Katherina II*, 391–8; and I. de Madariaga, *Russia*, 63.

50 Müller, "Puteshestvie g. D.S. sovetnika Millera K Sviatotroitskomu Sergievu Monastyriu," *Novyia ezhemesiachnyia sochineniia*, 41 (November 1789): 3–52, cited here, 12–15.

51 On Shcherbatov's *Kratkoe povest' o byvshikh v Rossii samozvantsakh* (St Petersburg 1774), see I.A. Fedosov, *Oz istorii russkoi obshchestvennoi mysli XVIII stoletiia. M.M. Shcherbatov* (Moscow 1967): 37–8.

52 Catherine II, *Zapiski kasatel'no rossiiskoi istorii*, part 1 (St Petersburg 1787): ii; part 2 (1738): 2, 6–10, 16, 32–3. The work was printed separately in six parts, 1787–93.

53 Müller, *Istoricheskii sochineniia o malorossii i malorossiianakh*. On the treaty of Pereiaslavl', see especially 11 ("subjected the Hetman and all Cossack troops and Little Russian towns on both sides of the Dnieper forever to the Russian Empire").

54 See "Pis'ma istorika," 373–90. Peshtich, *Russkaia istoriografiia*, 3 (1971): 87; on Sumarokov's requests for historical information, see P.M. Berkov, ed. "Shest' pisem A.P. Sumarokova k istoriografu F.-I. Milleru ... ," *XVII vek. Sbornik* 5, 376–82. For Sumarokov's plea to Shuvalov of 7 December 1760, see *Trudy Ia. K. Grota*, 3 (St Petersburg 1901), 65.

55 Kristina Müller to Vorontsov, 12 and 23 October 1783, *Arkhiv* ... *Vorontsova*, 30 (1884): 387–8.

56 Letters in Pekarskii, *Istoriia*, 1:397–8.

57 Müller to Dashkova, 1783, quoted at length in ibid. 398–9. Dashkova was appointed to head the Academy by Catherine in December 1782; the *ukaz* that made it official was dated 24 January 1783. See *The Memoirs of Princess Dashkov* [sic], ed. K. Fitzlyon (London 1958): 203–4.

58 Coxe, *Travels*, 294–5; see also Coxe, *Account*, 3rd ed., where he referred to the "celebrated" Müller, 20, 24.

59 *Materialy*, 6:404.

60 Printed in 1774; see Pekarskii, *Istoriia*, 1:418.

61 Taubert to Müller, 18 September 1767, in Schlözer, *August Ludwig v Schlözer und Russland*, 190–1; and *Istoricheskie arkhiv*, no. 6 (1960): 187–8. Tatischev, *Istoriia rossiiskaia s samykh drevneishkikh vremen*, 4 volumes (St Petersburg 1768–9, 1773, 1774).

62 For Müller's correspondence with Olsufiev, see Pekarskii in *Zapiski IAN*, 4:4 (1864): 8–46; for Pogodin's discovery, see *Moskvitianin*, 7 (1843): 229–31.

63 Polunin, *Geograficheskii leksikon Rossiiskago gosudarstva, ili slovar'* ... (Moscow 1773), "Predislovie"; *Protokoly*, 3 (25 October 1773): 104. On Müller's and Polunin's lexicon, see S.S. Ilizarov in *Arkh. ezheg. za 1977* (1978): 90–7.

64 [Büsching], *Anton Biushinga iz sokrashchennoi ego geografii tri glavu: o geografii vseobshche, o Evrope i o rossiiskoi imperii* (Moscow 1766). Dolinskii translated it under Müller's supervision.

65 *Kniga stepennaia tsarskago rodosloviia*, part 1 (St Petersburg 1775), "Predislovie ot izdatelia," vi. The project for publication had been in the works at least since 1771, when Müller wrote to I.I. Melissino about the possibility of printing it at the University of Moscow; see Golitsyn, *Portfeli*, 534–5.

66 Ikonnikov, *Opyt*, 1: 129.

67 Cited from the Müller archives by Miliukov, *Glavnyia techeniia*, 90. See also 168–9.

68 See, generally, Ikonnikov, *Opyt*, 1: 118–30, 221, 293, 296–300, 348, 896–7; N.N. Bantysh-Kamenski, *Obzor vneshnikh snoshenii Rossii (po 1800 god)* (St Petersburg 1894–1902); *Chteniia*, Book 3, section 5 (1846): 1–23; Book 5, section 5 (1847): 58–74; Book 6, section 4 (1847): 44–67.

69 Müller, "Istoricheskoe izvestie o kievskoi akademii," *Drevniaia rossiiskaia Vivliofika*, 2nd edition, part 16 (1791): 281–95. For other Müller materials in Novikov's serial, see: part 5 (1788): 1–134; part 6 (1788): 71–106; part 7 (1788): 305–71; part 8 (1789): 1–360; part 9 (1789): 387–484; part 15 (1790): 218–28; part 17 (1791): 363–90; part 18 (1791): 397–422.

70 Radishchev, *Polnoe sobranie sochinenii* (Moscow-Leningrad 1941): 145–63, 384–7.

71 *Sobranie ravnykh zapisok o sochinenii, sluzhashchikh k dostavleniiu podnago*

svedeniia o zhizni i deianiiakh Gosudaria Imperatora Petra Velikago, part 5 (1797): 117–80 (same three essays on Peter's youth; see above, note 21); part 7 (1787): 3–86.

72 "Vypiski iz bumag Iakutskago arkhiva, ob otkrytii i zavoevanii Ruskimi reki Amura," *Moskovskii telegraf*, 43 (1832): 167.

EPILOGUE

1 Catherine to Grimm, 28 September 1783 (n.s.); 19 December 1783 (n.s.), *SIRIO*, 23 (1878): 285–8, 290; see also Kristina Müller to A.R. Vorontsov, 12 October 1783 (o.s.), in *Arkhiv ... Vorontsova*, 30 (1884): 388.

2 On the Order of St. Vladimir, see *PSZR*, 21, no. 15.515 (22 September 1782): 671–5. See also Müller to Vorontsov, 28 September 1783, in *Arkhiv ... Vorontsova*, 30 (1884): 381.

3 On the diploma granted to Müller by the Free Economic Society, see Stählin to Müller, 9 March 1769, in *Der Gottschedkreis*, 279–80. On the award from the Free Russian Assembly, see Metropolitan Evgenii in *Slovar' russkikh svetskikh pisatelei*, 2:54.

4 *PSZR*, 21, no. 15.646 (24 January 1783): 800–1; Kozodavlev was made director of Russia's Pedagogical Seminary in 1785. He replaced Theodor Iankovich de Mirievo, the most prominent member of the Commission for the Establishment of Public Schools, who also was made a member of the Russian Academy of Letters. For the decree that established the Russian Academy, see *PSZR*, 21, no. 15.839 (30 September 1783): 1023–5.

5 On Dashkova and the Russian Academy, see *The Memoirs of Princess Dashkov*, [sic], ed. K. Fitzlyon, 217–20, and Sergei Nekrasov, *Rossiiskaia akademiia* (Moscow 1984). For the decree that established the new "Historical Assembly," see *PSZR*, 21, no. 15.890 (4 December 1783): 1066–7. The group was to include ten members, "three or four" of whom should be prepared to work full-time gathering historical sources on the eighth century and earlier.

6 Miliukov, *Glavnyia techeniia*, 62; Solovev, *Sobranie*, 1540.

7 Bacmeister to Müller, 28 February 1782, cited in Lauch, *Wissenschaft*, 53.

8 Strube de Piermont, *Razsuzhdenie*, "Predislovie." T. Mal'gin, *Zertsalo rossiiskikh gosudarei s 862 po 1789 god* (St Petersburg 1789): 1.

9 Schlözer, *Nestor*, 1: 344, 418–19.

10 *Kratkaia rossiiskaia istorii* (St Petersburg 1805), 3rd ed., 9–12. On this and Catherine's views, see Black, in "The Search."

11 Evgenii, *Slovar'*, 62. This entry on Müller was printed first in *Syn otechestve*, no. 22 (1821). Ewers, *Über den Ursprung der russischen Staats* (Dorpat 1808). This book was later regarded by many as the fountainhead of the Historico-Juridical School of Russian historians. N. Brusilov,

"Istoricheskoe razsuzhdenie o nachale russkago gosudarstva," *Vestnik evropy*, section 2, no. 55 (1811): 284–318. On the Historico-Juridical School ("State School"), see Black in *MERSH*, 39 (1984): 118–25.

12 Kachenovskii, "Ob istochnikakh dlia Russkoi istorii," *Vestnik evropy*, no. 3 (1809): 193–210; no. 5, 3–19; no. 6, 98–119; no. 15, 209–18; "O bezpristrastii istorika," ibid. no. 1 (1821): 35–44. See also his review of Artsybashev, "O pervobytnoi Rossii e eia Zhiteliakh," ibid. no. 17 (1809): 326–31.

13 Schlözer, *Probe russischer Annalen*, 151–2; see also his *Nestor*, 1:427–8. On the "Sceptical School", see also Black, "The Sceptical School of Russian Historians," *MERSH*, 33 (1983): 125–36.

14 Karamzin, *Istoriia gosudarstva Rossiiskago*, 1 (St Petersburg 1818): 231. See also 44–54, 113–14, 316–32. The last-named pages are footnotes, in which he outlines all the then-known theories about the origins of the Varangians and of the Russian state.

15 Ustrialov, *Nachertanie russkoi istorii* (St Petersburg 1835), 3–5. This book and an abbreviated version for the lower schools were adopted for use by S.S. Uvarov, the minister of public instruction under Nicholas I. See Uvarov, *Desiatiletie ministerstva narodnago prosveshcheniia, 1833–1843* (St Petersburg 1864), 97. See also Ustrialov, *O systeme pragmaticheskoi Russkoi istorii* (St Petersburg 1836), 18, 27–9, 46. Pogodin, *Nachertanie russkoi istorii dlia uchilishch* (Moscow 1835), 4–5; *Istoriko-kriticheskie otryvki* (Moscow 1846), 7, 21–2, 38, 40; and the three-volume *Izsledovaniia zamechaniia i lektsii M. Pogodina, o rosskoi istorii* (Moscow 1846). For the connection between Karamzin, Pogodin, and Ustrialov, see Black, *Karamzin*, chapter 5.

16 Solov'ev, *Istoriia Rossii*, 1:125–30; 13:545–54, and *Uchebnaia kniga russkoi istorii* (Moscow 1859), 8th ed. (1880): 5; Kliuchevskii, *Sochineniia*, 1:133–4, 138–41; 6:163–9; 7:400–11. For an English-language overview of early Soviet views on Normanism and its predominance in the nineteenth century, see Paszkiewicz, *Origin*, 109–32, 414–18. After Lomonosov, the first serious attack on Normanism came from J.P.G. Ewers in the 1820s, and later S. Gedeonov, N.I. Kostomarov, and D.I. Ilovaiskii became involved. But their motivation, method, and alternative explanations varied considerably. In the English language, the major criticisms of Normanism began after the Second World War, led in the main by the erudite and persuasive Riazanovsky family. See, for example, V. Riazanovsky, *Obzor russkoi kultury*, part 1 (New York 1947); N. Riazanovsky, "The Norman Theory of the Origin of the Russian State," *Russian Review*, no. 1 (1947): 96–110; A.V. Riazanovsky, "The Norman Theory," and, more recently, "Pseudo-Varangian Origins of the Kievo-Pechersky Monastery," *Russian History*, no. 7, part 3 (1980): 265–82. See also Nora K. Chadwick, *The Beginnings of Russian History: An Enquiry into Sources*

(Cambridge 1946), especially 12–15. Omeljian Pritsak outlines a new general theory in *Russian Review* (1977). The first volume of his proposed six-volume study under the same title was published by Harvard in 1981.

Bestuzhev-Riumin, *Russkaia istoriia*, 1:211; M.O. Koialovich, *Istoria*, 6, 9, 99; Solov'ev, *Sobranie sochinenii*, 1354; Kliuchevskii, *Sochineniia*, 8:400–5.

17 Abaza, *Rukovodstvo i etechestvennoi istorii* (St Petersburg 1889): 8–9; Abaza, *Istoriia Rossii: narodnoe izdanie* (St Petersburg 1885): 2–3; Ilovaiskii, *Kratkoe ocherki Russkoi istorii. Kurs starshago vosrasta* (Moscow 1880), 9th ed., 10–13; (1912), 36th ed., 8–11; M. Ostrogorskii, *Uchebnik russkoi istorii. Elementarnyi kurs* (Peking 1919): 8–9; see also K.V. Elpat'evskii, *Uchebnik Russkoi istorii* (St Petersburg 1909), 12th ed. of a textbook that first appeared in 1892:12–13.

18 A.N. Filippov in *Izvestiia AN SSSR* (1926), 428. Picheta, *Vvedenie v russkuiu istoriiu (istochniki i istoriografiia)* (Moscow 1922), 98–9; Ogorodnikov, *Ocherk istorii Sibiri do nachala XIX veka* (Irkutsk 1920), 45–51. Soviet historians also recognized the predominance of the "Normanist" interpretation throughout the 1920s. On this, see I.P. Shaskol'skii, *Normanskaia teoriia v sovremennoi burzhuaznoi nauk* (Moscow-Leningrad 1965), 11–12.

19 Rubinstein, *Russkaia istoriografiia*, 99–114; S.V. Bakhrushin in *Istoriia Sibiri*, 1: 5–6, 41, 54; A.N. Radishchev, *Polnoe sobranie sochinenii*, 384–5.

20 M. Tikhomirov, "Russkaia istoriografiia XVIII veka," *Voprosy istorii*, no. 2 (1948): 96–7; Rubinstein, *Russkaia istoriografiia*, 107.

21 *Ocherki istoricheskoi nauk v SSSR*, 1 (Moscow 1955): 190–2; Kosven in *Sibirskii etnograficheskii sbornik* 3 (1961): 167–212.

22 Chernyshevskii, *Polnoe sobranie sochineniia*, 16 (Moscow 1953): 73–4; Herzen, *Sobranii sochineniia*, 7 (Moscow 1956): 149.

23 L.V. Cherepnin, *Russkaia istoriografiia*, 188–91, 193–5, 214–17; D.M. Lebedev, *Ocherki po istorii geografii v Rossii. XVIII vek (1725–1800 gg.)* (Moscow 1957), 17; V.K. Iatsunskii, *Istoricheskaia geografiia. Istoriia ee vozniknoveniia i razvitiia v XIV–XVIII vekakh* (Moscow 1955): 219–20.

24 Peshtich, "Mesto G.F. Millera i A.L. Shletsera v russkoi istoriografii," chapter 5 in his *Russkaia istoriografiia XVIII veka*, 2:210–30; cited here, 212–13. Peshtich opens this chapter with a detailed account of the treatment accorded Müller in Russian writing. The third part of Peshtich's trilogy (1971) also has much to say about Müller, but it is very scattered. See also Radovskii, 69–72.

25 Mirzoev in *Uchenye Zapiski*. (1963), 45–71.

26 Illeritskii and Kudriavtsev, *Istoriografiia istorii SSSR*, 84–6, 92–4; and V.I. Astakhov, *Kurs lektsii po russkoi istoriografii*, 105–7.

27 See E.A. Rydzevskaia, *Drevniaia rus' i skandinaviia v IX–XIV vv.* (Moscow 1978): 128–9.

28 M.F. Shabaeva, *Ocherki istorii shkoly i pedagogicheskoi mysli narodov SSSR:*

XVIII v.–Pervaia polovina XIX v. (Moscow 1973): 68. See also *Istoriia Akademii nauk SSSR*, 1 (1958): 280; on this practice generally, see David M. Griffiths, "The Early Years."

29 Mirzoev, *Istoriografiia Sibiri (Domarksistskii period)*, 92.

30 Andreev's papers, one of which was a public lecture on Müller, were listed by T.I. Lysenko, "Fond," 292–300; see also Andreev, *Ocherki*, and "Trudy."

31 *Istoriia Sibiri*, 2:11–12. See also 255–9, 263–7.

32 *ES*, 17 (April 1763): 373.

33 Schlözer wrote that Müller was "unarguably the most honoured and best-known person abroad among scholars in Russia" (in 1761); see "Obshchestvennaia," 3.

34 *ES*, 17 (May 1763): 169.

35 Ibid. 20 (October 1764): 276.

36 On the "Sceptical School," see Black in *MERSH*, 33 (1983): 125–36.

37 Kachenovskii, *Vestnik evropy*, no. 17 (1830): 76.

38 When disputing Karamzin's argument that historians must be patriotic in their writing, Kachenovskii wrote that he was not embarrassed to admit that he owed his knowledge of old Russia to "Bayer, Müller, Tunmann, Stritter, and especially to the famous A. Schlözer"; see Kachenovskii, "O bespristrastii istorika," ibid. no. 17 (1809): 327.

39 *Teleskop* was shut down in 1836 because Nadezhdin printed P.I. Chaadayev's famous "Lettres sur la philosophie de l'histoire," which were very critical of Russian culture and history. Nadezhdin was sent to Siberia, and Chaadayev was declared insane and placed under house arrest.

40 On the popularity of Karamzin's history and the arguments against him by Kachenovskii, Artsybashev, and Polevoi, see Black, *Karamzin*, 129–55.

41 See I.N. Boltin, *Primechaniia na istoriiu gospodina Leklerka*, 2 vols. (St Petersburg 1788), and *Kriticheskie primechaniia gen.-maiora Boltina na pervy-vtoroi tom istorii kniazia Shcherbatova*, 2 vols. (St Petersburg 1793–4). On Shcherbatov and Boltin, see Peshtich, *Russkaia istoriografiia*, 3 (1971), *passim*, and Rogger, *National Consciousness*, 222–38.

42 Karamzin, *Izbrannye sochineniia*, 1 (Moscow-Leningrad 1964): 417–19.

43 See Evgenii in *Syn otechestva* (1821). Nadezhdin wrote that "it is sad to admit" that Müller was attacked in 1749 by the "immortal" Lomonosov; see Nadezhdin in "Ob istoricheskikh," 122. Another Kachenovskii student, N. Sazonov, wrote that Müller deserved the "eternal gratitude of all those who love the national history" and also regretted Lomonosov's stance as one of the "malevolent ones" in 1749; see Sazonov, "Ob istoricheskikh," 144. Kachenovskii edited the *Uchenyi zapiski*.

44 Barsukov, *Zhizn'*, 57, 69.

45 *ES*, 20 (October 1764): 286–7.
46 Solov'ev described Müller as an "archivist, professor, academician, historiographer, traveller, geographer, statistician, journalist," who was a "tireless worker for the vast machine of Russian civilization"; see *Sobranie*, 1539–40; see also Solov'ev, "Miuller."

Bibliography

Müller's huge manuscript collection, which for a long time was housed in the Ministry (College) of Foreign Affairs, is now located in the Central State Archives of Ancient Acts, Moscow (TSGADA, *fond* 199). The Archives of the Academy of Sciences (AAN) in Leningrad, which includes papers of Lomonosov, Euler, and others, is also a rich depository of information about Müller. Most of his Siberian portfolios are there (*fond* 21). I have not had access to this voluminous material. Instead, I have relied on the very extensive published documentation and collections compiled by scholars who drew on this material themselves.

The two most useful Academy publications in which Müller figures prominently are the ten volumes (each of approximately 1,000 pages) of *Materialy dlia istorii Imperatorskoi Akademii Nauk* (St. Petersburg 1885–1900), and the three-volume *Protokoly zasedanii Konferentsii imperatorskoi Akademii nauk a 1725 po 1803* (St Petersburg 1897–1911). *Materialy* is a documentary history of the Academy to 1750; the second volume of *Protokoly* (1744–70) encompasses the eleven-year period in which the minutes of the Conference were recorded by Müller himself (1754–65).

As we have seen, assorted Müller reports and papers were printed after his death in a wide variety of German and Russian periodicals. Large parts of his correspondence have been printed in conjunction with the letters of Leonhard Euler (the entire first volume of *Die Berliner*), Gottsched (*Der Gottschedkreis* – Müller's correspondence – nearly 300 letters with Gottsched, Köllner, Reichel, and Stählin), Bacmeister (Lauch, *Wissenscraft ... Bacmeisters* – 33 letters to Müller from Bacmeister), Schlözer, and Lomonosov. The collected works of Lomonosov, and the large documentary collections on him gathered and published by P.S. Biliarskii, P.P. Pekarskii, and V.I. Lamanskii, carry a wealth of information on Müller. Equally useful are memoirs and accounts left by Schlözer, Büsching, Gmelin, Rychkov, Pallas, Poroshin, and other academicians and scholars who were associates of Müller.

Several of Pekarskii's books are based on careful scrutiny of the Archives of the Ministry of Foreign Affairs, where he was employed from 1862 to 1872. The most important of these is his *Istoriia imperatorskoi Akademii Nauk v Peterburge* (1–2, 1870–2), the first volume of which contains over 100 pages devoted to Müller. Later pre-revolutionary historians, such as Paul Miliukov and A.N. Pypin, and the Soviet writers S.V. Bakhrushin, A.I. Andreev, M.O. Kosven, J.C. Mirzoev, and Iu.Kh. Kopelevich, have also drawn extensively on the archival resources.

Finally, Müller's own published works, most of which are readily available on microfiche cards by means of the Harvard Eighteenth Century Russia collection, and the *Ezhemesiachnyia sochineniia*, 20 vols. (1755–64), provided the data on which this study is based.

This bibliography is divided into two parts: Muller's works (including English translations) and correspondence, and general works. It does not include all the titles referred to in the notes; rather it holds titles that have to do specifically with Müller.

MÜLLER: WORKS, CORRESPONDENCE, AND TRANSLATIONS

"Avtobiografiia," In *Istoriia Sibiri*, 1 (Moscow-Leningrad 1937): 145–56.
Der Briefwechsel L. Eulers mit G.F. Miller, 1735–1767. Vol. 1 (1959) of *Die Berliner und die Petersburger Akademie der Wissenschaften im Briefswechsel Leonard Eulers*. 3 vols. Berlin 1959–76.
Chastitsa iz istorii Petra Velikago. Moscow 1778.
Conquest of Sibiria and the History of the Transactions, Wars, Commerce, carried on between Russia and China, London 1842.
Ezhemesiachnyia sochineniia. 20 vols. St Petersburg 1755–64.
Der Gottschedkreis und Russland. Deutsch-russische Literatur-beziehungen im Zeitsalter der Aufklärung. Ed. Ulf Lehmann. Berlin 1966.
Istoricheskiia sochineniia o malorossii i malorossiianakh G.F. Millera. Ed. O. Bodianskii. Moscow 1846.
Istoriia Sibiri. 2 vols. Moscow-Leningrad 1937–41.
Izvestie o dvorianakh rossiiskikh. I ikh drevnem proiskhozhdenii; o starinnykh chinakh, i kakiia ikh byli dolzhnosti pri gosudariakh ... St Petersburg 1790.
Joannis Georgii Gmelini. Reliquias quae supersunt commercii epistolici cum Carolo Linnaeo, Alberto Hallero, Guilielmo Stellero, etal. Ed. G.H.T. Plieninger. Stüttgart 1861. (Contains letters from Müller to Gmelin, 1741–2.)
Kopelevich, Iu.Kh., ed. "Pervaia zagranichnaia komandirovka peterburg-

skogo (iz zapisok G.F. Millera o ego puteshestvii 1730–1731 gg.)." *Voprosy istorii estvestvoznaniia i tekhniki*, 2 (1973): 47–52.

Leben herrn George Wilhelm Stellers. Frankfurt 1748. (This 38-page work has been attributed to Müller, but we have no evidence by which to demonstrate his authorship.)

A Letter from a Russian Sea-Officer to a Man of Distinction at the Court of St Petersburg. London 1754.

O narodakh izdrevle v Rossii obitavshikh. St Petersburg 1773.

Ob'iavlenie predlozheniia do ispravleniia rossiiskoi istorii kasaiushchagosia, kotoroe mozhet uchinit'sia chastym izdaniem sobraniia vsiakikh izvestii do istorii rossiiskago gosudarstva prinadlezhashchikh. St Petersburg 1732.

Opisanie o torgakh sibirskikh. St Petersburg 1756.

Opisanie Sibirskago Tsarstva i vsekh proizshedshikh v nem del, ot nachala a osoblivo ot pokoreniia ego Rossiiskoi derzhave po sii vremena. St Petersburg 1750.

Opisanie zhivushchikh v Kazanskoi gubernii iazycheskikh narodov, iako to Cheremis, Chuvash i Votiakov ... St Petersburg 1791.

"Origines gentis et nominis russorum" (1749) *Allgemeine historische Bibliothek.* Ed. Johann Christoph Gatterer. 5 (Halle 1768): 283–340.

"Pis'ma istorika Millera k grafu A.R. Vorontsovu." (1778–83). *Arkhiv kniazia Vorontsova.* Book 30 (Moscow 1884): 373–90.

Proizkhdozhdenie naroda i imeni rossiiskago v vysochaishee Tezoimenitstvo ... Elizavety Petrovny. St Petersburg 1749.

"Puteshestvie g. D.S. sovetnika Millera k Sviatotroitskomu Sergievu Monastyriu," *Novyia ezhemesiachnyia sochineniia*, 41 (November 1789): 3–52.

"Razsuzhdenie o predpriiatii voiny s kitaitsami" (1763) and "Razsuzhdenie o posol'stve v Kitai" (1764). In N. Bantysh-Kamenskii, ed. *Diplomaticheskoe sobranie del mezhdu Rossiiskim i kitaiskim gosudarstvami s 1619 po 1792–god*, 378–414. Kazan 1882.

Sammlung russischer Geschichte. 9 vols. St Petersburg 1732–64.

Sammlung russischer Geschichte des Herrn Collegienraths Müllers in Moscaw. Ed. Ulrich Weiss. 4 vols. Offenbach-am-Main 1777.

"Shest' pisem A.P. Sumarokova k istoriografu G.F. Milleru (1767–69) i chetyre zapiski poslednego k Sumarokovu." Ed. P.N. Berkov. *XVIII vek: Sbornik 5* (Moscow-Leningrad 1962): 376–82.

Urness, Carol, ed. *Bering's Expeditions: Reports from Russia by Gerard Friedrich Müller.* (Translations of Müller's reports, now in press, University of Alaska.)

Voyages et découvertes faites par les Russes le long côtes de la Mer Glaciale & sur l'Océan Oriental, tant vers le Japon que vers l'Amérique. On y a joint l'Histoire du Fleuve Amur. 2 vols. Amsterdam 1766.

Voyages from Asia to America, for Completing the Discoveries of the North West Coast of America. To Which is prefixed, A Summary of the Voyages Made by the Russians on the Frozen Sea ... Trans from the High Dutch of S. Muller[sic]. London 1761.

"Zur Geschichte der Akademie der Wissenschaften zu S. Petersburg." In *Materialy dlia istorii imperatorskoi akademii nauk*, 6 (St Petersburg 1890)

GENERAL

"Akademiki Miller i Fisher i opisanie Sibiri." *Chteniia*, Book 3, section 5 (1866): 15–30.

Akademiia nauk SSSR. Kratkii istoricheskii ocherk (v dvukh tomakh). 2 vols. Moscow 1977.

Andreev, A.I. *Ocherki po istochnikovedeniiu Sibiri. Vypusk vtoroi XVIII vek (pervaia polovina).* Moscow-Leningrad 1965.

– "Trudy G.F. Millera o vtoroi kamchatskoi ekspeditsii." *Izvestiia: Vsesoiuznoe geograficheskoe obshchestvo*, 91, no. 1 (January/February 1959): 3–16.

Andreev, A.I., ed. "Perepiska V.N. Tatishcheva za 1746–1750 gg." *Istoricheskii arkhiv* 6 (Moscow-Leningrad 1951): 245–314.

Astakhov, V.I. *Kurs lektsii po russkoi istoriografii.* Kharkov 1965.

Bagrow, Leo. *A History of Russian Cartography up to 1800.* Wolfe Island, Ont., 1975.

Barratt, Glynn. *Russia in Pacific Waters, 1715–1825.* Vancouver 1981.

Barsukov, N. *Zhizn' i trudov P.M. Stroeva.* St Petersburg 1878.

Bashkatova, Z.V. "Sibirskaia gorodskaia promyshlennost' v dvorianskoi istoriografii pervoi poloviny XVIII v." In *Istoriia Gorodov Sibiri dosovetskogo perioda (XVII–nachalo XXV.).* Novosibirsk 1977. 26–44.

Bayer, G.S. *Sochinenie o variagakh avtora Feofila Sigefra Beera.* St Petersburg 1767.

Belov, M.I. "O sostavlenii General'noi karty Vtoroi Kamchatskoi ekspeditsii." *Geograficheskii sbornik*, 3 (1954): 131–45.

Berg, L.S. *Ocherki po istorii russkikh geograficheskikh otkrytii.* Moscow-Leningrad 1949.

– *Otkrytie Kamchatki i ekspeditsii Beringa, 1725–1741.* Moscow-Leningrad 1946.

Bergholts, F.W. *Dnevnik kamer-iunkera F.V. Berkhgol'tsa, 1721–1725.* 4 parts. Moscow 1902.

Berkov, P.N. *Istoriia russkoi zhurnalistiki XVIII veka.* Moscow 1952.

– "Izuchenie russkoi literatury inostrantsami v xviii veke." In *Iazyk i literatura*, 5 (Leningrad 1930): 87–136.

– "Polemika v 'Ezhemesiachnykh sochineniiakh'." In *Lomonosov i literaturnaia polemika ego vremeni, 1750–1765.* Moscow-Leningrad 1936.

Bestuzhev-Riumin, K.N. *Biografii i kharakteristiki.* St Petersburg 1882.

– *Russkaia istoriia*, Vol. 1. St Petersburg 1772.

Biliarskii, P.S., ed. *Materialy dlia biografii Lomonosova.* St Petersburg 1865.

Black. J.L. "A.L. von Schlözer." In *Modern Encyclopedia of Russian and Soviet History.* 33 (Blacksburg, Va., 1983): 145–54.

- *Citizens for the Fatherland: Education, Educators, and Pedagogical Ideals in Eighteenth Century Russia.* Boulder, Col. 1979.
- "G.-F. Müller." In *Modern Encyclopedia of Russian and Soviet History.* 23 (Blacksburg, Va., 1981): 169–76.
- "G.-F. Müller and the Russian Academy of Sciences Contingent in the Second Kamchatka Expedition, 1733–43." *Canadian Slavonic Papers*, 25, no. 2 (June 1983): 235–52.
- *N. M. Karamzin and Russian Society in the Nineteenth Century.* Toronto 1975.
- "The Search for a 'Correct' Textbook of National History for 18th Century Russian Schools." *The New Review of East European History*, 16, no. 1 (March 1976): 1–19.

Boss, V. *Newton and Russia: The Early Influence, 1698–1796.* Cambridge, Mass., 1972.

Breitfuss, L. "Early Maps of North-Eastern Asia and of the Lands around the North Pacific: Controversy between G.F. Müller and N. Delisle." *Imago Mundi*, 3 (1939): 87–99.

Büsching, A.F., "Gerhard Friderich Muller." In *Beyträge zu der Lebensgeschichte denkwürdiger Personen, insonderheit Gelehrter Männer*, 3 (Halle 1785): 1–160.

Büsching, A.F. ed. *Magazin für die Historie und Geographie*. Vols. 1–4, Hamburg 1767-71. Vols. 7–23, Halle 1773–88.

Carver, J. Scott. "A Reconsideration of Eighteenth-Century Russia's Contributions to European Science." *Canadian / American Slavic Studies*, 14, no. 3 (fall 1980): 389–405.

Cherepnin, L.V. "G.F. Müllers Bedeutung für die Quellenkunde der russischen Geschichte." In *Ost und West in der Geschichte des Denken und der kulturellen Beziehungen* (Berlin 1966): 303–11.
- *Russkaia istoriografiia do XIV veka: kurs lektsii.* Moscow 1957.

Chteniia v Imperatorskom obshchestve istorii i drevnostei Rossiiskikh pri Moskovskom universitete. Moscow 1846–1918.

Coxe, William. *Account of the Russian Discoveries between Asia and America.* 2 vols. London 1787. Reprint 1955.
- *Travels in Poland, Russia, Sweden and Denmark.* 4 vols. London 1802. 5th edition reprinted 1970.

Cross, A.G. *'By the Banks of the Thames': Russians in Eighteenth Century Britain.* Newtonville, Mass., 1980.

Cross, S.H. "The Contribution of G.F. Mueller to Russian Historiography." PhD dissertation, Harvard University, 1916.

Daniels, Rudolph. *V.N. Tatishchev: Guardian of the Petrine Revolution.* Philadelphia 1973.

Die Berliner und die Petersburger Akademie der Wissenschaften im Briefwechsel Leonard Eulers. Ed. A.P. Iushkevich and E. Winter, 3 vols. Berlin 1959–76.

Dolgova, S.R. "'Sokrovishche rossiiskikh drevnosti' N.I. Novikova." *Kniga: Issledovanie i materialy. Sbornik XXXI.* (Moscow 1975): 141–7.

Dukes, Paul, ed. *Russia under Catherine the Great*. Vol. 1, Newtonville, Mass., 1977.

[Euler]. *Leonard Eiler 1707–1783. Sbornik statei i materialov k 150-letiiu so dnia smerti*. Moscow-Leningrad 1935.

Evgenii, Metropolitan. "Miller, Gerard Friderik." In *Slovar' russikh svetskikh pisatelei*, 2 (Moscow 1845): 54–68.

– "Rossiiskaia istoriia. Biografii Rossiiskikh Pisatelei. Gerard Friderik Miller." *Syn otechestva*, 22 (1821): 49–74; 23 (1821): 97–117.

Filippov, A.N. "K voprosu o pervoistochnikakh zhalovannov gramoty dvorianstvu." *Izvestiia AN SSSR*, 6th series (Leningrad 15 March–1 April 1926), 423–44.

Fisher, R.H. *Bering's Voyages: Whither and Why*. Seattle 1977.

– *The Voyage of Semen Dezhnev in 1648: Bering's Precursor. With Selected Documents*. London 1981.

Fradkin, N.G. *S.P. Krasheninnikov*. Moscow 1964.

Gleason, W. "The Course of Russian History According to an Eighteenth-Century Layman [Lomonosov]." *Laurentian University Review*, 10, no. 1 (November 1977): 17–31.

– *Moral Idealists, the Bureaucracy, and Catherine the Great*. New Brunswick, NJ, 1981.

Gmelin, J.G., *Reise durch Sibirien von den Jahr 1733 bis 1743*. 4 vols. Göttingen 1751–52. Volume 1 only was available to me.

– *Voyage en Sibérie*. 2 vols. Paris 1767.

Gmelin, Otto. *Johann Georg Gmelin. 1709–1755. Der Erforscher Sibiriens. Ein Gedenkbuch*. Munich 1911.

Gnucheva, V.F., ed. *Materialy dlia istorii ekspeditsii Akademii nauk v XVIII i XIX vekakh: khronologicheskie obzory i opisanie arkhivnykh materialov*. Moscow-Leningrad 1940.

Gogol, N.V. "Shletser, Miller i Gerder." [1834] *Sobranie sochinenii v semi tomakh*, 6 (Moscow 1967): 106–11.

Gol'denburg, L.A. *Fedor Ivanovich Soimonov (1692–1740)*. Moscow 1966.

Golder, F.A. *Bering's Voyages: An Account of the Efforts of the Russians to Learn the Relations of Asia and America*. 2 vols. New York 1922–5.

Golitsyn, N.V. "Portfeli G.F. Millera (Svedeniia o postuplenii ikh Arkhiv i opisani 3-x portfelei)." *Sbornik moskovskago glavnoe arkhiva Ministerstva Inostrannykh Del'*, issue 6 (Moscow 1899): 401–535.

Gorin, P.O., ed. "Iz istorii osvoeniia Severnogo morskogo puti (Ekspeditsiia Beringa 1732–1743 gg.)." *Krasnyi arkhiv*, 72 (1935): 137–43.

Grasshoff, H. "Gottsched als Popularisator und Übersetzer russischer Literatur." *Zeitschrift für Slawistik*, 15 (1970): 189–207.

Grau, Conrad. *Der Wirtschaftsorganisator Staatsmann und Wissenschaftler Vasilij N. Tatiščev (1686–1750)*. Berlin 1963.

Griffiths, D.M. "The Early Years of the Petersburg Academy of Sciences as

Reflected in Recent Soviet Literature." *Canadian / American Slavic Studies,* 14, no. 3 (fall 1980): 436–45.

Gur'ev, V.V. "Istoriograf Miller v Tomsk." *Russkii vestnik,* 11 (1881): 62–72.

Gurevich, M.M., and K.I. Shafronovskii. "Ob izdanii 1749 goda rechi G.F. Millera 'Proiskhozhdenie russkogo naroda i imeni rossiiskogo"' *Kniga. Issledovanie i materialy. Sbornik VI* (Moscow 1962): 282–5.

Gurliand, I. "K voprosu ob uchastii G.F. Millera v 'Drevnei Vivliofike' Novikova." *Chteniia,* Book 3, section 5 (1899): 20–4.

Hoffmann, P. "Die Briefe von Pallas an G.F. Müller." In *Lomonosov, Schlözer, Pallas,* edited by E. Winter, 310–14. Berlin 1962.

– "Gerhard Friedrich Müller." *Zeitschrift für Slawistik,* 3 (1958): 771–6.

– "Gerhard Friedrich Müller als Geograf." In *Jahrbüch für Geschichte der sozialistischen Länder Europas,* 20, no. 2 (1976): 43–59.

– "O perepiske G.F. Millera i A.F. Biuzhinga." *Arkheograficheskii ezhegodnik za 1977 god* (Moscow 1978): 290–5.

Home, R.W. *Aepinus's Essay on the Theory of Electricity and Magnetism.* Princeton, NJ, 1979.

Ikonnikov, V.S. *Avgust Liudvig Shletser. Istoriko-biograficheskii ocherk.* Kiev 1911.

– *Opyt russkoi istoriografii.* 4 vols. Kiev 1891–1908.

Ilizarov, S.S. "Istoriia sozdaniia i publikatsii pervogo russkogo geograficheskogo slovaria." *Arkheograficheskii ezhegodnik za 1977 god* (Moscow 1978): 90–7.

Illeritskii, V.E., and I.A. Kudriavtsev. *Istoriografiia istorii SSSR.* Moscow 1961.

Istoriia Akademii Nauk SSSR. Vol. 1. Moscow-Leningrad 1958.

Istoriia Biblioteki Akademii Nauk SSSR (1714–1964). Moscow-Leningrad 1964.

Istoriia Sibiri s drevneishikh vremen do nashikh dnei v piati tomakh. Vol. 2. Leningrad 1968.

Ivanov, P.I. "Sledstvennoe delo o sovetnike Akademii nauk' Shumakhere." *Chteniia,* Book 3, section 5 (1860): 64–122.

"Iz protokolov istoricheskago sobraniia peterburgskoi Akademii Nauk." *Bibliograficheskiia zapiski,* 3 (1861): 515–18.

Kaganov, I.Ia. "G.A. Poletika i ego knizhnye interesy. (Iz istorii knizhnoi kul'tury XVIII v.)." *Rol' i znachenie literatury XVIII veka v istorii russkoi kul'tury* (Moscow-Leningrad 1966): 138–44.

Kalaidovich, K. "Zapiska o zhizni N.N. Bantysh-Kamenskago Upravliavshchago Moskovskim arkhivom Kollegii inostrannykh del'." *Vestnik evropy,* 6 (1814): 114–34.

Kirchner, Walter. *A Siberian Journey. The Journal of Hans Jakob Fries. 1774–1776.* London 1974.

Kliuchevskii, V.O. *Sochineniia.* 8 vols. Moscow 1956–9.

Kniazev, G.A. "Gerard Fridrikh Miller. K 150-letiiu so dnia smerti." *Vestnik AN SSSR,* 11 (1933): 29–40.

Kniazhetskaia, E.A. "Nauchnye sviazi Rossii i Frantsii pri Petre I." *Voprosy istorii*, 5 (1981): 91–100.

Koialovich, M.O. *Istoriia russkago samosoznaniia po istoricheskim pamiatnikam i nauchnym sochineniiam*. St Petersburg 1884.

Kopelevich, Iu. Kh. *Osnovanie peterburgskoi Akademii Nauk*. Leningrad 1977.

– "V dni osnovaniia Akademiia nauk i khudozhestv." *Vestnik AN SSSR*, 10 (1973): 121–31.

Kosven, M.O. "Etnograficheskie rezul'taty Velikoi Severnoi Ekspeditsii 1733–1743 gg." *Sibirskii etnograficheskii sbornik*, 3 (1961): 167–212.

Krasheninnikov, S.P. *Explorations of Kamchatka. Report of a Journey Made to Explore Eastern Siberia in 1735–1741*. Trans. and ed. E.A.P. Crownhart-Vaughn. Portland, Ore., 1972.

– *Opisanie zemli Kamchatki*. 2 vols. St Petersburg 1755. Reprint Moscow 1949.

– *S.P. Krasheninnikov v Sibiri: neopublikovannye materialy*. Ed. N.N. Stepanov. Moscow-Leningrad 1966.

Kuliabko, E.S. *M.V. Lomonosov i uchebnaia deiatel'nost' Petersburgskoi Akademii nauk*. Moscow-Leningrad 1962.

– "Pervye prezidenty." *Vestnik AN SSSR*, 2 (1974): 144–51 (refers to the first five presidents of the Academy of Sciences).

Kuliabko, E.S., and N.V. Sokolava. "Istochniki vol'terovskoi 'Istorii Petra'." In *Frantsuskii ezhgodnik. Stat'i i materialy po istorii Frantsik. 1964* (Moscow 1965): 247–8.

Kunik, A.A. "Ob uchenykh sbornikakh i periodicheskikh izdanniiakh imp. Akademii nauk s 1726 po 1825 i ob izdanii 'Uchenykh zapisok'." *Zapiski IAN*, 1 (1853): I–CXXX.

Lamanskii, V.I. comp. "Lomonosov i Peterburgskaia Akademiia Nauk. Materialy k stoletei pamiati ego: 1765–1865." *Chteniia*, Book 1, section 5 (1865): 37–192.

Lauch, Annelies. *Wissenschaft und kulturelle Bezeihungen in der russischen Aufklärung: zum Wirken H.L.Ch. Bacmeisters*. Berlin 1969.

Lauridsen, Peter. *Vitus Bering: The Discoverer of Bering Strait*. New York 1889. Reprint 1969.

Lavrent'ev, M.A., et al., eds. *Leonard Eiler: Sbornik statei v chest' 250 letiia so dnia rozhdeniia, predstavlennykh Akademii nauk SSSR*. Moscow 1959.

Leonhard Euler und Christian Goldbach. Briefwechsel 1729–1764. Berlin 1965.

Letopis' zhizni i tvorchestva M.V. Lomonosova. Ed. V.L. Chenakal. Moscow-Leningrad 1961.

Likhareva-Bokii, N.I. "Iz istorii pedagogicheskoi mysli. (Voprosy metodiki istorii v Rossii XVIII veka)." In *K 25-letiiu ucheno-pedagogicheskoi deiatel'nosti I.M. Grevsa. Sbornik statei* (St Petersburg 1911): 445–76.

Locatelli, Francesco. *Lettres moscovites*. Paris 1736.

Lomonosov, M.V. *Polnoe sobranie sochinenii*. 10 vols. Moscow-Leningrad 1950–9.

Luppov, S.P. *Kniga v Rossii v pervoi chetverti XVIII veka*. Leningrad 1973.

Lysenko, T.I. "Fond A.I. Andreeva v Leningradskom otdelenii arkhiva Akademii nauk sssr." In *Arkheograficheskii ezhegodnik za 1978 god* (Moscow 1979): 292–300.

Madariaga, I. de. *Russia in the Age of Catherine II*. London 1981.

Maier, L.A. "Der Krise der St. Petersburger Akademie der Wissenschaften nach der Thronbesteignung Elisabeth Petrovna und die 'Affäre Gmelin'." *Jahrbücher für Geschichte Osteuropas*, 27, no. 3 (1979): 353–73.

– "Gerhard Friedrich Müller's Memoranda on Russian Relations with China and the Reconquest of the Amur." *Slavonic and East European Review*, 59, no. 2 (April 1981): 219–40.

– "K istorii russko-nemetskikh nauchnykh sviazei v xviii v. (neopublikovannoe pis'mo M.V. Lomonosova k I.G. Gmelinu)." *Vestnik moskovskogo universiteta*, 4 (1978): 29–35.

Maikov, P.M. *Ivan Ivanovich Betskoi: opyt ego biografii*. St Petersburg 1904.

Marker, Gary. *Publishing, Printing, and the Origins of Intellectual Life in Russia, 1700–1800*. Princeton, nj, 1985.

Mashkova, M.V. *P.P. Pekarskii. Kratkii ocherk zhizni i deiatel'nosti*. Moscow 1957.

Materialy dlia istorii Imperatorskoi Akademii Nauk, 9 vols. St Petersburg 1885–1900.

Mazour, A.G. *Modern Russian Historiography*. London 1975.

Miliukov, P.N. *Glavnyia techeniia russkoi istoricheskoi mysli*. Vol. 1. Moscow 1897.

Miliutin, V.A. "Ocherki russkoi zhurnalistiki, preimushchestvenno staroi: 1, 'Ezhemesiachnyia sochineniia, (1755–1764)'." *Sovremennik*, 25, no. 1, section 2 (1851): 1–52; no. 2, section 2 (1851): 151–82; 26, no. 3, section 2 (1851): 1–48.

"Millerovy 'Sochineniia'." *Ezhemesiachnyia sochineniia*, 10 (1900): 148–55.

Mirzoev, V.G. "G.F. Miller kak istorik Sibiri v otsenke russkoi dorevoliutsionnoi i sovetskoi istoriografii." *Uchenye zapiski Kamerovskogo pedagog. instituta*, 5 (1963): 45–71.

– *Istoriografiia Sibiri (Domarksistikii period)*. Moscow 1970.

Modzalevskii, A.B. "Literaturnaia polemika Lomonosova i Trediakovskogo v 'Ezhemesiachnykh sochineniiakh' 1755 goda." *XVIII vek: Sbornik 4* (Moscow-Leningrad 1959): 45–65.

Moiseeva, G. "Iz istorii izucheniia russkikh letopisei v xviii veke (G.F. Miller)." *Russkaia literatura*, 1 (1967): 130–7.

– K istorii literaturno-obshchestvennoi polemiki xviii veka." In *Iskusstvo slova* (Moscow 1973): 55–64 (about Miller as middle man in literary polemics during 1750s–60s).

– "Otryvok Troitskii pergamennoi letopisi, perepisannyi G.F. Millerom." *Trudy otdela drevnerusskoi literatury*, 25 (Leningrad 1971): 93–9.

Nadezhdin, N.L. "Ob istoricheskikh trudakh v Rossii." *Biblioteka dlia Chteniia*, 20 (1837), section 2: 93–136.

Nekrasov, Sergei. *Rossiiskaia Akademiia*. Moscow 1984.

Neubauer, Helmut. "August Ludwig Schlözer (1735–1809) und die Geschichte Osteuropas." *Jahrbücher für Geschichte Osteuropas*, 36, no. 2 (1970): 205–30.

Neuschäffer, Hubertus. *Katerina II und die baltischen Provinzen. Beiträge zur baltischen Geschichte*. Bd. 2. Hannover-Döhren n.d.

Neustroev, A.N. *Istoricheskoe rozyskanie o russkikh povremennykh i sbornikam za 1703–1802 gg.* St Petersburg 1975.

– *Ukazatel' k russkim povremennym izdaniiam i sbornikam za 1703–1802 gg. i k istoricheskomu rozyskaniiu' o nikh*. St Petersburg 1898.

Nevskaia, N.I. "Zhosef Nikola Delil' i Peterburgskaia Akademiia nauk (XVIII v.)." *Voprosy istorii astronomii, sbornik 3* (Moscow 1974): 61–93.

Novikov, N. *Drevniaia rossiiskaia Vivliofika*. 20 vols. St Petersburg 1788–9.

– *Opyt istoricheskago slovaria o rossiiskikh pisateliakh*. St Petersburg 1772.

Novyia ezhemesiachnyia sochineniia. 121 vols. St Petersburg 1786–96.

Obolensky, D. "The Varangian-Russian Controversy: The First Round." In H. Lloyd-Jones, V. Pearly, B. Worden, et al., ed. *History and Imagination: Essays in Honour of H.R. Trevor-Roper*, London 1981. 323–42.

Oglobin, N. "K russkoi istoriografii (G. Miller i ego otnosheniia k pervoistochnikam)." *Bibliograf*, 1 (1189): 1–11.

Opyt trudov Vol'nago Rossiiskago sobraniia pri Moskovskom universitete. 6 parts. Moscow 1774–83.

Papmehl, K.A. *Freedom of Expression in Eighteenth Century Russia*. The Hague 1971.

Paszkiewicz, H. *The Origin of Russia*. London 1954.

Pavlova, G.E., ed. *M.V. Lomonosov v vospominaniiakh i kharakteristikakh sovremennikov*. Moscow-Leningrad 1962.

Pekarskii, P.P. *Dopolnitel'nyia izvestiia dlia biografii Lomonosova*. St Petersburg 1865.

– *Istoriia imperatorskoi Akademii Nauk v Peterburge*. 2 vols. St Petersburg 1870–3 (on Müller see especially 1: 308–430).

– "Materialy dlia istorii biblioteki Moskovskago Glavnago Arkhiva Ministerstva Inostrannykh Del'." *Zapiski IAN*, 12, book 1 (1867): 92–8.

– *Zhizn' i literaturnaia perepiska P.I. Rychkova*. St Petersburg 1867.

– "Materialy dlia istorii obrazovaniia v Rossii. (Pervye professory Akademii nauyk i pervye ucheniki ikh." *Atenei*, 14 (1858): 376–92.

– *Nauka i literatura v Rossii pri Petre Velikom*. Vol. 1 (St Petersburg 1862).

– "Novye izvestiia o V.N. Tatishcheva." *Zapiski IAN*, 4 book 4 (1864): 1–55. (Müller's corrrespondence with A.V. Olsuf'ev).

– "O perepiske akademika Shtelina, khranishcheisia v imperatorskoi publichnoi biblioteke." *Zapiski IAN*, 7 (1865): 117–33.

- "Pis'ma Poroshina k Akademiku Milleru." *Russkii arkhiv*, 1 (1969): 72–4.
- "Redaktor sotrudiki i tsensura v russkom zhurnale 1755–1764 godov." *Sbornik statei chitannykh v otdelenii russkago iazyka i slovestnosti imp. Akademii Nauk*. Vol. 2. St Petersburg 1868.
- *Snosheniia P.I. Rychkova s Akademieiu nauk v XVIII stoletii.* St Petersburg 1866.

Peshtich, S.L. *Russkaia istoriografiia XVIII veka.* 3 vols. Moscow-Leningrad 1961–71.

Piatkovskii, A.P. *Iz istorii nashego literaturnago i obshchestvennago razvitiia.* Vol. 2 (St Petersburg 1876).

Picchio, Riccardo. "La 'Introductio in Historiam et rem Literariam Slavorum' di J.P. Kohl." *Ricerche slavistiche*, 2 (1953): 3–28.

Polevoi, B.P. "Nakhodka podlinnykh dokumentov S.I. Dezhneva o ego istoricheskom pokhode 1648 g." *Vestnik leningradskogo universiteta*, 6 (1962): 145–52.

Poroshin, S.A. "Zapiski vospitatelia velikago kniazia Pavla Petrovicha, S. Poroshina." *Russkaia starina*, 31 (1881): 149–405.

Pritsak, O. *The Origin of Rus'.* Vol. 1. Cambridge, Mass., 1981.
- "The Origin of Rus'." *Russian Review*, 36, no. 3 (July 1977): 249–73.

Protokoly zasedanii konferentsii imperatorskoi Akademii nauk s 1725 po 1803 goda. 4 vols. St Petersburg 1897–1911.

Pypin, A.N. *Istoriia russkoi etnografii.* Vol. 4 St Petersburg 1892.

Radlov, V. "Iz sochinenii akademikov G.F. Millera i I.G. Gmelina." *Materialy po arkheologii Rossii*, 15 (1894), "Prilozhenie" to *Sibirskiia drevnosti*, 1, issue 3 (St Petersburg 1894): 55–126.

Radovskii, M.I. *M.V. Lomonosov i Peterburgskaia Akademiia Nauk.* Moscow-Leningrad 1961.

Ransel, David. "Ivan Betskoi and the Institutionalization of the Enlightenment in Russia." *Canadian/American Slavic Studies*, 14, no. 3 (fall 1980): 327–38.

Riazanovsky, A.V. "The Norman Theory of the Origin of the Russian State: A Critical Analysis." PhD dissertation, Stanford University, 1959.

Robel, Gert. "Der Wandel des deutschen Sibirienbildes im 18. Jahrhündert." *Canadian/American Slavic Studies*, 14, no. 3 (fall 1980): 406–26.

Roggers, Hans. *National Consciousness in Eighteenth-Century Russia.* Cambridge, Mass., 1960.

Rosenberg, Karen. "The Norman Theory and the Language Question in Mid-Eighteenth Century Russia." *Study Group on Eighteenth Century Russia: Newsletter*, 10 (1982): 37–49.

Rozhdestvenskii, S.V. "Akademii nauk i Kommissiia o sochinenii proekta Novago Ulozheniia." In *Sbornik statei v chest' M.K. Liubavskago*, Petrograd 1917. 637–42.

Rozhdestvenskii, S.V. ed. *Materialy dlia istorii uchebnykh v Rossii v XVIII-XIX vekakh.* St Petersburg 1910.

Rubinstein, N.L. *Russkaia istoriografiia*. Ogiz 1941.

Sazonov, I. "Ob istoricheskikh trudakh i zaslugakh Millera. Soobshch. zasl. Professorum Kachenovskim." *Uchenyia zapiski Imp. Moskovskago Universiteta*. Vol. 9, no. 1, section 3 (1985): 130–51; no. 1 (1835): 306–27.

Sbornik moskovskago glavnago arkhiva Ministerstva Inostrannykh Del'. 7 vols. Moscow 1880–1900.

Schlözer, August Ludwig. *August Ludwig Schlözers offentlich und Privatleben*. 2 vols. Leipzig 1828.

- *August Ludwig v Schlözer und Russland*. Ed. E. Winter. Berlin 1961.

- *Nestor: Russkie letopisi na drevle-slavenskom*. 4 vols. St Petersburg 1809–14.

- "Obshchestvennaia i chastnaia zhizn' Avgusta Liudviga Shletsera, im samim opisanie." *Sbornik otdeleniia russkago iazyka i slovesnosti imp. Akademii Nauk*, 13 (St Petersburg 1875): 1–532.

- *Probe russischer Annalen*. Bremen und Göttingen 1768.

Schottenstein, Isaac M. "The Russian Conquest of Kamchatka, 1697–1731." PhD dissertation, University of Wisconsin, 1969.

Shchapov, A.P. *Sochineniia A.P. Shchapova*. Vol. 3. St Petersburg 1908.

Shcherbatov, M.M. *Istoriia Rossiiskaia ot drevneishikh vremen*. 5 vols. St Petersburg 1901.

Shmurlo, E. *Voltaire et son oeuvre 'Histoire de l'Empire de Russie sous Pierre le Grand'*. Prague 1929.

Sinopsis' ili kratkoe opisanie ot razlichnykh letopistseve o nachale slavenskago naroda ... St Petersburg 1810. 9th edition.

Skriabin, G.K., et al., eds. *Akademiia nauk SSSR. Personal'nyi sostav*. Vol. 1, Moscow 1974.

Sokolov, A. "Istoriia: Severnaia ekspeditsii, 1733–1743 goda." *Zapiski. Gidrograficheskoe upravlenie*, part 9 (1851): 190–469.

Solov'ev, S.M. "Gerard Fridrikh Miuller (Fridrikh Ivanovich Miller)." *Sovremennik*, 10 (1854): 115–50.

- *Istoriia Rossii s drevneishikh vremen*. Books 11–12. Moscow 1963–4.

- *Sobranie sochinenii S.M. Solov'eva*. St Petersburg 1901.

Stählin, Karl. *Aus den Papierien Jacob von Stählin*. Königsberg and Berlin 1926.

Stejneger, Leonhard. *Georg Wilhelm Steller. The Pioneer of Alaskan Natural History*. Cambridge, Mass., 1936.

Strube de Piermont, F.-H. *Razsuzhdenie o drevnikh rossianakh*. St Petersburg 1791.

Svodnyi katalog russkoi knigi grazhdanskoi pechati XVIII veka 1725–1800. 4 volumes. Moscow 1963–75.

Tatishchev, V.N. *Istoriia Rossiiskaia*. 7 vols. Leningrad 1962–8.

- *Izbrannye trudy po geografii Rossii*. Moscow 1950.

- "Razgovor dvukh priatelei o pol'ze nauk i uchilishch." *Chteniia*. Book 1, section 5 (1887): 1–171.

Tetzner, J. "Die Leipziger Neuen Zeitungen von gelehrten Sachen über die Anfange der Petersburger Akademie." *Zeitschrift für Slawistik*, 1 (1956): 93–120.

Tolstoi, D.A. "Akademicheskaia gimnasiia v xviii stoletii, po rukopisnym dokumentam Arkhiva Akademii Nauk." *Zapiski IAN*, vol. 51, book 1, appendix 2 (St Petersburg 1885): 1–114.

Tompkins, S.R. *The Russian Mind from Peter the Great through the Enlightenment.* Norman, Okla., 1953.

Uchenaia korrespondentsiia Akademii Nauk XVIII veka. Nauchnoe opisanie. 1766–1782 gg. Moscow-Leningrad 1937.

Vasenko, P.G. "Pechatnoe izdanie 'kniga stepennoi tsarskago rodosloviia' i tipy eia spiskov." *Izvestiia otdeleniia Russkago Iazyka i slovesnosti imperatorskoi Akademii Nauk*, 8, book 3 (1903): 59–126.

Vernadsky, G. *Russian Historiography: A History.* Belmont, Mass., 1979.

Veselovskii, K.S. "Zapreshchenie istoriografu Milleru zanimat'sia genealo-gieiu." *Russkaia starina*, 9 (1896): 626.

Vorob'eva, T. "Izuchenie vostochnoi sibiri uchastnikami vtoroi kamchatskoi ekspeditsii." *Sibirskii geograficheskii sbornik*, 3 (1964): 198–233.

Vucinich, A. *Science in Russian Culture: A History to 1860.* London 1965.

Winter, E. "I,-v. Paus o svoei deiatel'nosti v kachestve filologa i istorik (1732)." *XVIII vek. Sbornik 4* (Moscow-Leningrad 1959): 313–26.

– "L. Blumentrost und die Anfänge der Petersburger Akademie der Wissenschaften. Nach Aufzeichnung von K.F. Swenskie." *Jahrbücher fur Geschichte der UdSSE und der Volksdemokratischen Länder Europe*, 8 (1964): 247–69.

Winter, E., and A.P. Iushkevich. "O perepiske Leonarda Eilera i G.F. Millera." In M.A. Lavren'tev et al. *Leonard Eiler: Sbornik statei v chest' 250-letiia so dnia rozhdeniia predstavlennykh Akademii nauk SSSR.* (Moscow 1959): 465–98.

Winter, E., ed. *Lomonosov, Schlözer, Pallas. Deutsch-Russische Wissenschaftbeziehungen im 18. Jahrhundert.* Berlin 1962.

Zagorskii, F.N. *Andrei Konstantinovich Nartov, 1693–1756.* Leningrad 1969.

Zapadov, A.V. *Russkaia zhurnalistika 30-x-60-x godov XVIII veka.* Moscow 1966.

"Zapiski Petra Ivanovicha Rychkova." *Russkii arkhiv*, 11 (1905): 289–340.

"Zhaloba sekretaria akademii nauk Volchkova na deistviia onoi protiv nego pravitel'stvuiushchemu senatu." Ed. P.I. Ivanov. *Chteniia*, book 2, section 5 (1859): 153–62.

Zinner, E.P. *Sibir' v izvestiiakh zapadnoevropeiskikh puteshestvennikov i uchenykh XVIII veka.* Vostochno-sibirskoe knizhnoe izdatel'stvo 1968.

Index

ACT7570